Disney

ST MURAI

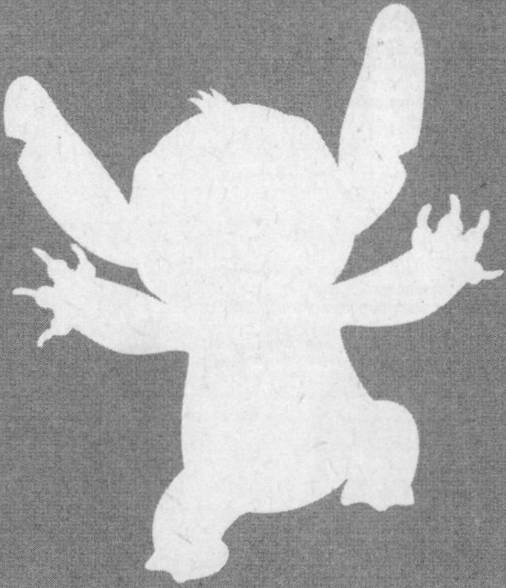

3

HIROTO WADA

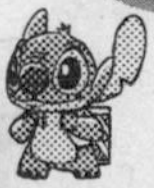

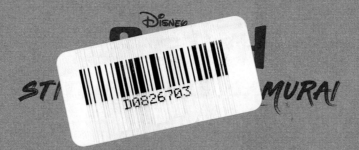

CONTENTS

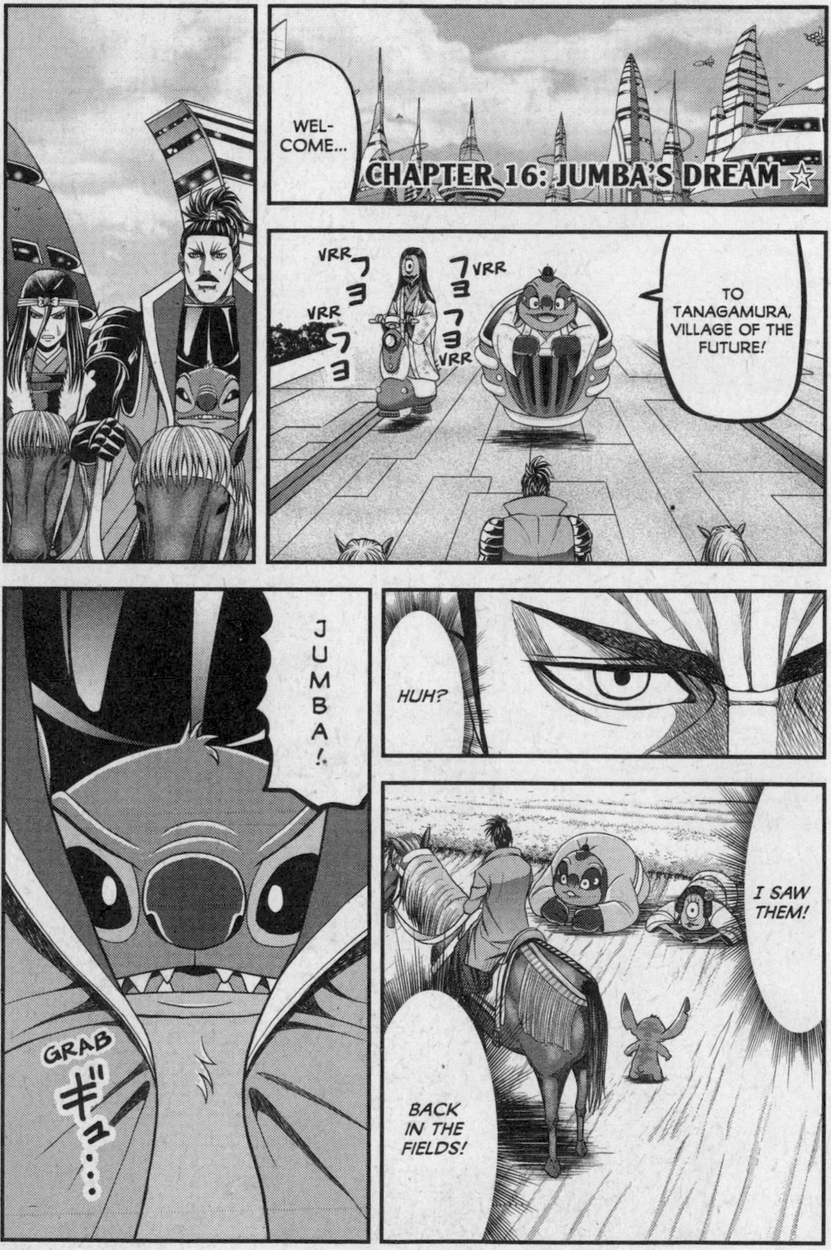
WEL-
COME...
CHAPTER 16: JUMBA'S DREAM ☆
TO TANAGAMURA, VILLAGE OF THE FUTURE!
VRR フヨ
VRR フヨ
VRR フヨ
VRR フヨ
HUH?
I SAW THEM!
BACK IN THE FIELDS!
JUMBA!
GRAB ギュ...

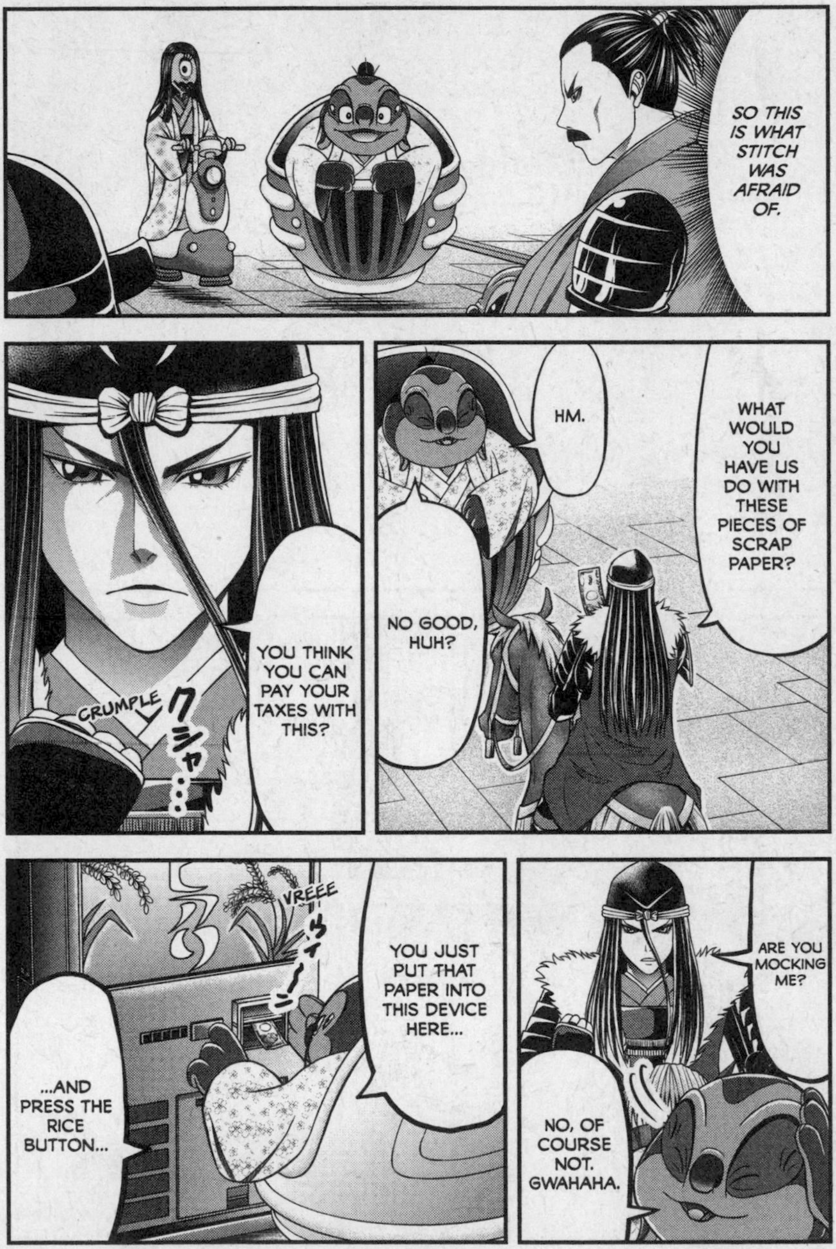
SO THIS IS WHAT STITCH WAS AFRAID OF.
WHAT WOULD YOU HAVE US DO WITH THESE PIECES OF SCRAP PAPER?
HM.
NO GOOD, HUH?
YOU THINK YOU CAN PAY YOUR TAXES WITH THIS?
CRUMPLE
クシャ…
ARE YOU MOCKING ME?
NO, OF COURSE NOT. GWAHAHA.
YOU JUST PUT THAT PAPER INTO THIS DEVICE HERE...
VREEE
...AND PRESS THE RICE BUTTON...

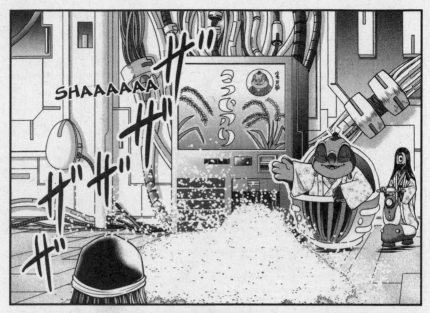

SHAAAAAA
SHAAAAAA
I...I...
SHAAAAAA
ONE OF THESE PAPERS CAN SUMMON THAT MUCH RICE?
TEN BAGS OF RICE!
WHA??

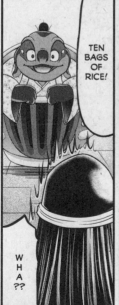

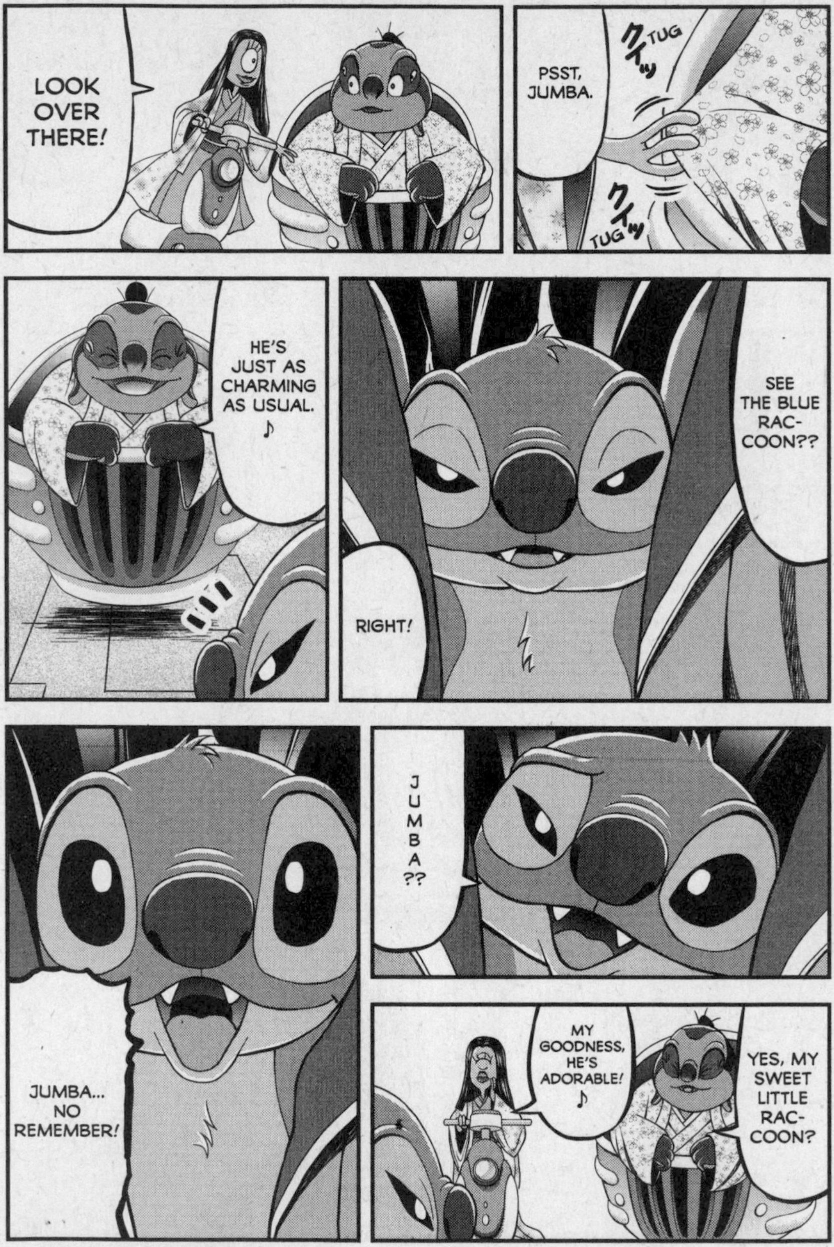
PSST, JUMBA.
クイッ TUG
クイッ TUG
LOOK OVER THERE!
SEE THE BLUE RAC-COON??
RIGHT!
HE'S JUST AS CHARMING AS USUAL. ♪
JUMBA??
YES, MY SWEET LITTLE RAC-COON?
MY GOODNESS, HE'S ADORABLE! ♪
JUMBA... NO REMEMBER!

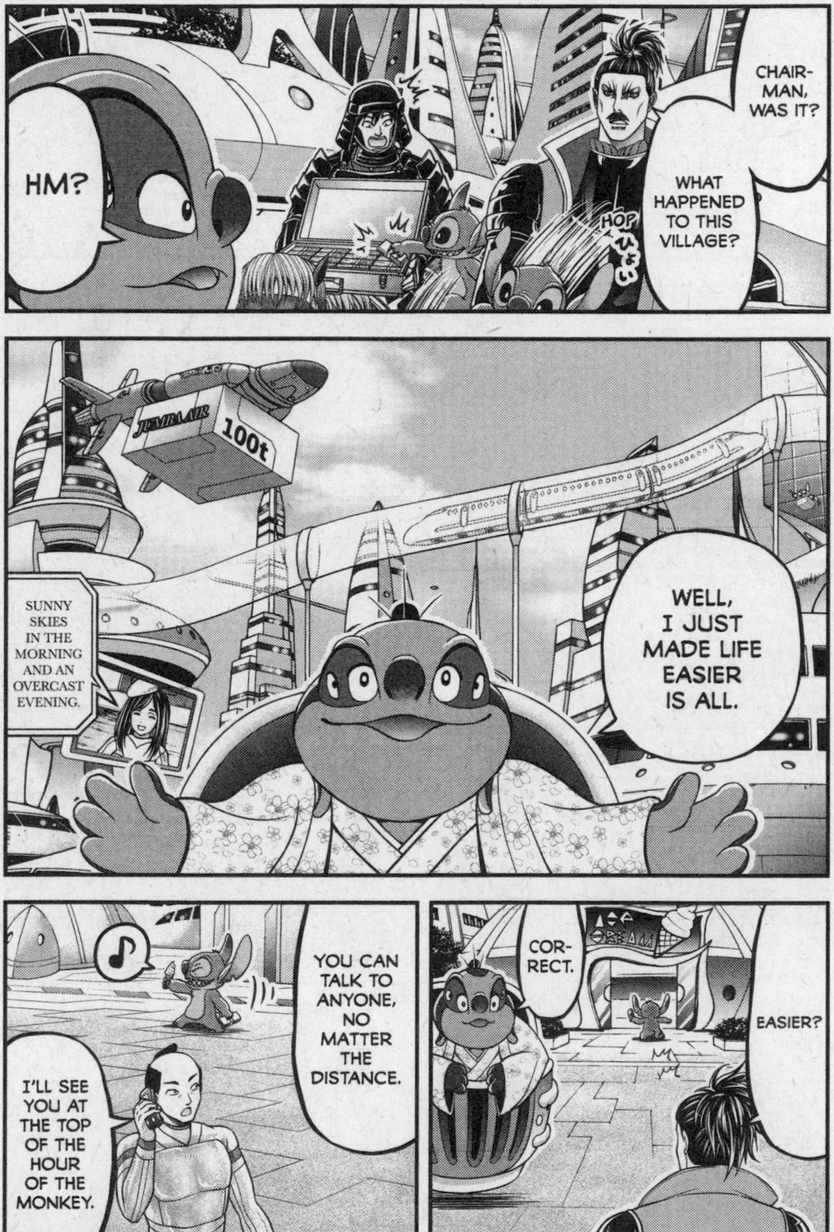
CHAIR-MAN, WAS IT?
WHAT HAPPENED TO THIS VILLAGE?
HOP
HM?
JUMBAAIR
100t
WELL, I JUST MADE LIFE EASIER IS ALL.
SUNNY SKIES IN THE MORNING AND AN OVERCAST EVENING.
EASIER?
COR-RECT.
YOU CAN TALK TO ANYONE, NO MATTER THE DISTANCE.
I'LL SEE YOU AT THE TOP OF THE HOUR OF THE MONKEY.

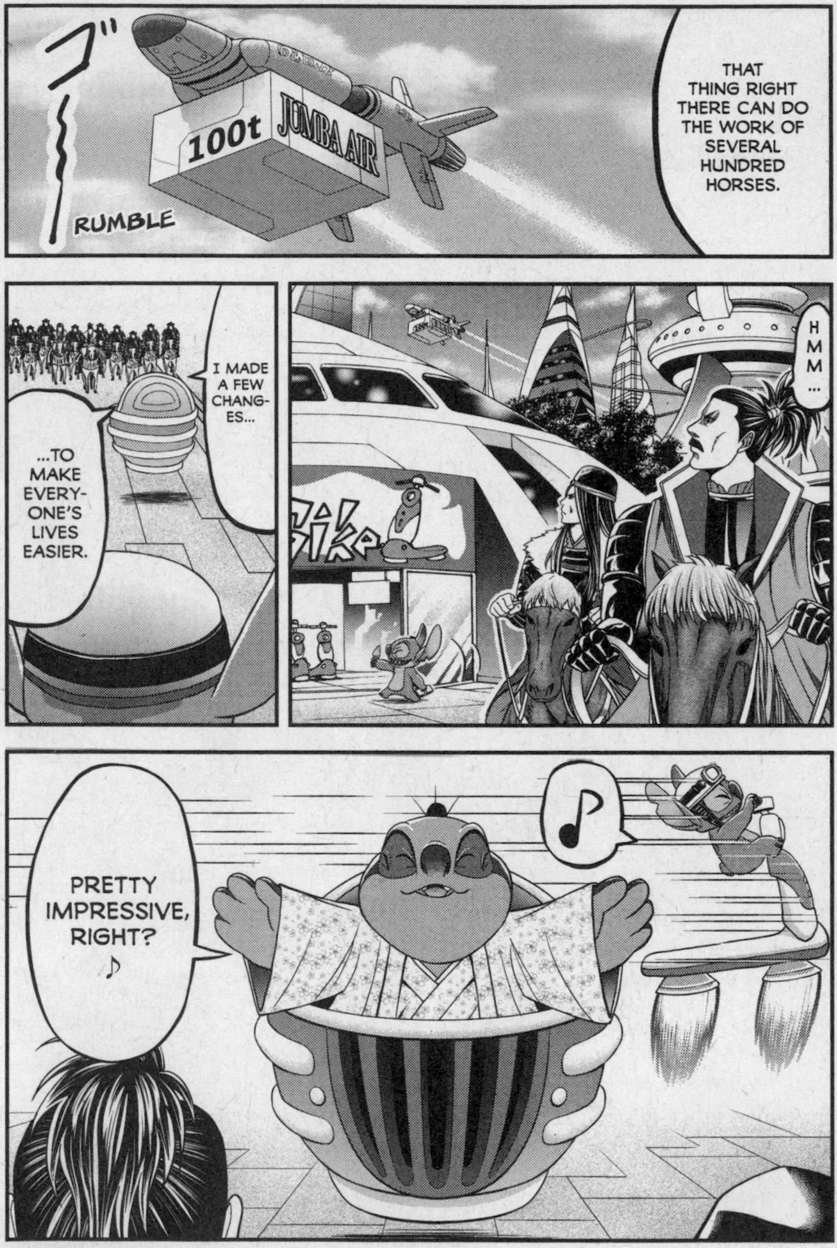
THAT THING RIGHT THERE CAN DO THE WORK OF SEVERAL HUNDRED HORSES.
100t
JUMBA AIR
ゴー
RUMBLE
HMM...
I MADE A FEW CHANGES...
...TO MAKE EVERYONE'S LIVES EASIER.
♪
PRETTY IMPRESSIVE, RIGHT? ♪

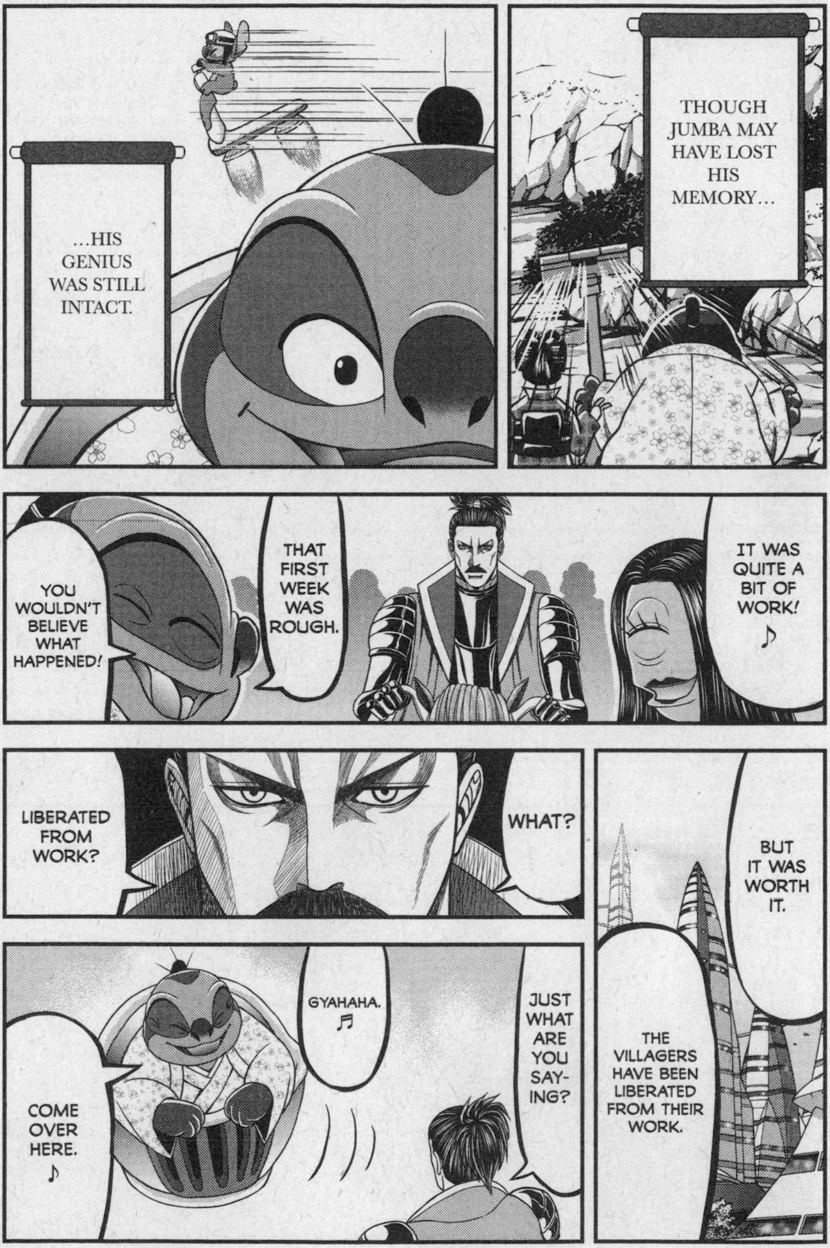
THOUGH JUMBA MAY HAVE LOST HIS MEMORY...
...HIS GENIUS WAS STILL INTACT.
IT WAS QUITE A BIT OF WORK! ♪
THAT FIRST WEEK WAS ROUGH.
YOU WOULDN'T BELIEVE WHAT HAPPENED!
BUT IT WAS WORTH IT.
THE VILLAGERS HAVE BEEN LIBERATED FROM THEIR WORK.
WHAT?
LIBERATED FROM WORK?
JUST WHAT ARE YOU SAY-ING?
GYAHAHA. ♬
COME OVER HERE. ♪

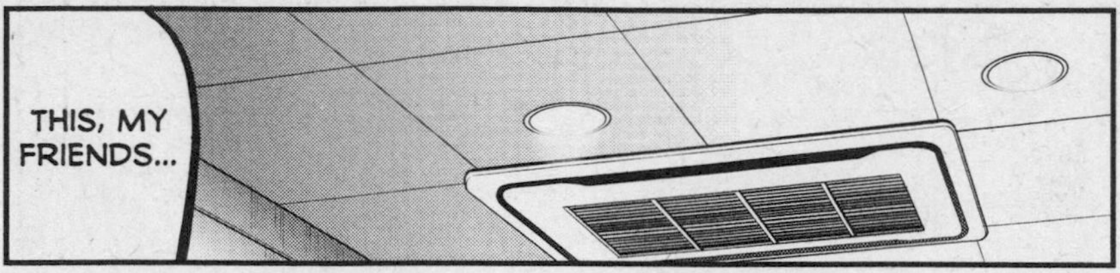
THIS, MY FRIENDS...

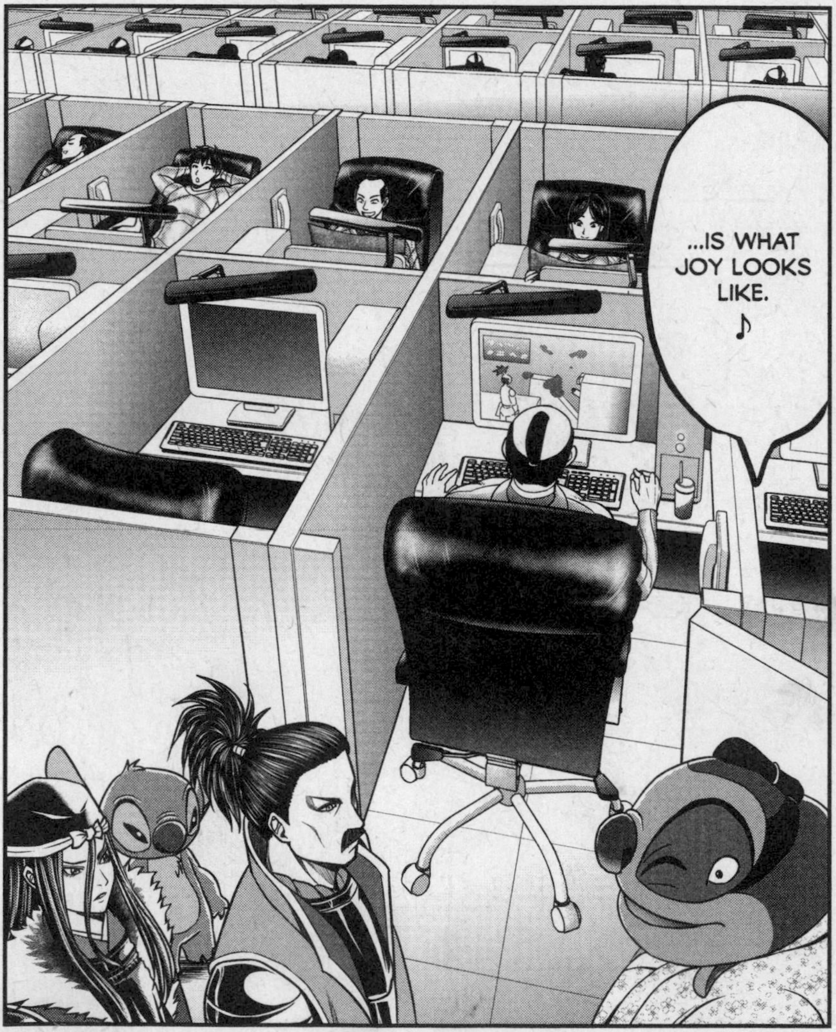
...IS WHAT JOY LOOKS LIKE. ♪

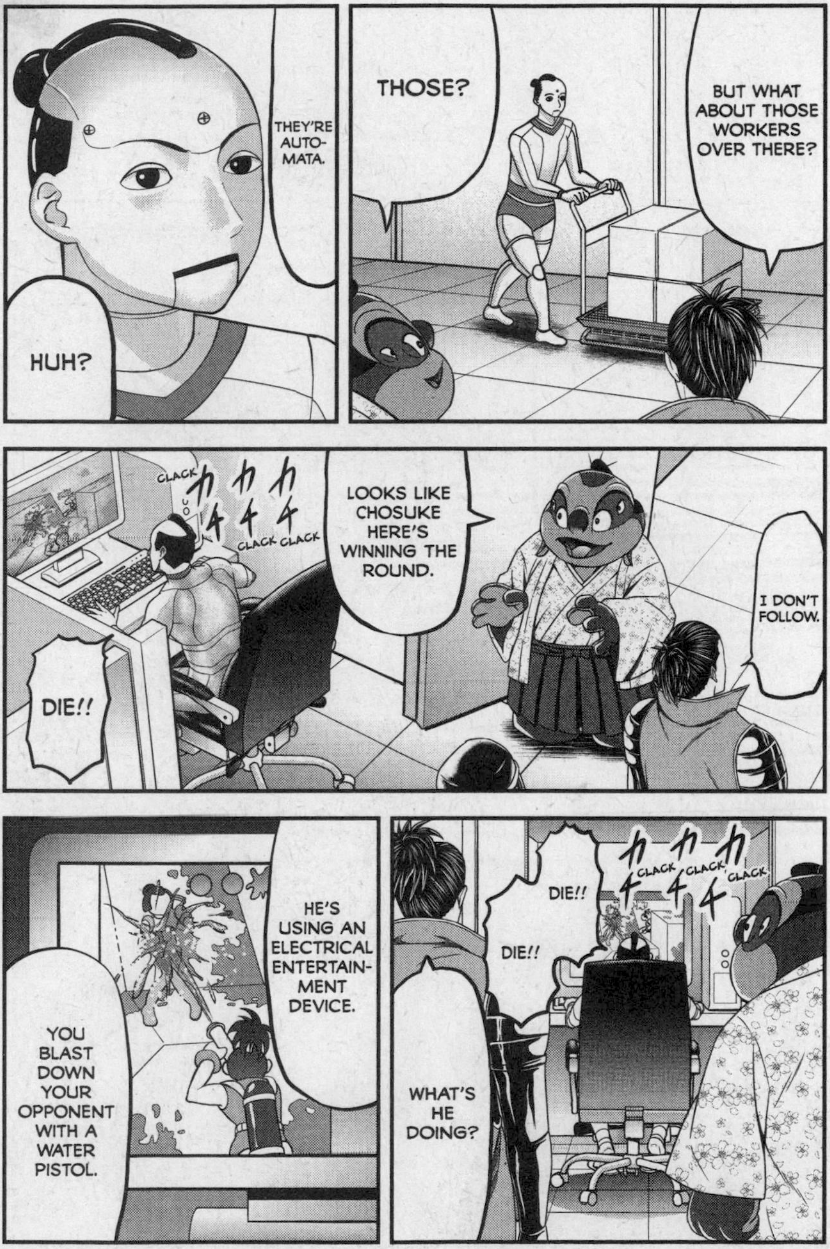
BUT WHAT ABOUT THOSE WORKERS OVER THERE?
THOSE?
THEY'RE AUTO-MATA.
HUH?
CLACK
CLACK
CLACK
LOOKS LIKE CHOSUKE HERE'S WINNING THE ROUND.
I DON'T FOLLOW.
DIE!!
CLACK
CLACK
CLACK
DIE!!
DIE!!
WHAT'S HE DOING?
HE'S USING AN ELECTRICAL ENTERTAIN-MENT DEVICE.
YOU BLAST DOWN YOUR OPPONENT WITH A WATER PISTOL.

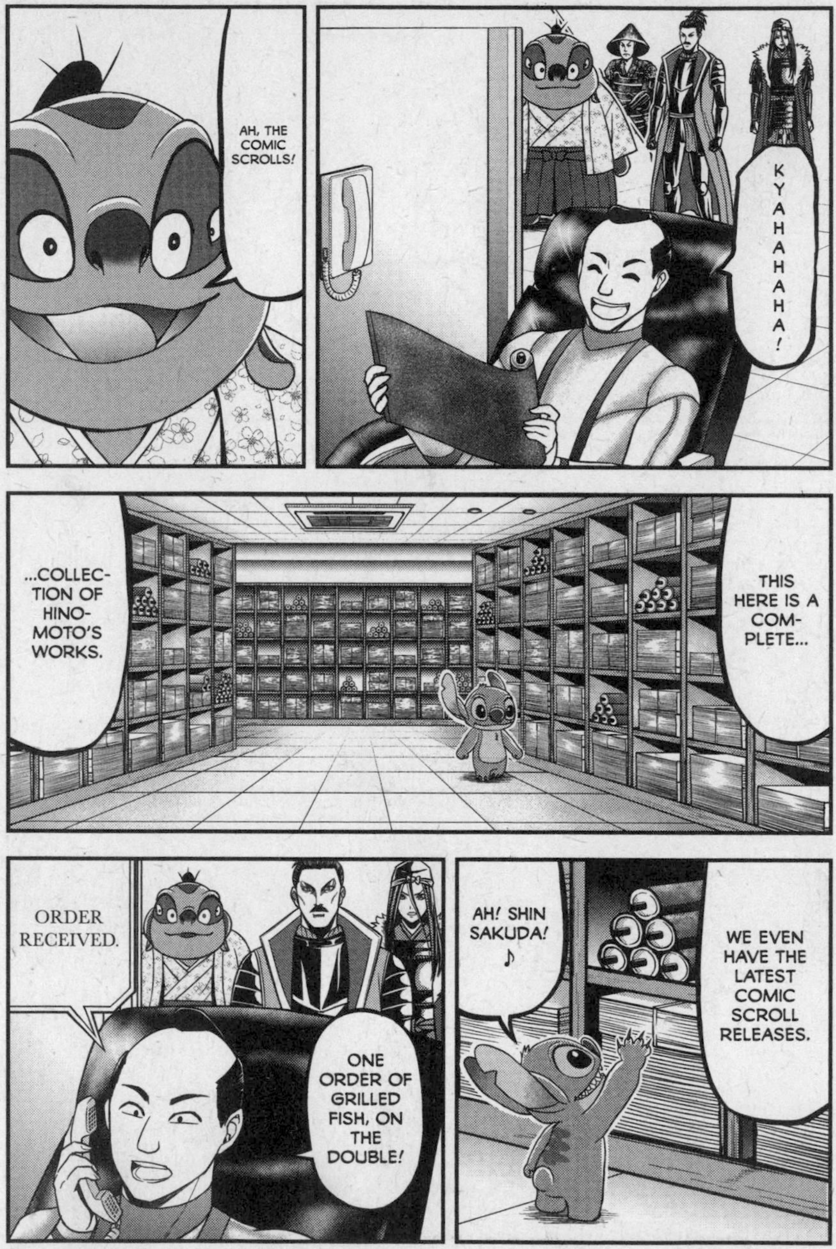
KYAHAHAHA!
AH, THE COMIC SCROLLS!
THIS HERE IS A COMPLETE...
...COLLECTION OF HINO-MOTO'S WORKS.
WE EVEN HAVE THE LATEST COMIC SCROLL RELEASES.
AH! SHIN SAKUDA! ♪
ONE ORDER OF GRILLED FISH, ON THE DOUBLE!
ORDER RECEIVED.

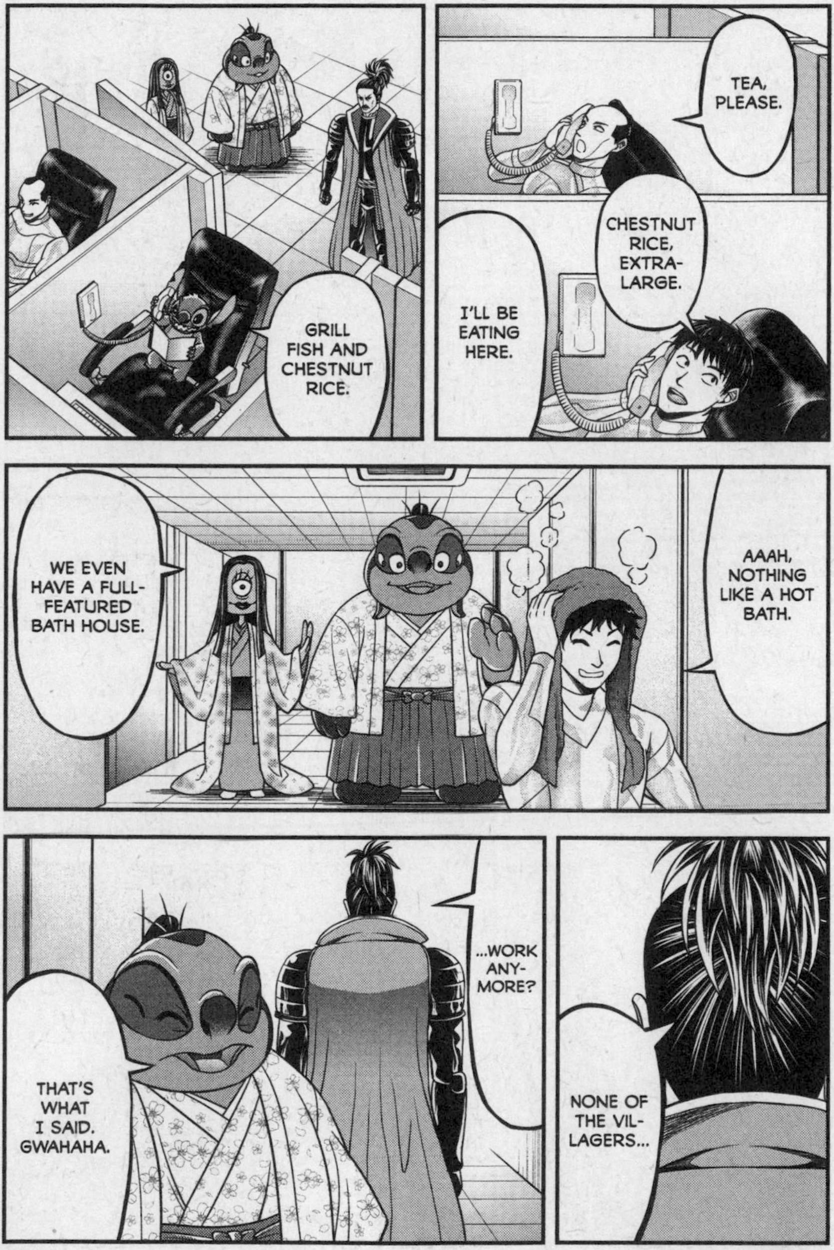
TEA, PLEASE.
CHESTNUT RICE, EXTRA-LARGE.
I'LL BE EATING HERE.
GRILL FISH AND CHESTNUT RICE.
AAAH, NOTHING LIKE A HOT BATH.
WE EVEN HAVE A FULL-FEATURED BATH HOUSE.
NONE OF THE VILLAGERS...
...WORK ANYMORE?
THAT'S WHAT I SAID. GWAHAHA.

EVERYTHING HERE IS AUTOMATED.
THERE'S NO NEED TO EVER WORK AGAIN. ♪
IT'S THE PICTURE OF PERFECTION!

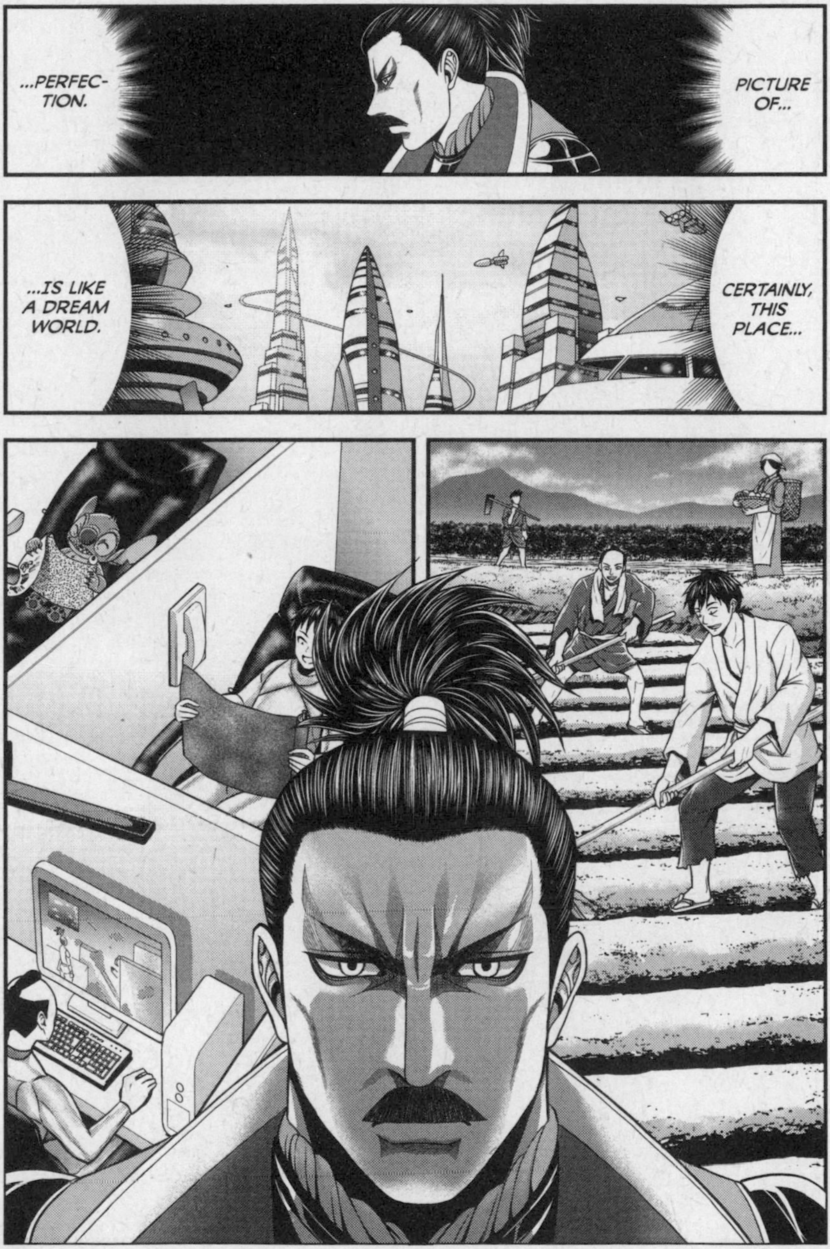
PICTURE OF...
...PERFEC-TION.
CERTAINLY, THIS PLACE...
...IS LIKE A DREAM WORLD.

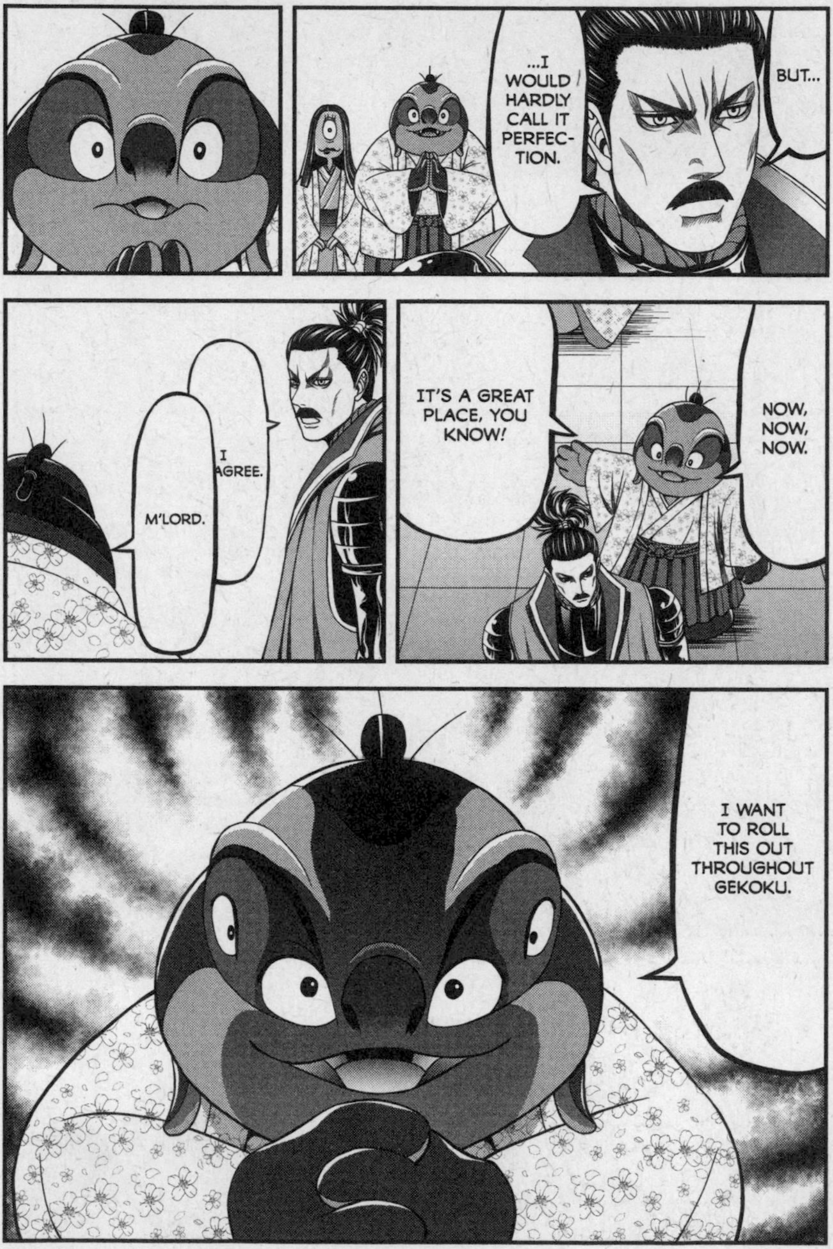
BUT...
...I WOULD HARDLY CALL IT PERFECTION.
NOW, NOW, NOW.
IT'S A GREAT PLACE, YOU KNOW!
I AGREE.
M'LORD.
I WANT TO ROLL THIS OUT THROUGHOUT GEKOKU.

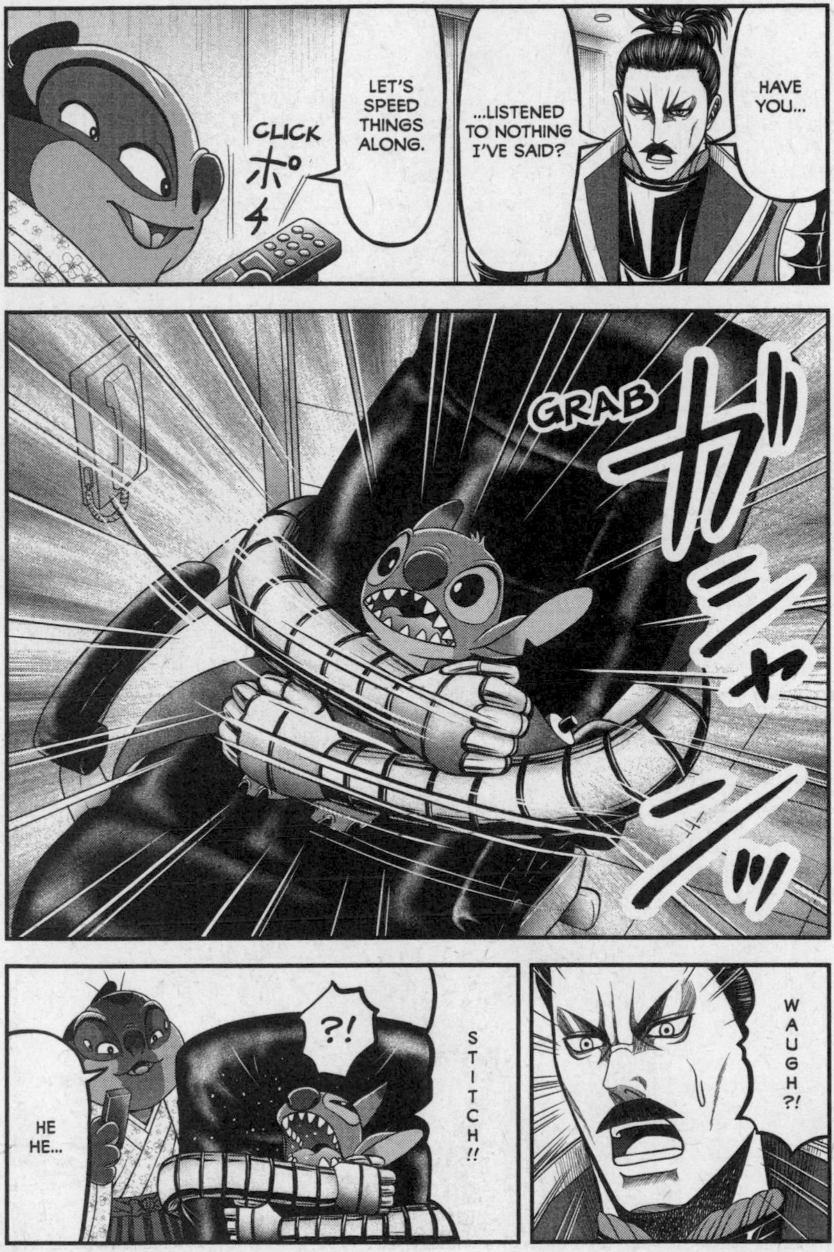
HAVE YOU...
...LISTENED TO NOTHING I'VE SAID?
LET'S SPEED THINGS ALONG.
CLICK
ポチ
GRAB
ガシャーンッ
WAUGH?!
STITCH!!
?!
HE HE...

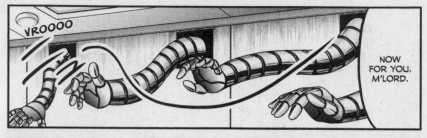

VROOOO

NOW FOR YOU, M'LORD.

GRAB

GRAB

HUANG?!

WHAT'S GOING ON HERE?!

I GUESS I'LL JUST HAVE TO TAKE YOU PRISONER, THEN.

CHAPTER 16: FIN

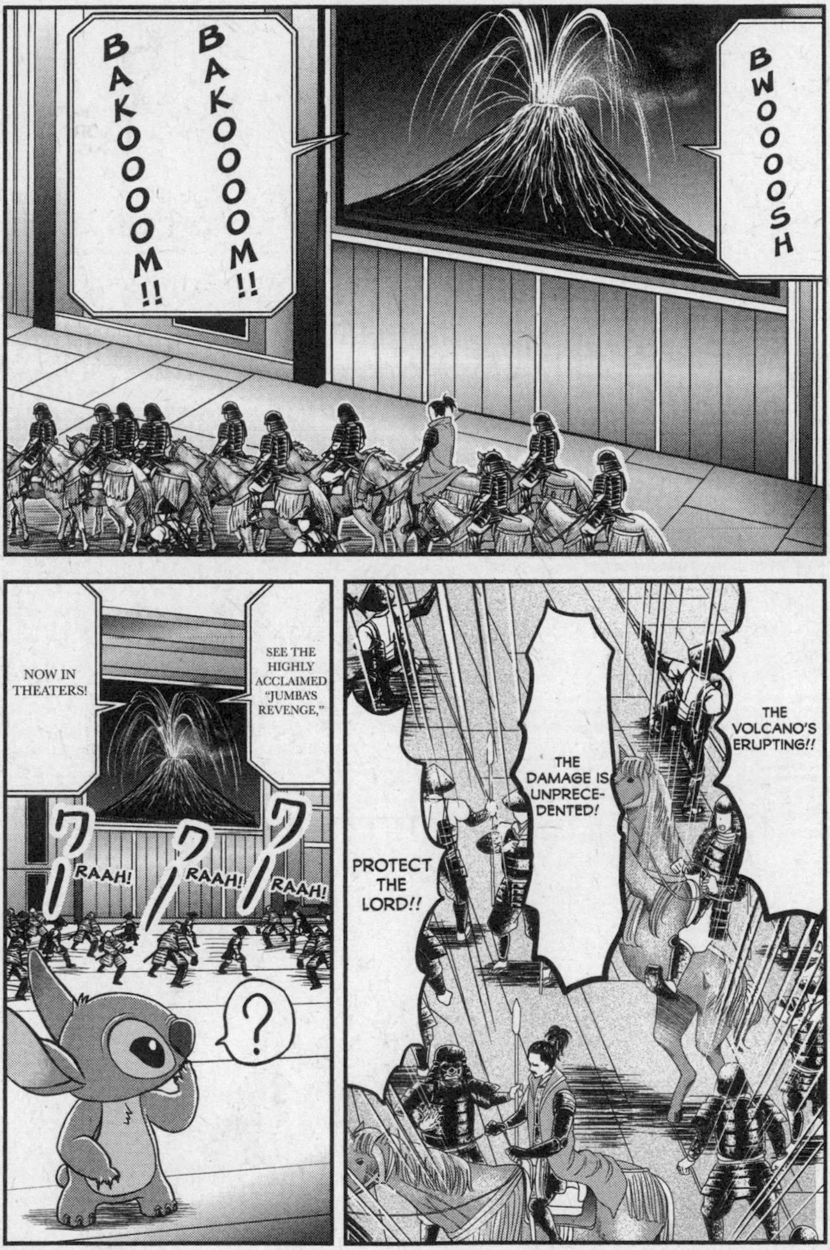
BWOOOOSH
BAKOOOOM!!
BAKOOOOM!!
THE VOLCANO'S ERUPTING!!
THE DAMAGE IS UNPRECE-DENTED!
PROTECT THE LORD!!
SEE THE HIGHLY ACCLAIMED "JUMBA'S REVENGE,"
NOW IN THEATERS!
ワ RAAH!
ワ RAAH!
ワ RAAH!
?

Disney Stitch

STITCH & THE SAMURAI

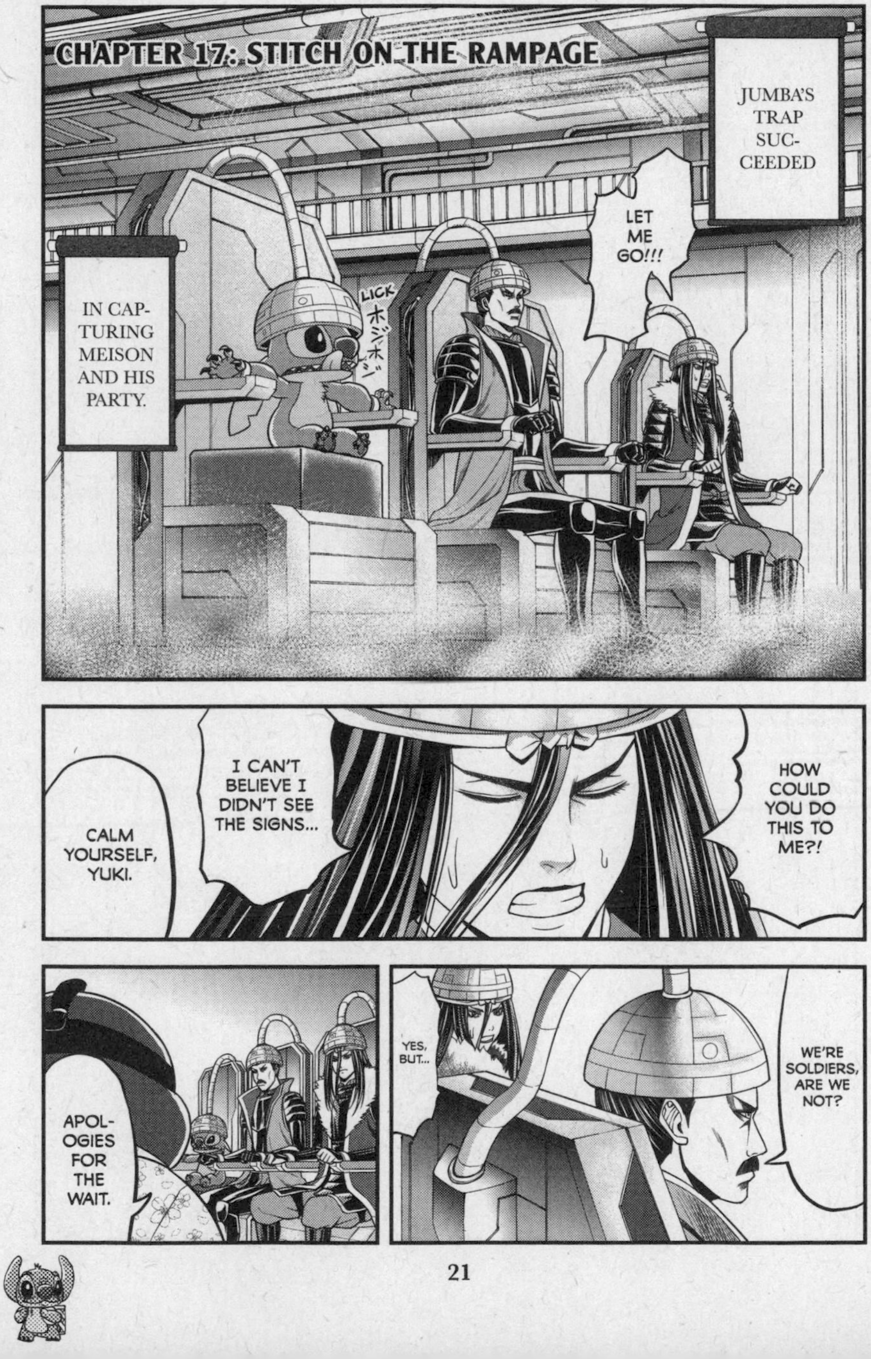
CHAPTER 17: STITCH ON THE RAMPAGE
JUMBA'S TRAP SUCCEEDED
LET ME GO!!!
IN CAPTURING MEISON AND HIS PARTY.
LICK
ホジホジ
HOW COULD YOU DO THIS TO ME?!
I CAN'T BELIEVE I DIDN'T SEE THE SIGNS...
CALM YOURSELF, YUKI.
WE'RE SOLDIERS, ARE WE NOT?
YES, BUT...
APOLOGIES FOR THE WAIT.

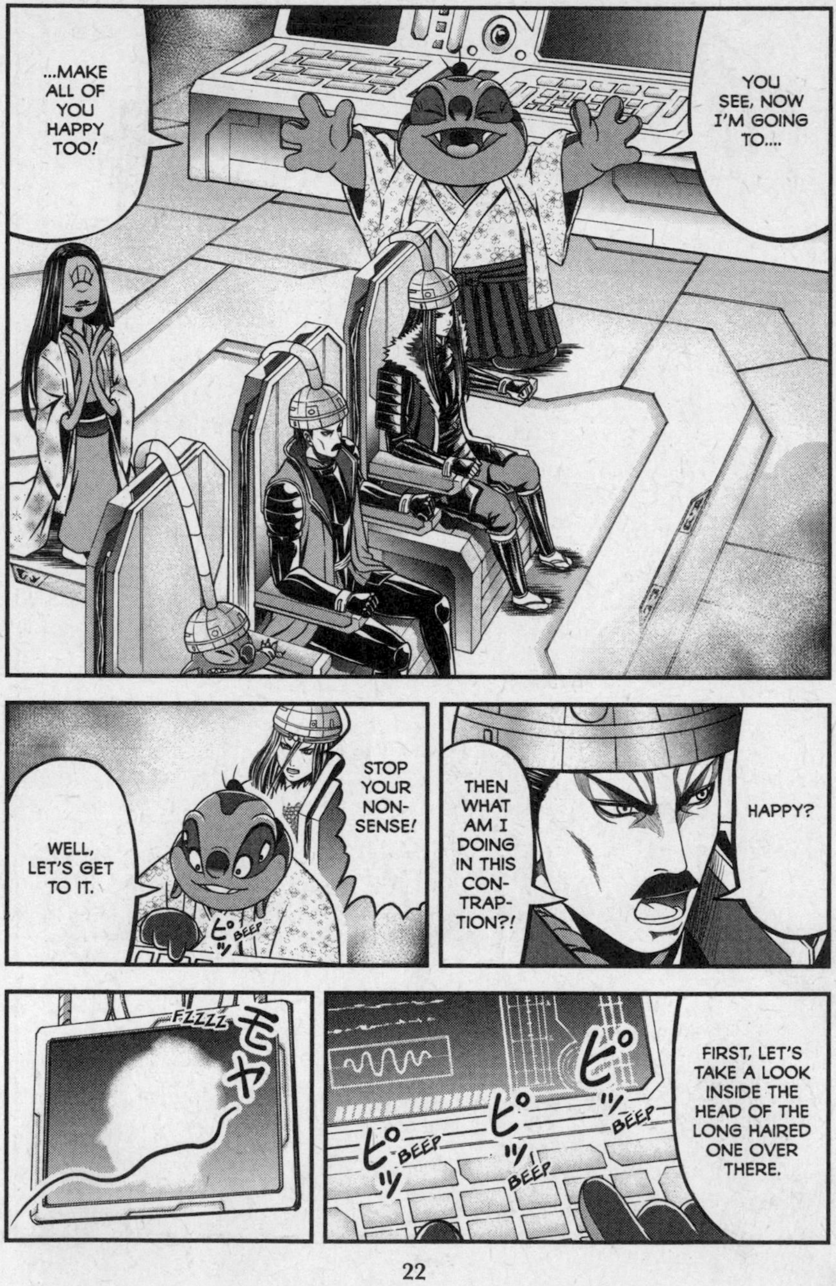
YOU SEE, NOW I'M GOING TO....
...MAKE ALL OF YOU HAPPY TOO!
HAPPY?
THEN WHAT AM I DOING IN THIS CONTRAPTION?!
STOP YOUR NONSENSE!
WELL, LET'S GET TO IT.
ピッ BEEP
FIRST, LET'S TAKE A LOOK INSIDE THE HEAD OF THE LONG HAIRED ONE OVER THERE.
ピッ BEEP
ピッ BEEP
ピッ BEEP
FZZZZ
モヤ

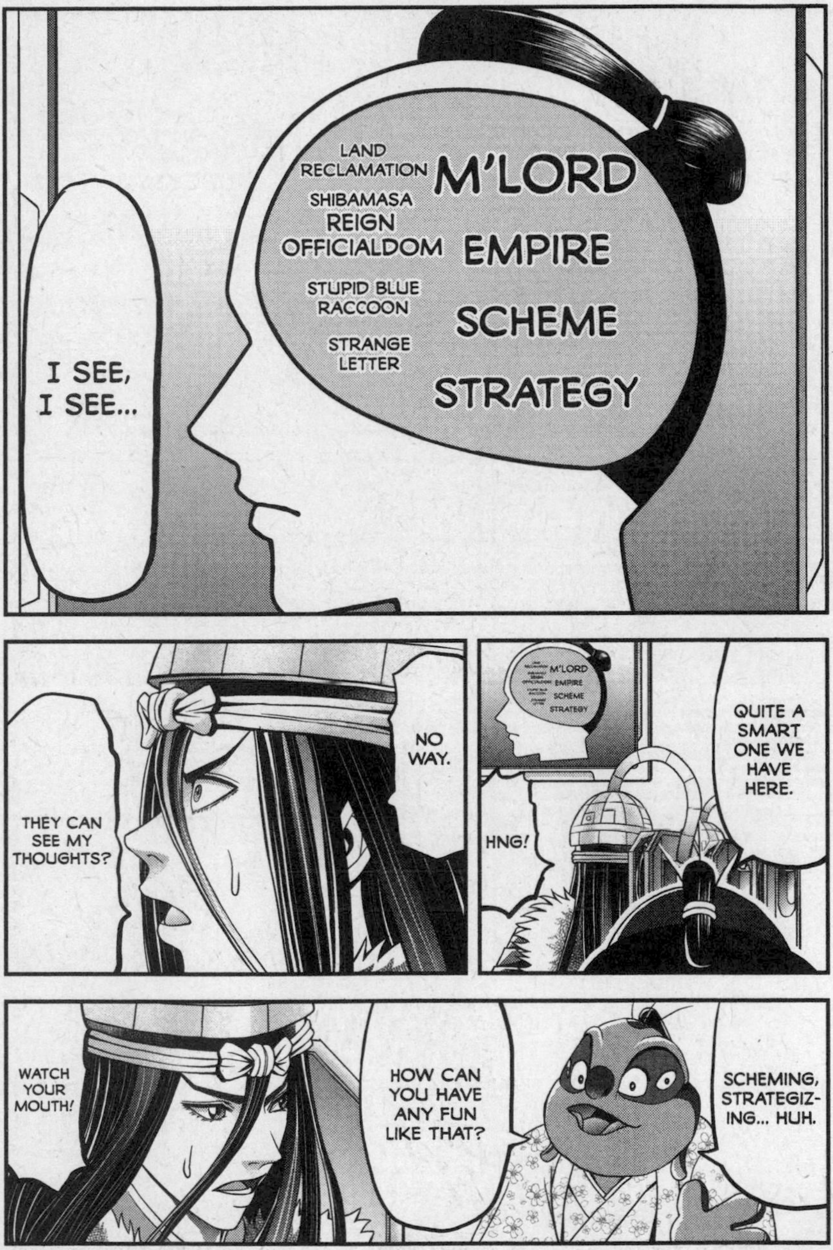
M'LORD
EMPIRE
SCHEME
STRATEGY
LAND RECLAMATION
SHIBAMASA
REIGN
OFFICIALDOM
STUPID BLUE RACCOON
STRANGE LETTER
I SEE, I SEE...
QUITE A SMART ONE WE HAVE HERE.
HNG!
NO WAY.
THEY CAN SEE MY THOUGHTS?
SCHEMING, STRATEGIZ-ING... HUH.
HOW CAN YOU HAVE ANY FUN LIKE THAT?
WATCH YOUR MOUTH!

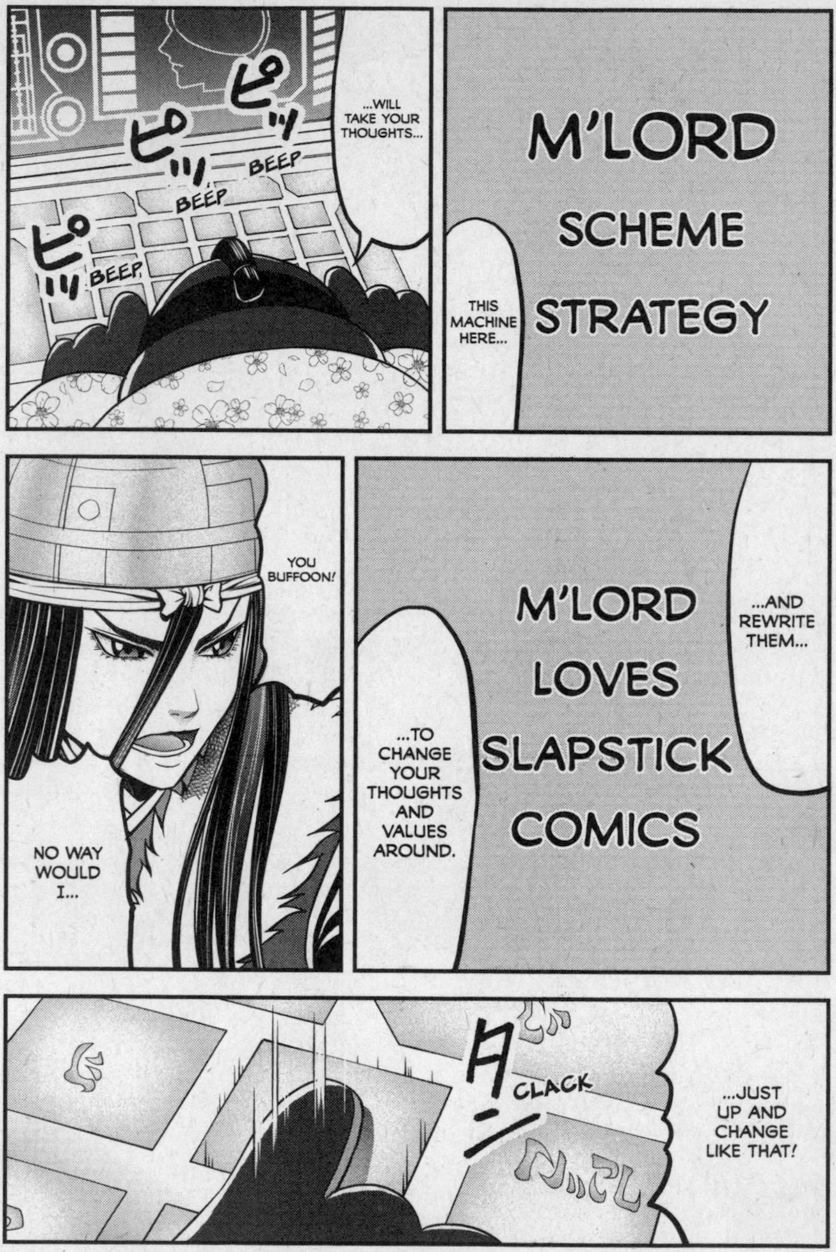
M'LORD
SCHEME
STRATEGY
THIS MACHINE HERE...
...WILL TAKE YOUR THOUGHTS...
ピッ
BEEP
ピッ
BEEP
ピッ
BEEP
...AND REWRITE THEM...
M'LORD
LOVES
SLAPSTICK
COMICS
...TO CHANGE YOUR THOUGHTS AND VALUES AROUND.
YOU BUFFOON!
NO WAY WOULD I...
...JUST UP AND CHANGE LIKE THAT!
CLACK

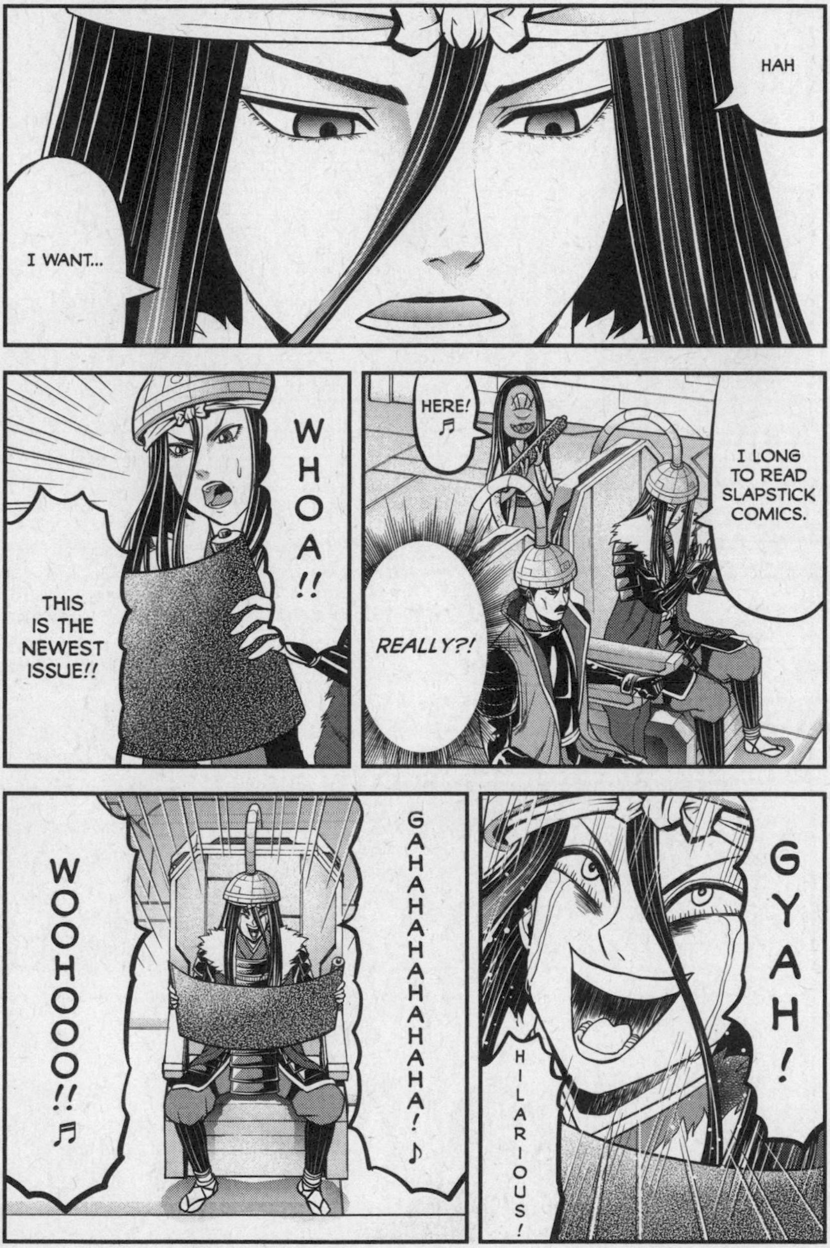
HAH
I WANT...
I LONG TO READ SLAPSTICK COMICS.
HERE! ♪
REALLY?!
WHOA!!
THIS IS THE NEWEST ISSUE!!
GYAH!
HILARIOUS!
GAHAHAHAHAHAHAHA! ♪
WOOHOOOO!! ♬

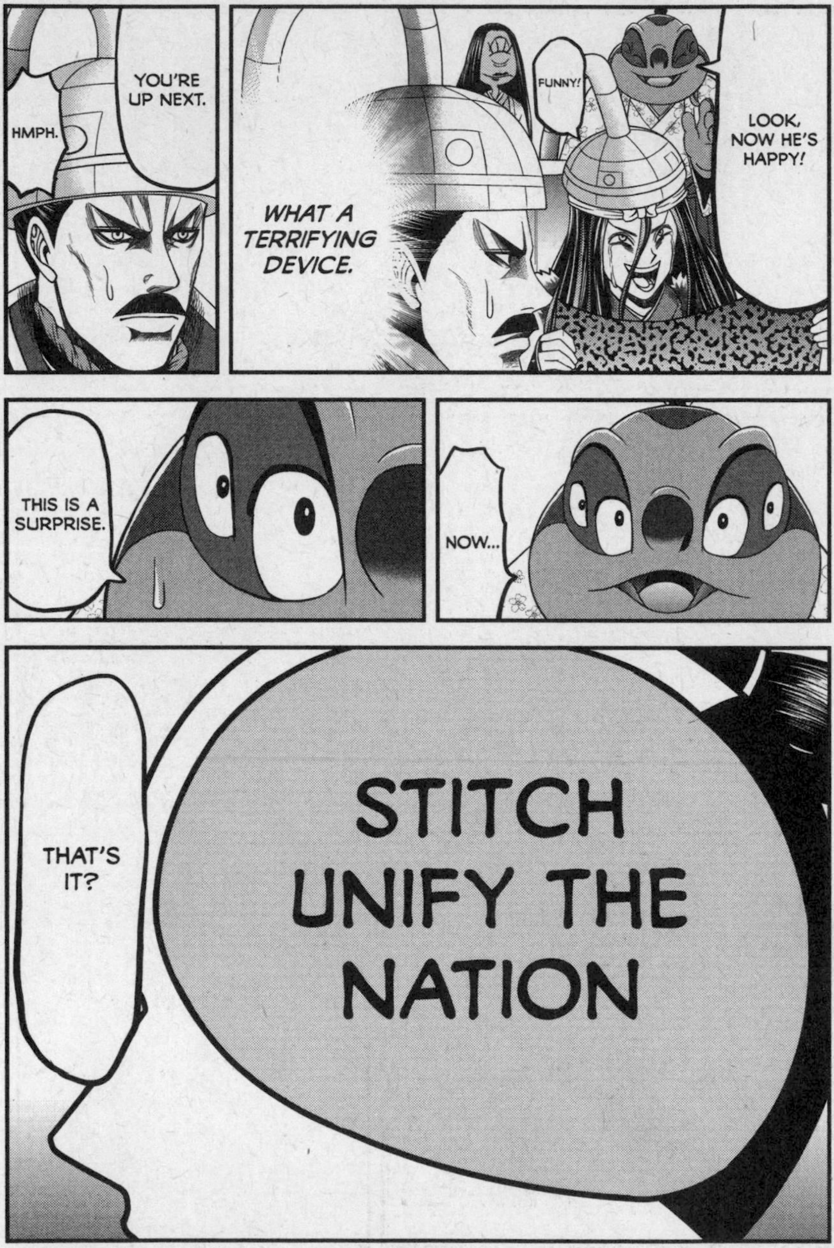
LOOK, NOW HE'S HAPPY!
FUNNY!
WHAT A TERRIFYING DEVICE.
YOU'RE UP NEXT.
HMPH.
NOW...
THIS IS A SURPRISE.
STITCH UNIFY THE NATION
THAT'S IT?

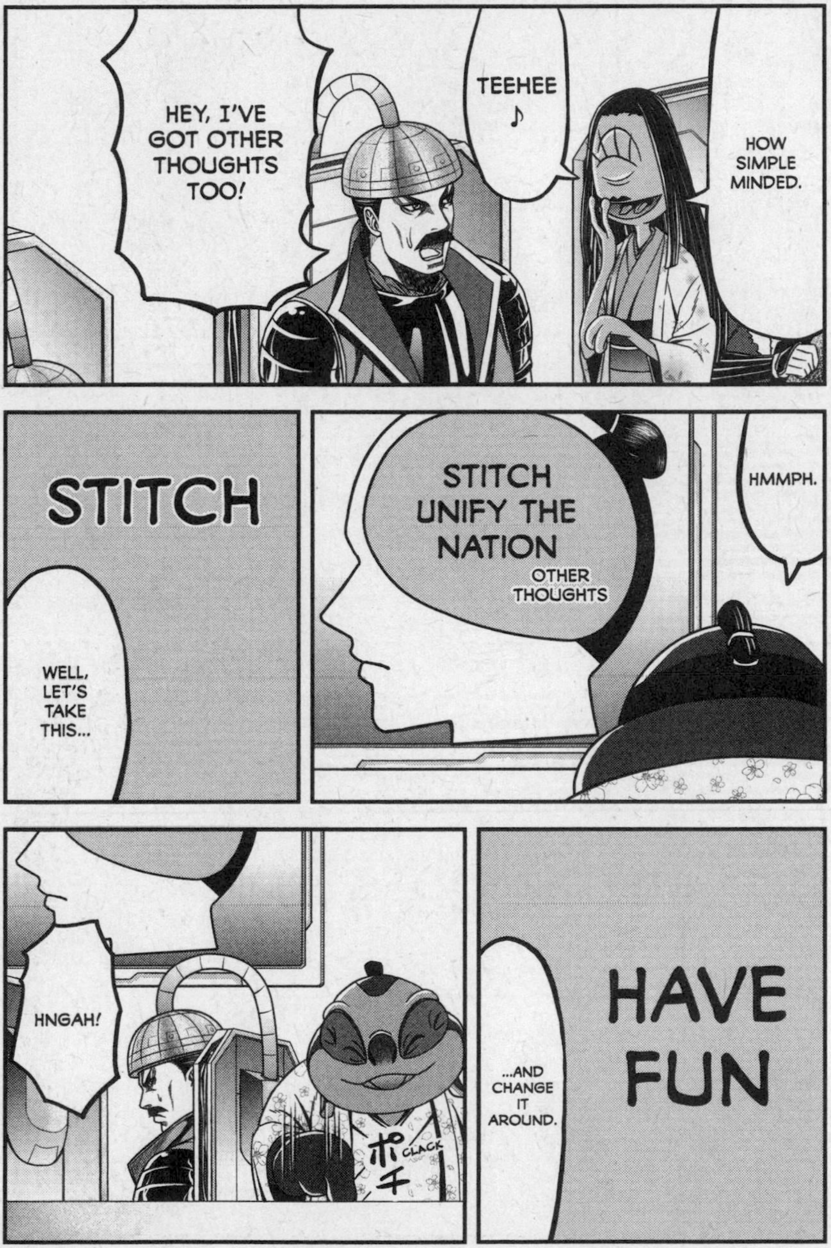
HOW SIMPLE MINDED.
TEEHEE ♪
HEY, I'VE GOT OTHER THOUGHTS TOO!
HMMPH.
STITCH UNIFY THE NATION
OTHER THOUGHTS
STITCH
WELL, LET'S TAKE THIS...
HAVE FUN
...AND CHANGE IT AROUND.
HNGAH!
ポチ
CLACK

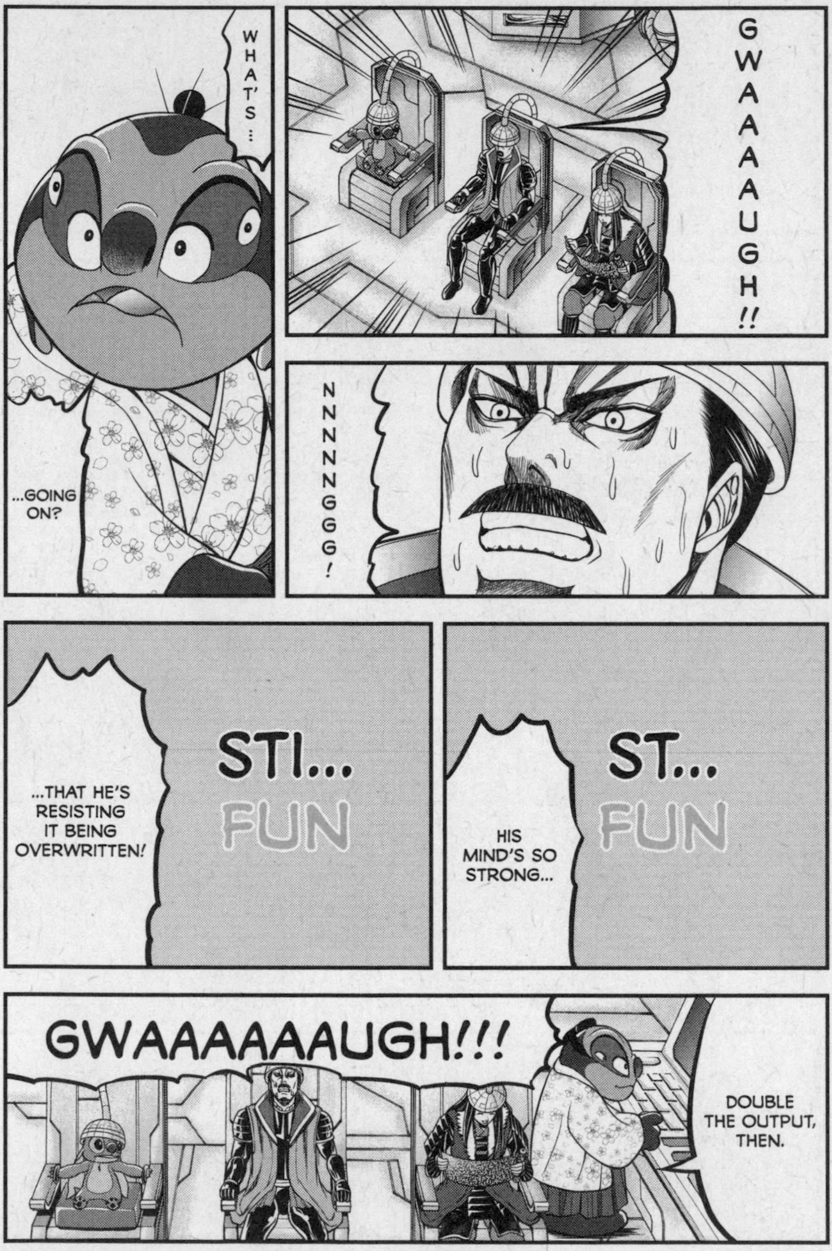
GWAAAAAUGH!!
NNNNNGGG!
WHAT'S...
...GOING ON?
ST...
FUN
HIS MIND'S SO STRONG...
STI...
FUN
...THAT HE'S RESISTING IT BEING OVERWRITTEN!
DOUBLE THE OUTPUT, THEN.
GWAAAAAAUGH!!!

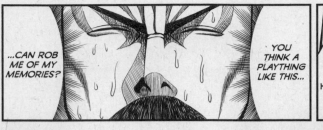

HNG
YOU THINK A PLAYTHING LIKE THIS...
...CAN ROB ME OF MY MEMORIES?
STITCH!
STITCH!
STITCH!
STITCH!
STITCH!
STITCH! STITCH! STITCH! STITCH! STITCH! STITCH! STITCH! STITCH! STITCH! STITCH! STITCH! STITCH!
...?!

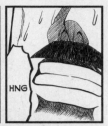

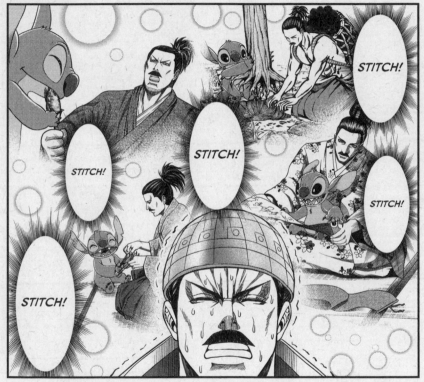

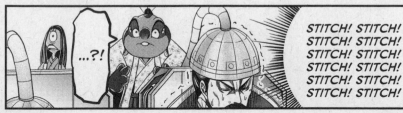

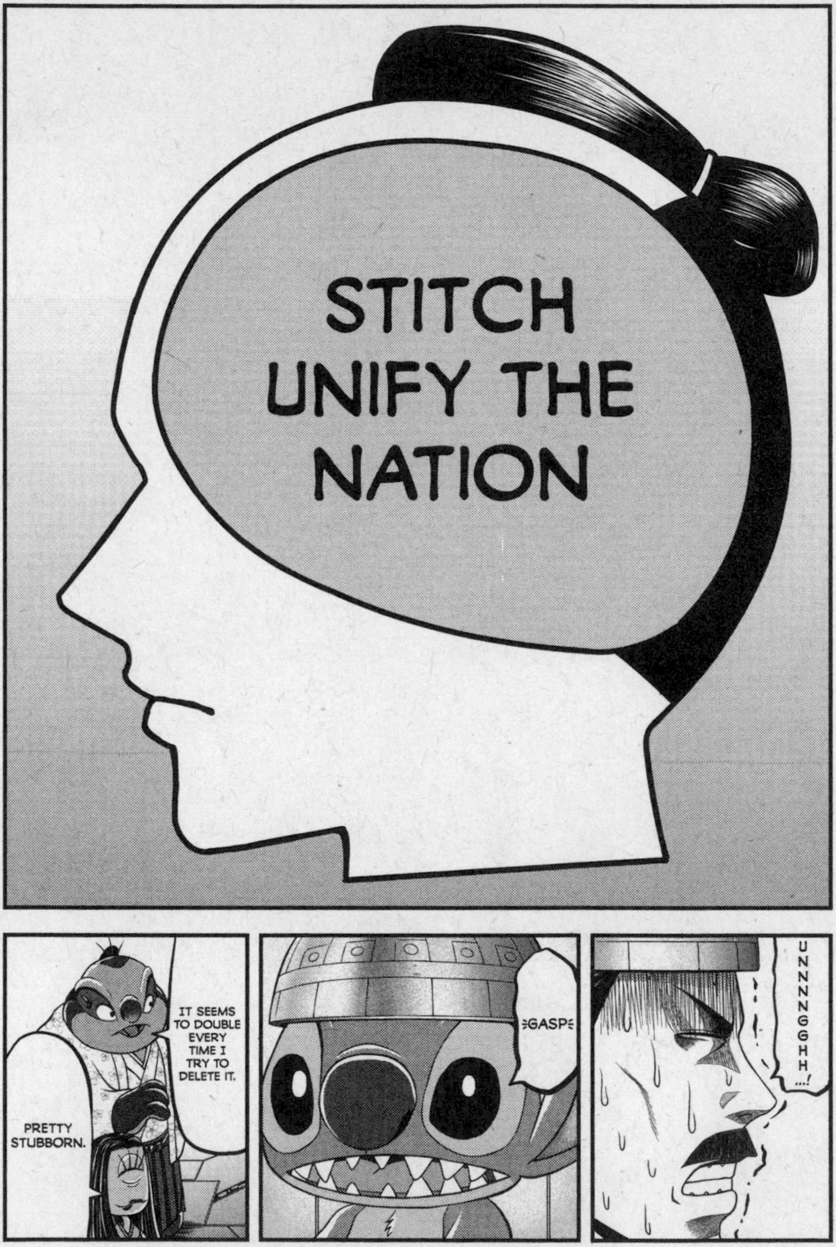
STITCH UNIFY THE NATION
UNNNNGGHH...!
GASP
IT SEEMS TO DOUBLE EVERY TIME I TRY TO DELETE IT.
PRETTY STUBBORN.

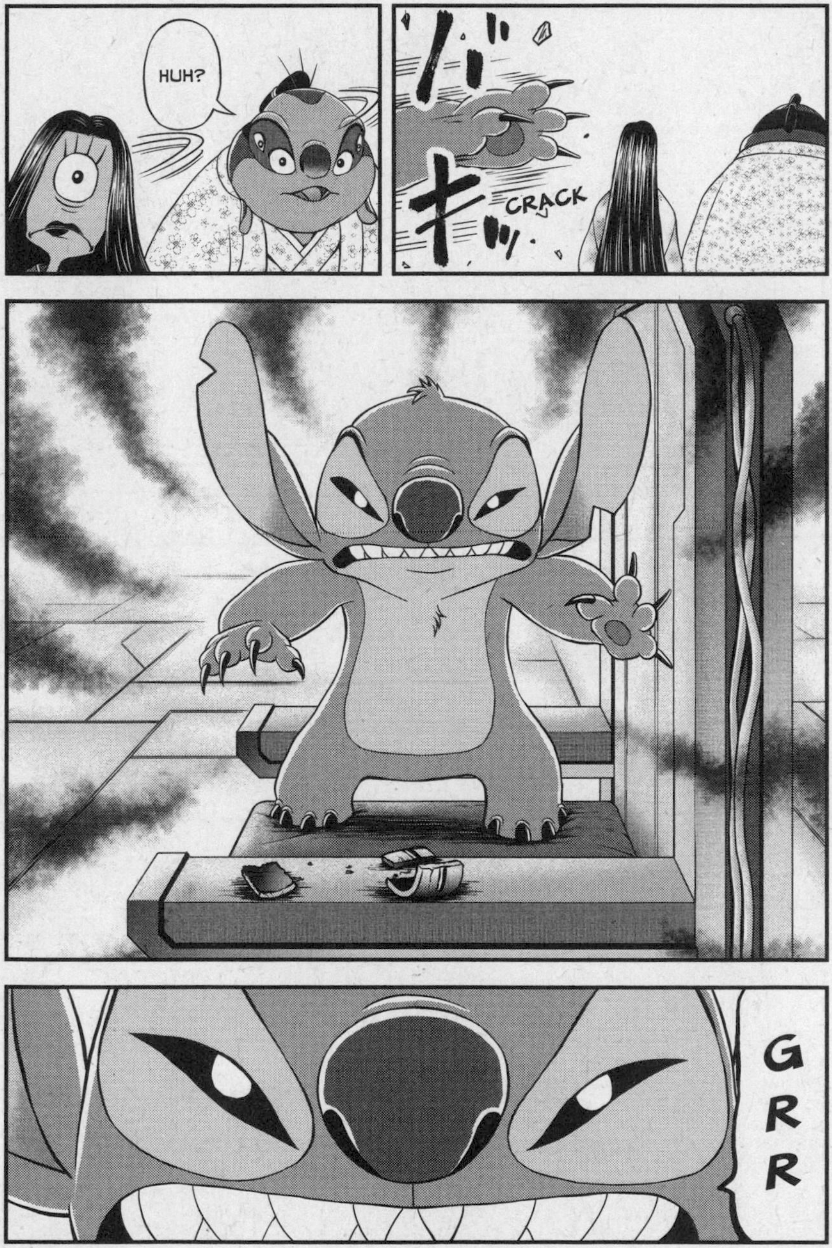
バキッ
CRACK
HUH?
GRR

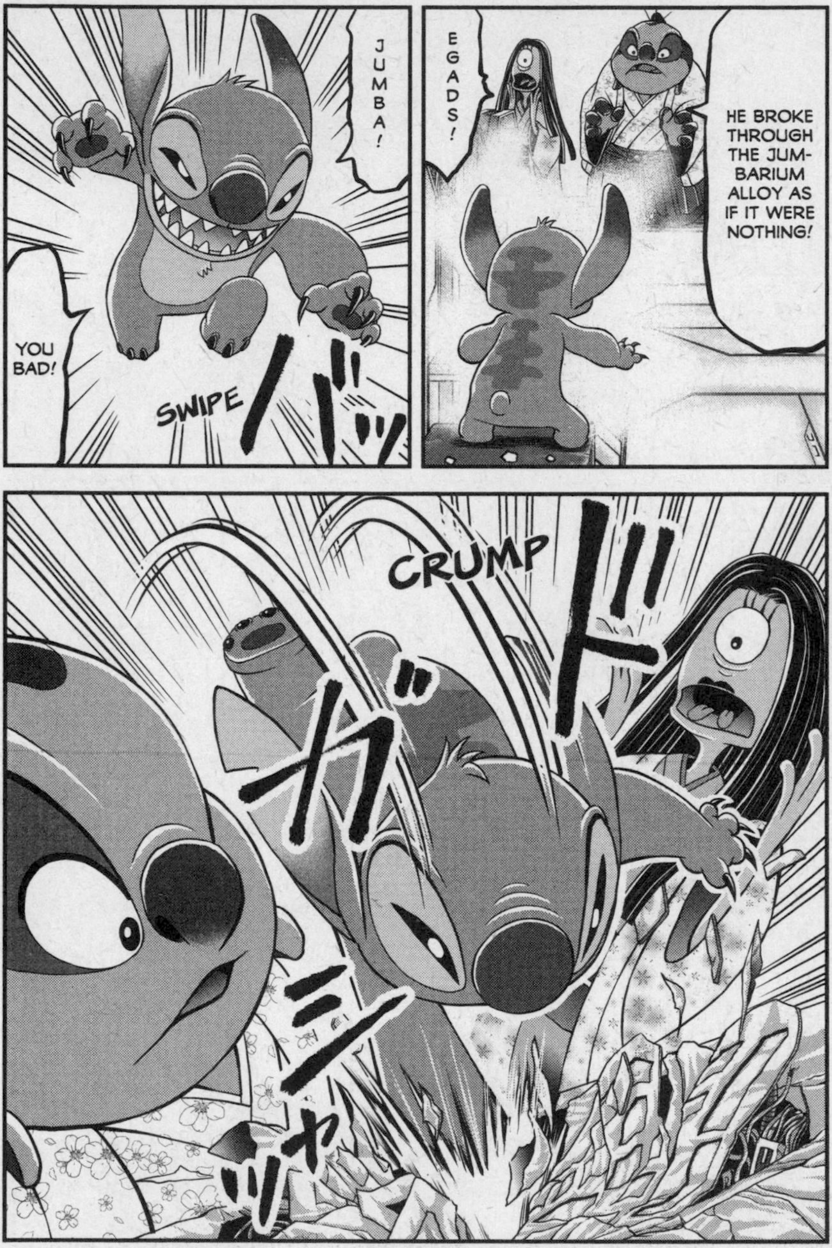
HE BROKE THROUGH THE JUM-BARIUM ALLOY AS IF IT WERE NOTHING!
EGADS!
JUMBA!
YOU BAD!
SWIPE
CRUMP

MY WONDERFUL INVENTION, YOU'VE...!

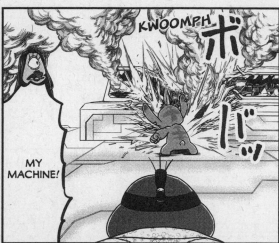

KWOOMPH

ボ

ゴッ

MY MACHINE!

CLINK

カシュ

HUH?

STITCH!!

ド

ー

ン

BOOM

NO!!

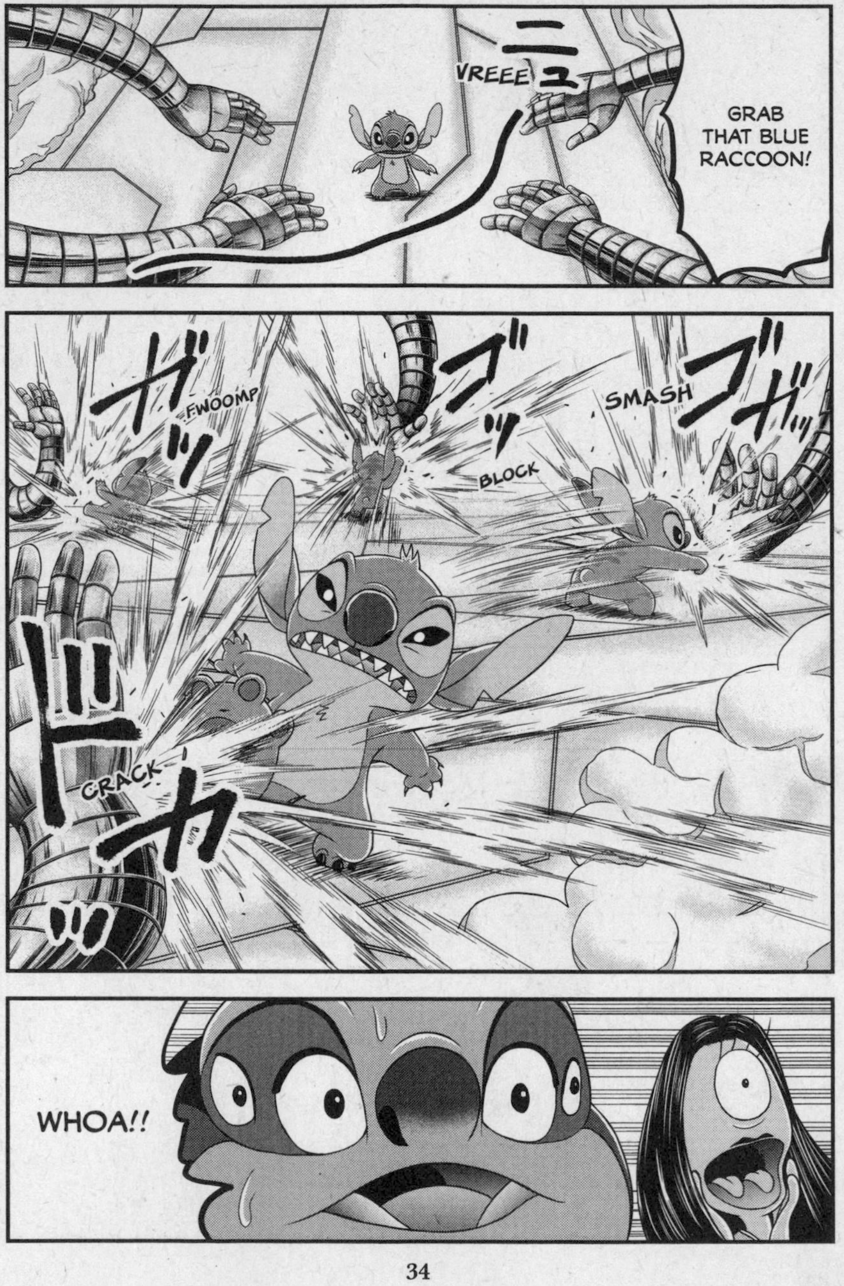
GRAB THAT BLUE RACCOON!
VREEE
SMASH
FWOOMP
BLOCK
CRACK
WHOA!!

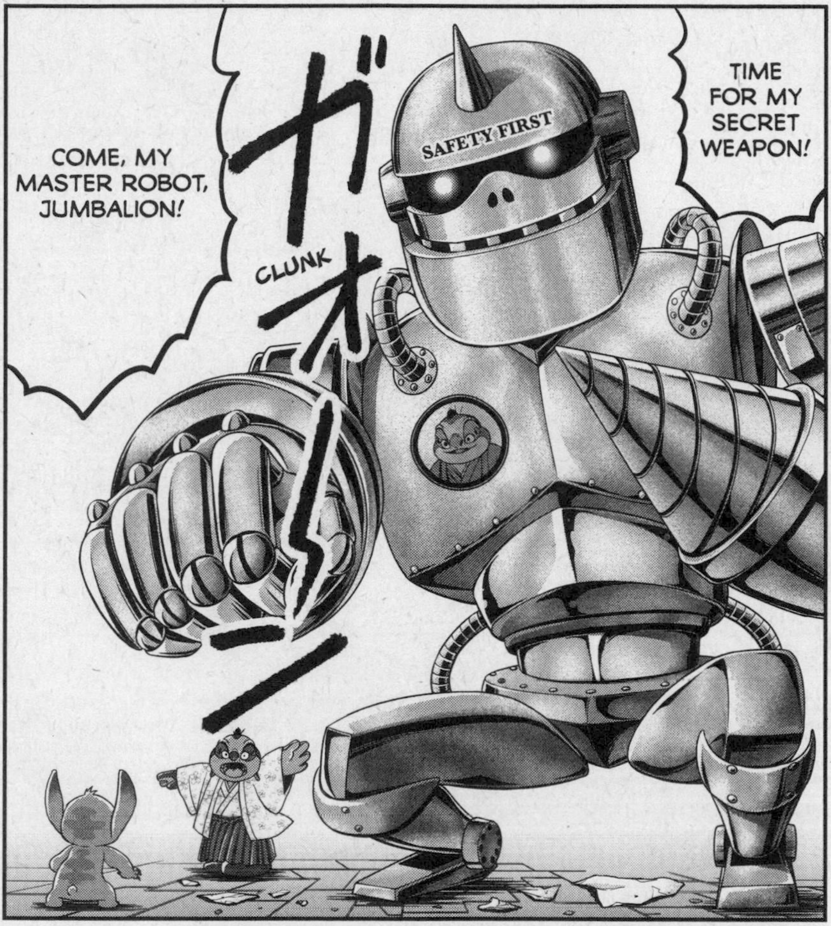
TIME FOR MY SECRET WEAPON!
COME, MY MASTER ROBOT, JUMBALION!
SAFETY FIRST
CLUNK

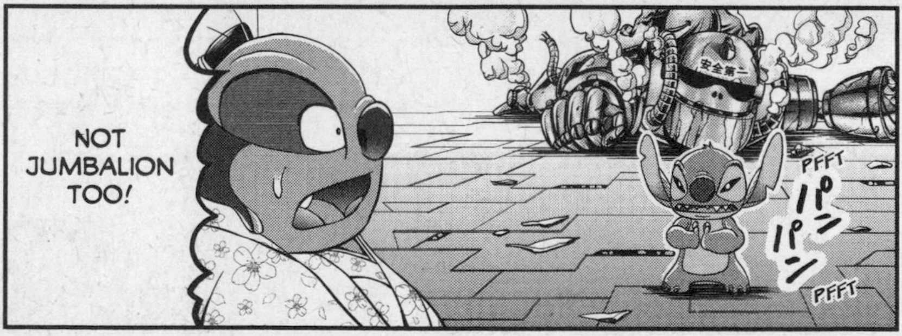
安全第二
PFFT
パン
パン
PFFT
NOT JUMBALION TOO!

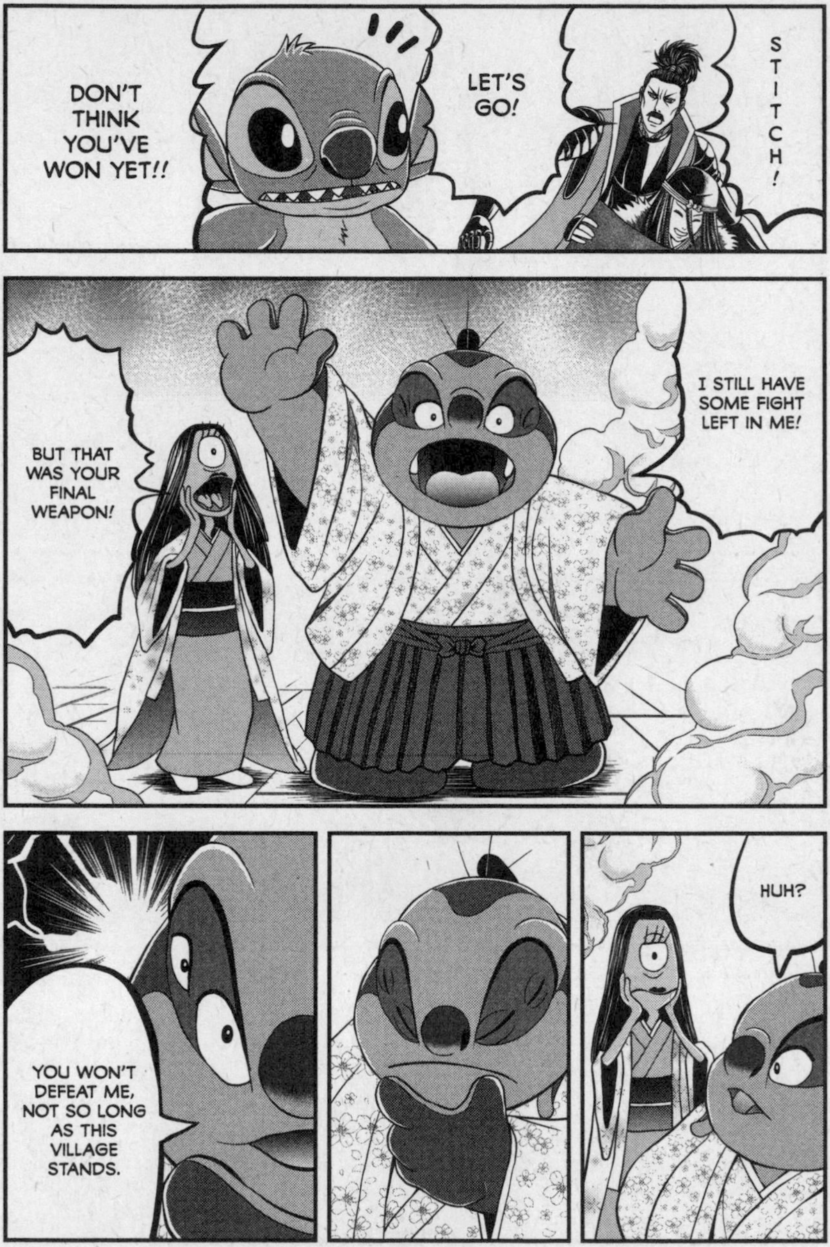
STITCH!
LET'S GO!
DON'T THINK YOU'VE WON YET!!
I STILL HAVE SOME FIGHT LEFT IN ME!
BUT THAT WAS YOUR FINAL WEAPON!
HUH?
YOU WON'T DEFEAT ME, NOT SO LONG AS THIS VILLAGE STANDS.

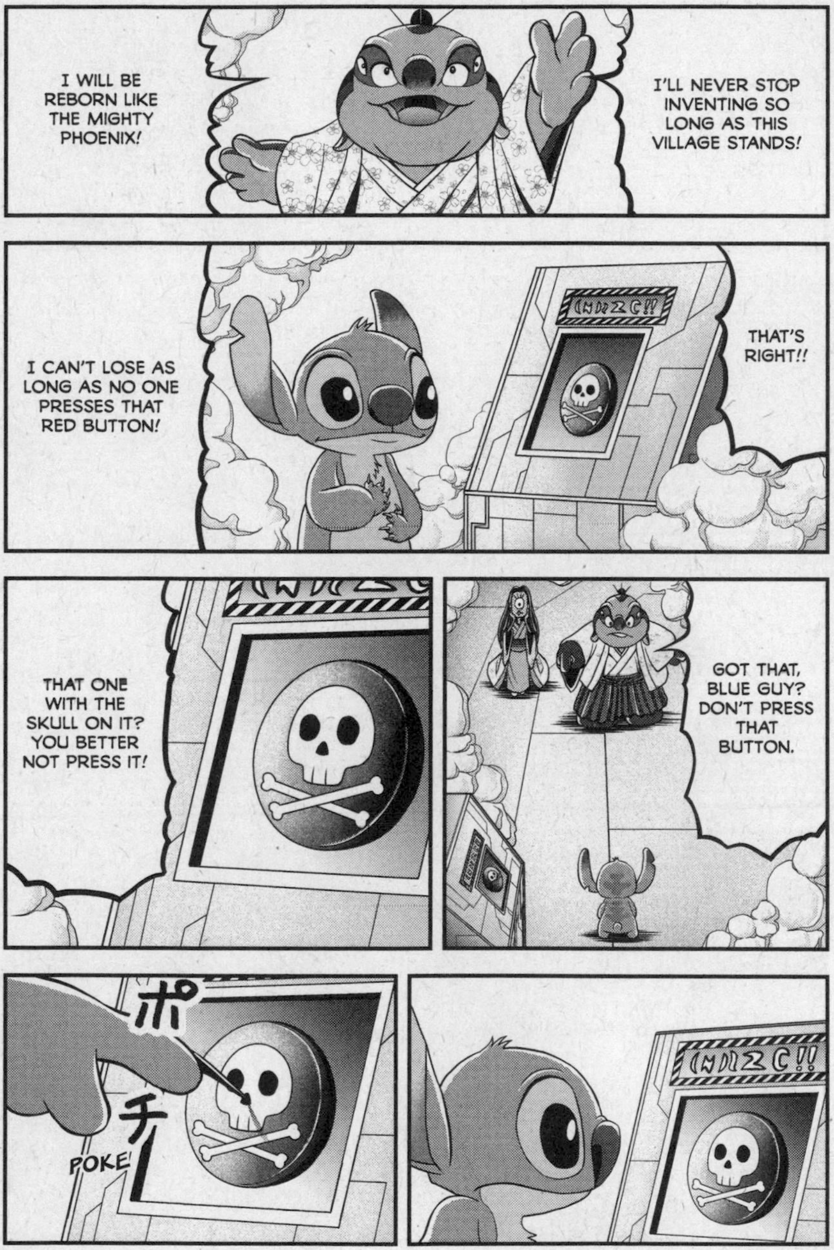
I'LL NEVER STOP INVENTING SO LONG AS THIS VILLAGE STANDS!
I WILL BE REBORN LIKE THE MIGHTY PHOENIX!
THAT'S RIGHT!!
I CAN'T LOSE AS LONG AS NO ONE PRESSES THAT RED BUTTON!
GOT THAT, BLUE GUY? DON'T PRESS THAT BUTTON.
THAT ONE WITH THE SKULL ON IT? YOU BETTER NOT PRESS IT!
ポチ
POKE

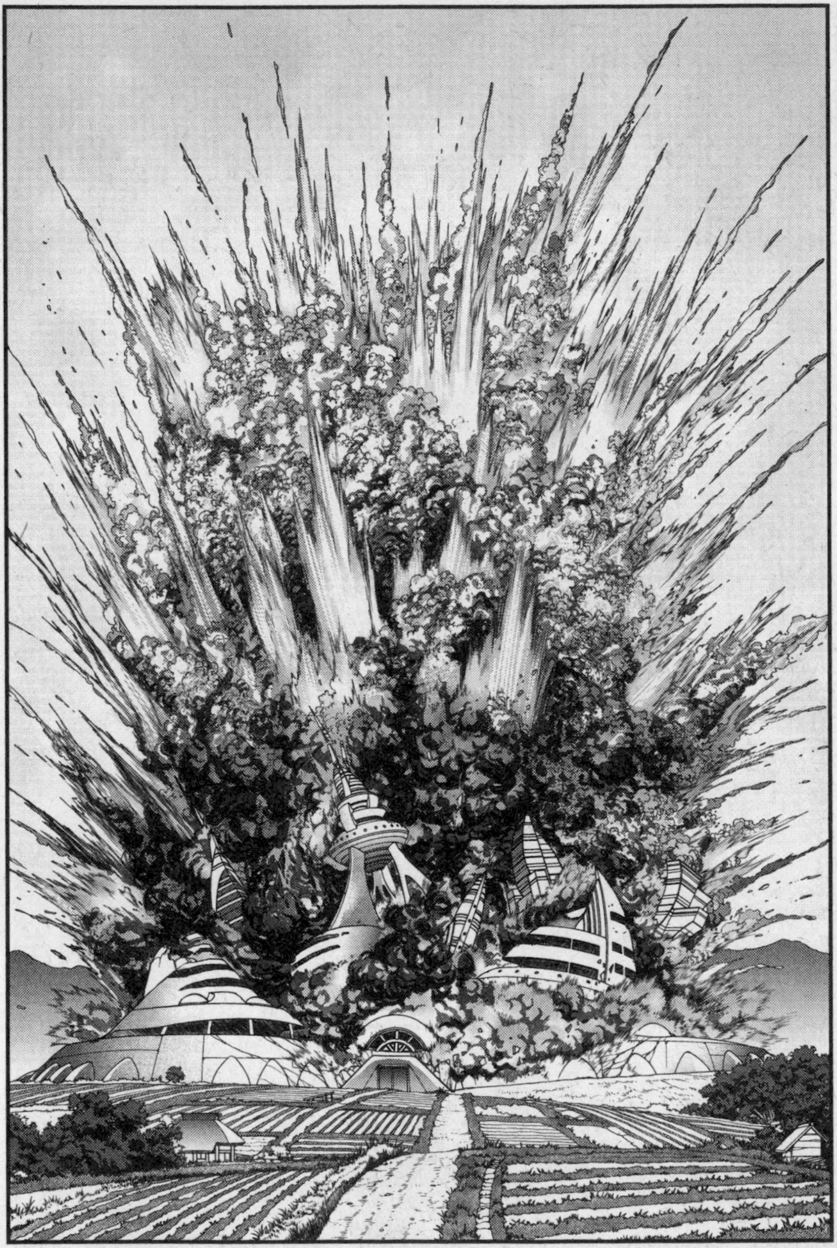

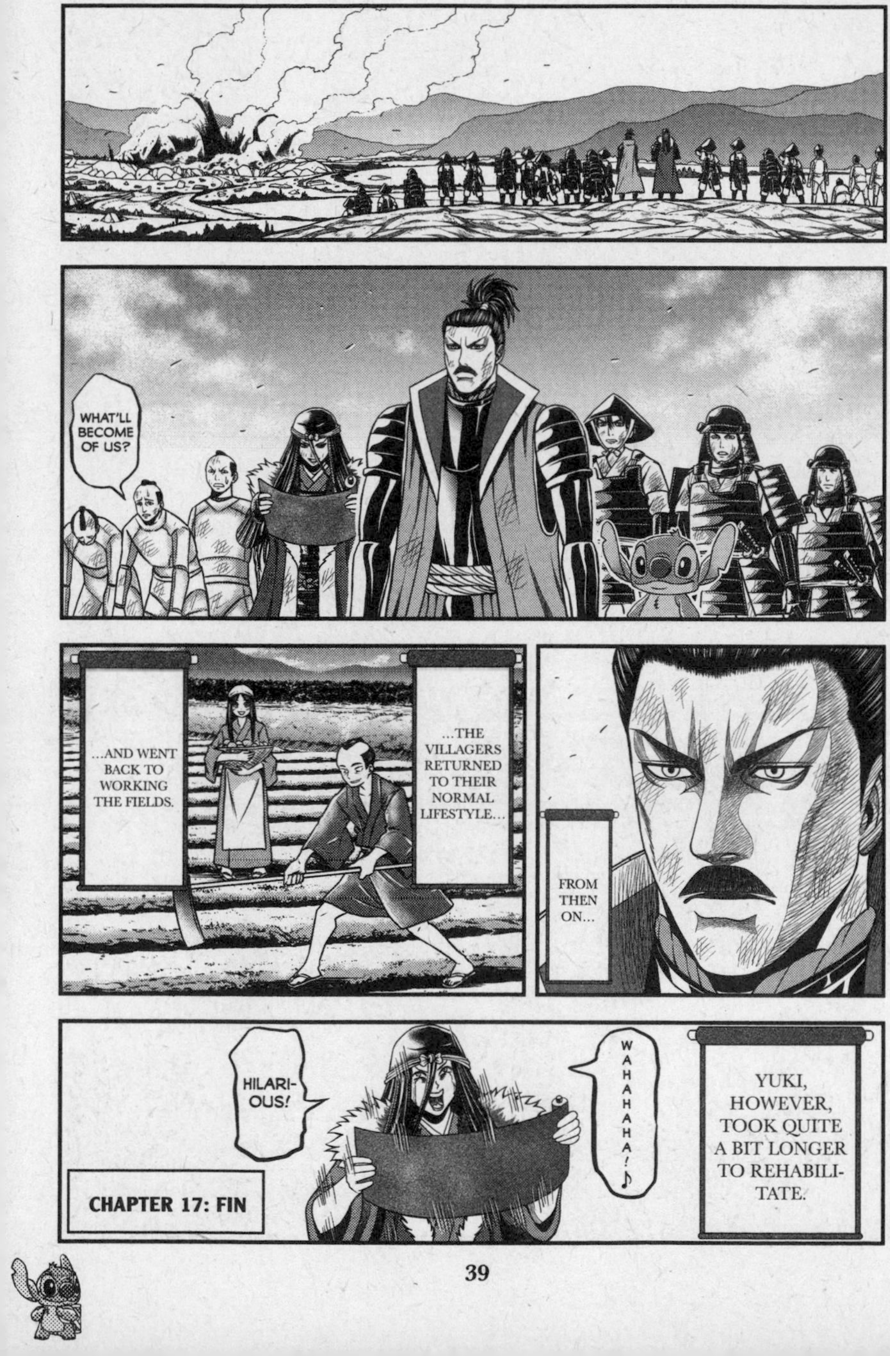
WHAT'LL BECOME OF US?
FROM THEN ON...
...THE VILLAGERS RETURNED TO THEIR NORMAL LIFESTYLE...
...AND WENT BACK TO WORKING THE FIELDS.
YUKI, HOWEVER, TOOK QUITE A BIT LONGER TO REHABILI-TATE.
WAHAHAHA!♪
HILARI-OUS!
CHAPTER 17: FIN

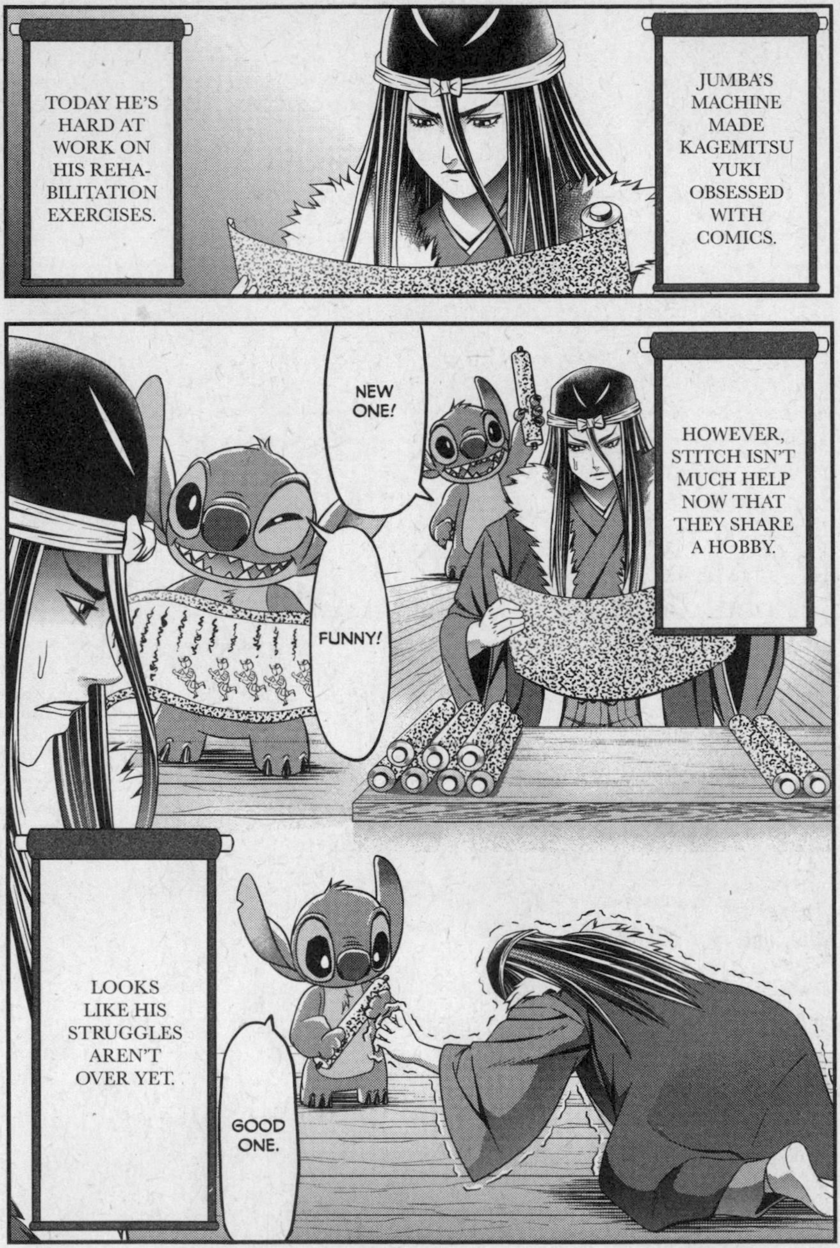
JUMBA'S MACHINE MADE KAGEMITSU YUKI OBSESSED WITH COMICS.
TODAY HE'S HARD AT WORK ON HIS REHABILITATION EXERCISES.
HOWEVER, STITCH ISN'T MUCH HELP NOW THAT THEY SHARE A HOBBY.
NEW ONE!
FUNNY!
GOOD ONE.
LOOKS LIKE HIS STRUGGLES AREN'T OVER YET.

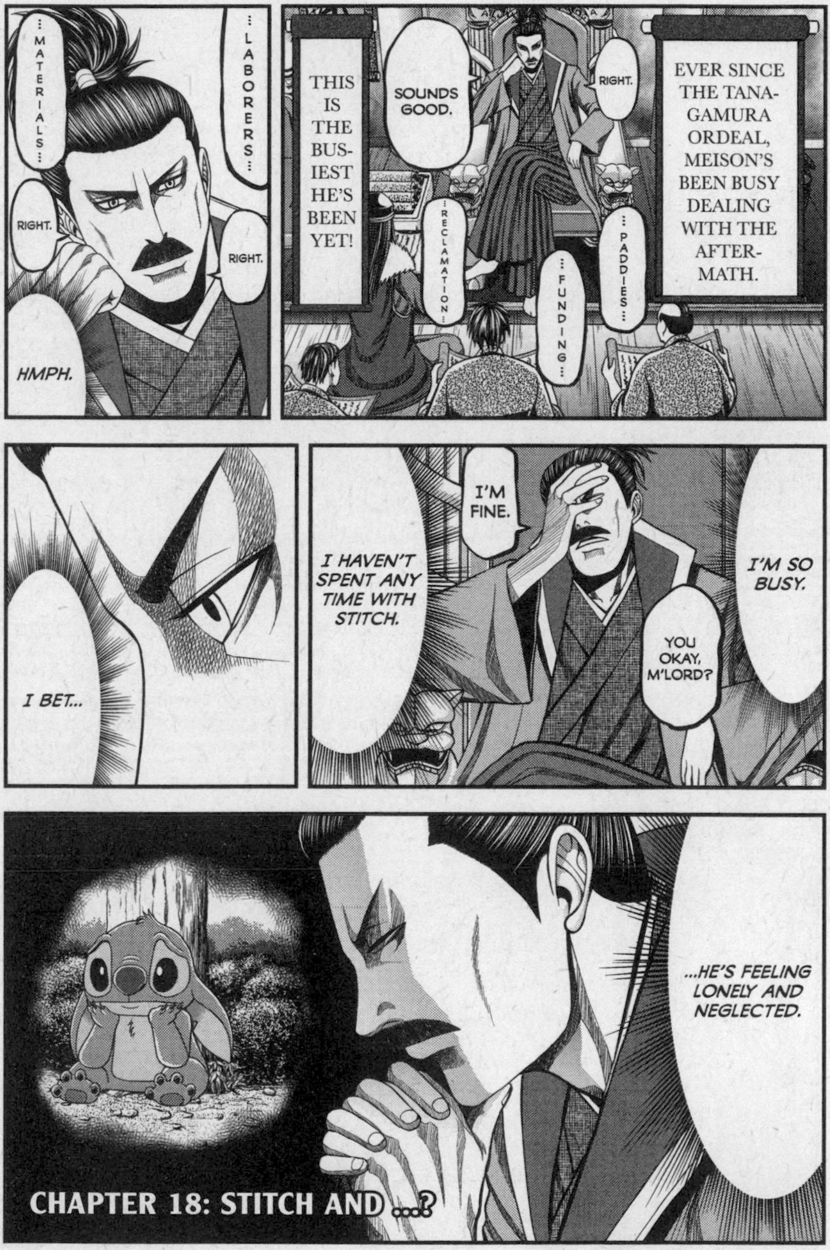
EVER SINCE THE TANAGAMURA ORDEAL, MEISON'S BEEN BUSY DEALING WITH THE AFTERMATH.
RIGHT.
SOUNDS GOOD.
THIS IS THE BUSIEST HE'S BEEN YET!
...PADDIES...
...FUNDING...
...RECLAMATION...
...LABORERS...
...MATERIALS...
RIGHT.
RIGHT.
HMPH.
I'M SO BUSY.
YOU OKAY, M'LORD?
I'M FINE.
I HAVEN'T SPENT ANY TIME WITH STITCH.
I BET...
...HE'S FEELING LONELY AND NEGLECTED.
CHAPTER 18: STITCH AND ...?

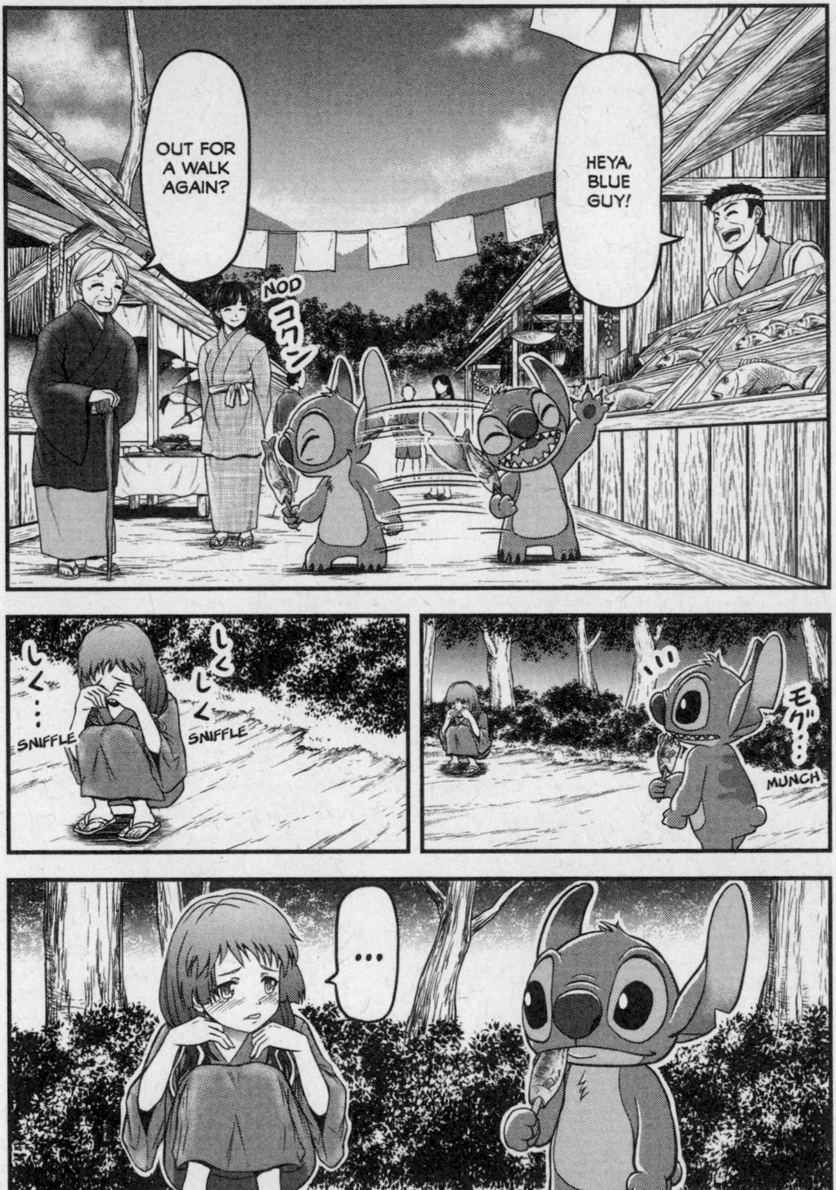

HEYA, BLUE GUY!
OUT FOR A WALK AGAIN?
コクン
NOD
モグ…
MUNCH
しくしく
SNIFFLE
しく…
SNIFFLE
...

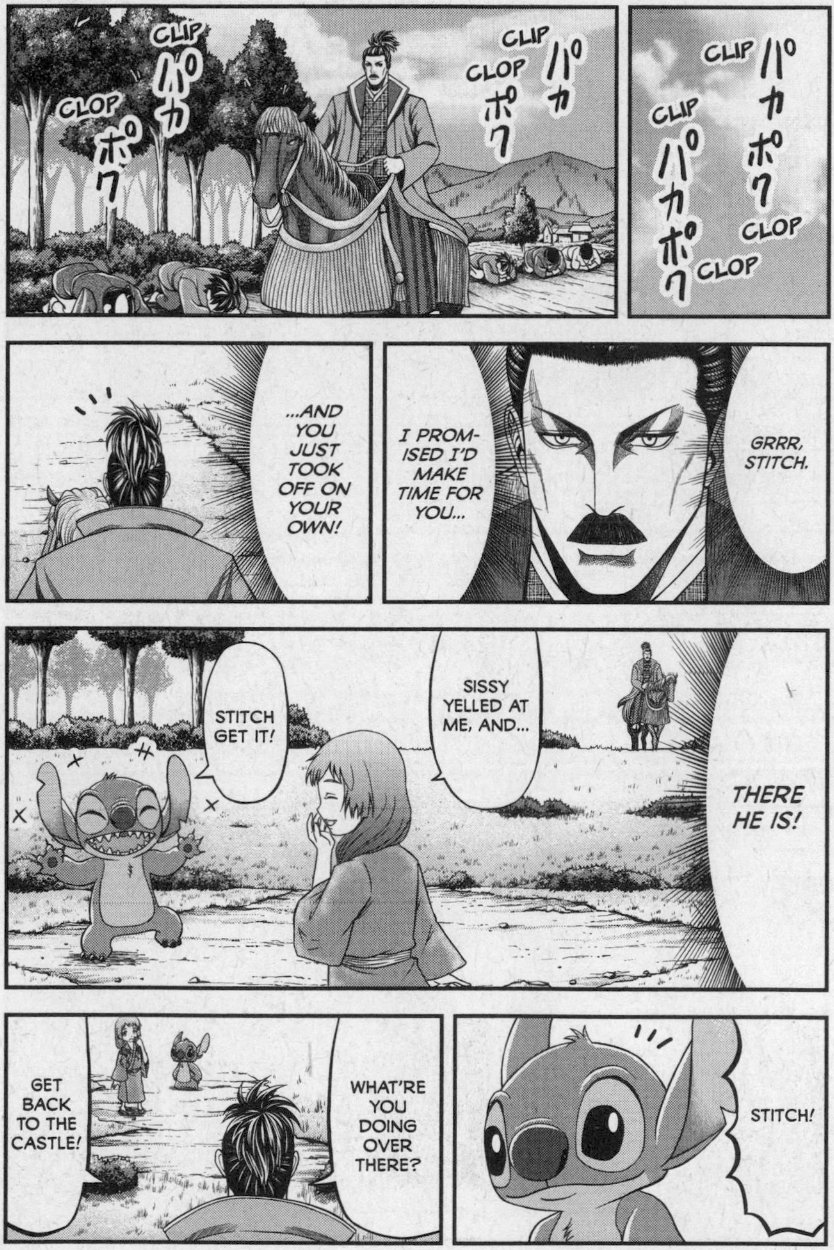
CLIP
パカポク
CLOP
CLIP
パカポク
CLOP
CLIP
パカ
CLOP
ポク
CLIP
パカ
CLOP
ポク
GRRR, STITCH.
I PROMISED I'D MAKE TIME FOR YOU...
...AND YOU JUST TOOK OFF ON YOUR OWN!
THERE HE IS!
SISSY YELLED AT ME, AND...
STITCH GET IT!
STITCH!
WHAT'RE YOU DOING OVER THERE?
GET BACK TO THE CASTLE!

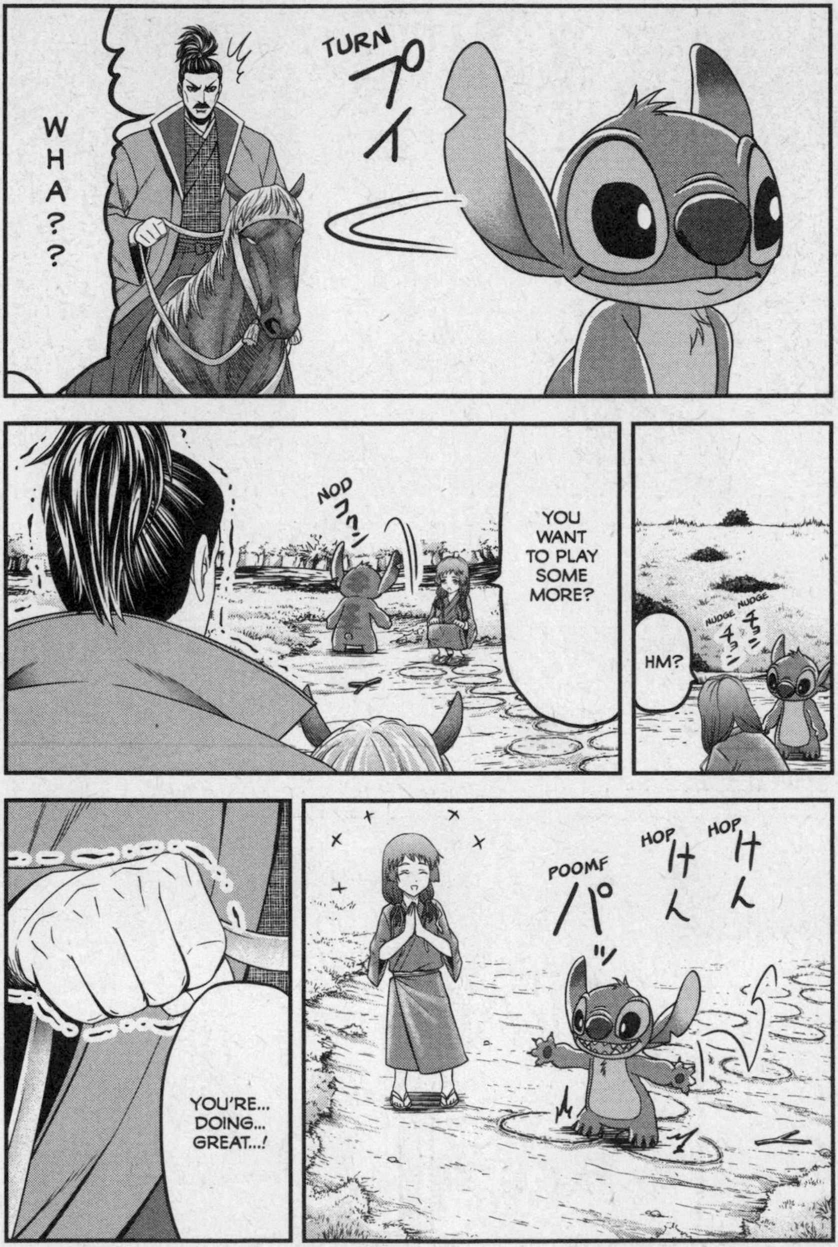
TURN
プイ
WHA??
NUDGE NUDGE
チョン チョン
HM?
YOU WANT TO PLAY SOME MORE?
NOD
コクン
HOP
けん
HOP
けん
POOMF
パッ
YOU'RE... DOING... GREAT...!

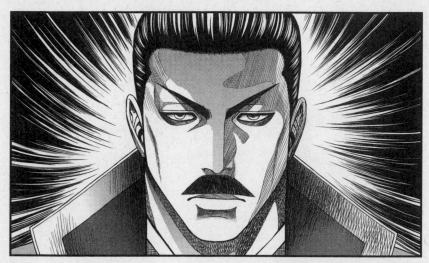

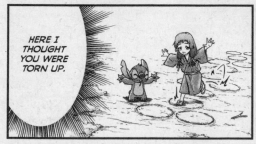

LOOK AT THAT SMILE.
HERE I THOUGHT YOU WERE TORN UP.
SO I HURRIED THROUGH MY WORK.
THIS FEELING…
…WAS ONE UN-FAMILIAR TO MEISON.
CLENCH

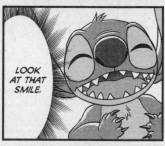

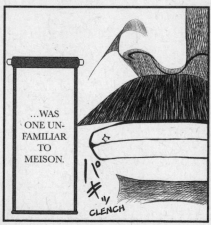

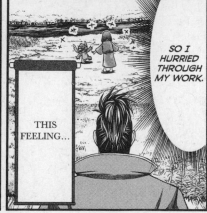

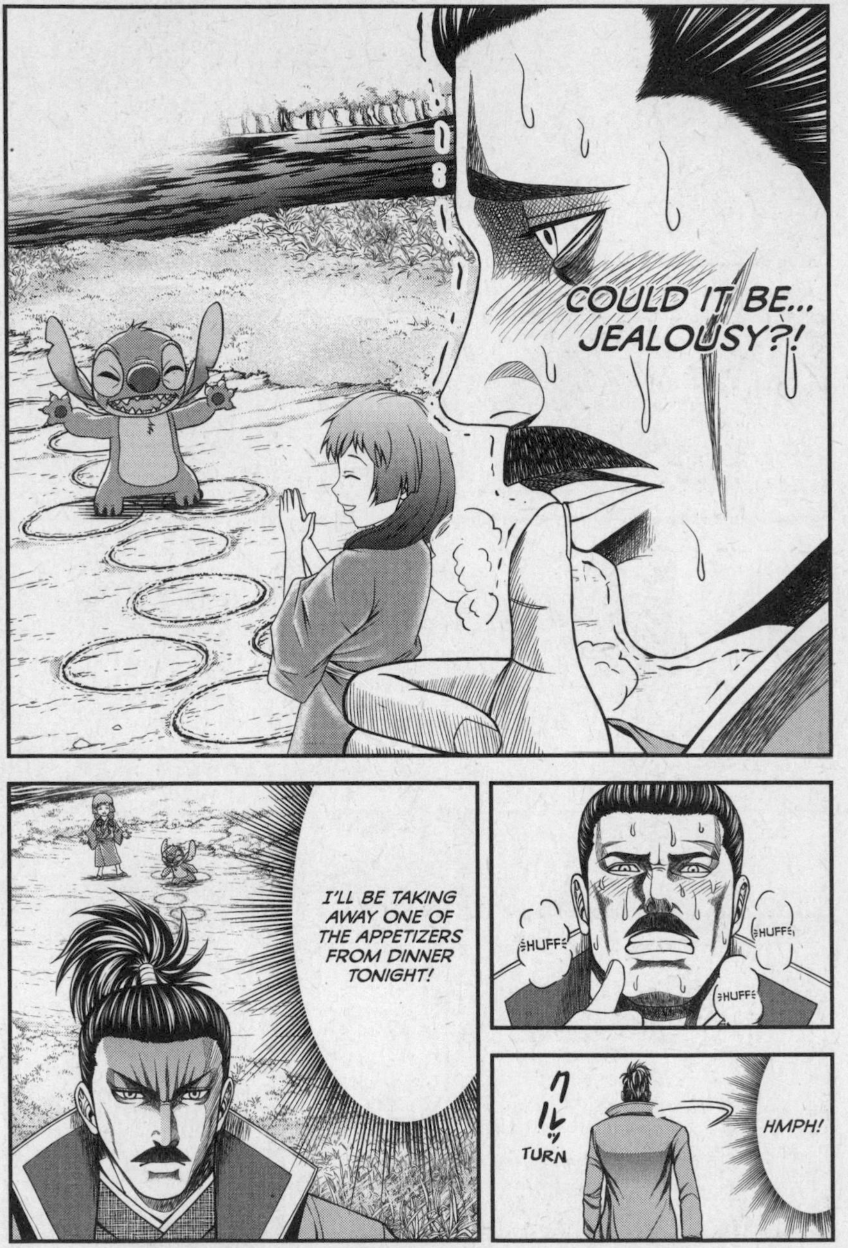
COULD IT BE... JEALOUSY?!
HUFF
HUFF
HUFF
クルッ
TURN
HMPH!
I'LL BE TAKING AWAY ONE OF THE APPETIZERS FROM DINNER TONIGHT!

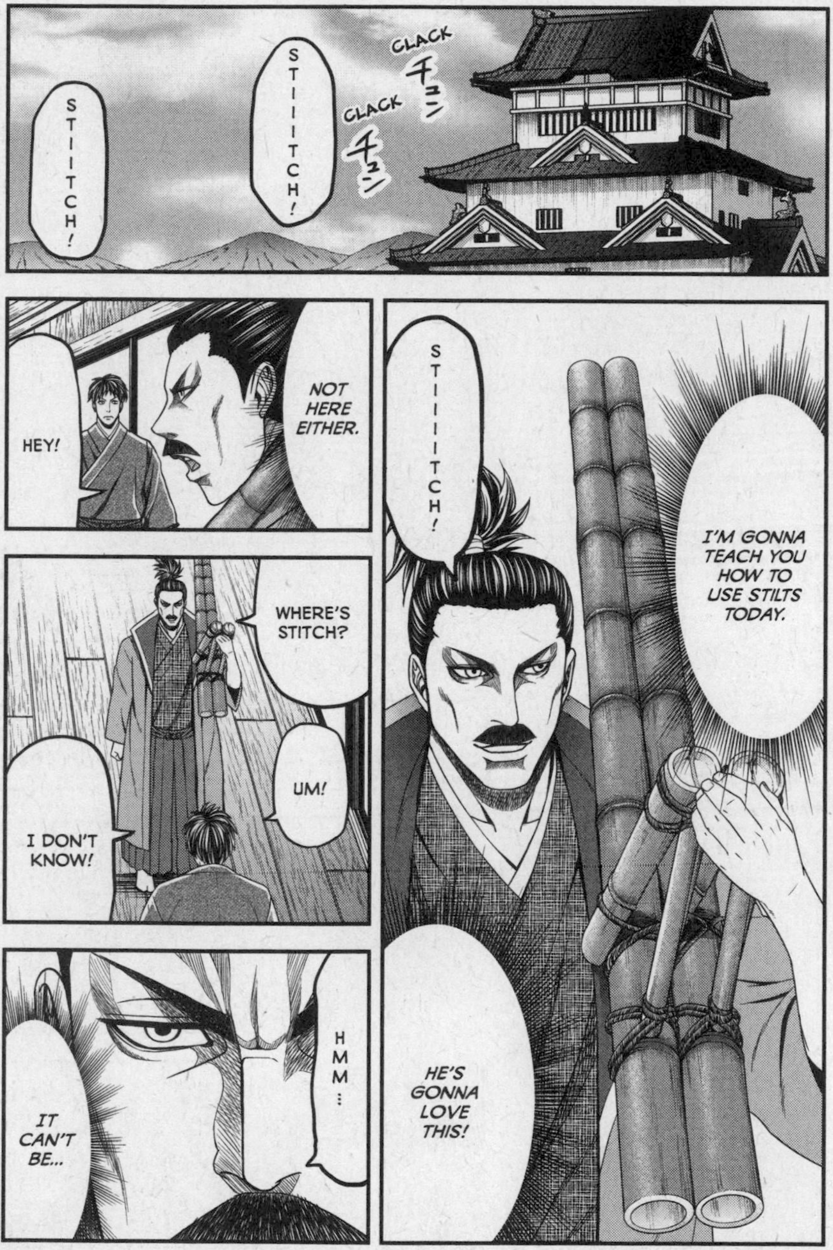
CLACK
チュン
CLACK
チュン
STIIITCH!
STIITCH!
STIIIITCH!
I'M GONNA TEACH YOU HOW TO USE STILTS TODAY.
HE'S GONNA LOVE THIS!
NOT HERE EITHER.
HEY!
WHERE'S STITCH?
UM!
I DON'T KNOW!
HMM...
IT CAN'T BE...

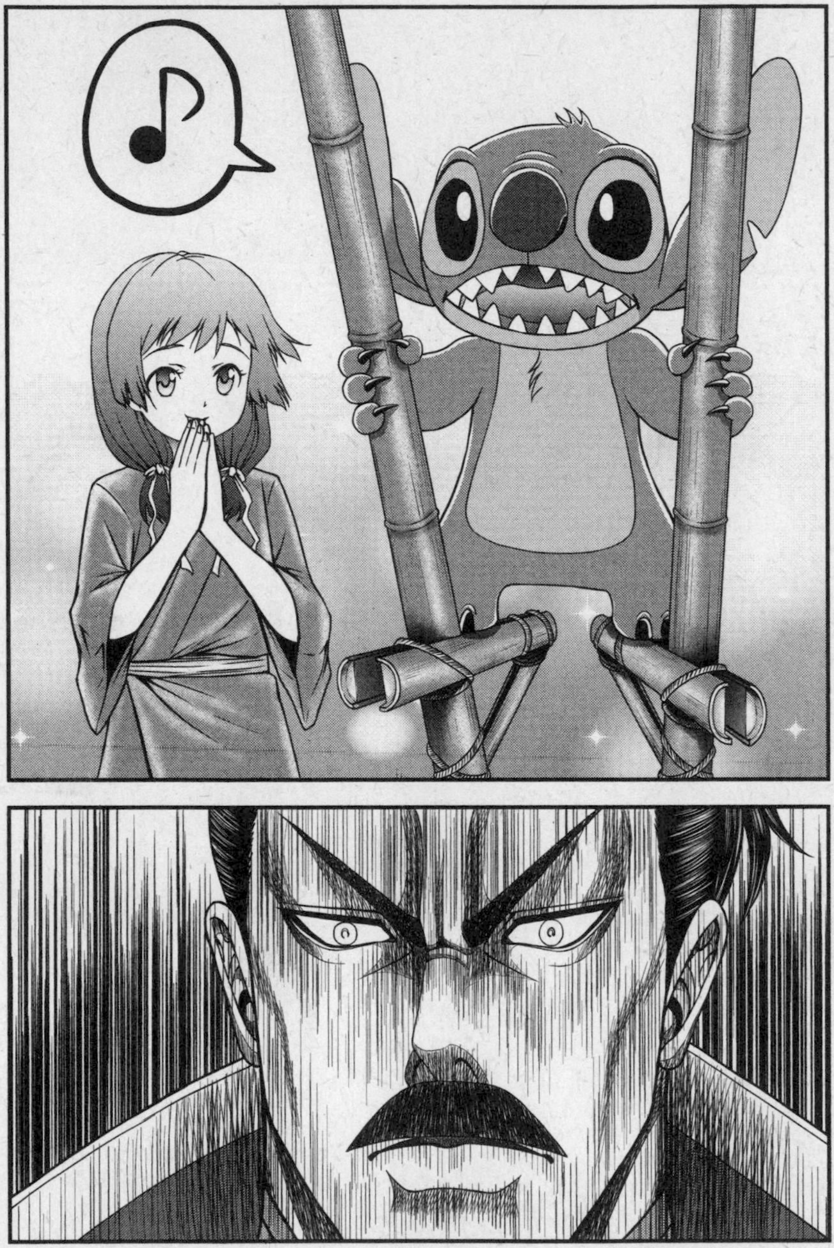

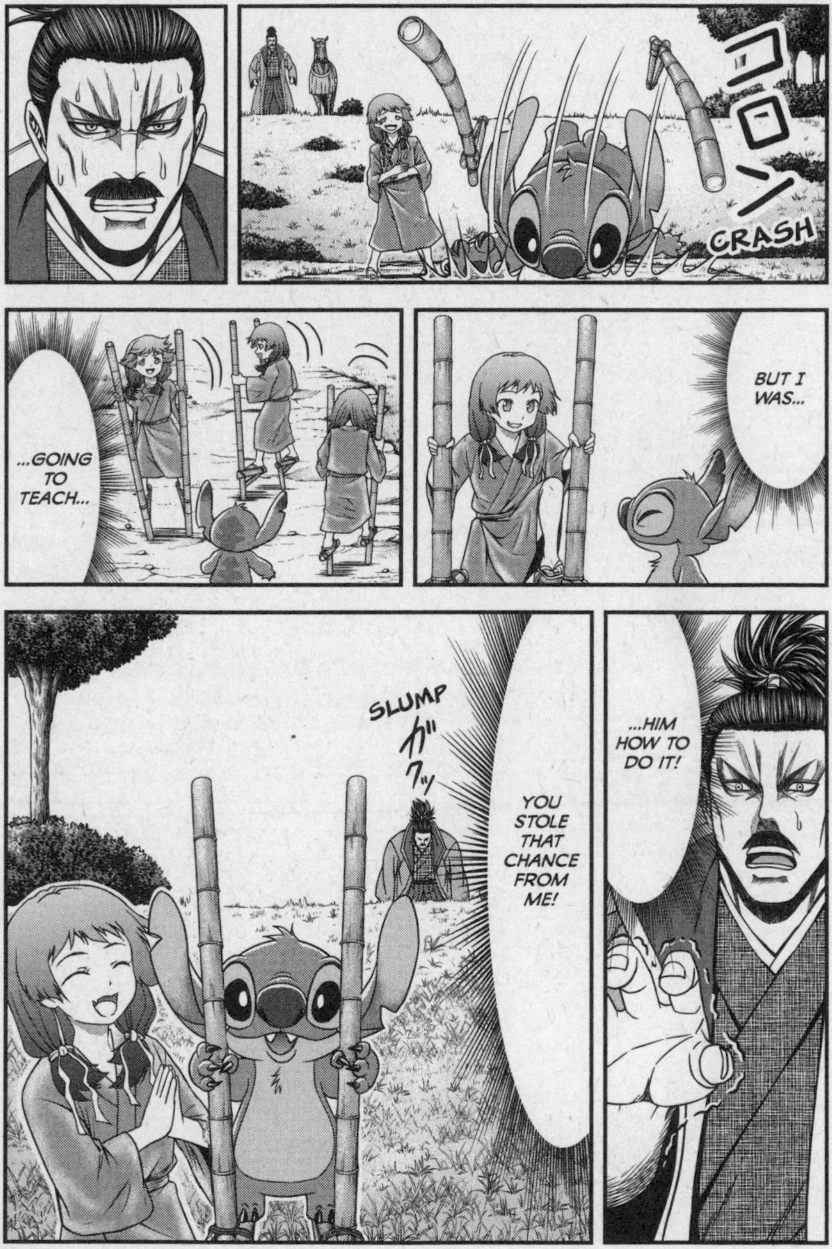
コロン
CRASH
BUT I WAS...
...GOING TO TEACH...
...HIM HOW TO DO IT!
YOU STOLE THAT CHANCE FROM ME!
SLUMP
ガクッ

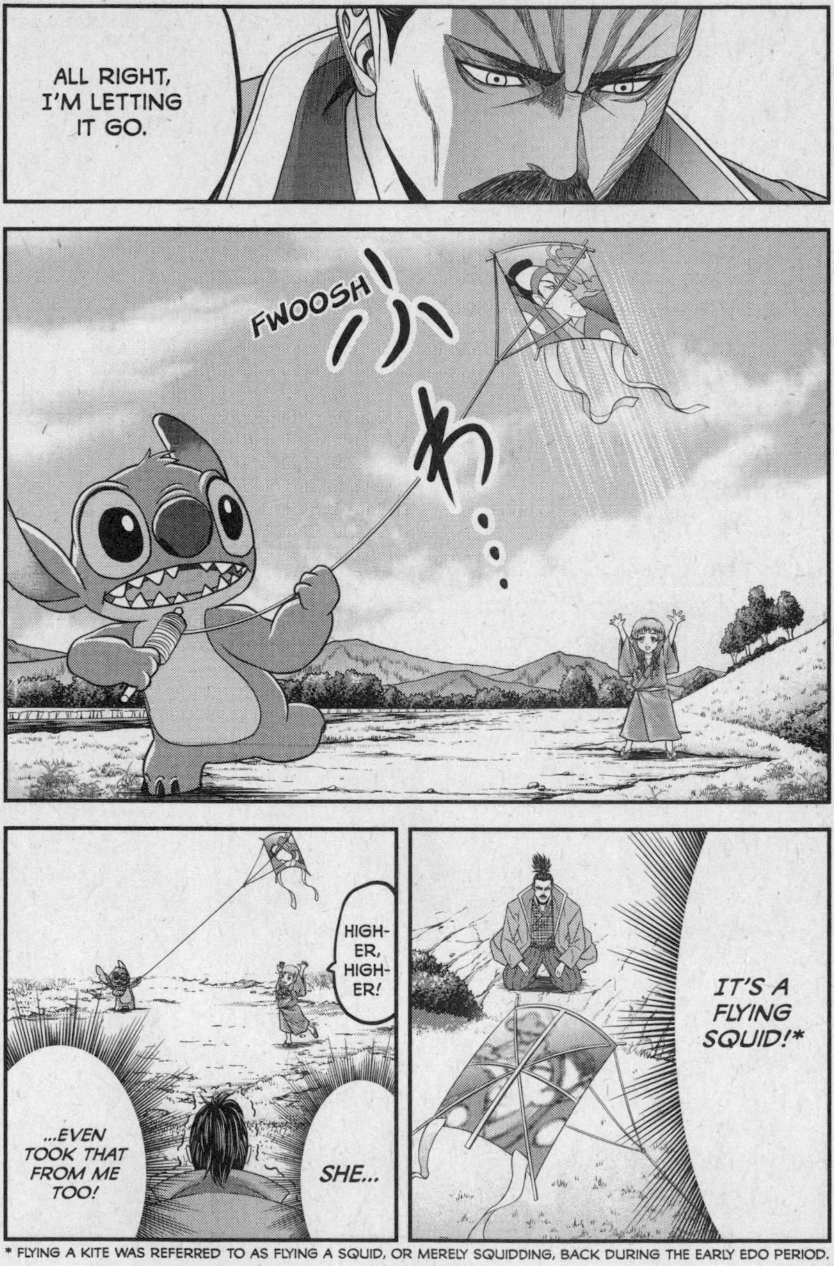
ALL RIGHT, I'M LETTING IT GO.
FWOOSH
ふわ…
IT'S A FLYING SQUID!*
HIGH-ER, HIGH-ER!
SHE...
...EVEN TOOK THAT FROM ME TOO!

* FLYING A KITE WAS REFERRED TO AS FLYING A SQUID, OR MERELY SQUIDDING, BACK DURING THE EARLY EDO PERIOD.

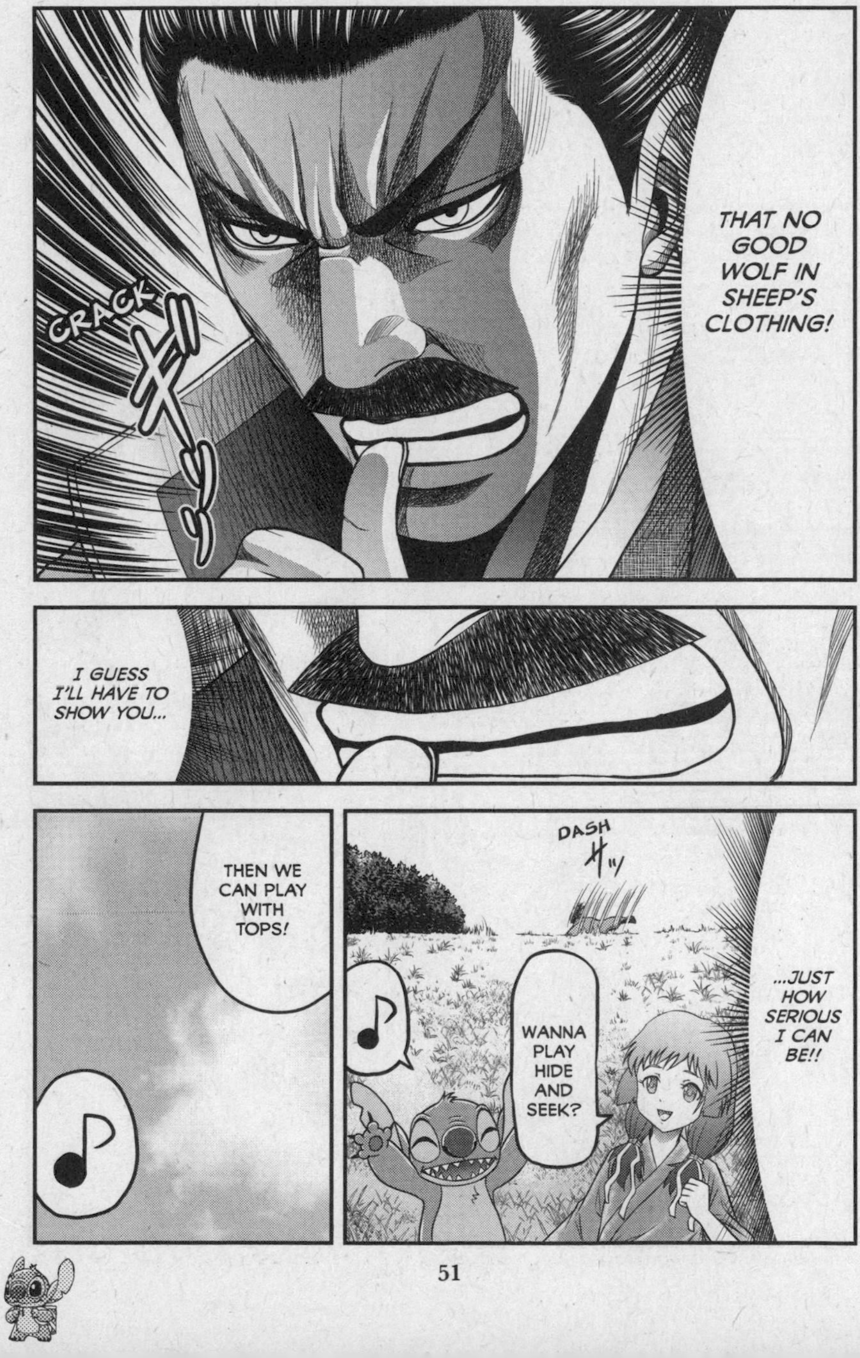
THAT NO GOOD WOLF IN SHEEP'S CLOTHING!
CRACK
I GUESS I'LL HAVE TO SHOW YOU...
DASH
...JUST HOW SERIOUS I CAN BE!!
WANNA PLAY HIDE AND SEEK?
THEN WE CAN PLAY WITH TOPS!

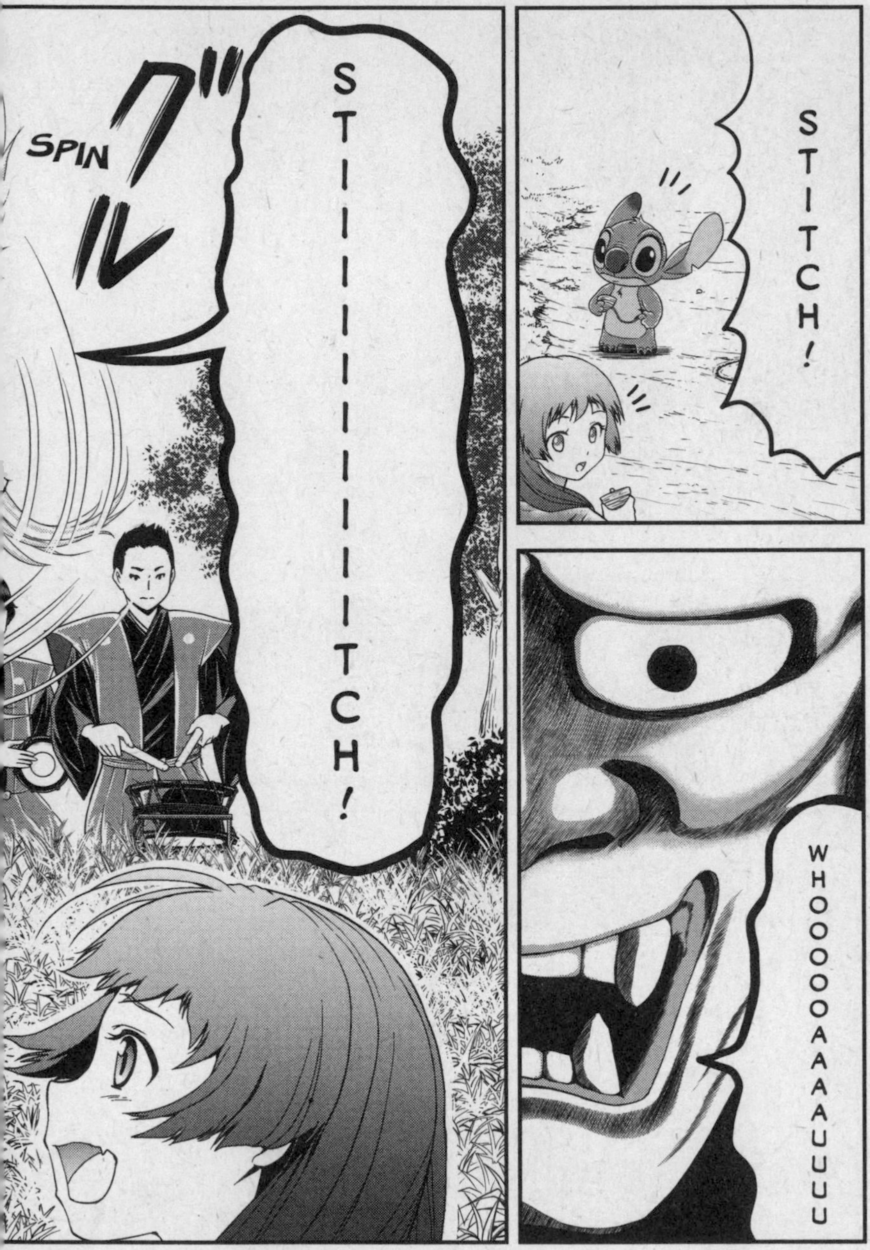
STITCH!
WHOOOOOOAAAAUUUU
SPIN
STIIIIIIIIIIIIITCH!

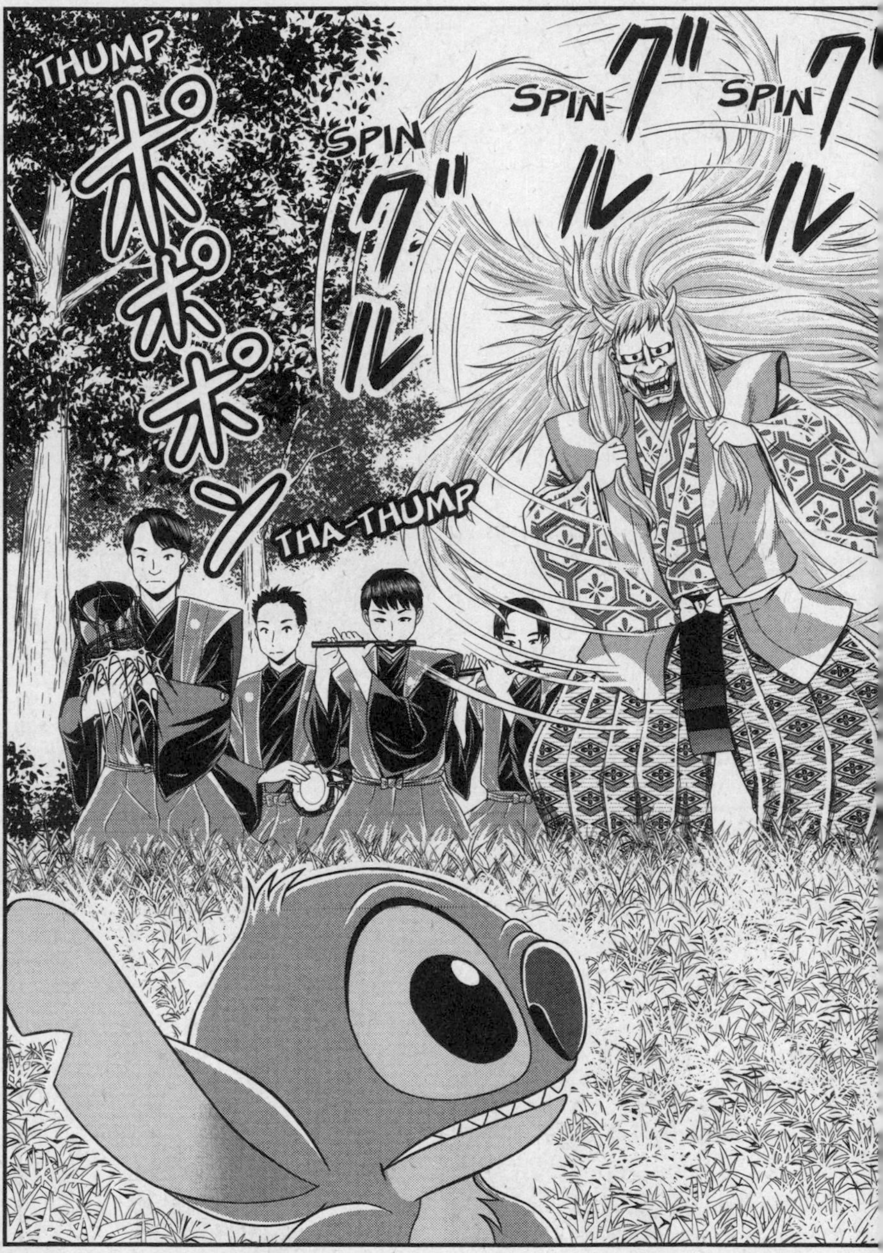
SPIN
グル
SPIN
グル
SPIN
グル
THUMP
ポポポン
THA-THUMP

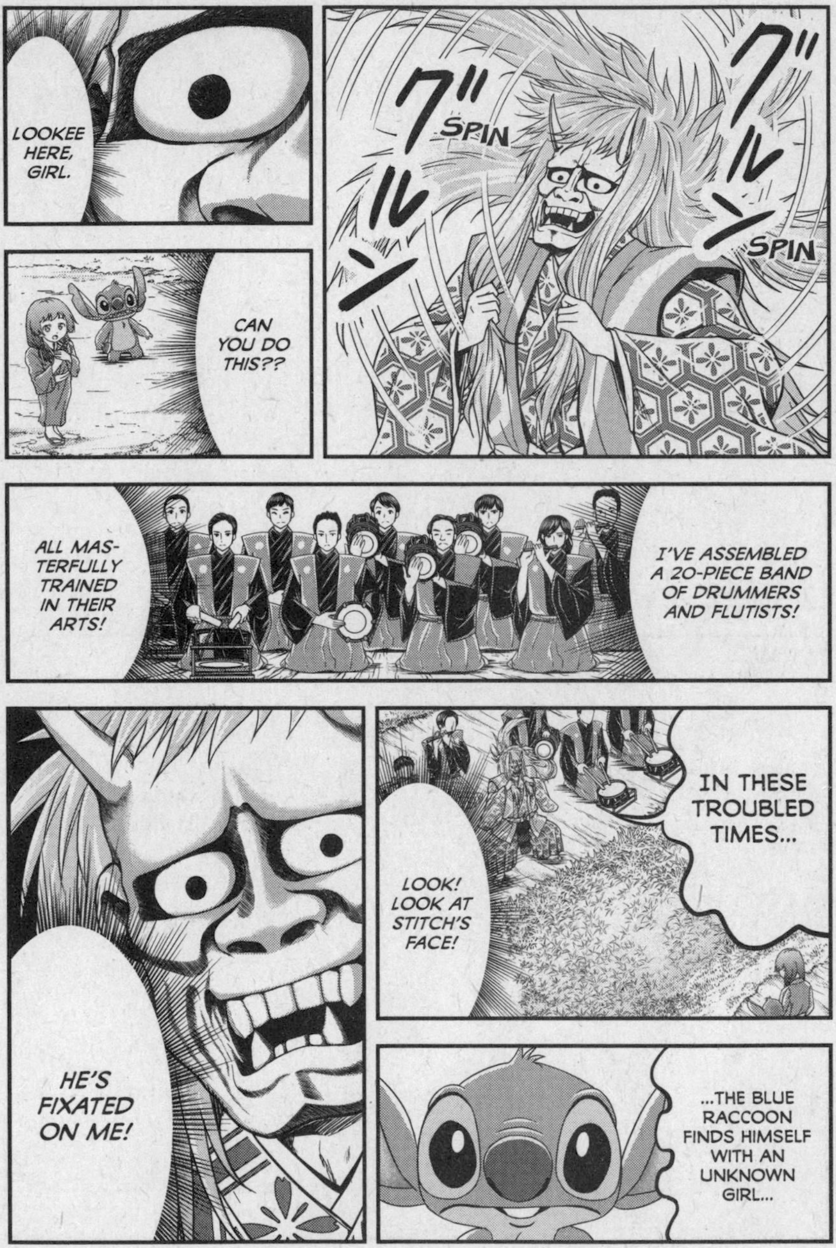
グルン
SPIN
グルン
SPIN
LOOKEE HERE, GIRL.
CAN YOU DO THIS??
I'VE ASSEMBLED A 20-PIECE BAND OF DRUMMERS AND FLUTISTS!
ALL MASTERFULLY TRAINED IN THEIR ARTS!
IN THESE TROUBLED TIMES...
LOOK! LOOK AT STITCH'S FACE!
...THE BLUE RACCOON FINDS HIMSELF WITH AN UNKNOWN GIRL...
HE'S FIXATED ON ME!

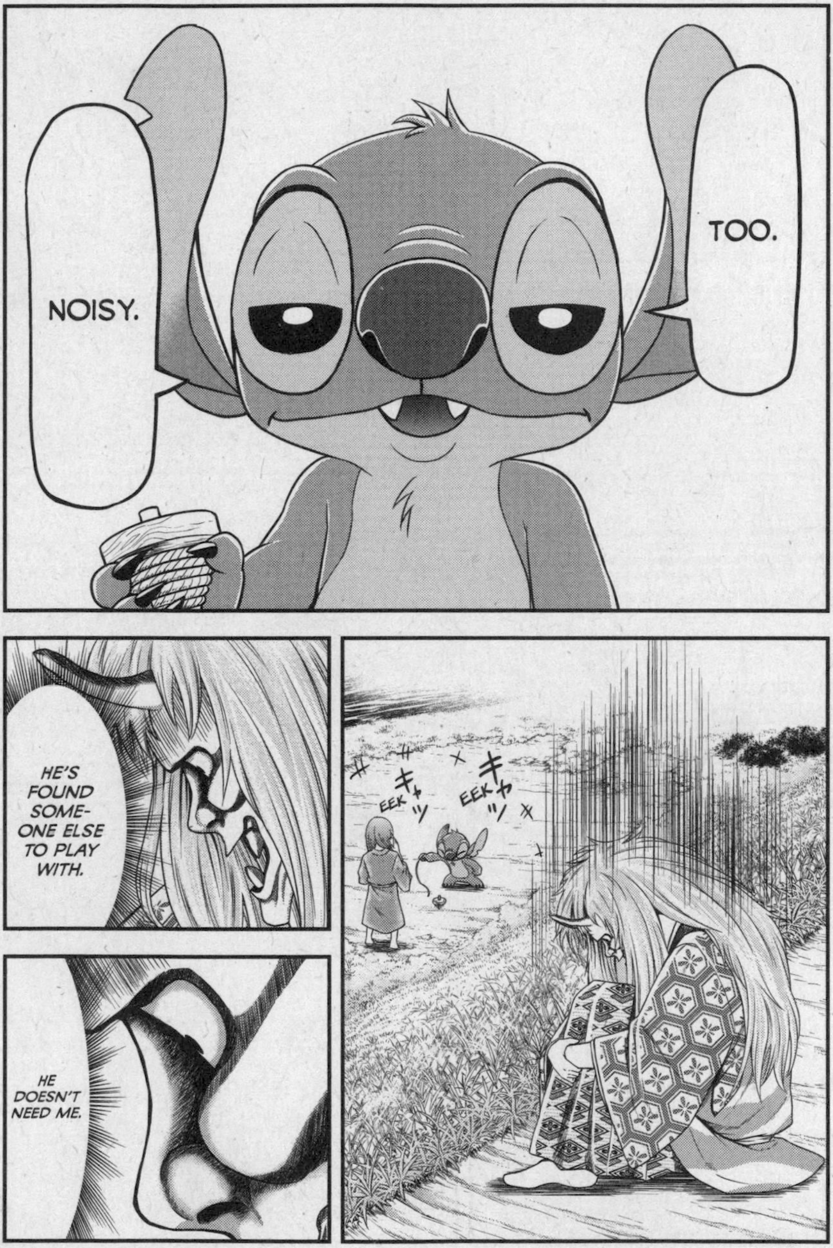
TOO.
NOISY.
EEK
EEK
HE'S FOUND SOME-ONE ELSE TO PLAY WITH.
HE DOESN'T NEED ME.

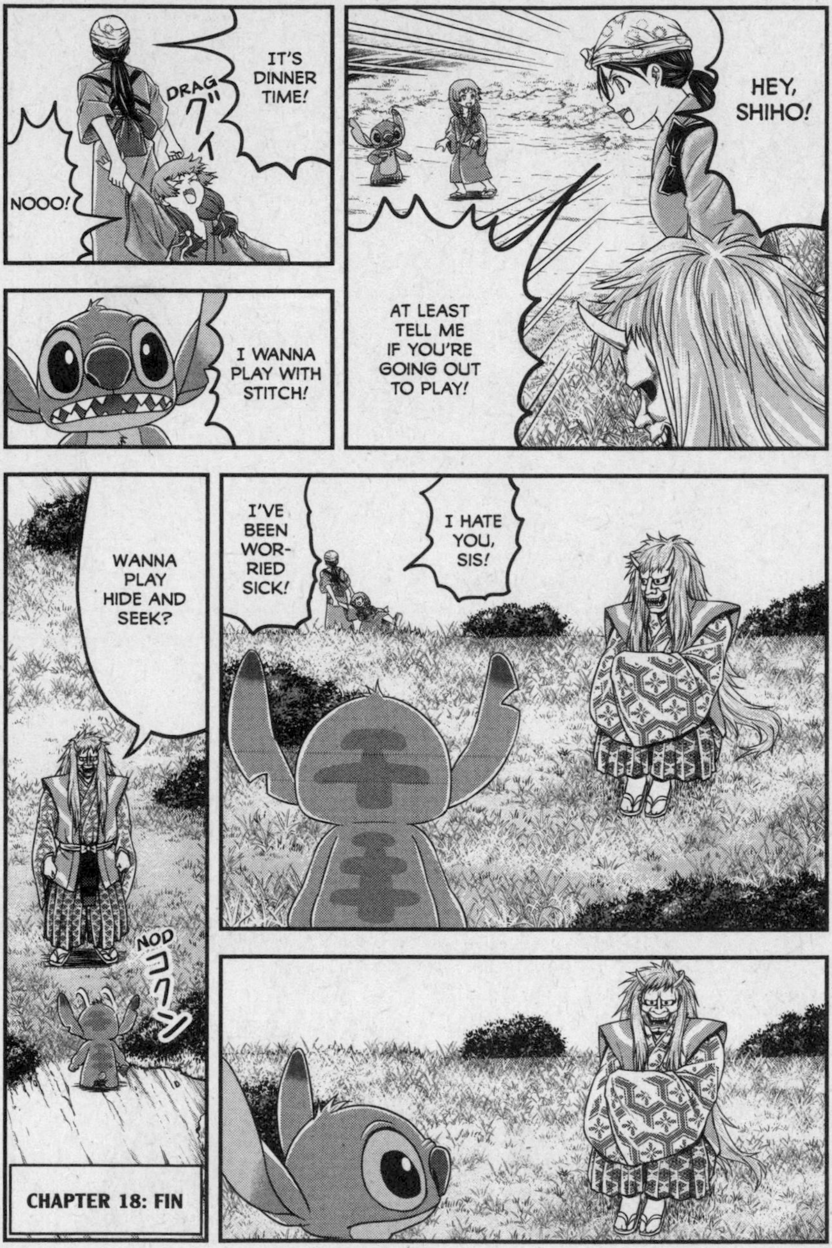
HEY, SHIHO!
AT LEAST TELL ME IF YOU'RE GOING OUT TO PLAY!
IT'S DINNER TIME!
DRAG グイ
NOOO!
I WANNA PLAY WITH STITCH!
I HATE YOU, SIS!
I'VE BEEN WOR-RIED SICK!
WANNA PLAY HIDE AND SEEK?
NOD コクン
CHAPTER 18: FIN

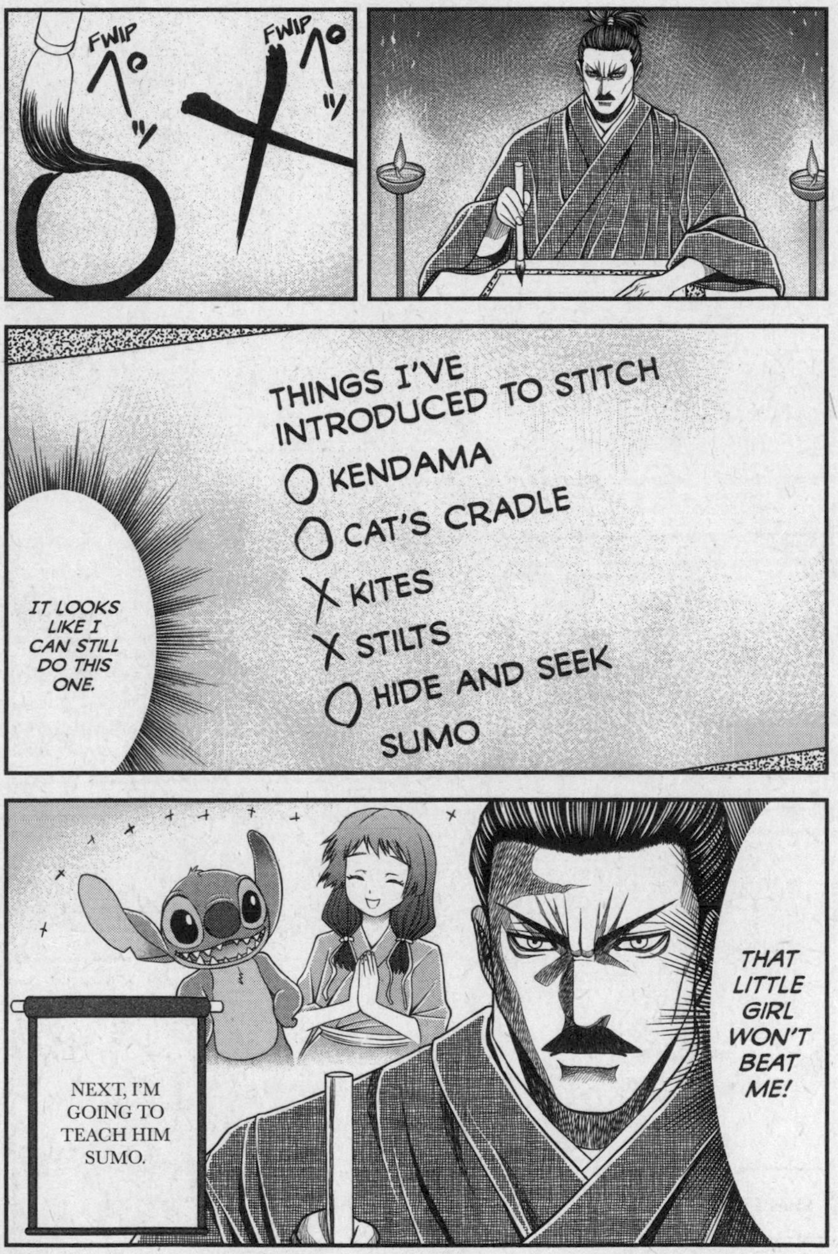
FWIP
FWIP
THINGS I'VE INTRODUCED TO STITCH
O KENDAMA
O CAT'S CRADLE
X KITES
X STILTS
O HIDE AND SEEK
SUMO
IT LOOKS LIKE I CAN STILL DO THIS ONE.
THAT LITTLE GIRL WON'T BEAT ME!
NEXT, I'M GOING TO TEACH HIM SUMO.

Disney

Stitch

STITCH & THE SAMURAI

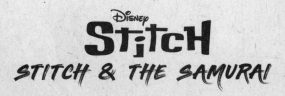

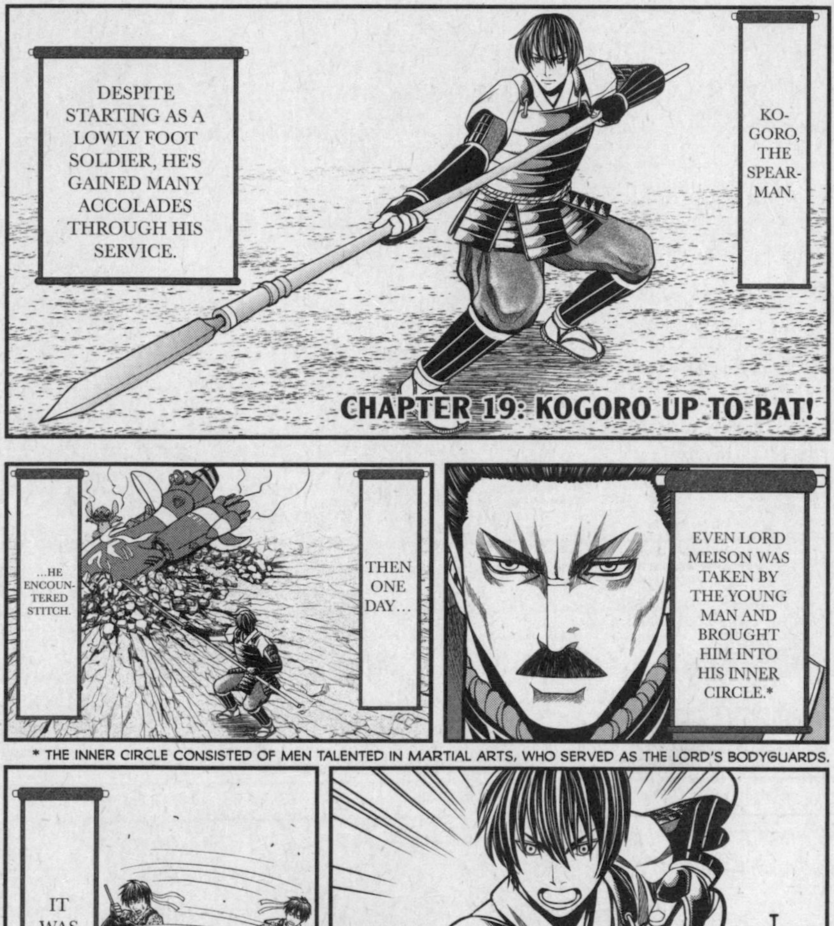
KOGORO, THE SPEARMAN.
DESPITE STARTING AS A LOWLY FOOT SOLDIER, HE'S GAINED MANY ACCOLADES THROUGH HIS SERVICE.
CHAPTER 19: KOGORO UP TO BAT!
EVEN LORD MEISON WAS TAKEN BY THE YOUNG MAN AND BROUGHT HIM INTO HIS INNER CIRCLE.*
THEN ONE DAY…
...HE ENCOUNTERED STITCH.

* THE INNER CIRCLE CONSISTED OF MEN TALENTED IN MARTIAL ARTS, WHO SERVED AS THE LORD'S BODYGUARDS.

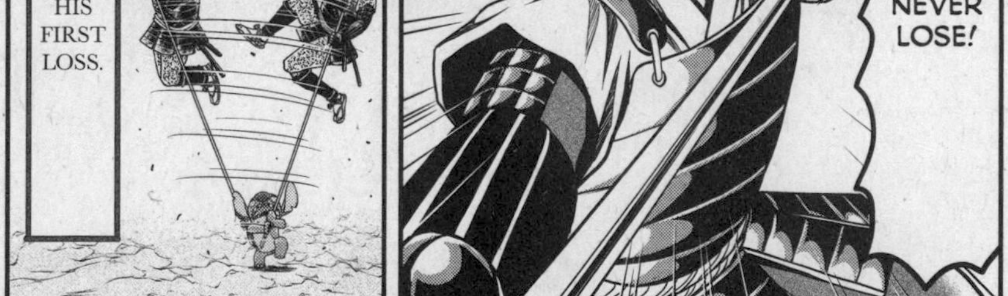
I NEVER LOSE!
IT WAS HIS FIRST LOSS.

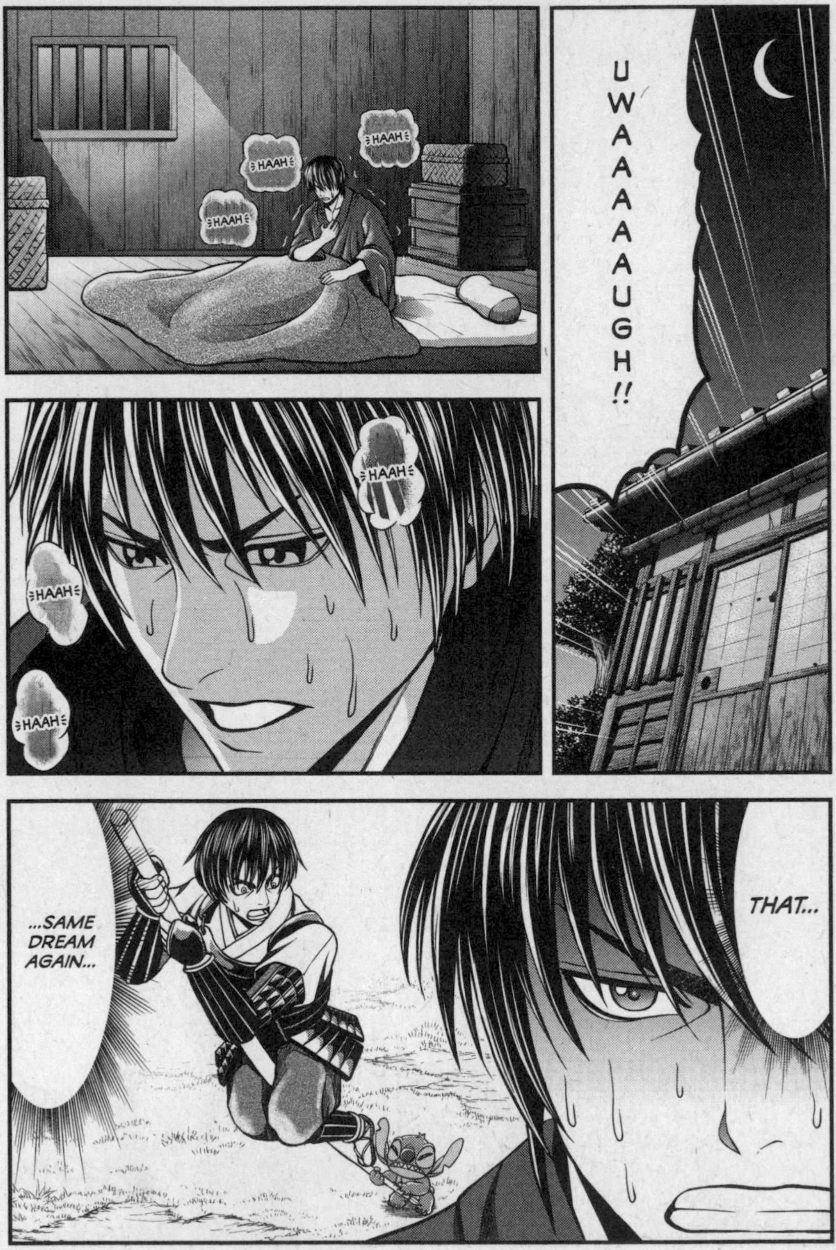
UWAAAAAAUGH!!
HAAH
HAAH
HAAH
HAAH
HAAH
HAAH
HAAH
THAT...
...SAME DREAM AGAIN...

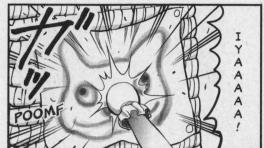

HYAH!!
HYAH!!
HANGF!
IYAAAAAA!
POOMF
STUPID BLUE RAC-COON!
STUPID BLUE RAC-COON!
CLACK
CLACK
CLACK
ALWAYS LORDING YOUR SINGLE VICTORY OVER ME!
ALWAYS HANGING BY MASTER'S SIDE!
ARE YOU TRYING TO JOIN HIS INNER CIRCLE?!
♪
I'M THE TOP DOG OF THAT GROUP!
AND I'LL SHOW YOU JUST HOW FAR APART WE ARE!

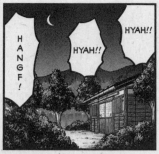

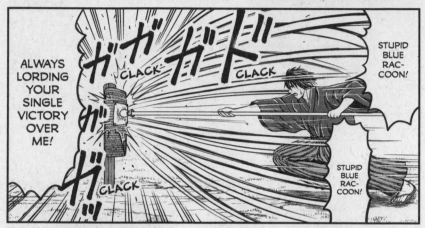

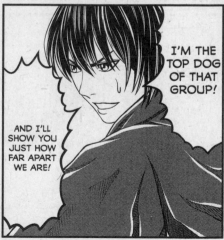

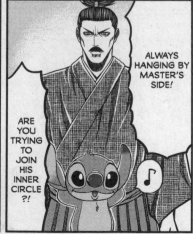

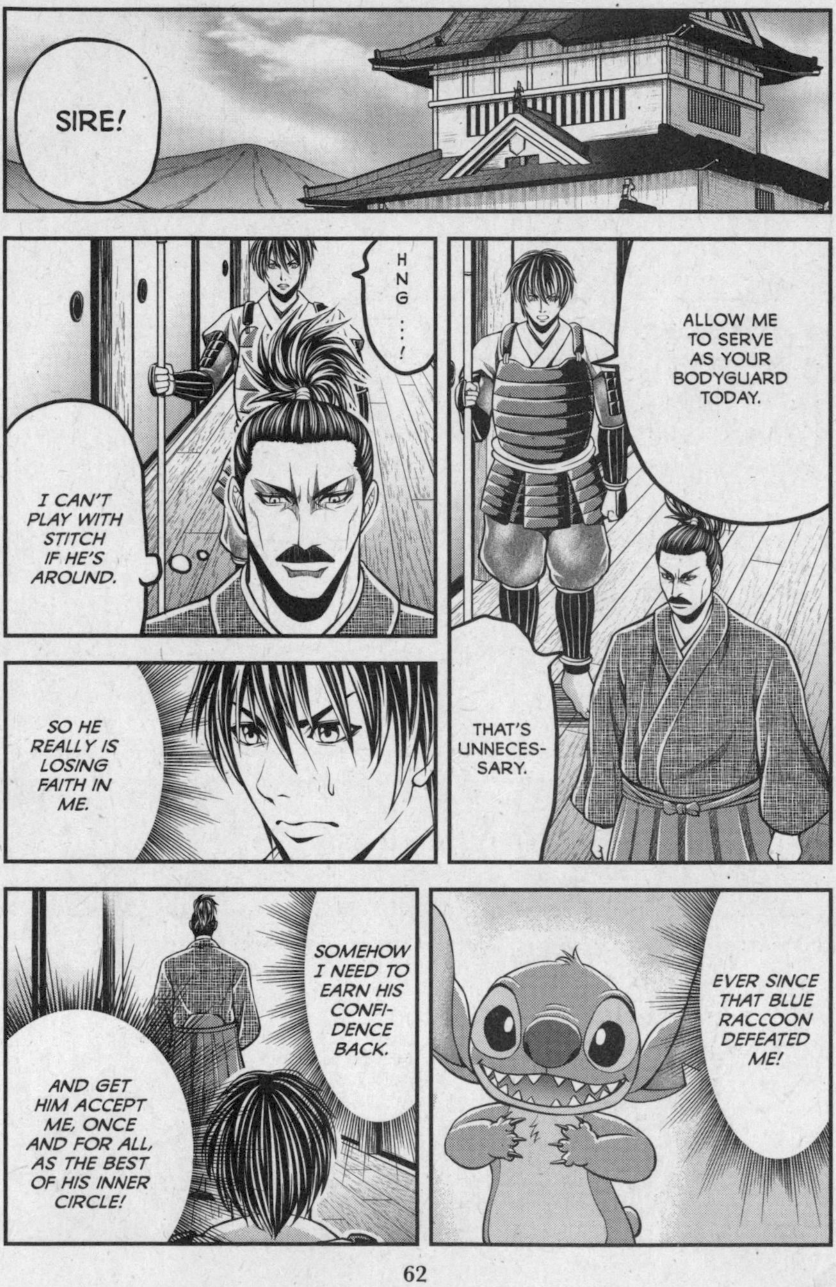
SIRE!
ALLOW ME TO SERVE AS YOUR BODYGUARD TODAY.
THAT'S UNNECES-SARY.
HNG ...!
I CAN'T PLAY WITH STITCH IF HE'S AROUND.
SO HE REALLY IS LOSING FAITH IN ME.
EVER SINCE THAT BLUE RACCOON DEFEATED ME!
SOMEHOW I NEED TO EARN HIS CONFI-DENCE BACK.
AND GET HIM ACCEPT ME, ONCE AND FOR ALL, AS THE BEST OF HIS INNER CIRCLE!

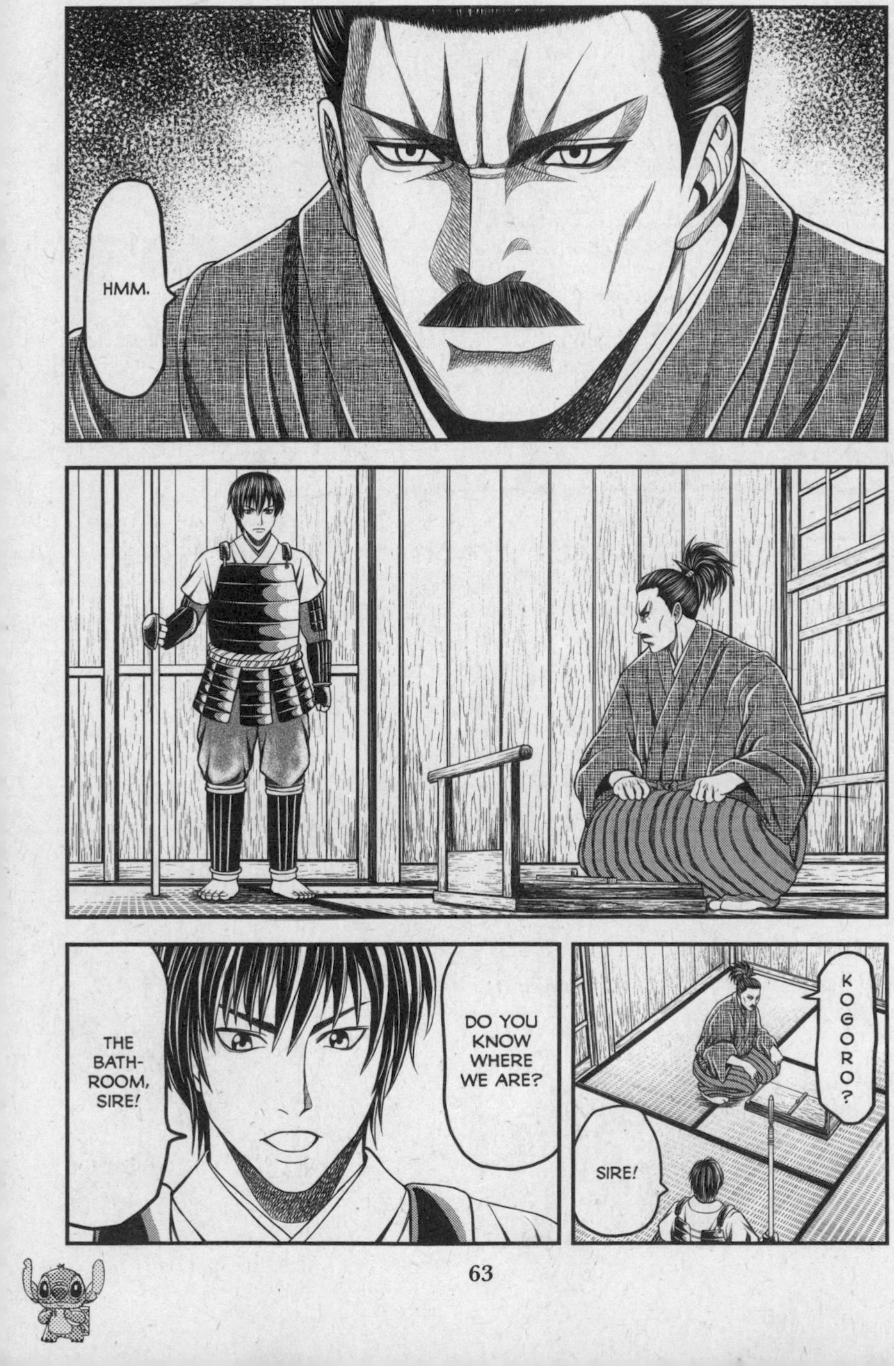
HMM.
KOGORO?
SIRE!
DO YOU KNOW WHERE WE ARE?
THE BATH-ROOM, SIRE!

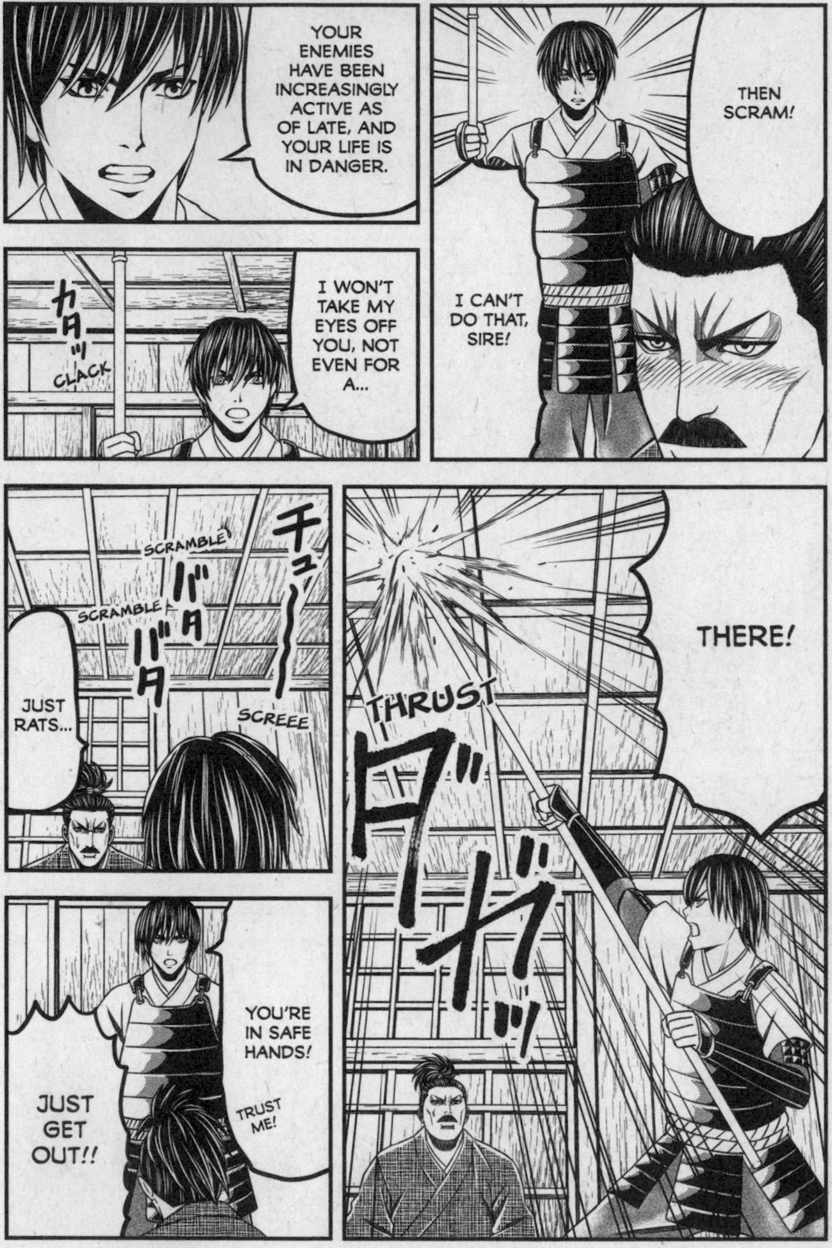
THEN SCRAM!
I CAN'T DO THAT, SIRE!
YOUR ENEMIES HAVE BEEN INCREASINGLY ACTIVE AS OF LATE, AND YOUR LIFE IS IN DANGER.
I WON'T TAKE MY EYES OFF YOU, NOT EVEN FOR A...
カタッ
CLACK
THERE!
THRUST
チューーー
SCREEE
バタ
SCRAMBLE
バタ
SCRAMBLE
JUST RATS...
YOU'RE IN SAFE HANDS!
TRUST ME!
JUST GET OUT!!

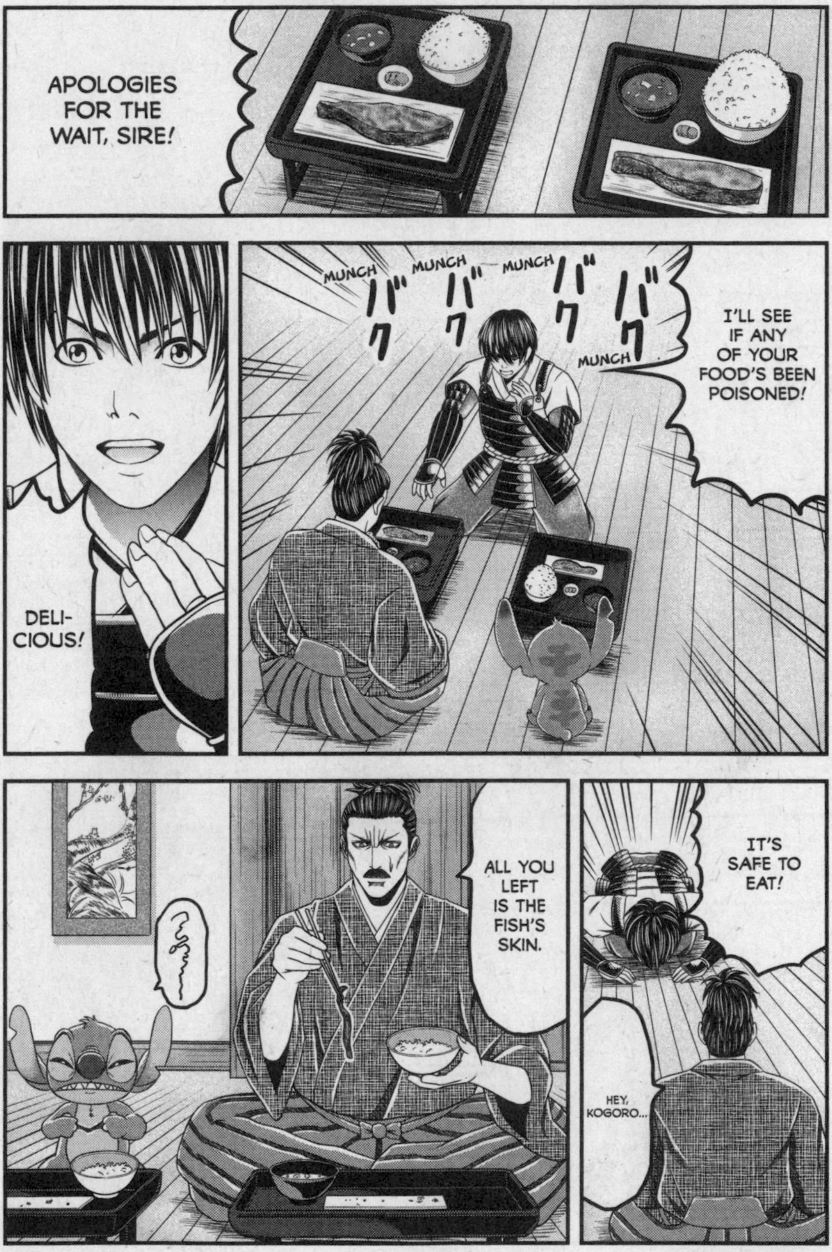
APOLOGIES FOR THE WAIT, SIRE!
I'LL SEE IF ANY OF YOUR FOOD'S BEEN POISONED!
MUNCH MUNCH MUNCH MUNCH
DELI-CIOUS!
IT'S SAFE TO EAT!
HEY, KOGORO...
ALL YOU LEFT IS THE FISH'S SKIN.

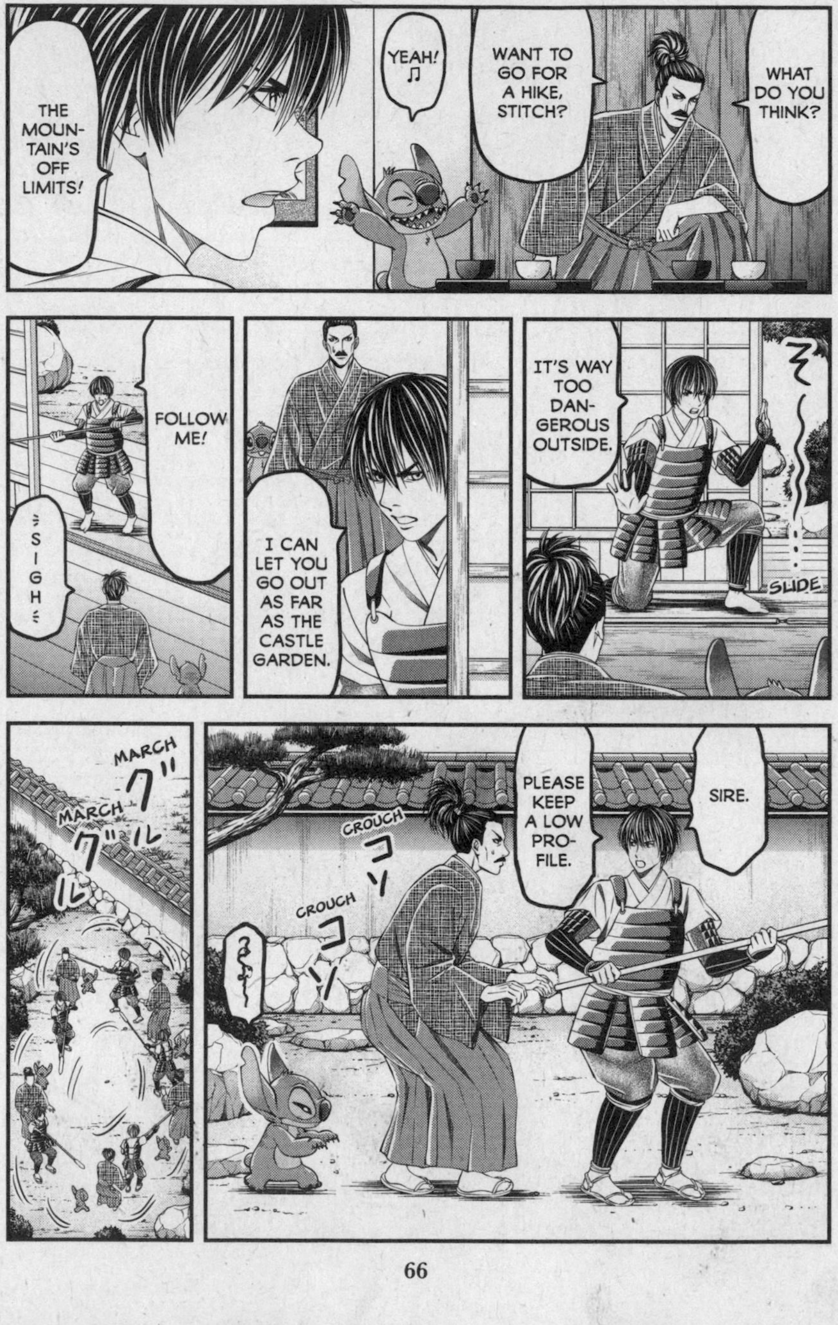
WHAT DO YOU THINK?
WANT TO GO FOR A HIKE, STITCH?
YEAH! ♫
THE MOUNTAIN'S OFF LIMITS!
SLIDE
IT'S WAY TOO DANGEROUS OUTSIDE.
I CAN LET YOU GO OUT AS FAR AS THE CASTLE GARDEN.
FOLLOW ME!
SIGH
SIRE.
PLEASE KEEP A LOW PROFILE.
CROUCH
CROUCH
MARCH
MARCH

HOOT HOOT
ホー ホー
WHAT A DAY...
TIME FOR BED!
WAIT A MOMENT, SIRE!
YOUR TOYS ARE PILED UP ALL OVER THE PLACE.
YOU MIGHT FIND YOURSELF UNABLE TO HOLD YOUR GROUND IN A MELEE!
LET'S TIDY UP.
GRRR
AWW...
I WAS GONNA PLAY WITH THOSE.
CALM DOWN, STITCH.
YOU CAN ALWAYS BRING THEM OUT AGAIN.

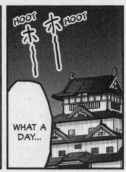

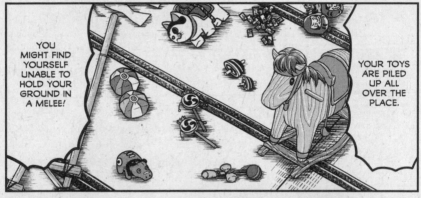

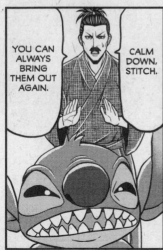

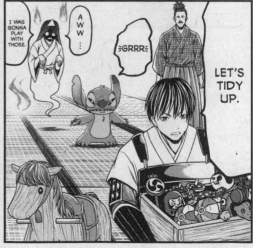

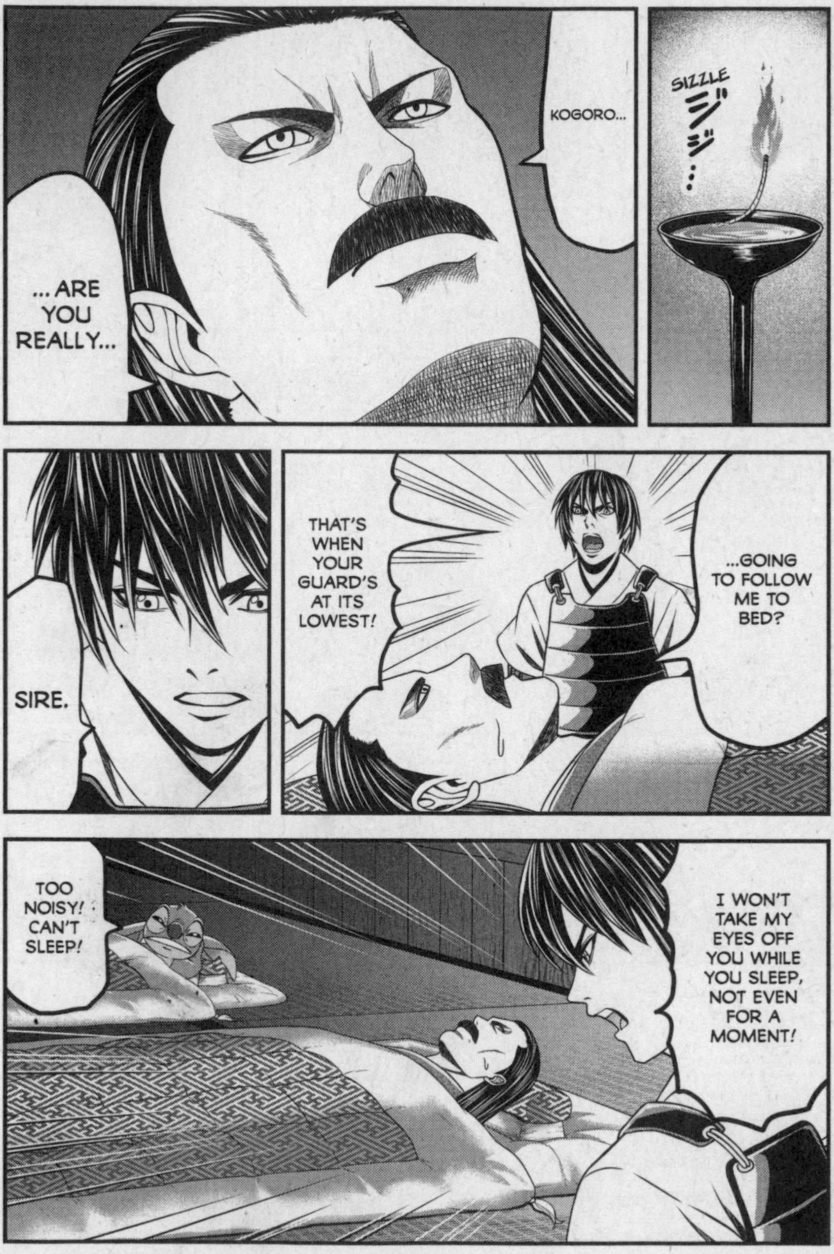
SIZZLE
ジジ…
KOGORO...
...ARE YOU REALLY...
...GOING TO FOLLOW ME TO BED?
THAT'S WHEN YOUR GUARD'S AT ITS LOWEST!
SIRE.
I WON'T TAKE MY EYES OFF YOU WHILE YOU SLEEP, NOT EVEN FOR A MOMENT!
TOO NOISY! CAN'T SLEEP!

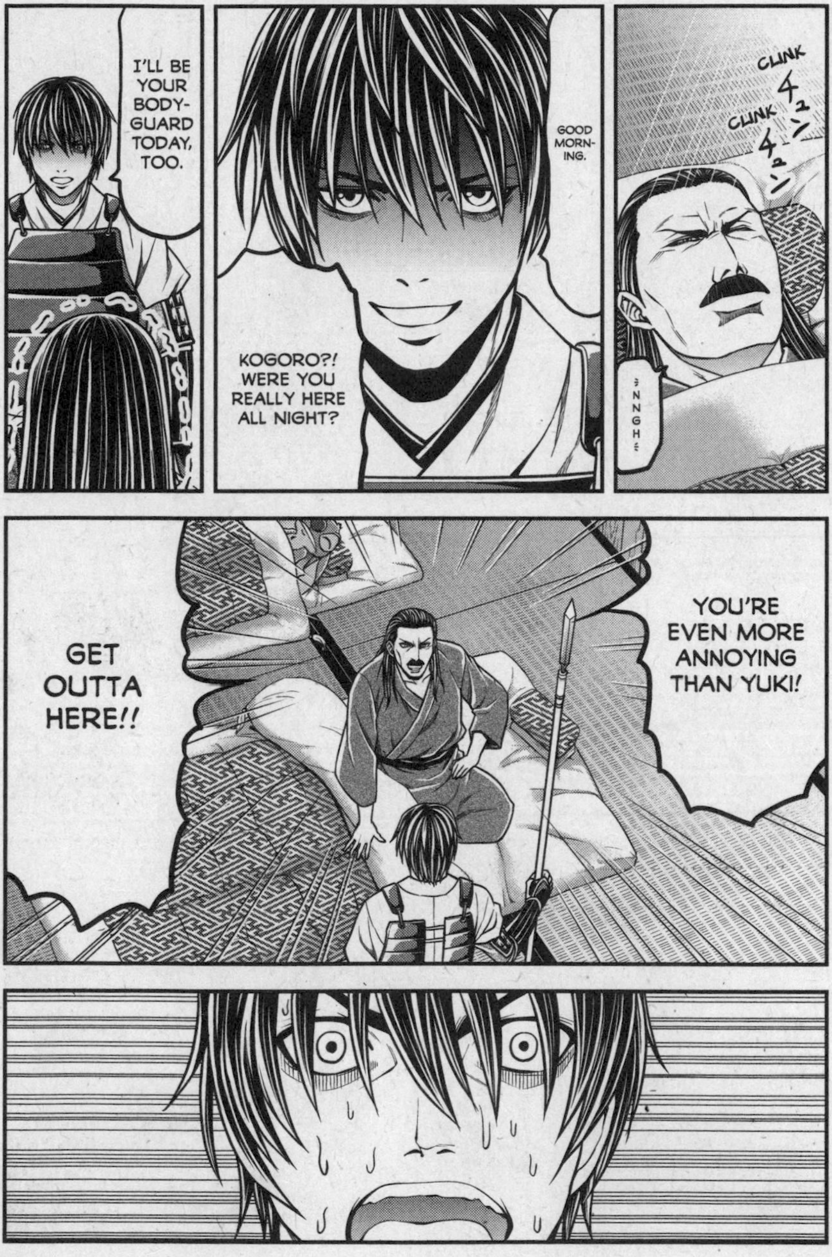
CLINK
CLINK
NNGH
GOOD MORNING.
KOGORO?! WERE YOU REALLY HERE ALL NIGHT?
I'LL BE YOUR BODYGUARD TODAY, TOO.
YOU'RE EVEN MORE ANNOYING THAN YUKI!
GET OUTTA HERE!!

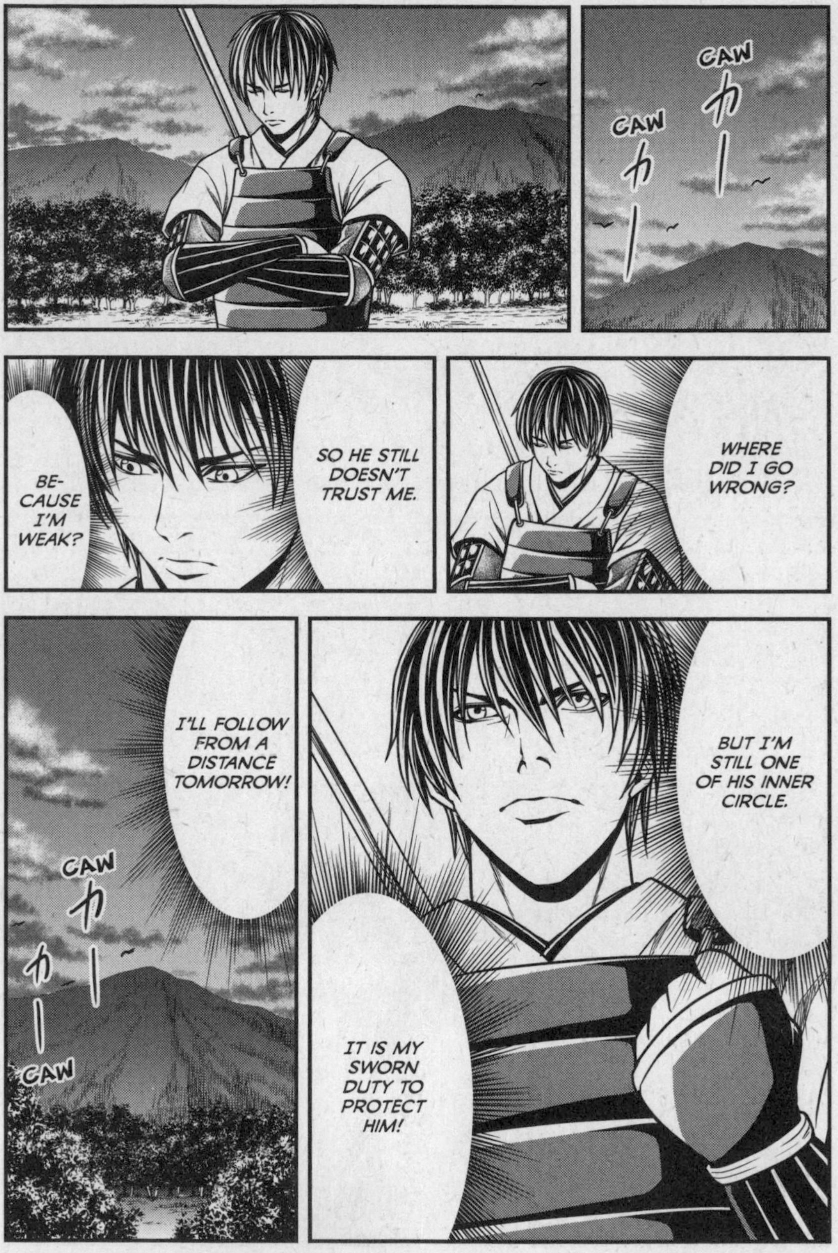
CAW
カー
CAW
カー
WHERE DID I GO WRONG?
SO HE STILL DOESN'T TRUST ME.
BE-CAUSE I'M WEAK?
BUT I'M STILL ONE OF HIS INNER CIRCLE.
IT IS MY SWORN DUTY TO PROTECT HIM!
I'LL FOLLOW FROM A DISTANCE TOMORROW!
CAW
カー
カー
CAW

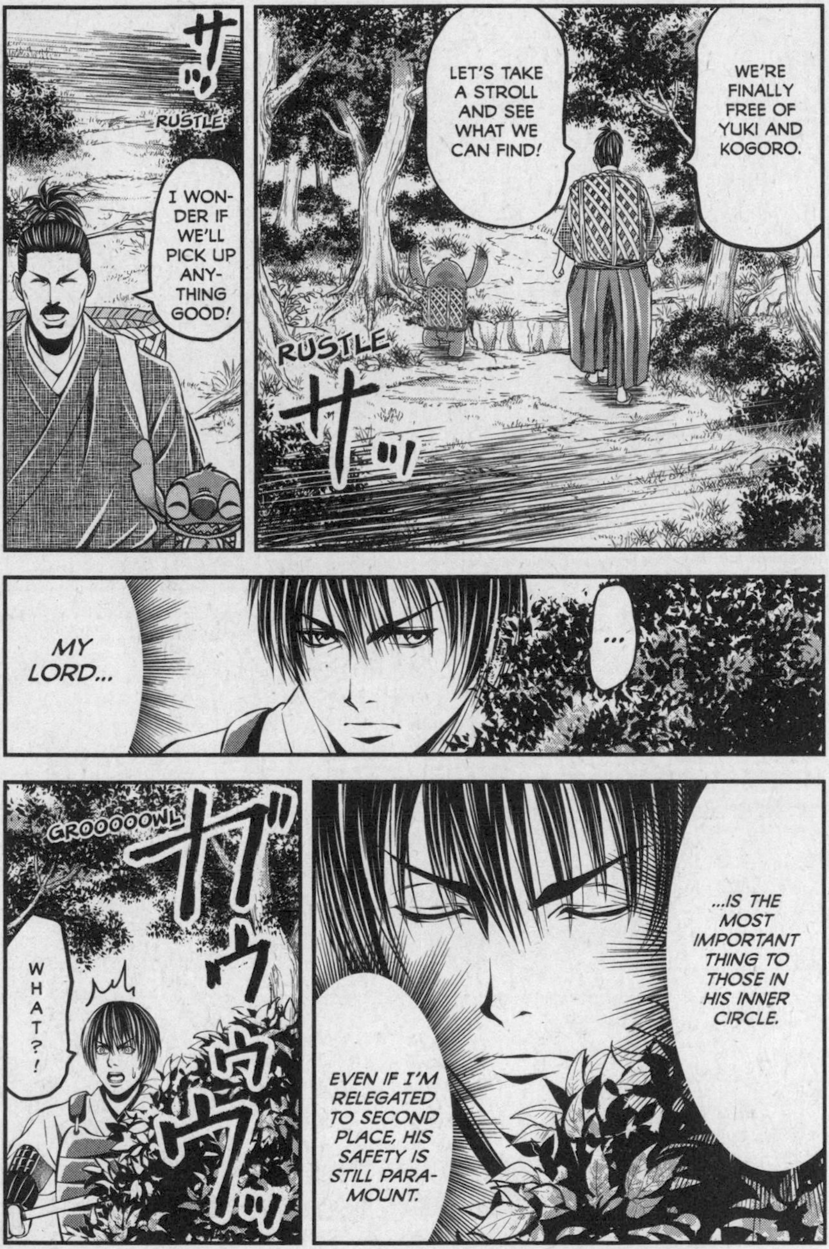
WE'RE FINALLY FREE OF YUKI AND KOGORO.
LET'S TAKE A STROLL AND SEE WHAT WE CAN FIND!
RUSTLE
RUSTLE
I WONDER IF WE'LL PICK UP ANYTHING GOOD!
...
MY LORD...
...IS THE MOST IMPORTANT THING TO THOSE IN HIS INNER CIRCLE.
EVEN IF I'M RELEGATED TO SECOND PLACE, HIS SAFETY IS STILL PARAMOUNT.
GROOOOOWL
WHAT?!

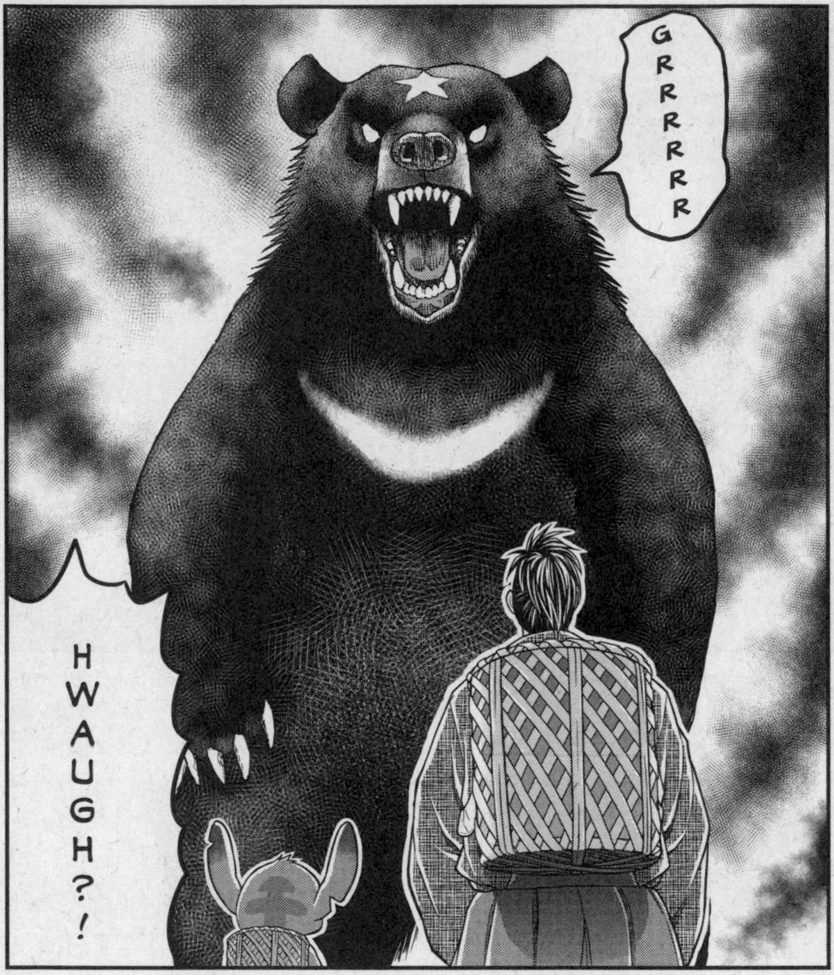
GRRRRRR
HWAUGH?!
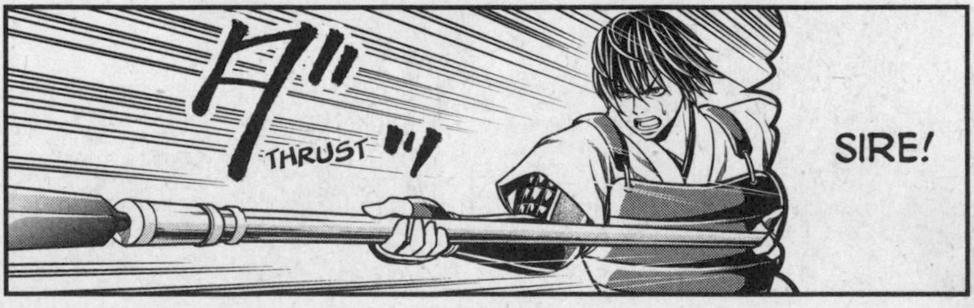
SIRE!
THRUST

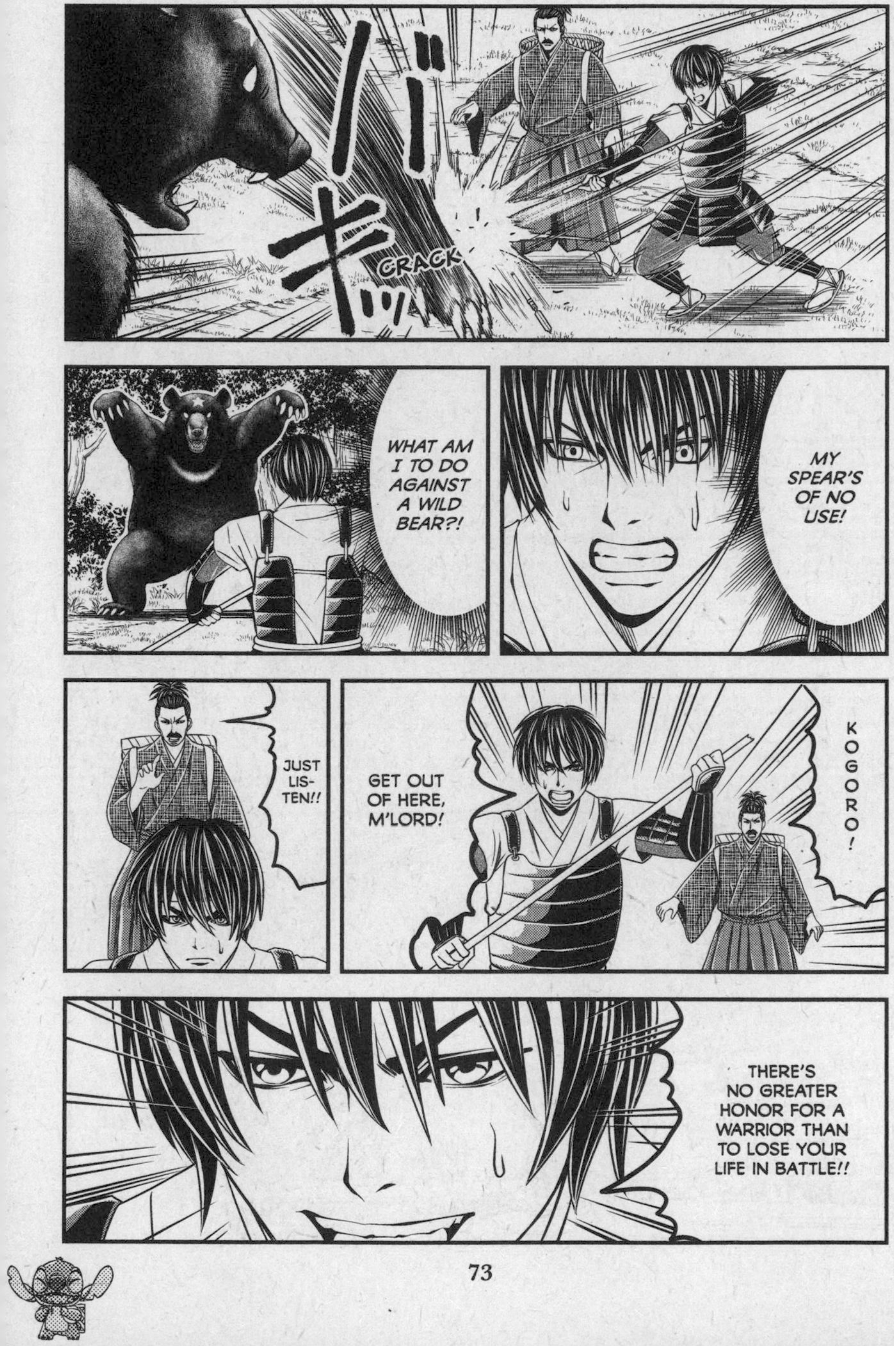
バギッ
CRACK
MY SPEAR'S OF NO USE!
WHAT AM I TO DO AGAINST A WILD BEAR?!
KOGORO!
GET OUT OF HERE, M'LORD!
JUST LIS-TEN!!
THERE'S NO GREATER HONOR FOR A WARRIOR THAN TO LOSE YOUR LIFE IN BATTLE!!

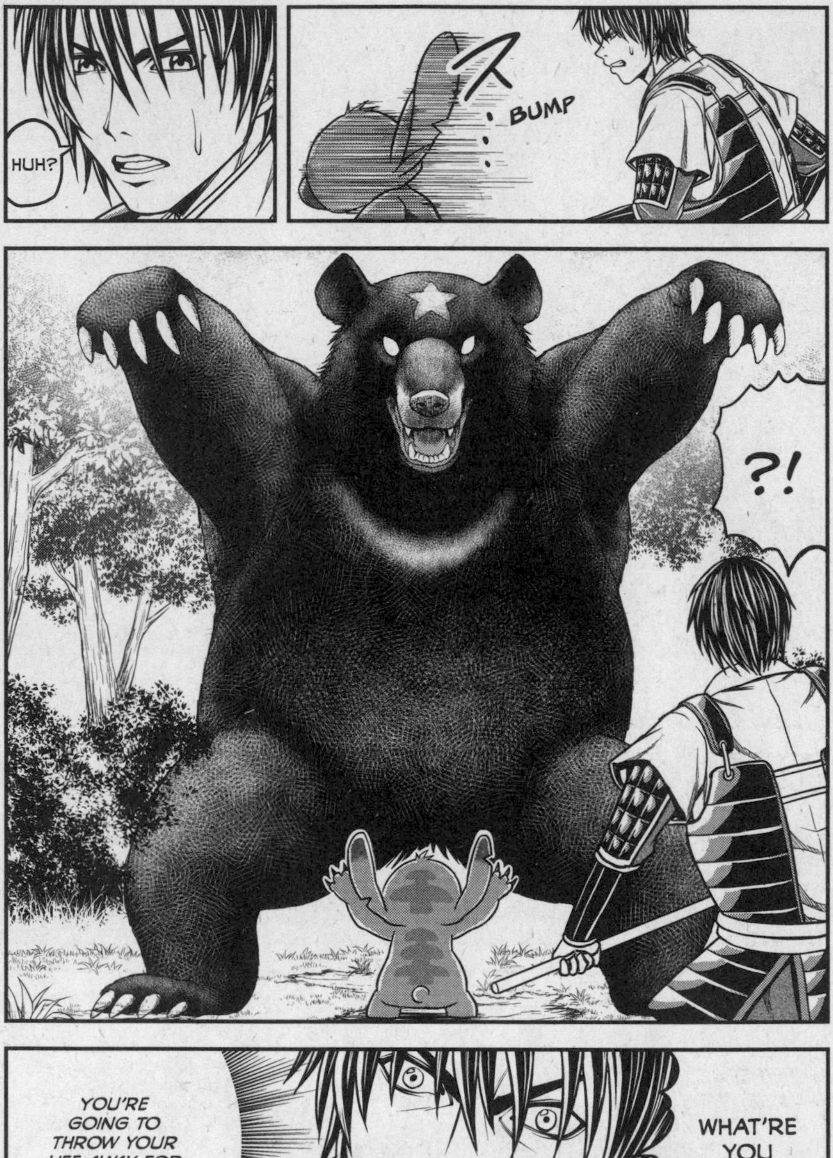
BUMP
HUH?
?!
WHAT'RE YOU DOING?!
YOU'RE GOING TO THROW YOUR LIFE AWAY FOR US??

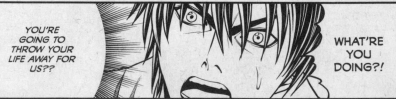

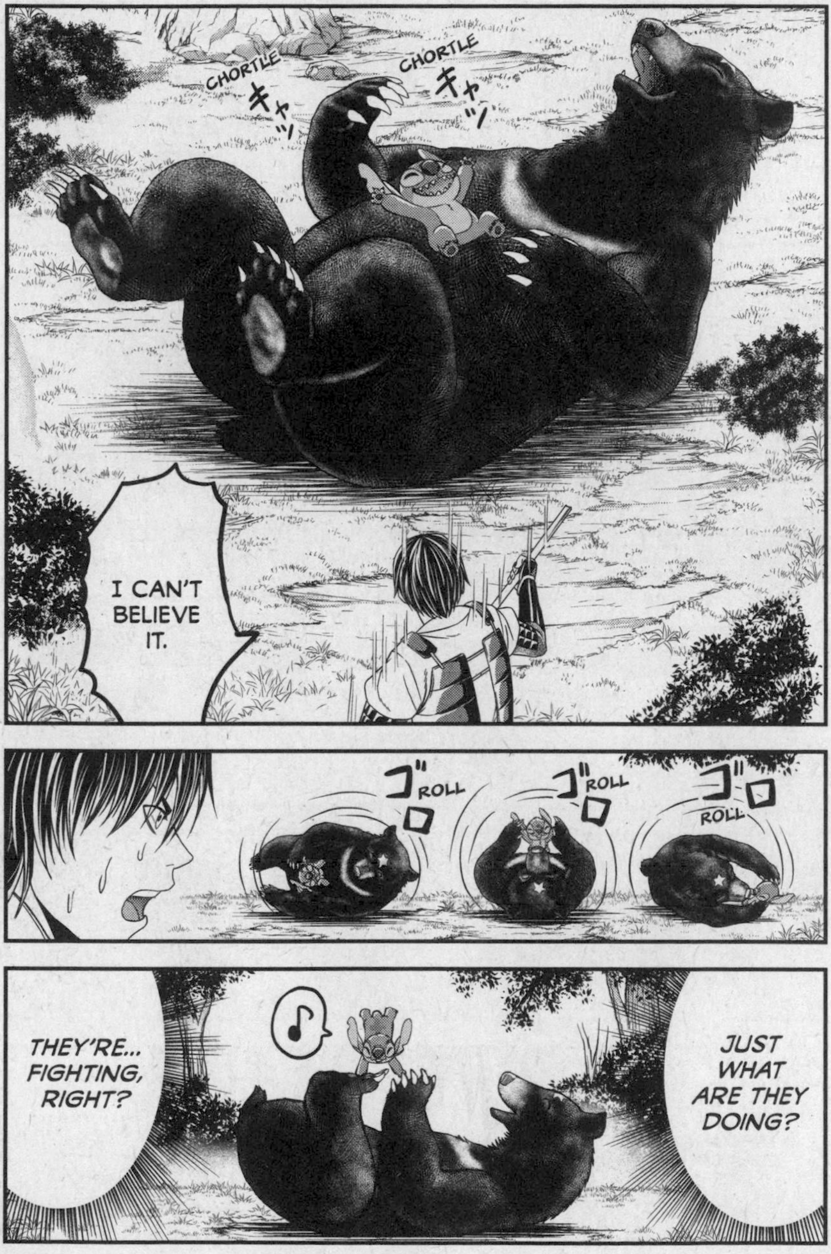
CHORTLE
キャッ
CHORTLE
キャッ
I CAN'T BELIEVE IT.
ゴロ ROLL
ゴロ ROLL
ゴロ ROLL
JUST WHAT ARE THEY DOING?
♪
THEY'RE... FIGHTING, RIGHT?

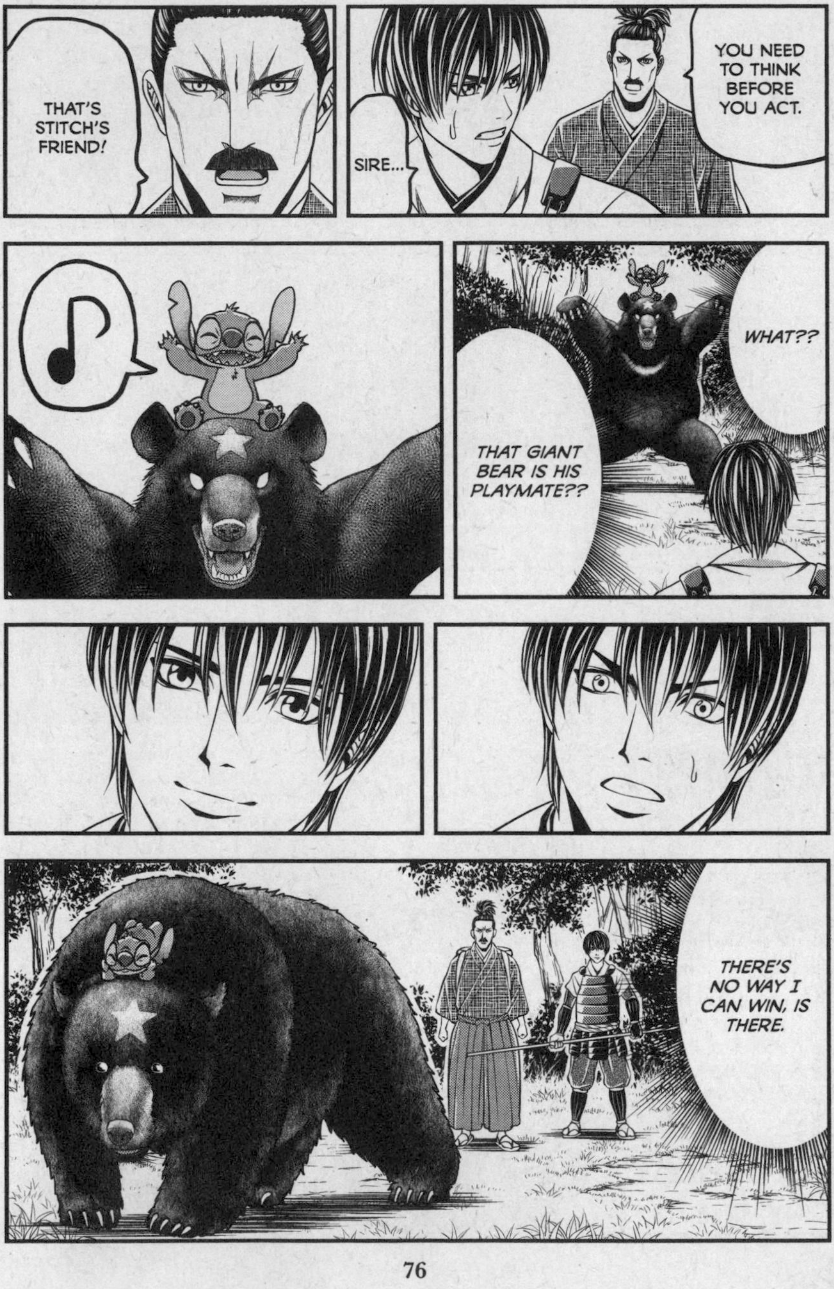
YOU NEED TO THINK BEFORE YOU ACT.
SIRE...
THAT'S STITCH'S FRIEND!
WHAT??
THAT GIANT BEAR IS HIS PLAYMATE??
♪
THERE'S NO WAY I CAN WIN, IS THERE.

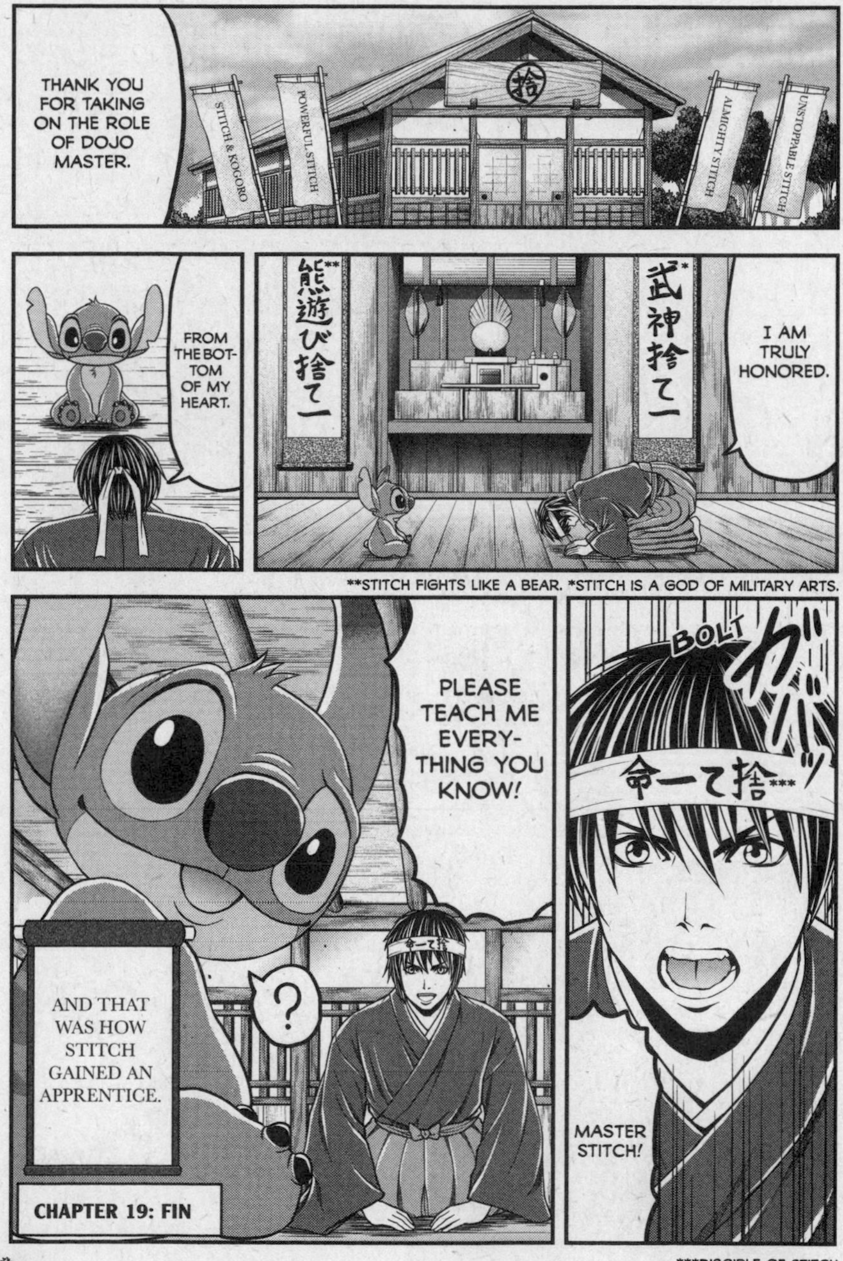
THANK YOU FOR TAKING ON THE ROLE OF DOJO MASTER.
UNSTOPPABLE STITCH
ALMIGHTY STITCH
POWERFUL STITCH
STITCH & KOGORO
I AM TRULY HONORED.
武神捨て一*
熊遊び捨て一**
FROM THE BOT-TOM OF MY HEART.
**STITCH FIGHTS LIKE A BEAR. *STITCH IS A GOD OF MILITARY ARTS.
BOLT
ガバッ
命一て捨***
MASTER STITCH!
PLEASE TEACH ME EVERY-THING YOU KNOW!
?
AND THAT WAS HOW STITCH GAINED AN APPRENTICE.
CHAPTER 19: FIN
***DISCIPLE OF STITCH

TRAINING

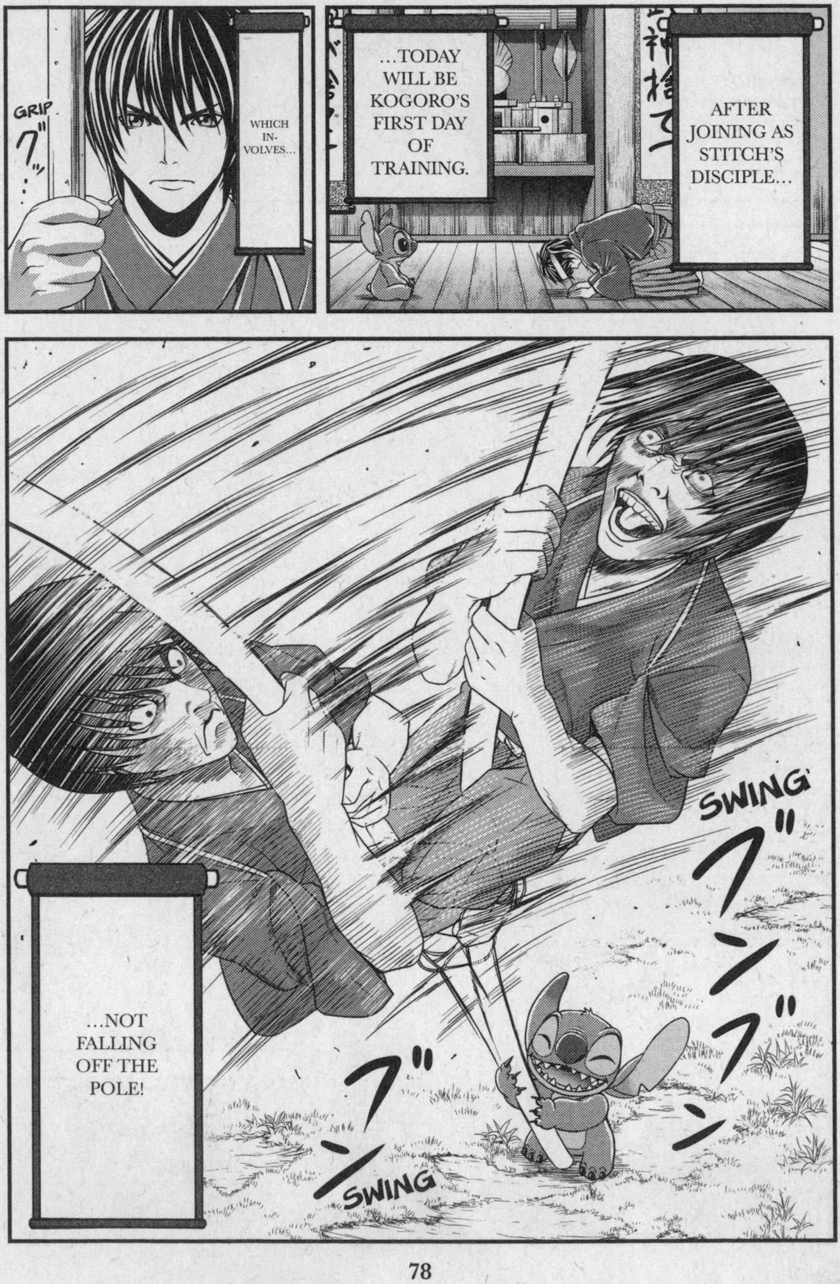
AFTER JOINING AS STITCH'S DISCIPLE...
...TODAY WILL BE KOGORO'S FIRST DAY OF TRAINING.
GRIP
WHICH IN-VOLVES...
SWING
...NOT FALLING OFF THE POLE!
SWING

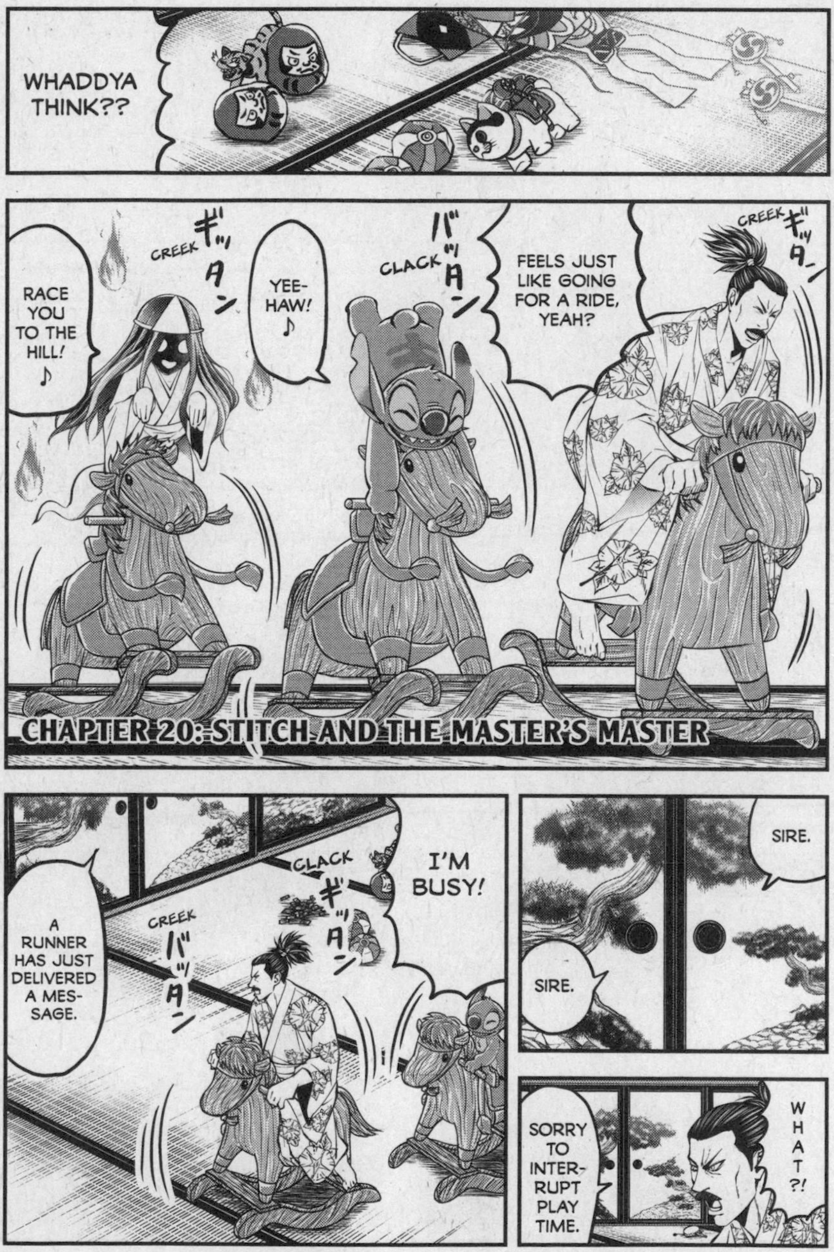
WHADDYA THINK??
CREEK ギッタン
FEELS JUST LIKE GOING FOR A RIDE, YEAH?
CLACK バッタン
YEE-HAW! ♪
CREEK ギッタン
RACE YOU TO THE HILL! ♪
CHAPTER 20: STITCH AND THE MASTER'S MASTER
SIRE.
SIRE.
WHAT?!
SORRY TO INTERRUPT PLAY TIME.
CLACK ギッタン
I'M BUSY!
CREEK バッタン
A RUNNER HAS JUST DELIVERED A MESSAGE.

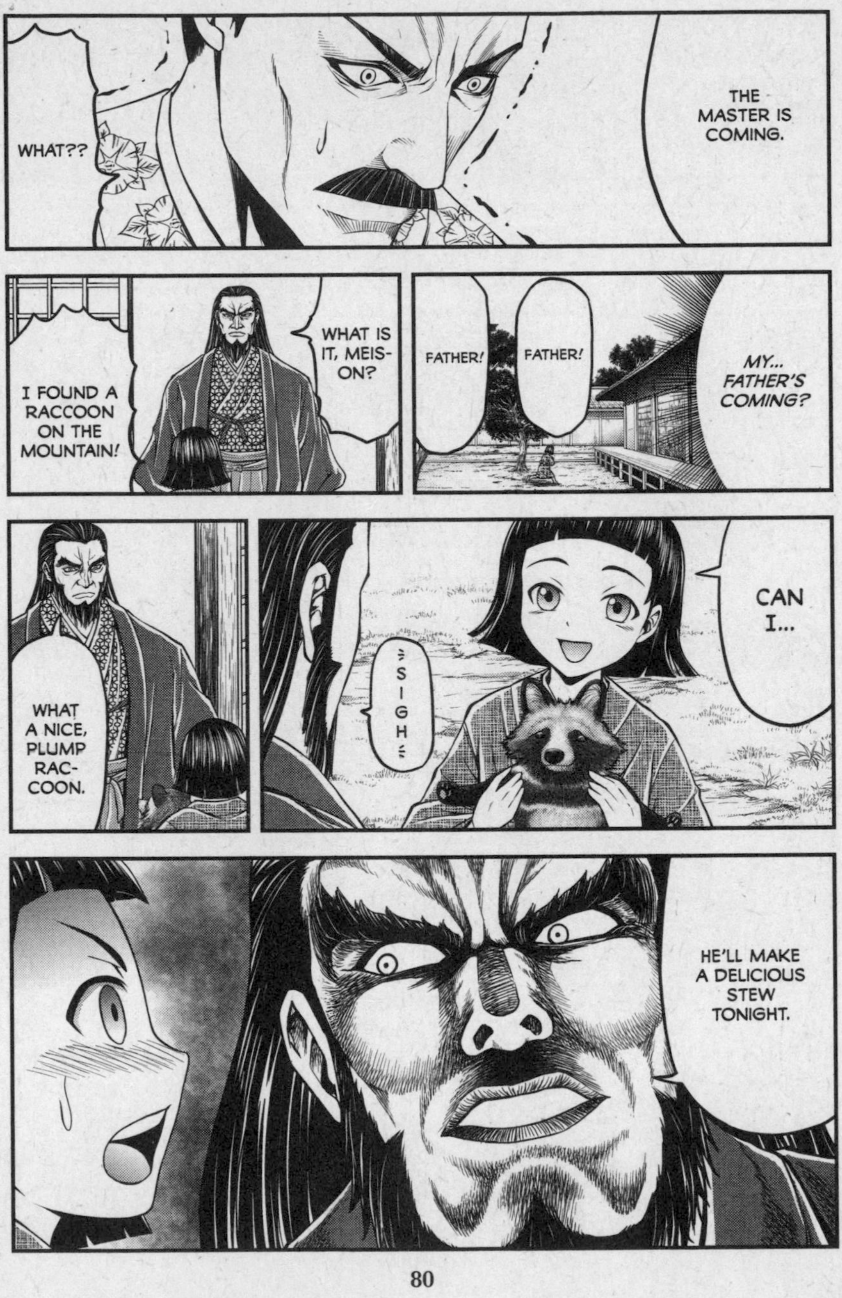
THE MASTER IS COMING.
WHAT??
MY... FATHER'S COMING?
FATHER!
FATHER!
WHAT IS IT, MEIS-ON?
I FOUND A RACCOON ON THE MOUNTAIN!
CAN I...
SIGH
WHAT A NICE, PLUMP RAC-COON.
HE'LL MAKE A DELICIOUS STEW TONIGHT.

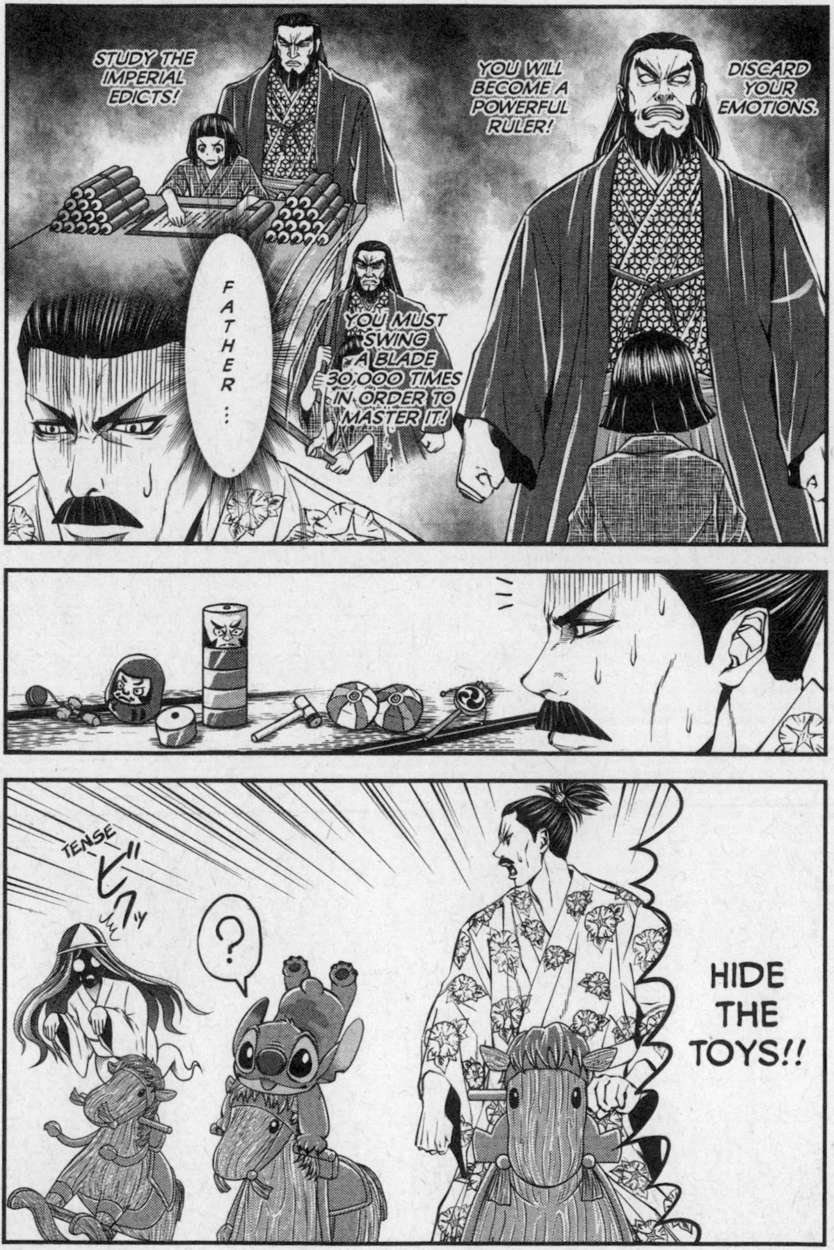
DISCARD YOUR EMOTIONS.
YOU WILL BECOME A POWERFUL RULER!
STUDY THE IMPERIAL EDICTS!
YOU MUST SWING A BLADE 30,000 TIMES IN ORDER TO MASTER IT!
FATHER ...
HIDE THE TOYS!!
?
TENSE

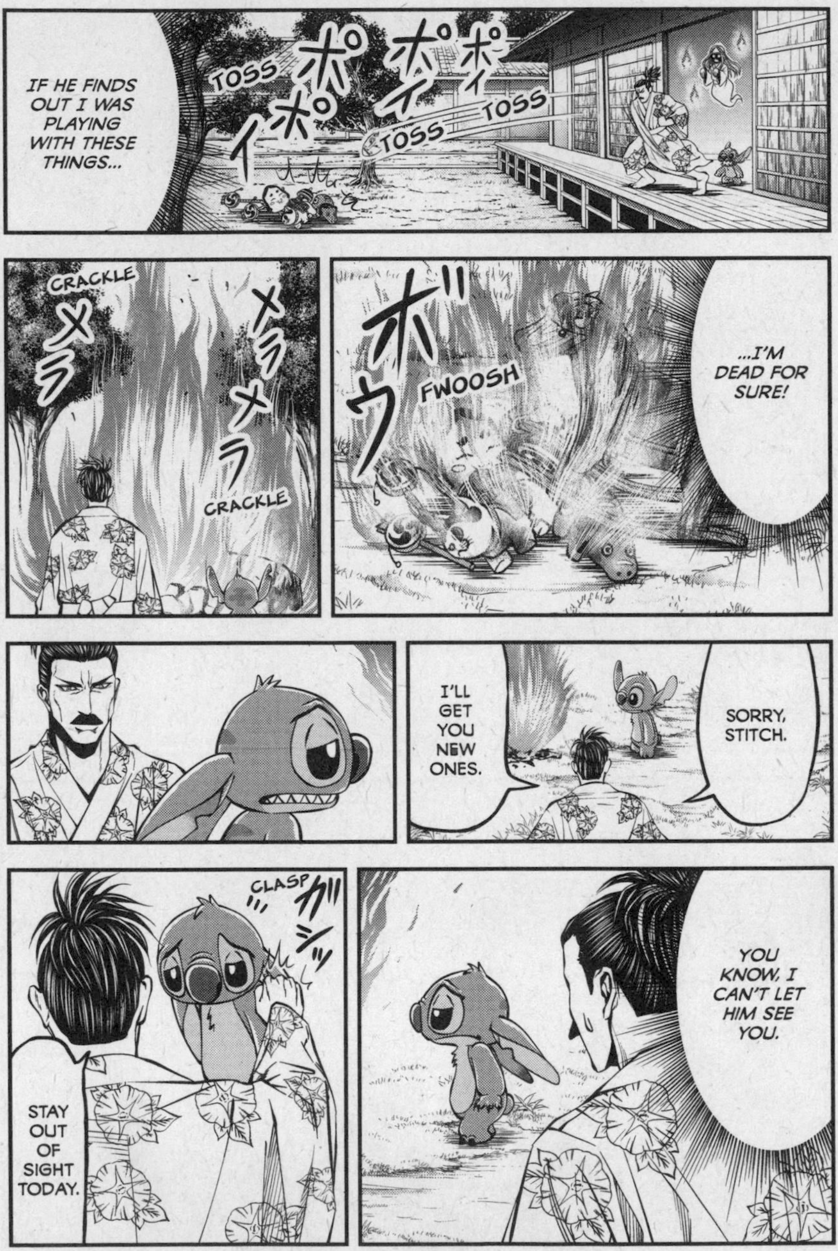
ポイ
TOSS TOSS
ポイ
ポイ
TOSS
ポイ
TOSS
IF HE FINDS OUT I WAS PLAYING WITH THESE THINGS...
...I'M DEAD FOR SURE!
FWOOSH
ボウ
メラメラ
CRACKLE
CRACKLE
メラ
SORRY, STITCH.
I'LL GET YOU NEW ONES.
YOU KNOW, I CAN'T LET HIM SEE YOU.
ガシッ
CLASP
STAY OUT OF SIGHT TODAY.

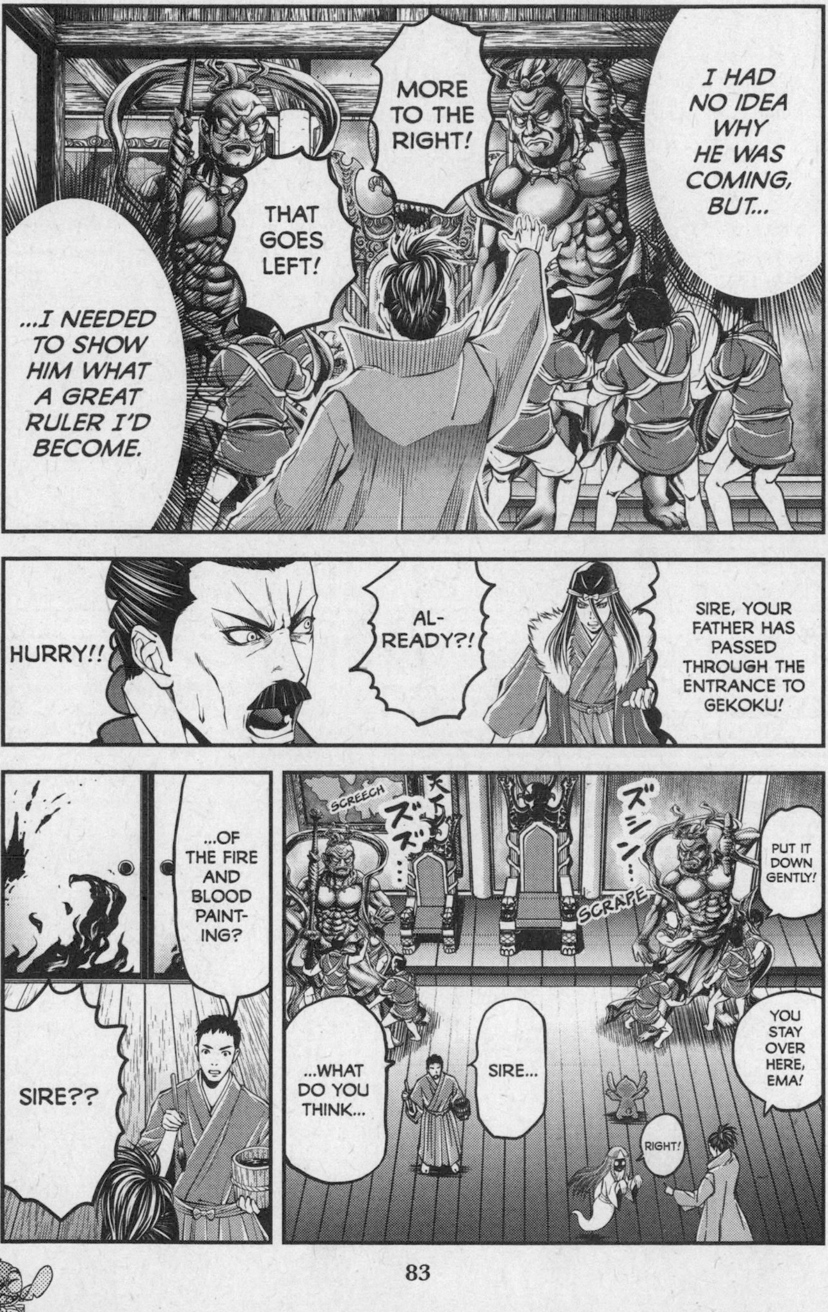
I HAD NO IDEA WHY HE WAS COMING, BUT...
MORE TO THE RIGHT!
THAT GOES LEFT!
...I NEEDED TO SHOW HIM WHAT A GREAT RULER I'D BECOME.
SIRE, YOUR FATHER HAS PASSED THROUGH THE ENTRANCE TO GEKOKU!
AL-READY?!
HURRY!!
PUT IT DOWN GENTLY!
ズシン…
SCRAPE
ズズ…
SCREECH
YOU STAY OVER HERE, EMA!
RIGHT!
SIRE...
...WHAT DO YOU THINK...
...OF THE FIRE AND BLOOD PAINT-ING?
SIRE??

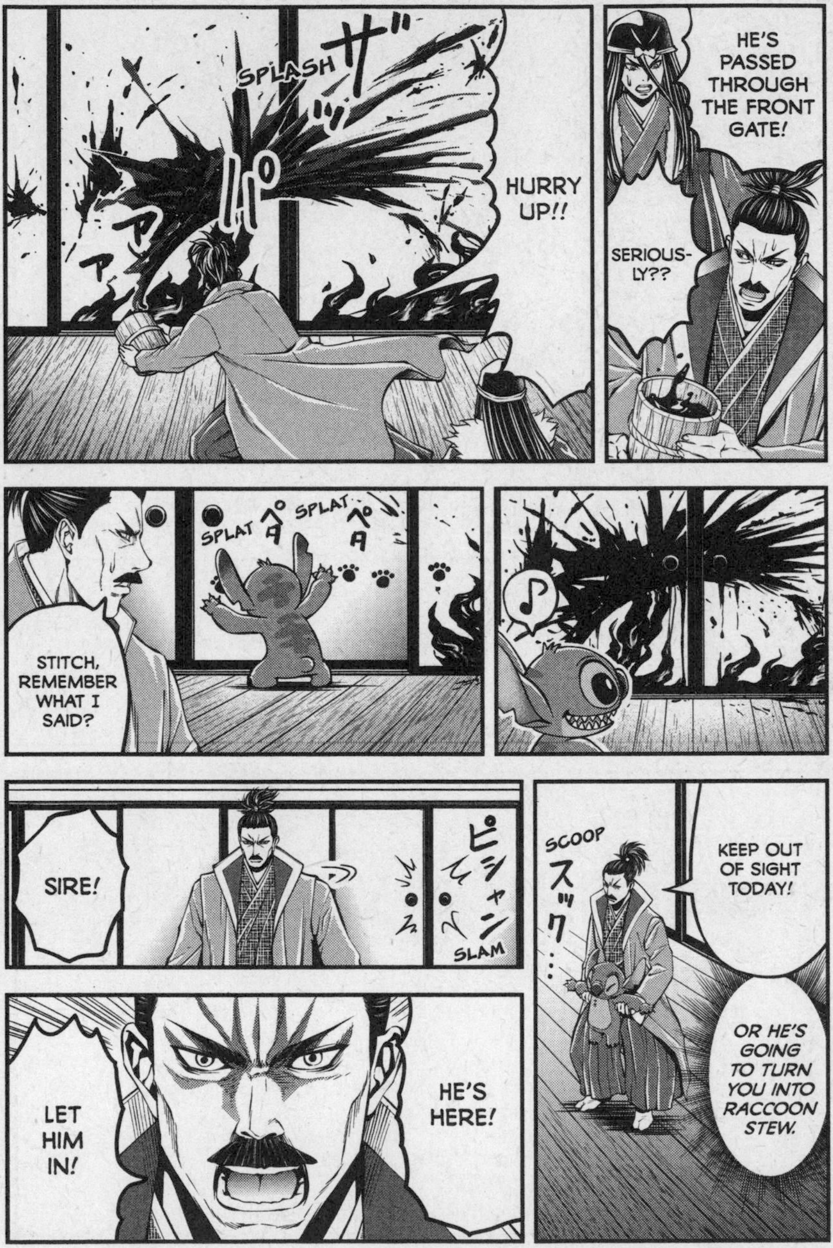
HE'S PASSED THROUGH THE FRONT GATE!
SERIOUS-LY??
SPLASH
HURRY UP!!
SPLAT
SPLAT
STITCH, REMEMBER WHAT I SAID?
♪
SCOOP
KEEP OUT OF SIGHT TODAY!
OR HE'S GOING TO TURN YOU INTO RACCOON STEW.
SLAM
SIRE!
HE'S HERE!
LET HIM IN!

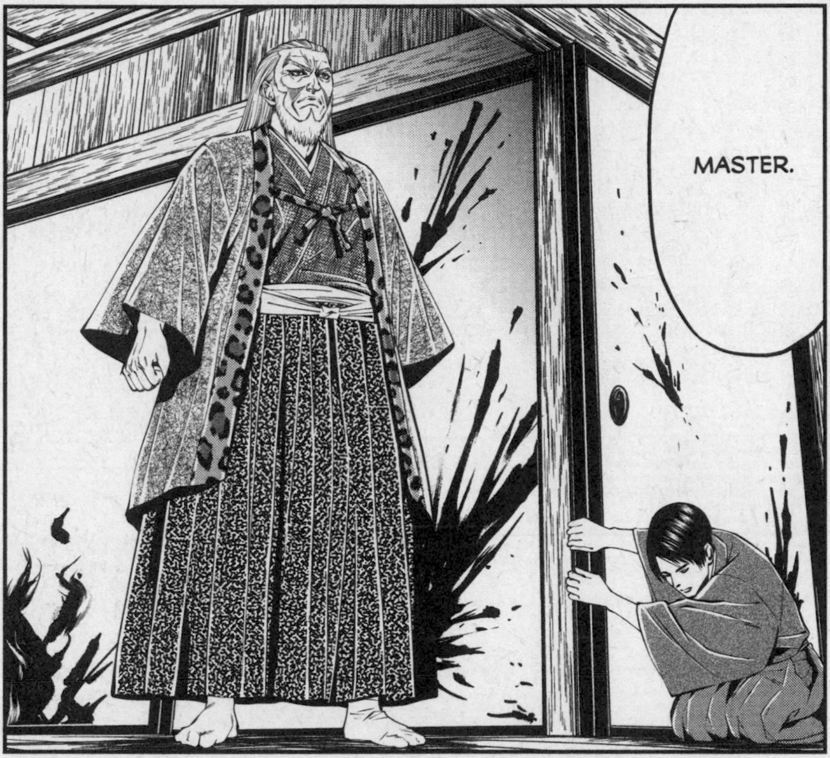
MASTER.

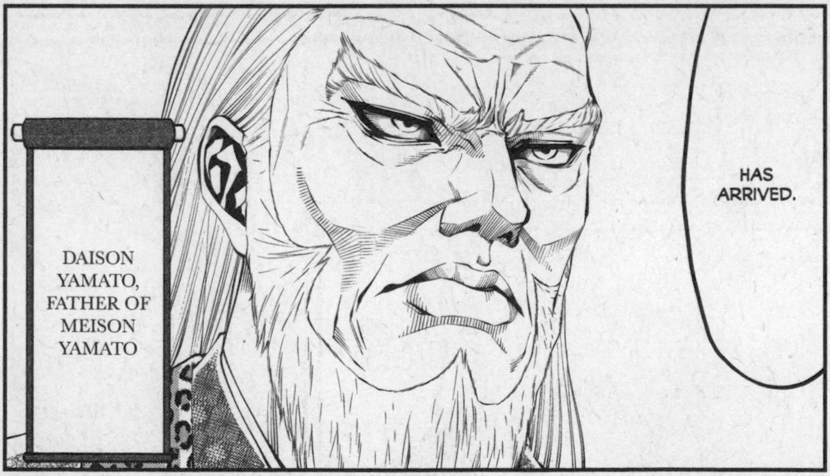
HAS
ARRIVED.
DAISON
YAMATO,
FATHER OF
MEISON
YAMATO

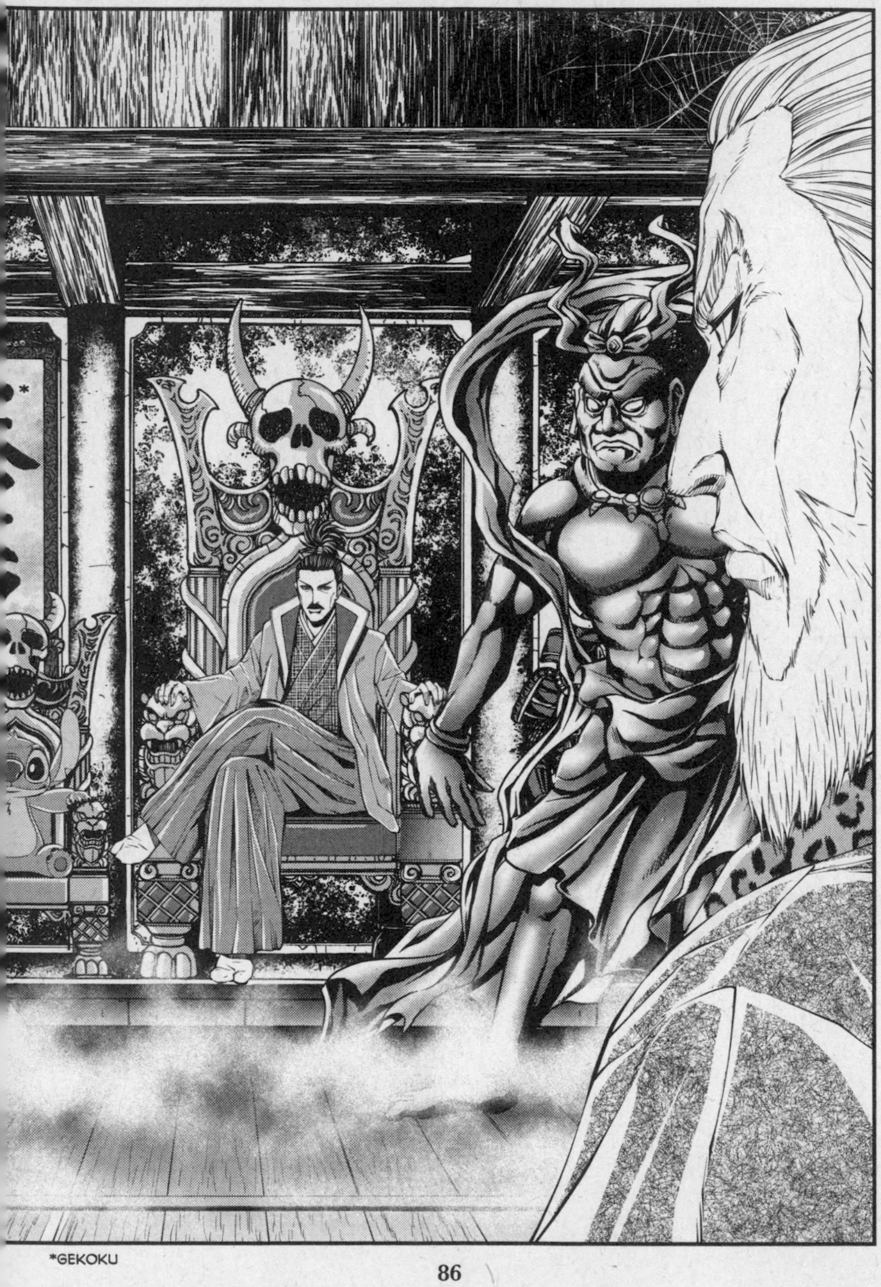

*GEKOKU

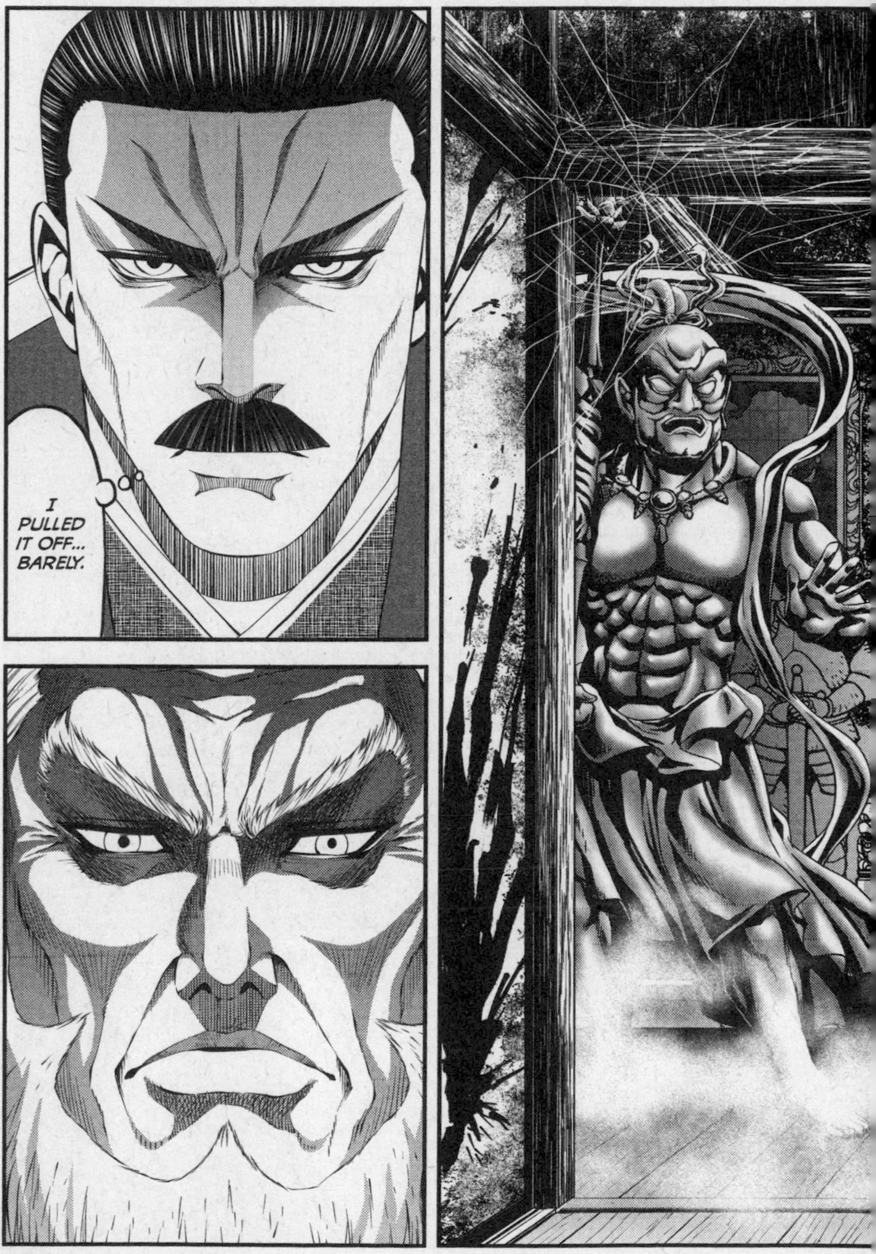
I PULLED IT OFF... BARELY.

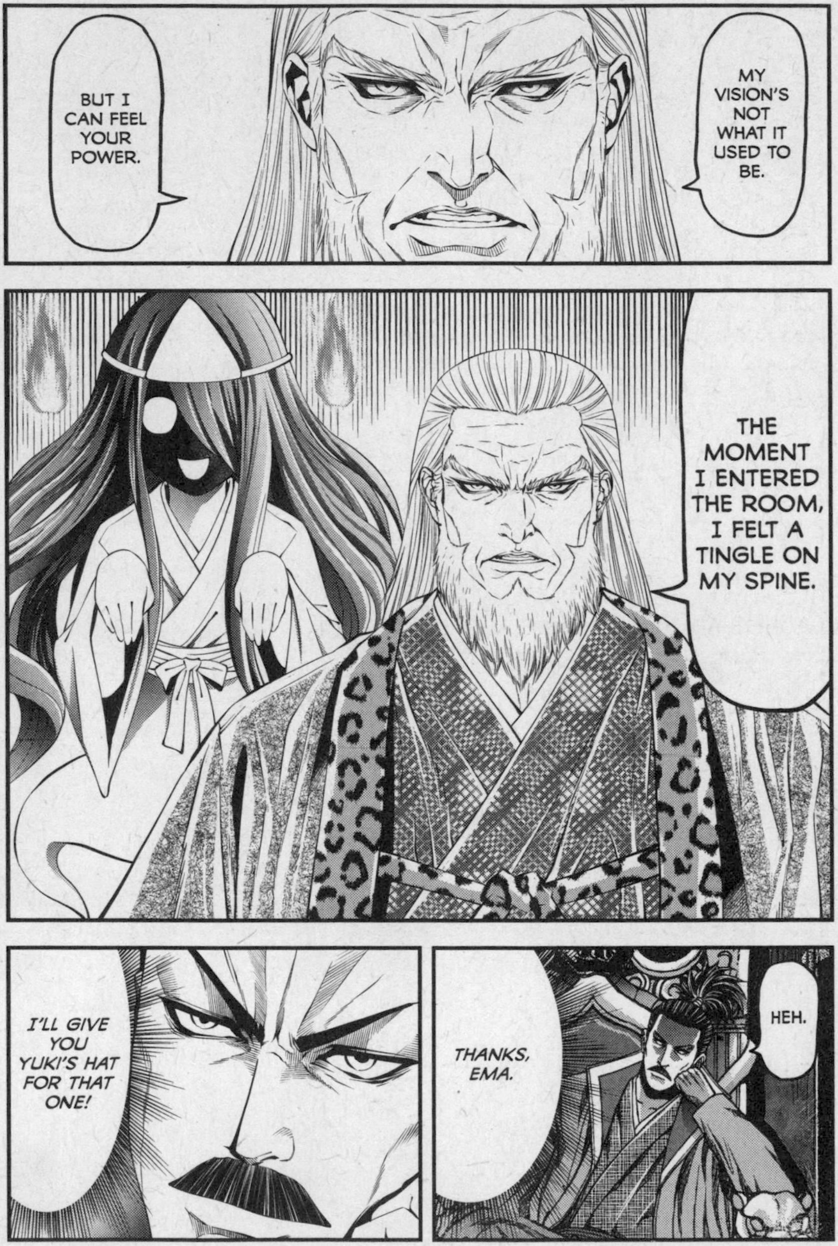
MY VISION'S NOT WHAT IT USED TO BE.
BUT I CAN FEEL YOUR POWER.
THE MOMENT I ENTERED THE ROOM, I FELT A TINGLE ON MY SPINE.
HEH.
THANKS, EMA.
I'LL GIVE YOU YUKI'S HAT FOR THAT ONE!

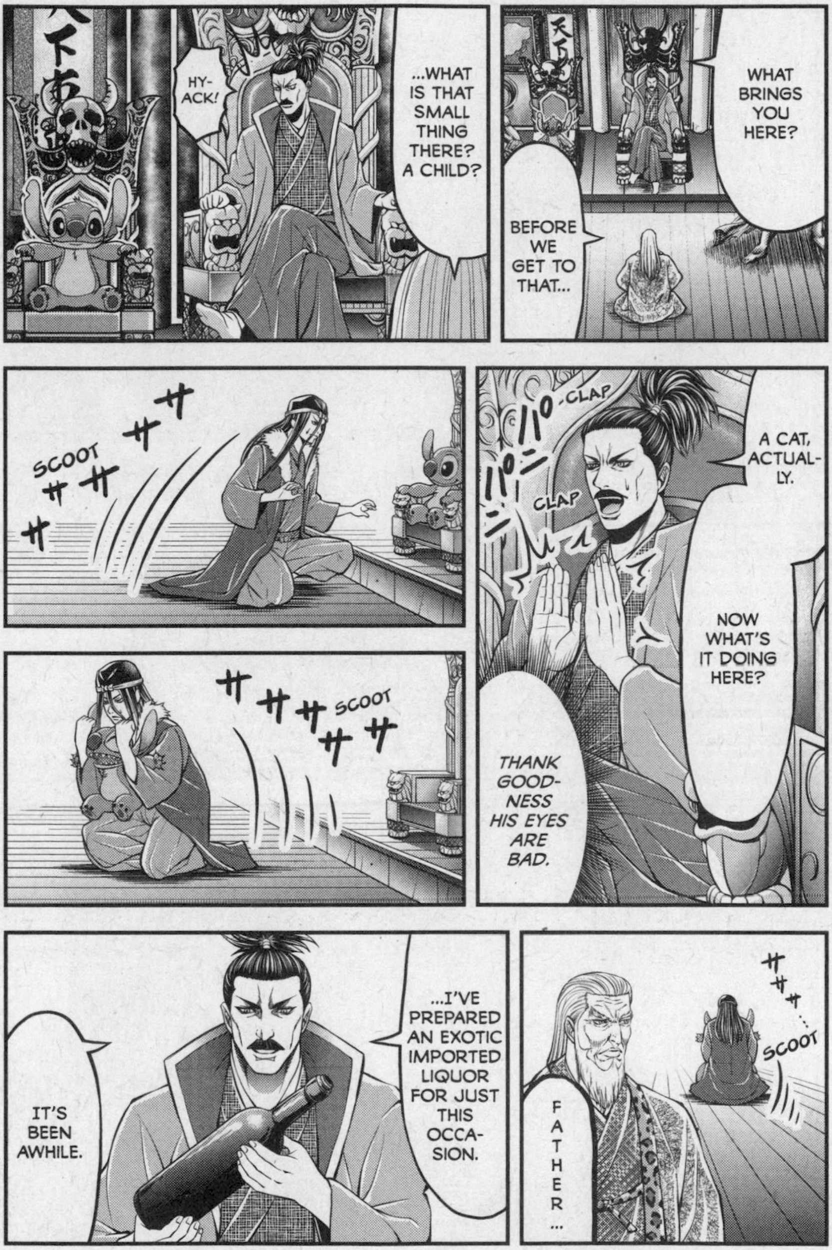
WHAT BRINGS YOU HERE?
BEFORE WE GET TO THAT...
...WHAT IS THAT SMALL THING THERE? A CHILD?
HY-ACK!
CLAP
CLAP
A CAT, ACTUAL-LY.
NOW WHAT'S IT DOING HERE?
THANK GOODNESS HIS EYES ARE BAD.
SCOOT
SCOOT
SCOOT
FATHER...
...I'VE PREPARED AN EXOTIC IMPORTED LIQUOR FOR JUST THIS OCCA-SION.
IT'S BEEN AWHILE.

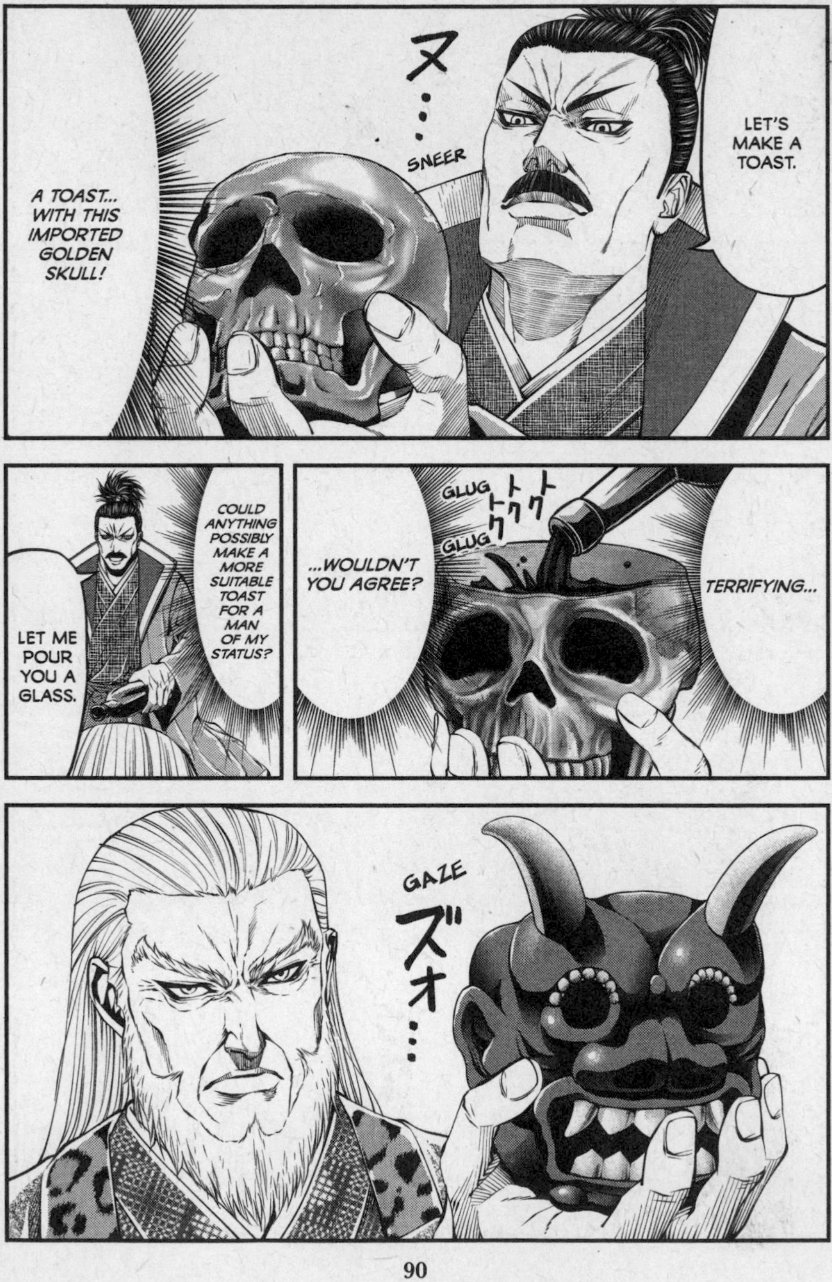

LET'S MAKE A TOAST.
ヌ…
SNEER
A TOAST... WITH THIS IMPORTED GOLDEN SKULL!
TERRIFYING...
トクトクトク
GLUG
GLUG
...WOULDN'T YOU AGREE?
COULD ANYTHING POSSIBLY MAKE A MORE SUITABLE TOAST FOR A MAN OF MY STATUS?
LET ME POUR YOU A GLASS.
GAZE
ズオ…

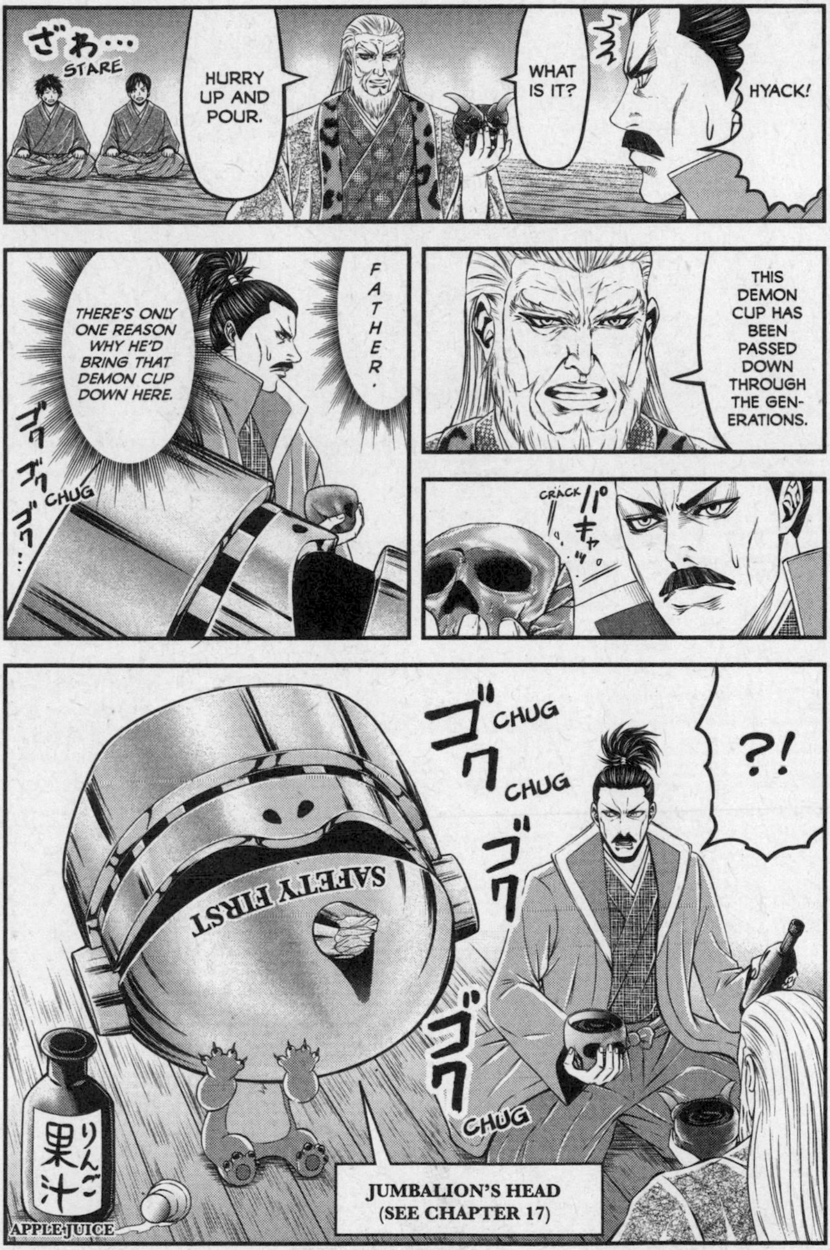
HYACK!
WHAT IS IT?
HURRY UP AND POUR.
ざわ… STARE
THIS DEMON CUP HAS BEEN PASSED DOWN THROUGH THE GENERATIONS.
パキャ CRACK
FATHER.
THERE'S ONLY ONE REASON WHY HE'D BRING THAT DEMON CUP DOWN HERE.
ゴクゴクゴク… CHUG
?!
ゴク CHUG CHUG
ゴクゴク CHUG
SAFETY FIRST
JUMBALION'S HEAD (SEE CHAPTER 17)
りんご果汁
APPLE JUICE

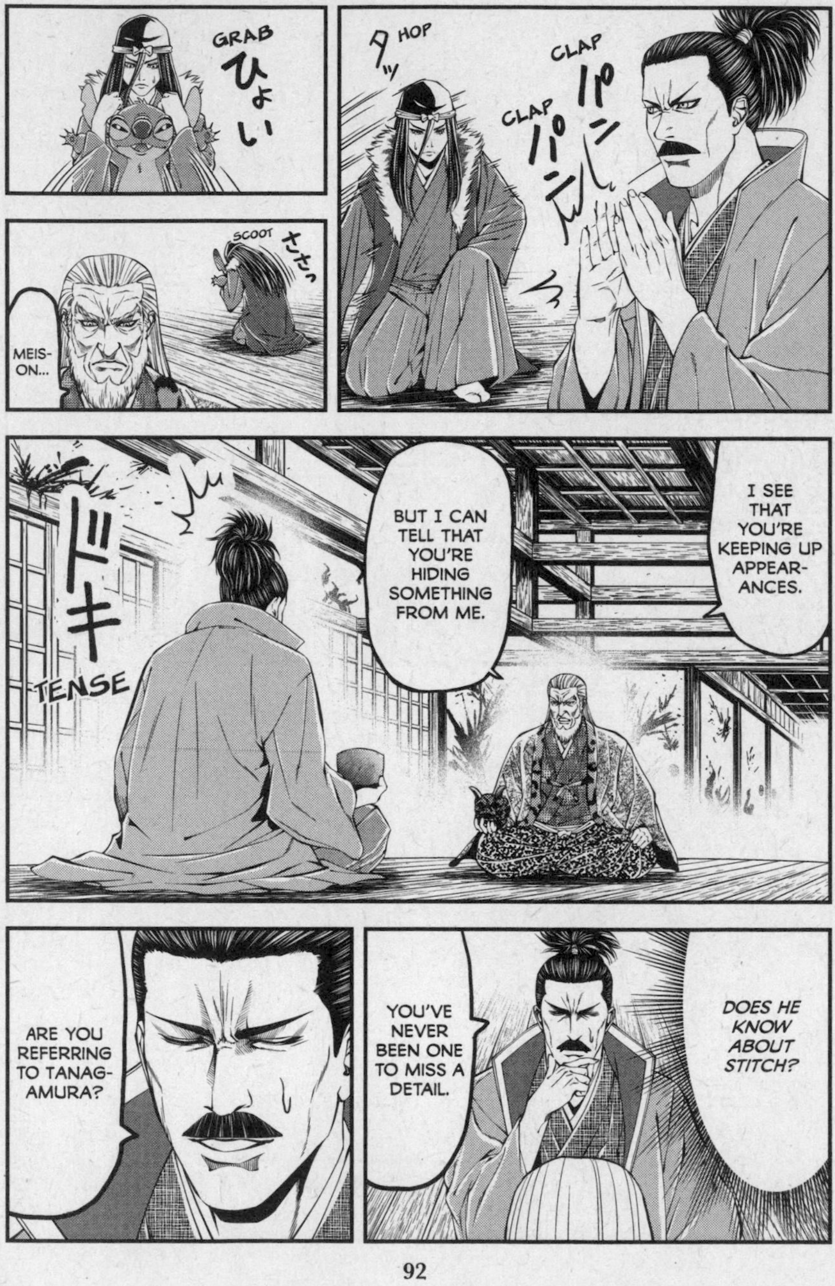
タッ HOP
CLAP パン
CLAP パン
GRAB ひょい
SCOOT ささっ
MEIS-ON...
I SEE THAT YOU'RE KEEPING UP APPEAR-ANCES.
BUT I CAN TELL THAT YOU'RE HIDING SOMETHING FROM ME.
ドキ TENSE
DOES HE KNOW ABOUT STITCH?
YOU'VE NEVER BEEN ONE TO MISS A DETAIL.
ARE YOU REFERRING TO TANAG-AMURA?

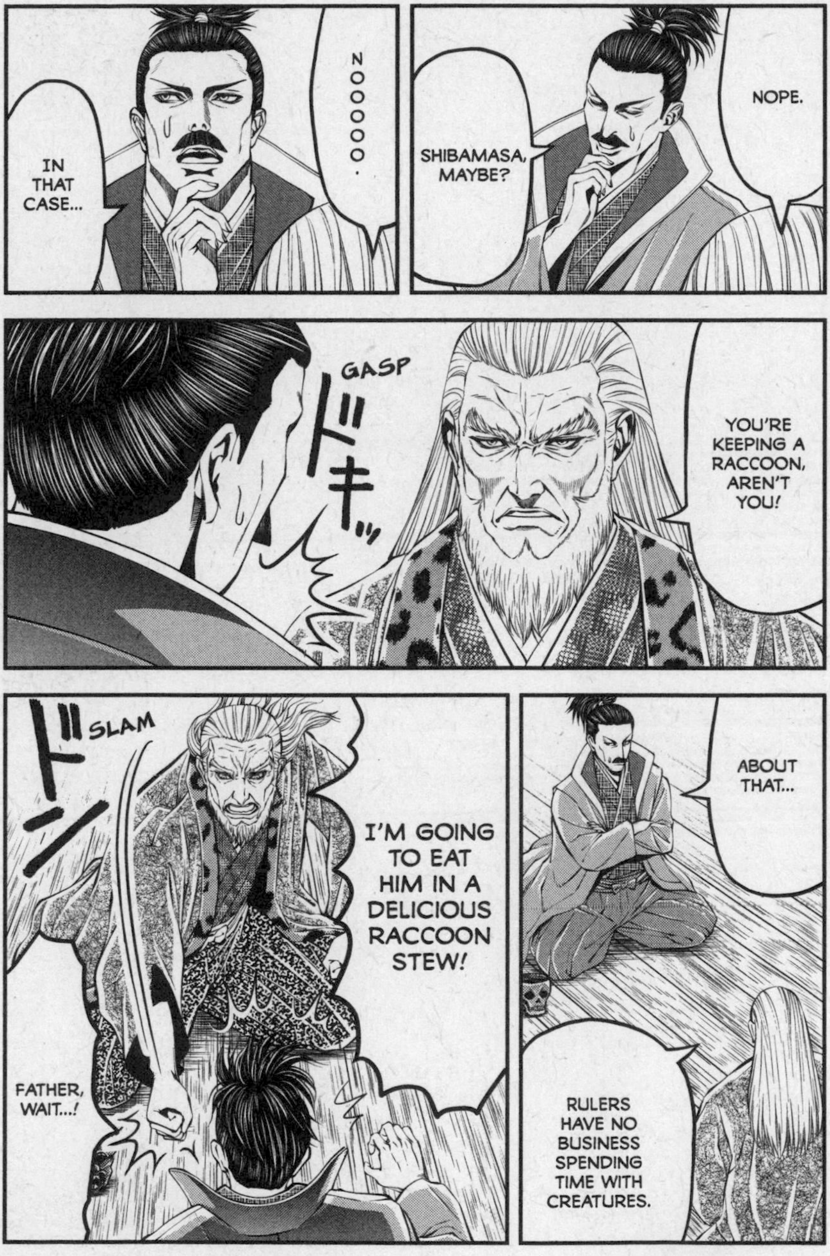
NOPE.
SHIBAMASA, MAYBE?
NOOOOO.
IN THAT CASE...
YOU'RE KEEPING A RACCOON, AREN'T YOU!
GASP
ドキッ
ABOUT THAT...
RULERS HAVE NO BUSINESS SPENDING TIME WITH CREATURES.
I'M GOING TO EAT HIM IN A DELICIOUS RACCOON STEW!
ドーン
SLAM
FATHER, WAIT...!

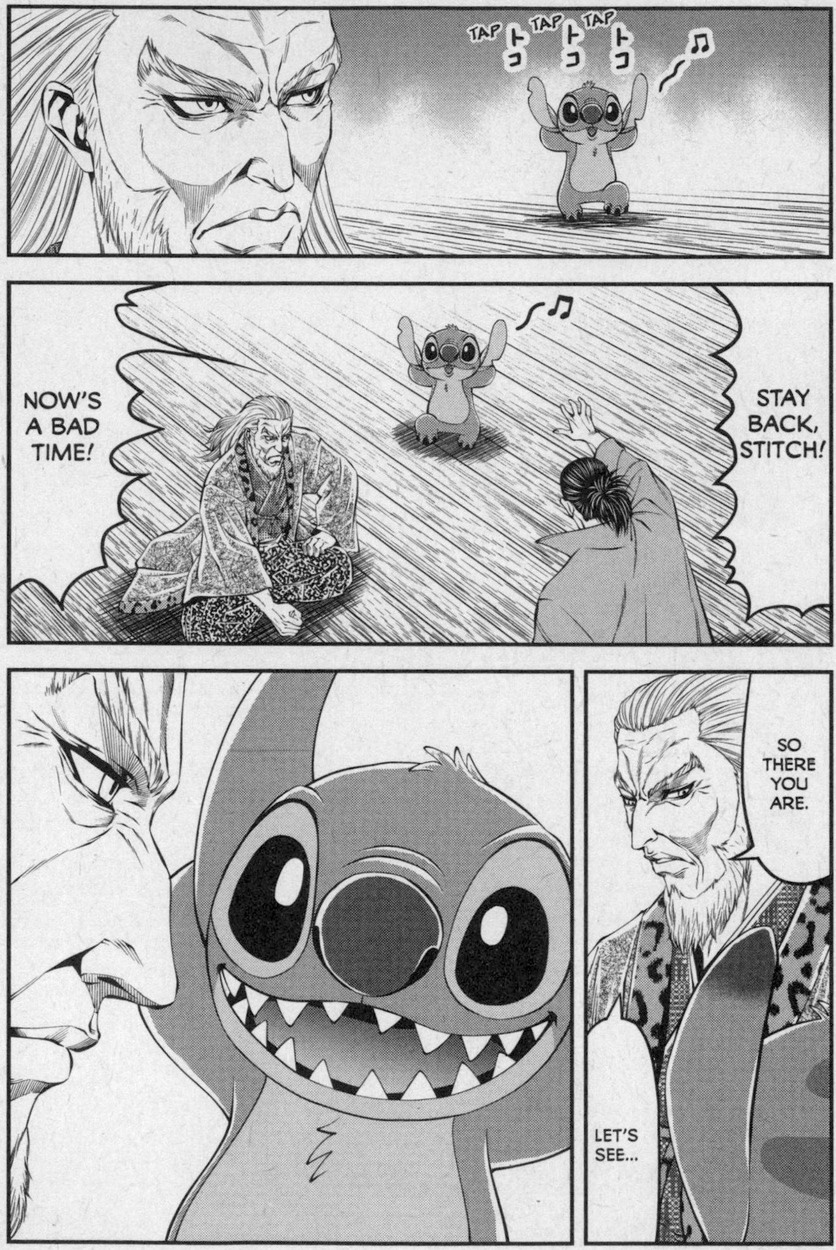
TAP TAP TAP
トコ トコ トコ
STAY BACK, STITCH!
NOW'S A BAD TIME!
SO THERE YOU ARE.
LET'S SEE...

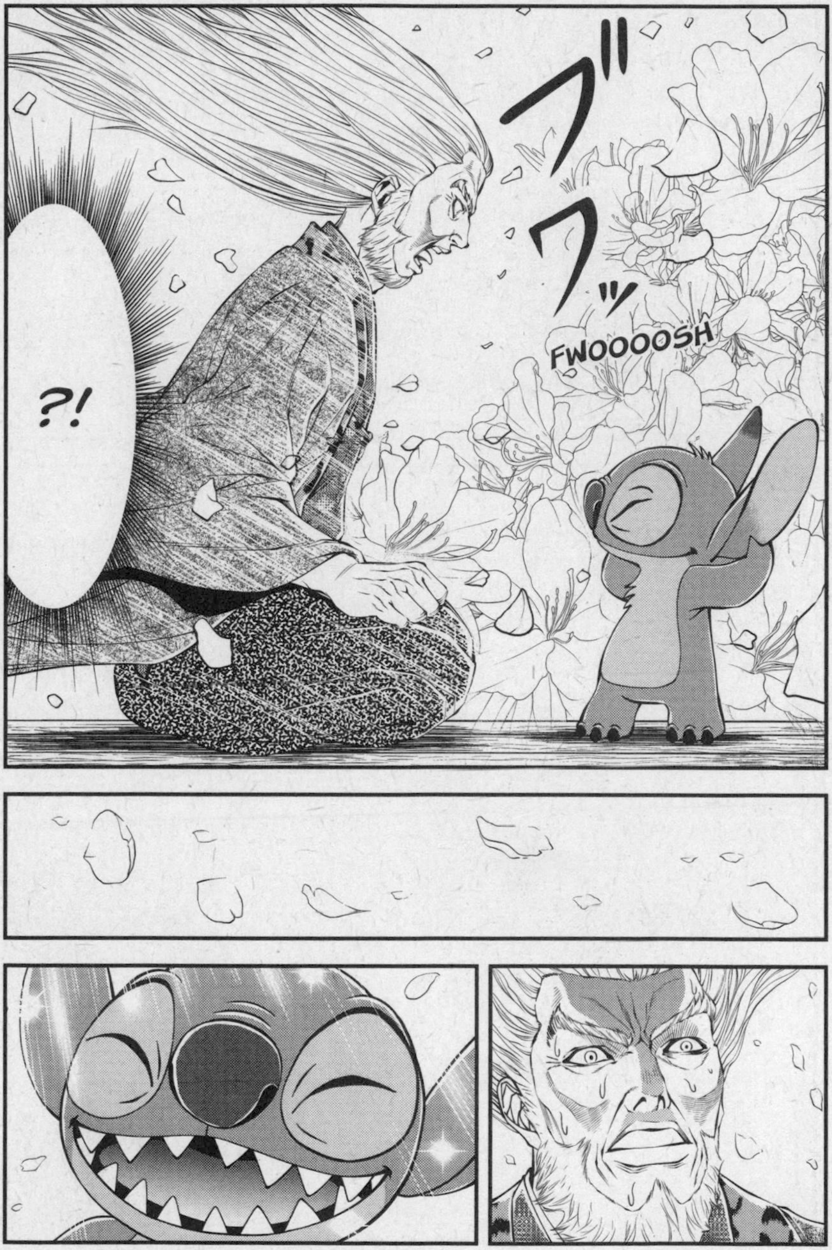
ブワッ
FWOOOOSH
?!

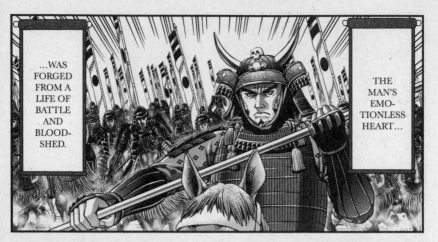

THE MAN'S EMOTIONLESS HEART…
…WAS FORGED FROM A LIFE OF BATTLE AND BLOODSHED.
I WISH I COULD JUST BREATHE YOU IN.
AND RUB MY FACE AGAINST YOUR SOFT CHEEKS.
THIS WAS THE FIRST TIME HE'D EVER FELT THIS WAY.
LOVE!!

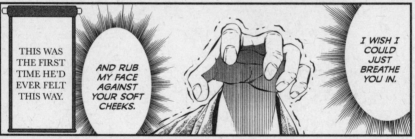

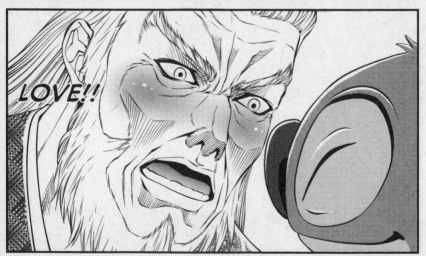

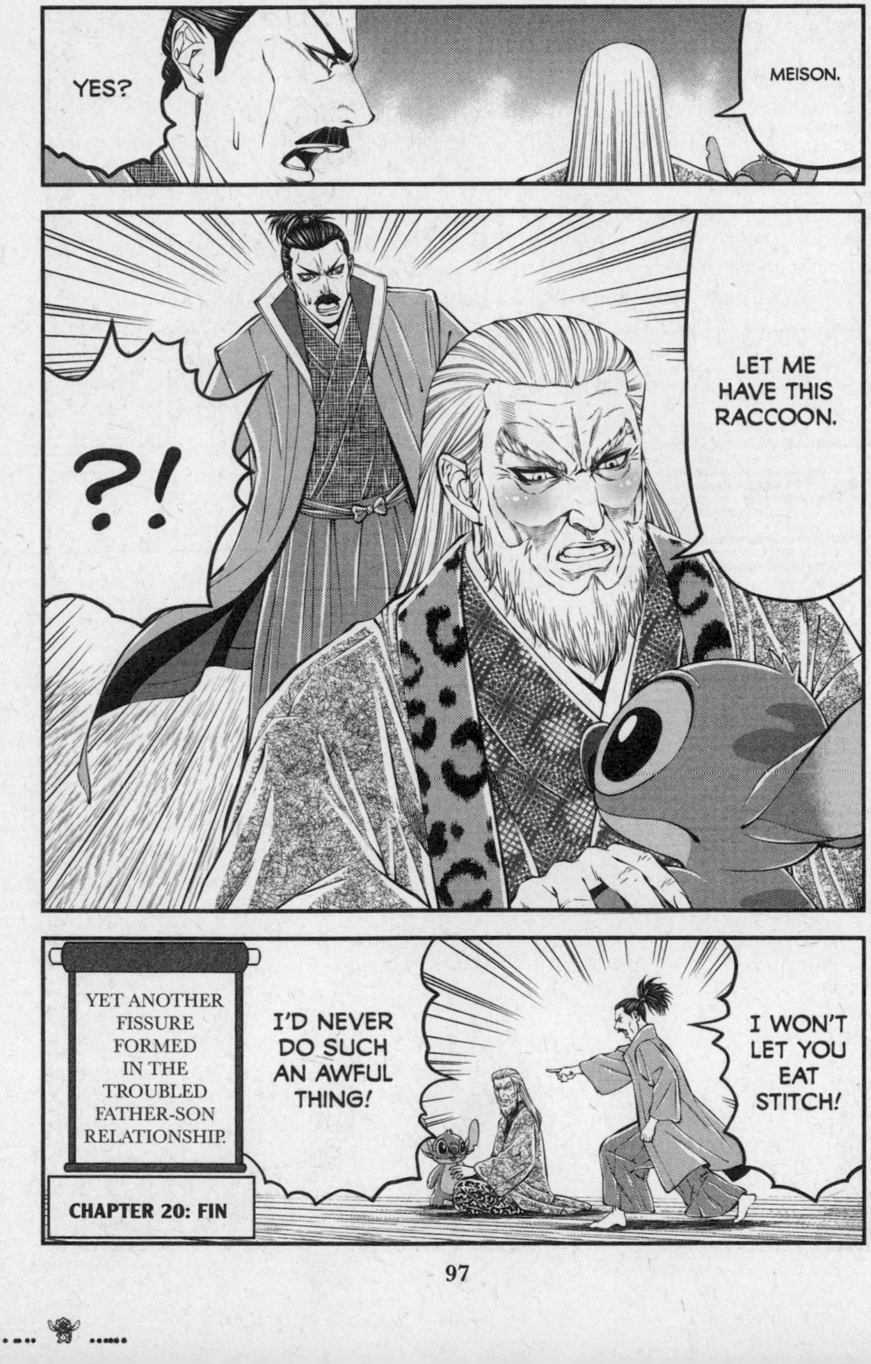
MEISON.
YES?
LET ME HAVE THIS RACCOON.
?!
I WON'T LET YOU EAT STITCH!
I'D NEVER DO SUCH AN AWFUL THING!
YET ANOTHER FISSURE FORMED IN THE TROUBLED FATHER-SON RELATIONSHIP.
CHAPTER 20: FIN

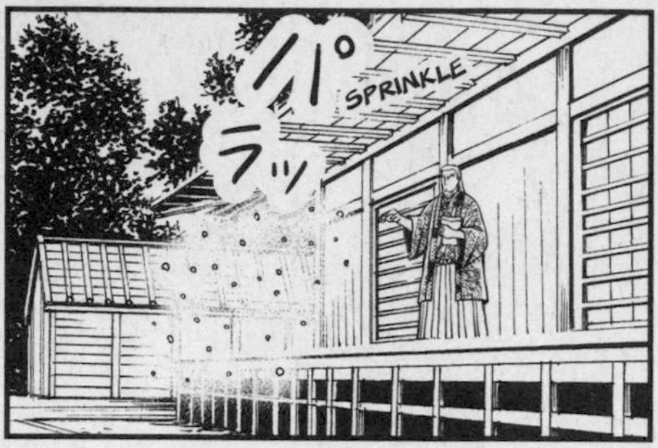
パラッ
SPRINKLE

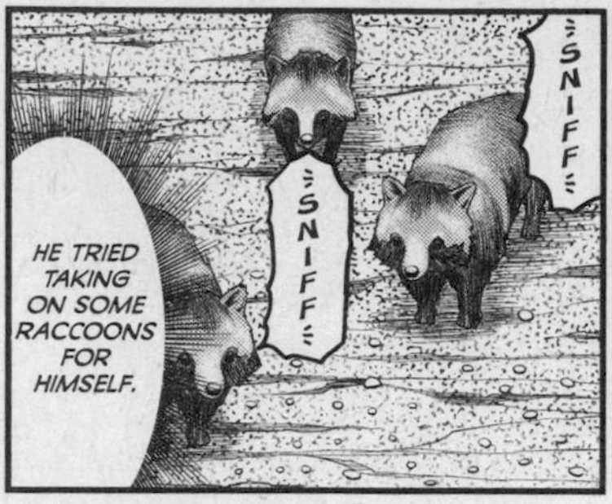
SNIFF
SNIFF
HE TRIED TAKING ON SOME RACCOONS FOR HIMSELF.

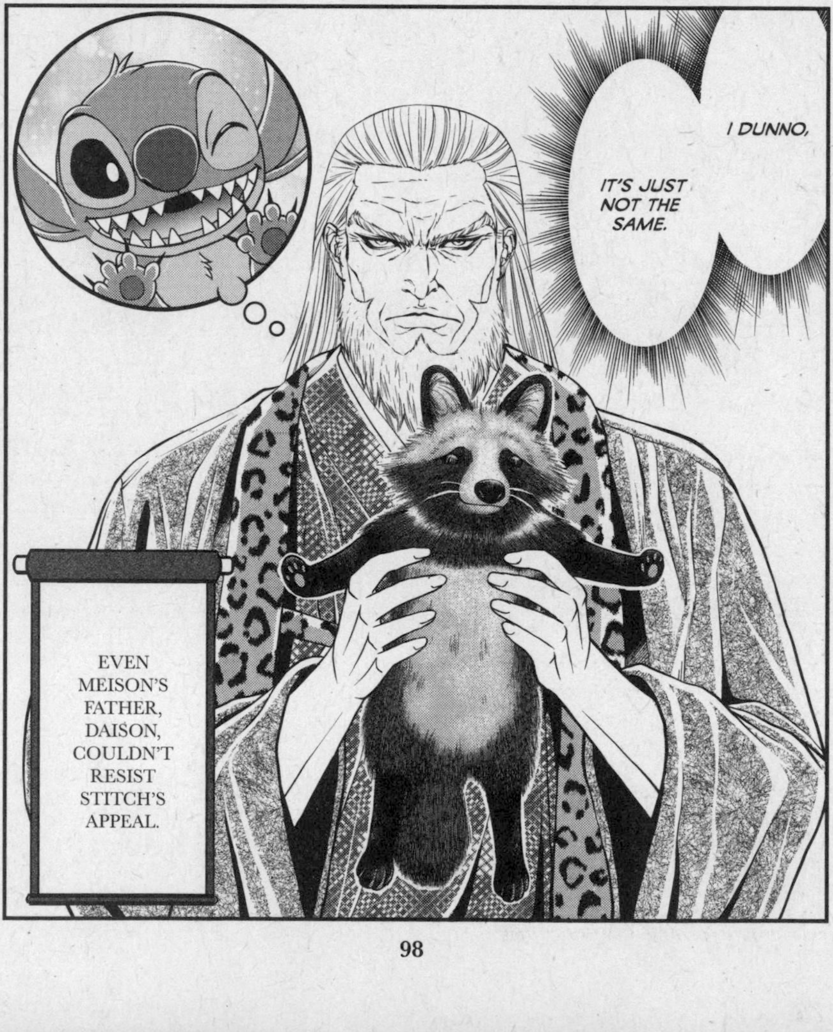
I DUNNO,
IT'S JUST NOT THE SAME.
EVEN MEISON'S FATHER, DAISON, COULDN'T RESIST STITCH'S APPEAL.

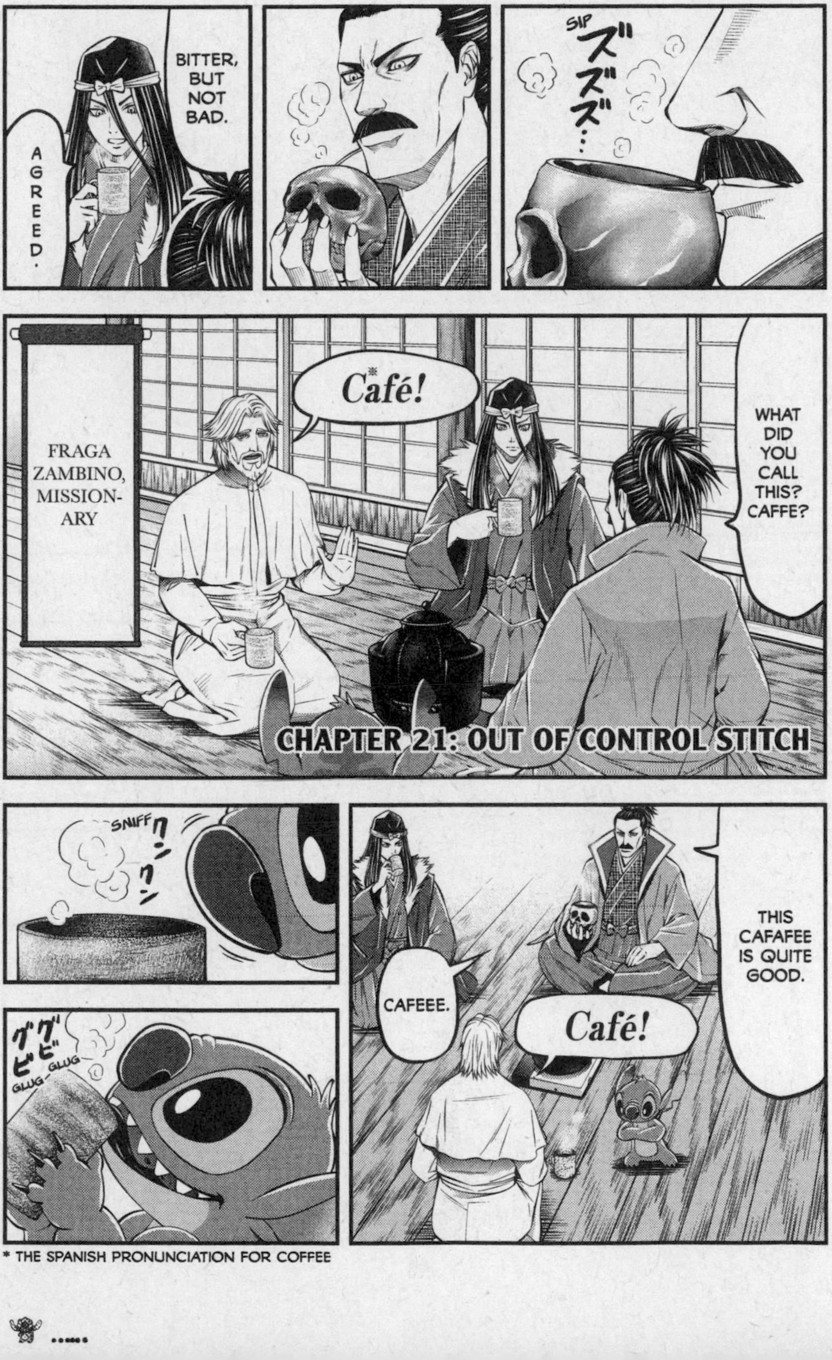
SIP ズズズ…
BITTER, BUT NOT BAD.
AGREED.
WHAT DID YOU CALL THIS? CAFFE?
Café!
FRAGA ZAMBINO, MISSIONARY
CHAPTER 21: OUT OF CONTROL STITCH
THIS CAFAFEE IS QUITE GOOD.
CAFEEE.
Café!
SNIFF クン クン
グビ グビ GLUG GLUG

* THE SPANISH PRONUNCIATION FOR COFFEE

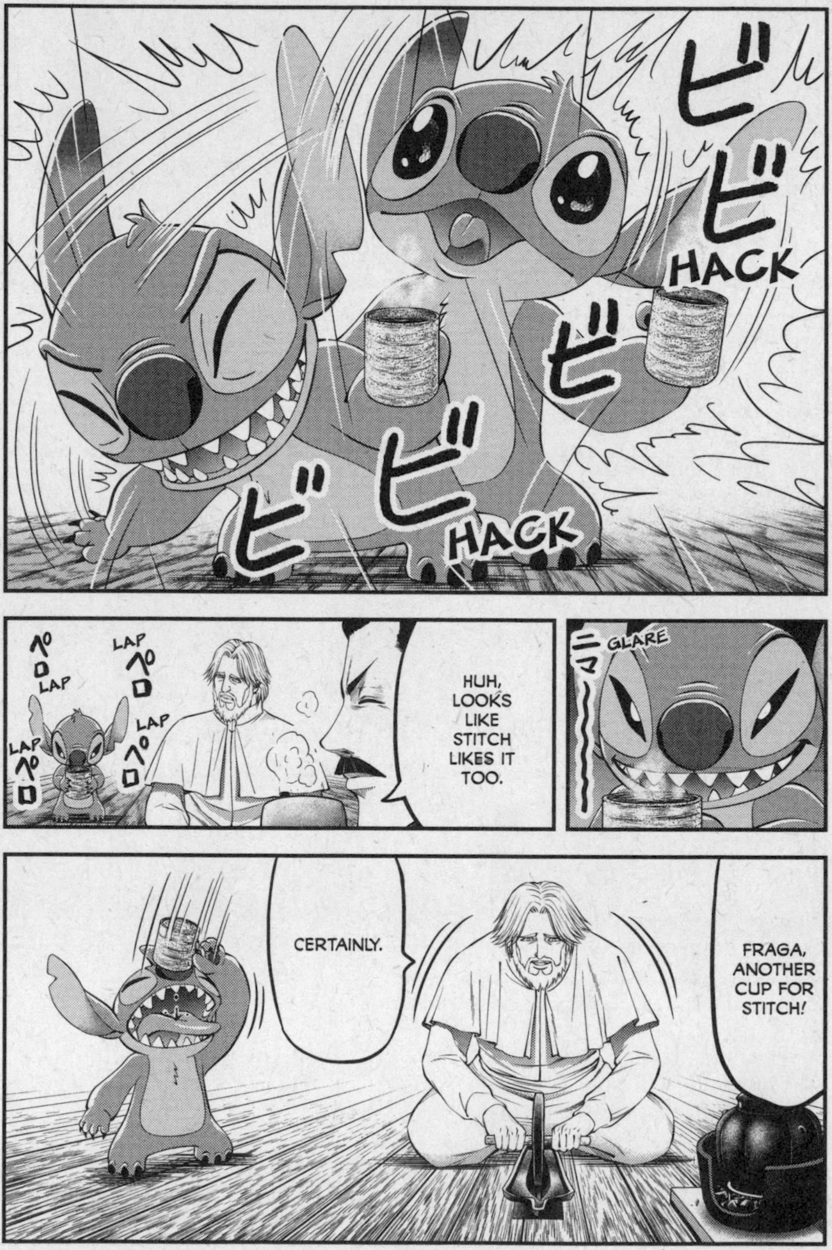
ビビ
HACK
ビ
ビビ
HACK
ニマ～～～
GLARE
HUH, LOOKS LIKE STITCH LIKES IT TOO.
ペロ
LAP
ペロ
LAP
ペロ
LAP
ペロ
LAP
FRAGA, ANOTHER CUP FOR STITCH!
CERTAINLY.

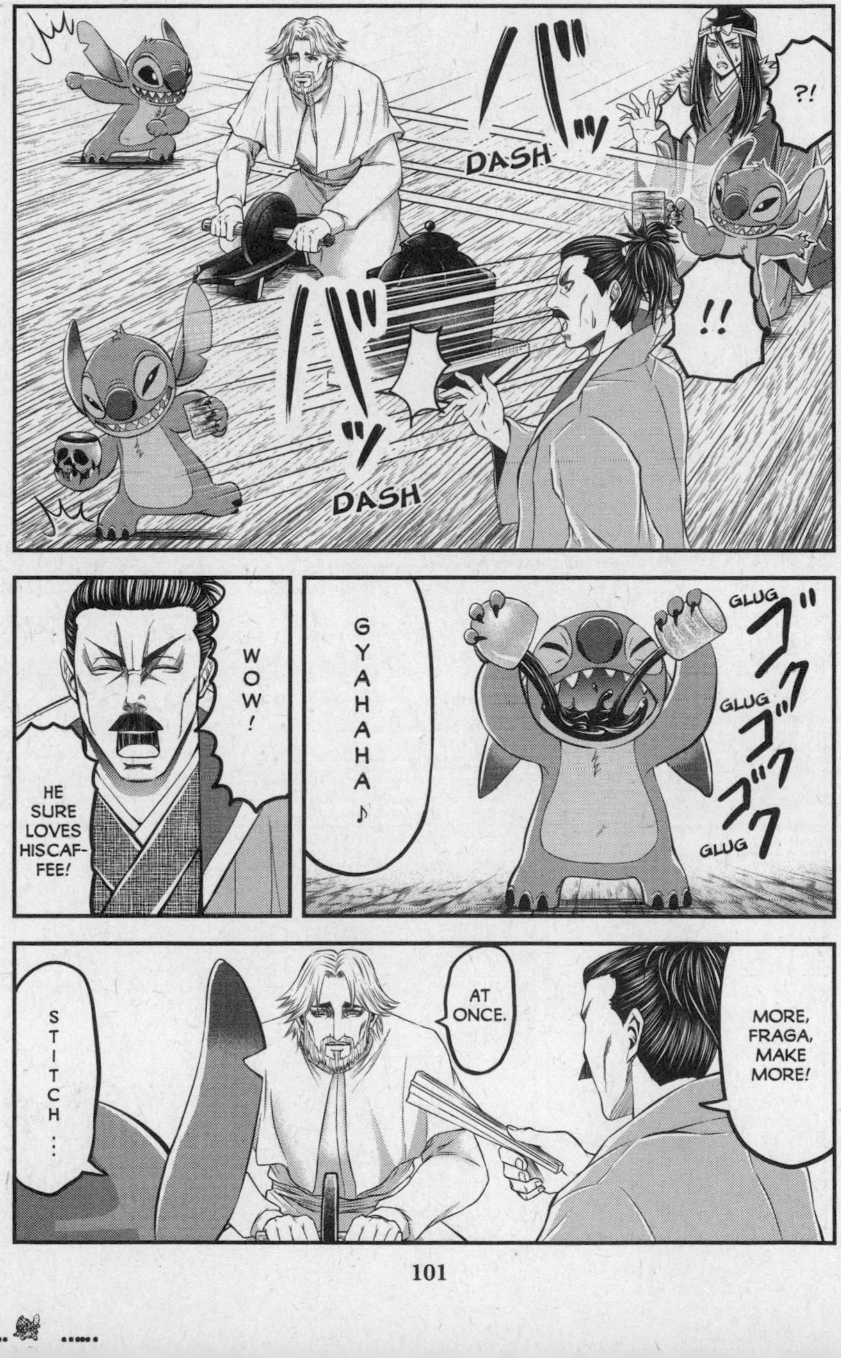
?!
バッ
DASH
!!
バッ
DASH
GLUG
ゴク
GLUG
ゴク
ゴク
GLUG
GYAHAHA ♪
WOW!
HE SURE LOVES HISCAF-FEE!
MORE, FRAGA, MAKE MORE!
AT ONCE.
STITCH ...

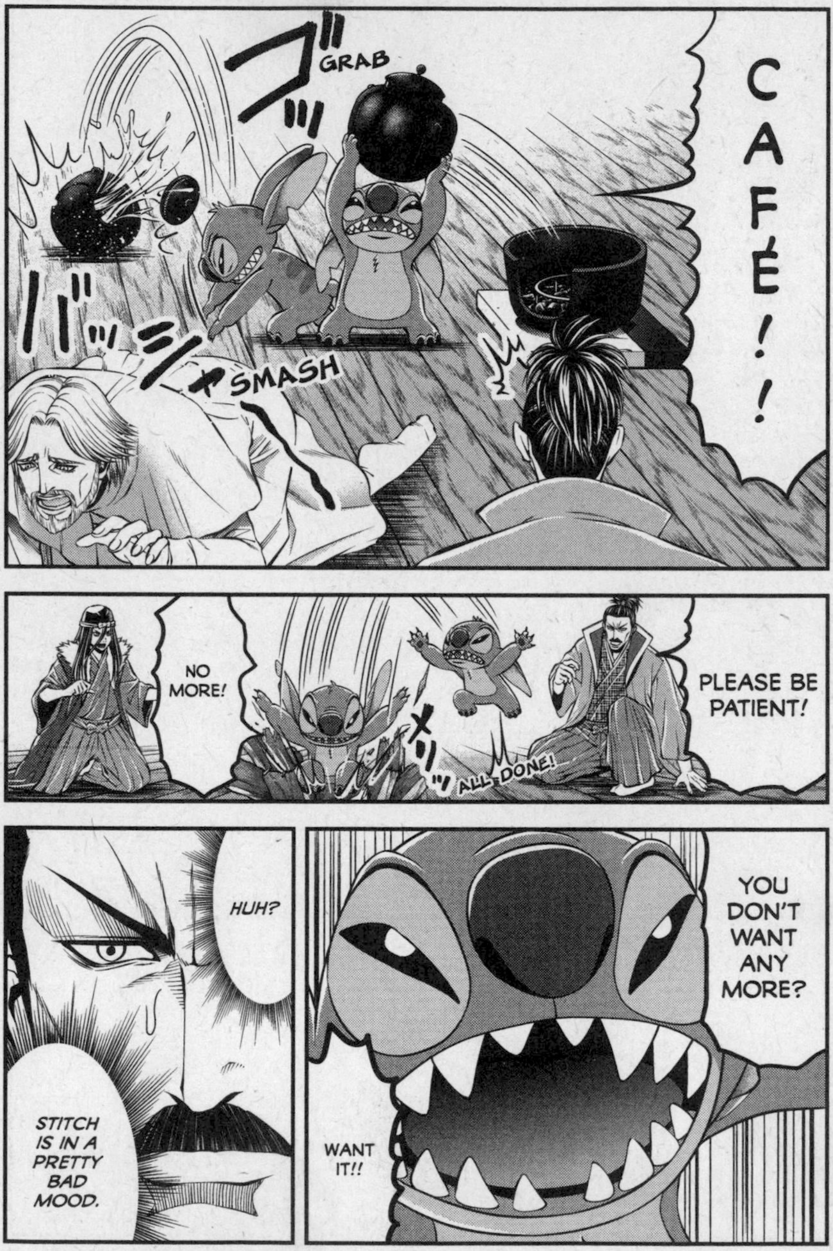

CAFÉ!!
GRAB
SMASH
PLEASE BE PATIENT!
ALL DONE!
NO MORE!
YOU DON'T WANT ANY MORE?
WANT IT!!
HUH?
STITCH IS IN A PRETTY BAD MOOD.

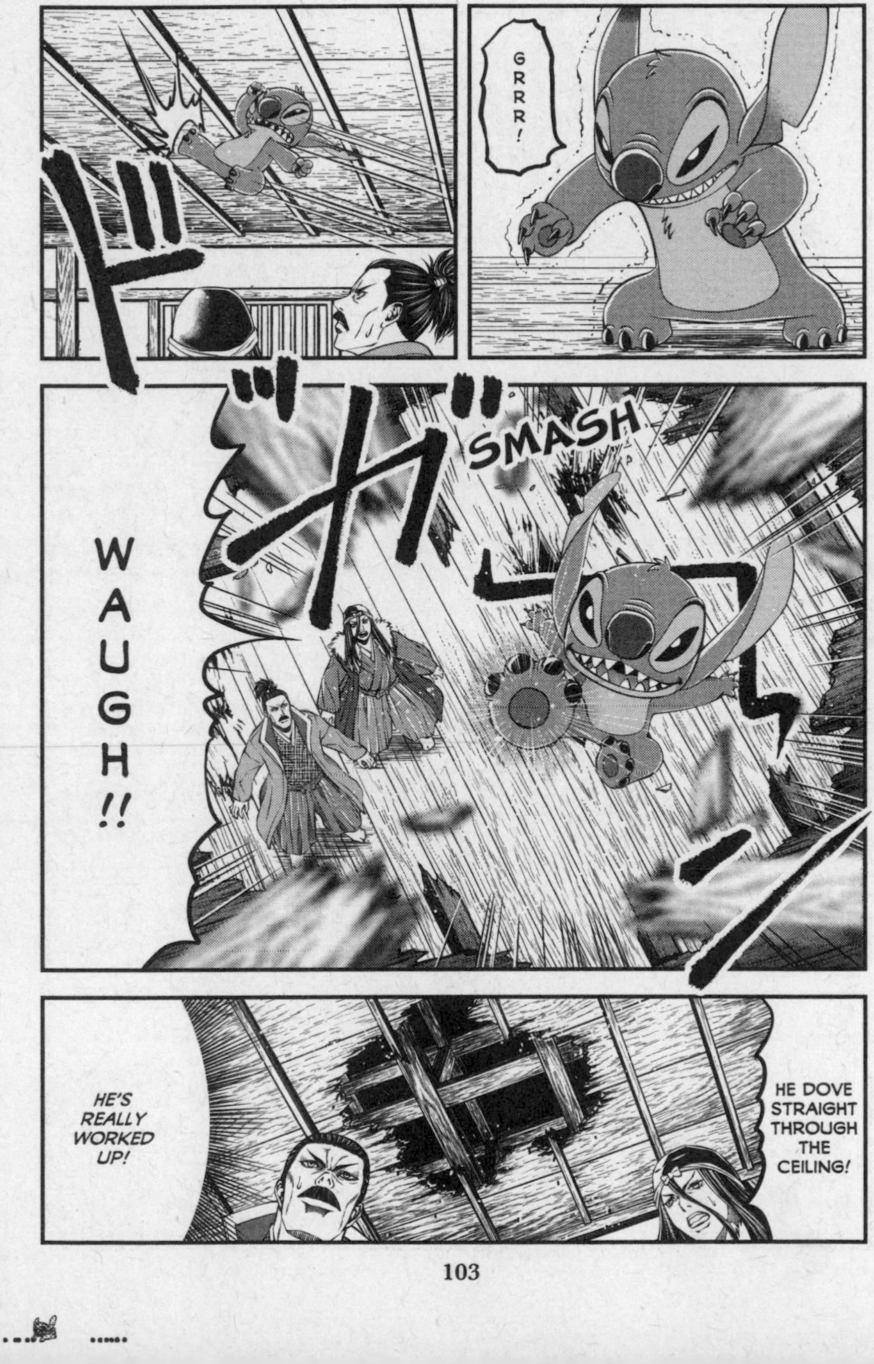
GRRR!
SMASH
WAUGH!!
HE DOVE STRAIGHT THROUGH THE CEILING!
HE'S REALLY WORKED UP!

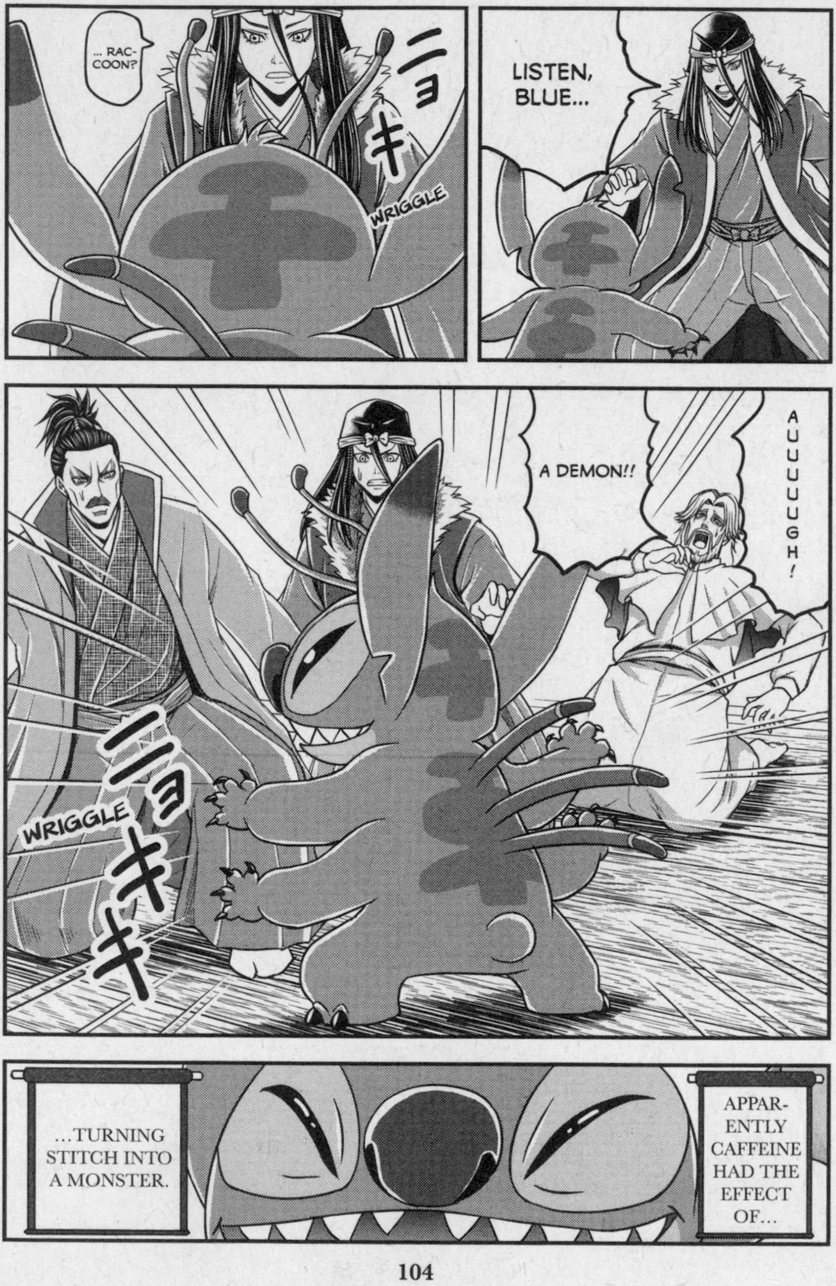
LISTEN, BLUE...
... RAC-COON?
ニョキ
WRIGGLE
AUUUUUGH!
A DEMON!!
ニョキキ
WRIGGLE
APPAR-ENTLY CAFFEINE HAD THE EFFECT OF...
...TURNING STITCH INTO A MONSTER.

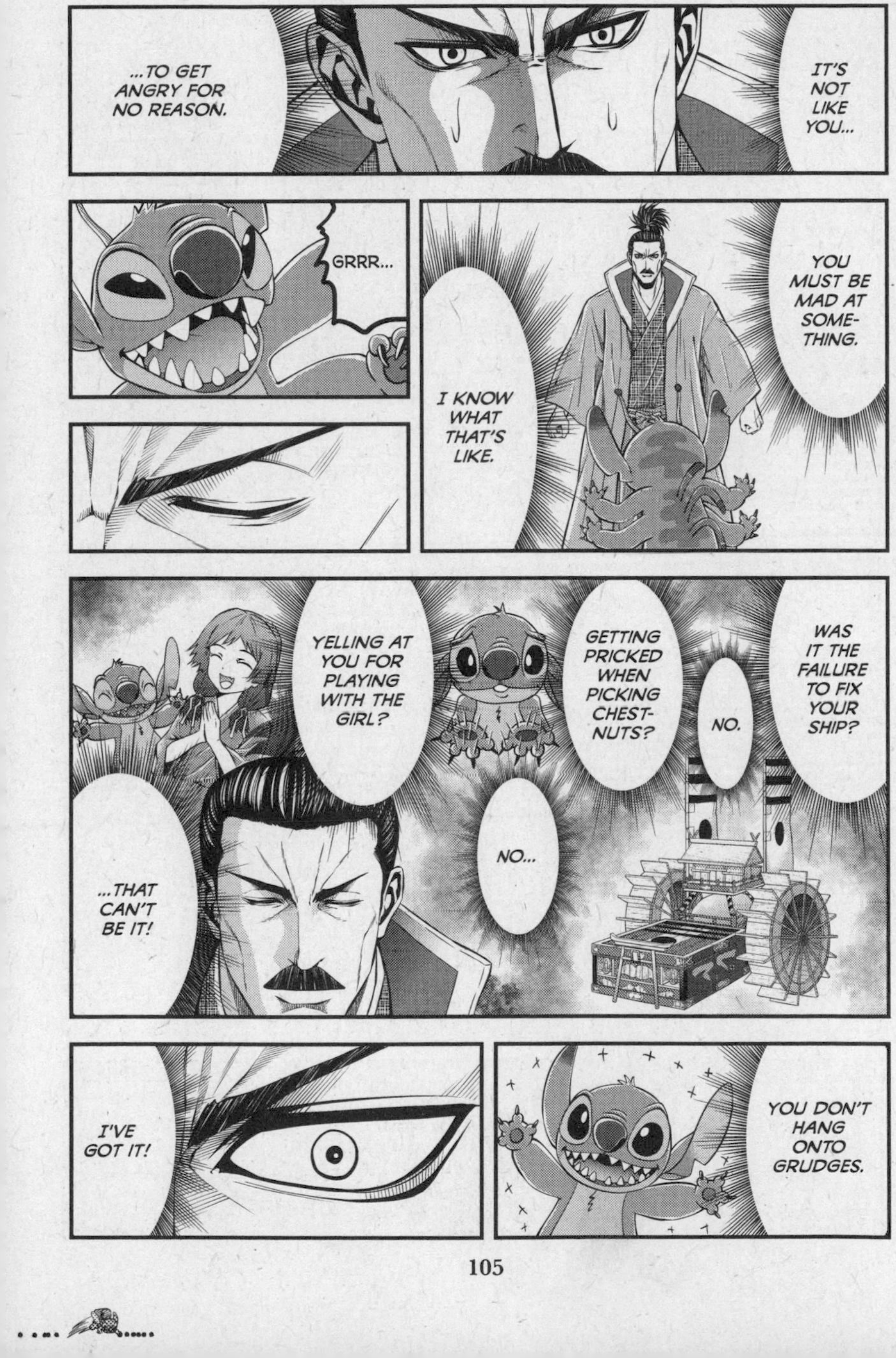
IT'S NOT LIKE YOU...
...TO GET ANGRY FOR NO REASON.
YOU MUST BE MAD AT SOME-THING.
I KNOW WHAT THAT'S LIKE.
GRRR...
WAS IT THE FAILURE TO FIX YOUR SHIP?
NO.
GETTING PRICKED WHEN PICKING CHEST-NUTS?
NO...
YELLING AT YOU FOR PLAYING WITH THE GIRL?
...THAT CAN'T BE IT!
YOU DON'T HANG ONTO GRUDGES.
I'VE GOT IT!

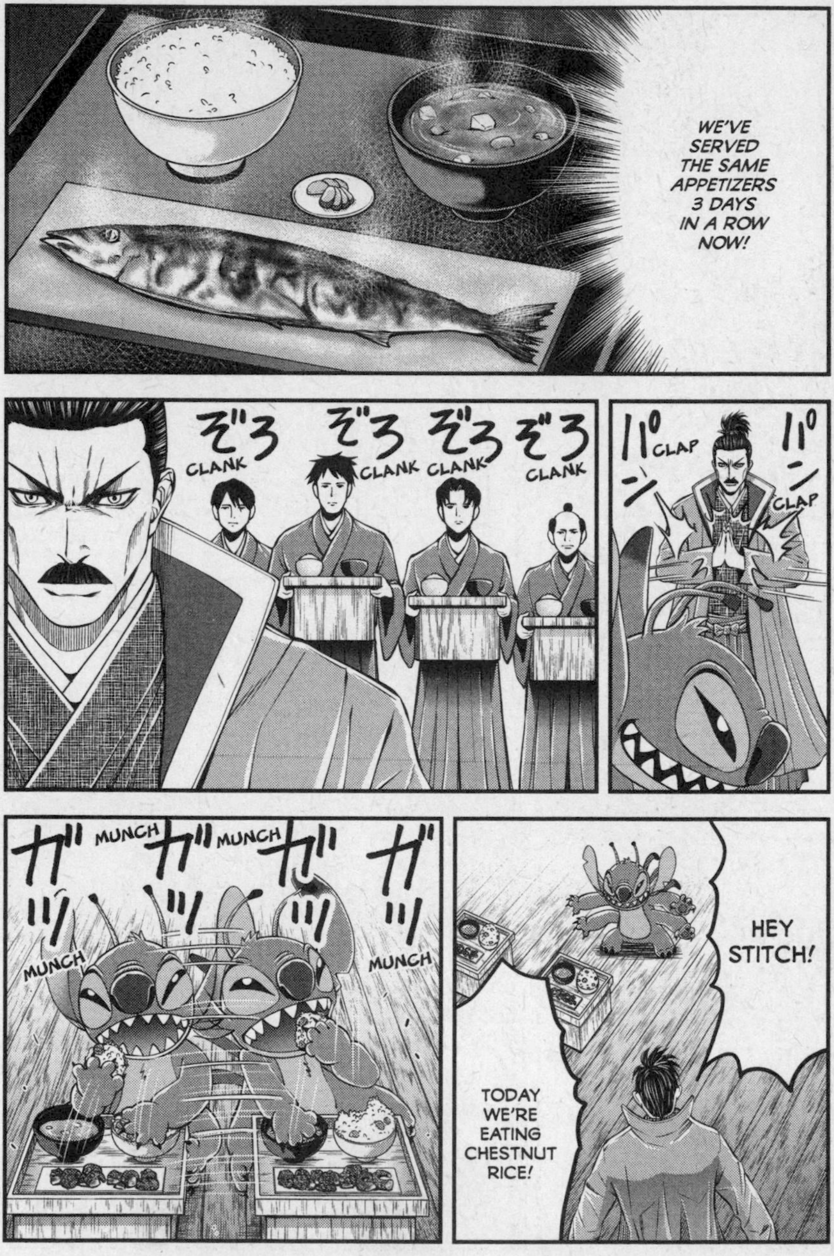
WE'VE SERVED THE SAME APPETIZERS 3 DAYS IN A ROW NOW!
パン
CLAP
パン
CLAP
ぞろ
CLANK
ぞろ
CLANK
ぞろ
CLANK
ぞろ
CLANK
HEY STITCH!
TODAY WE'RE EATING CHESTNUT RICE!
ガツ
MUNCH
ガツ
MUNCH
ガツ
MUNCH
ガツ
MUNCH

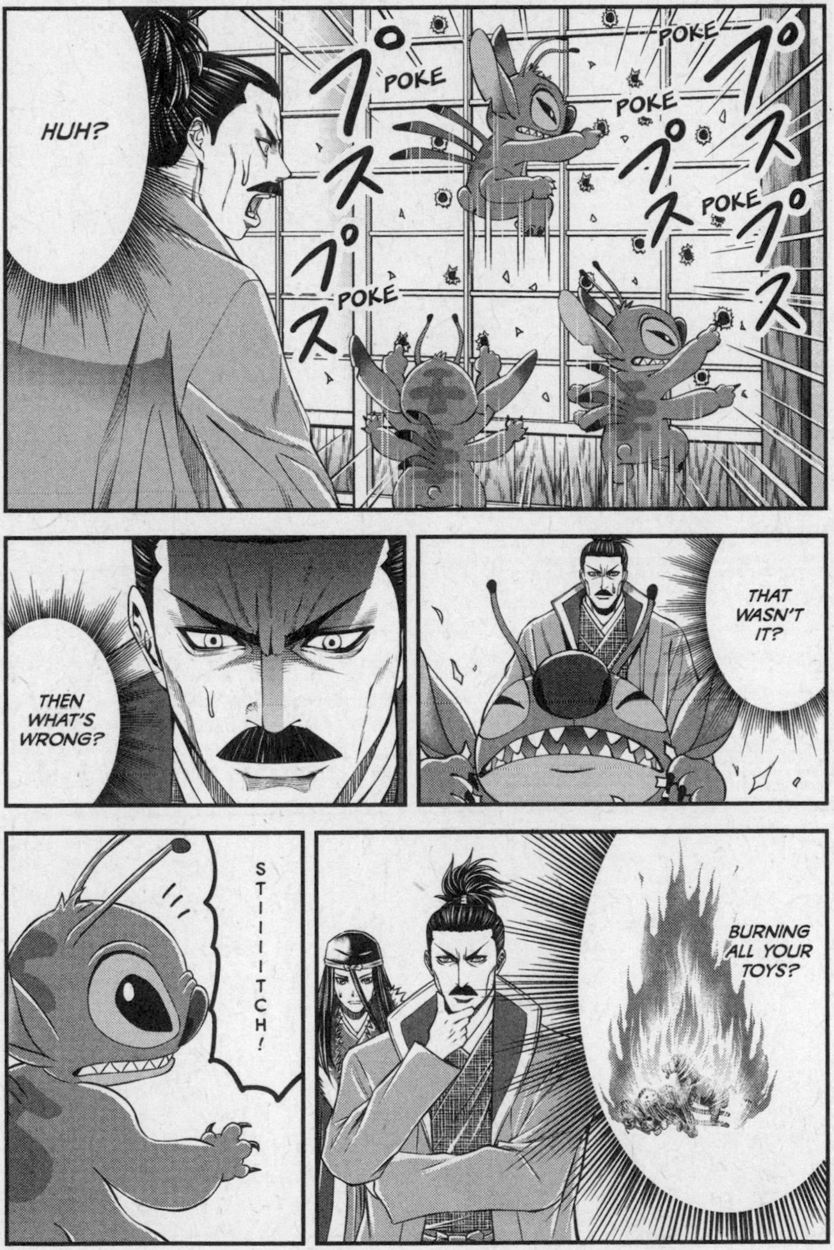
POKE
プスプス
POKE
プス
POKE
POKE
プスプス
POKE
HUH?
THAT WASN'T IT?
THEN WHAT'S WRONG?
BURNING ALL YOUR TOYS?
STIIIITCH!

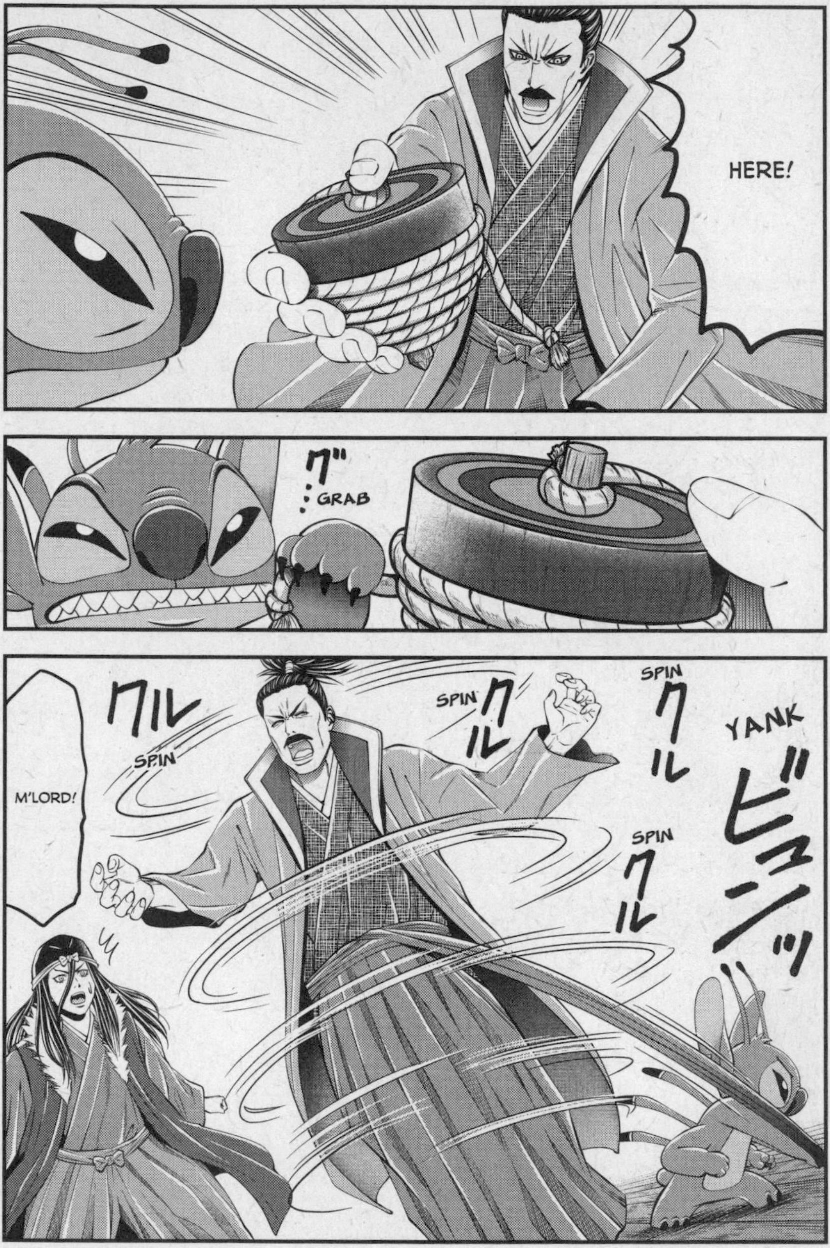
HERE!
グ
GRAB
YANK
ビュンッ
SPIN
クル
SPIN
クル
SPIN
クル
SPIN
クル
M'LORD!

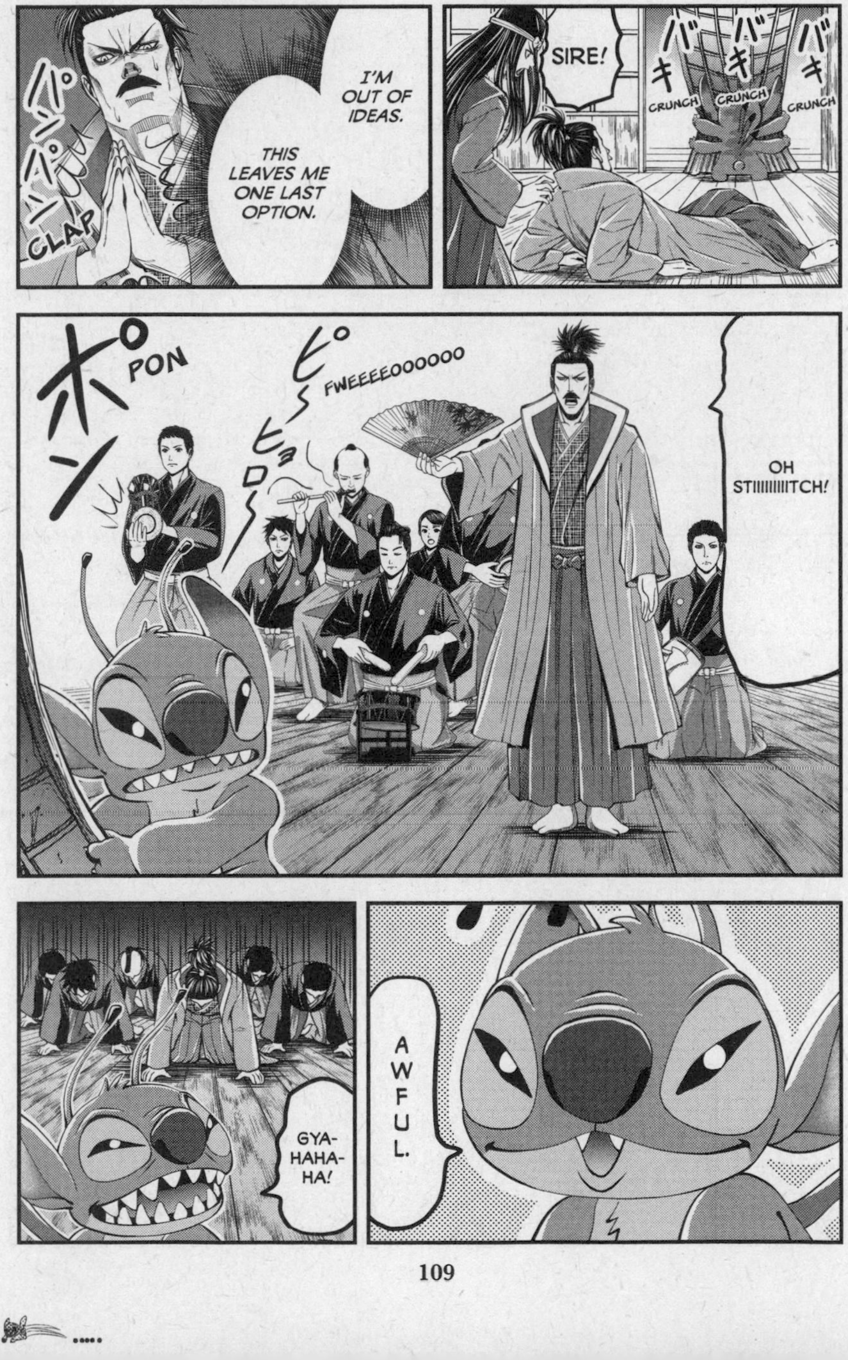
SIRE!
バキ バキ バキ
CRUNCH CRUNCH CRUNCH
I'M OUT OF IDEAS.
THIS LEAVES ME ONE LAST OPTION.
パンパン
CLAP
OH STIIIIIIITCH!
FWEEEEOOOOOO
ポン
PON
AWFUL.
GYA-HAHAHA!

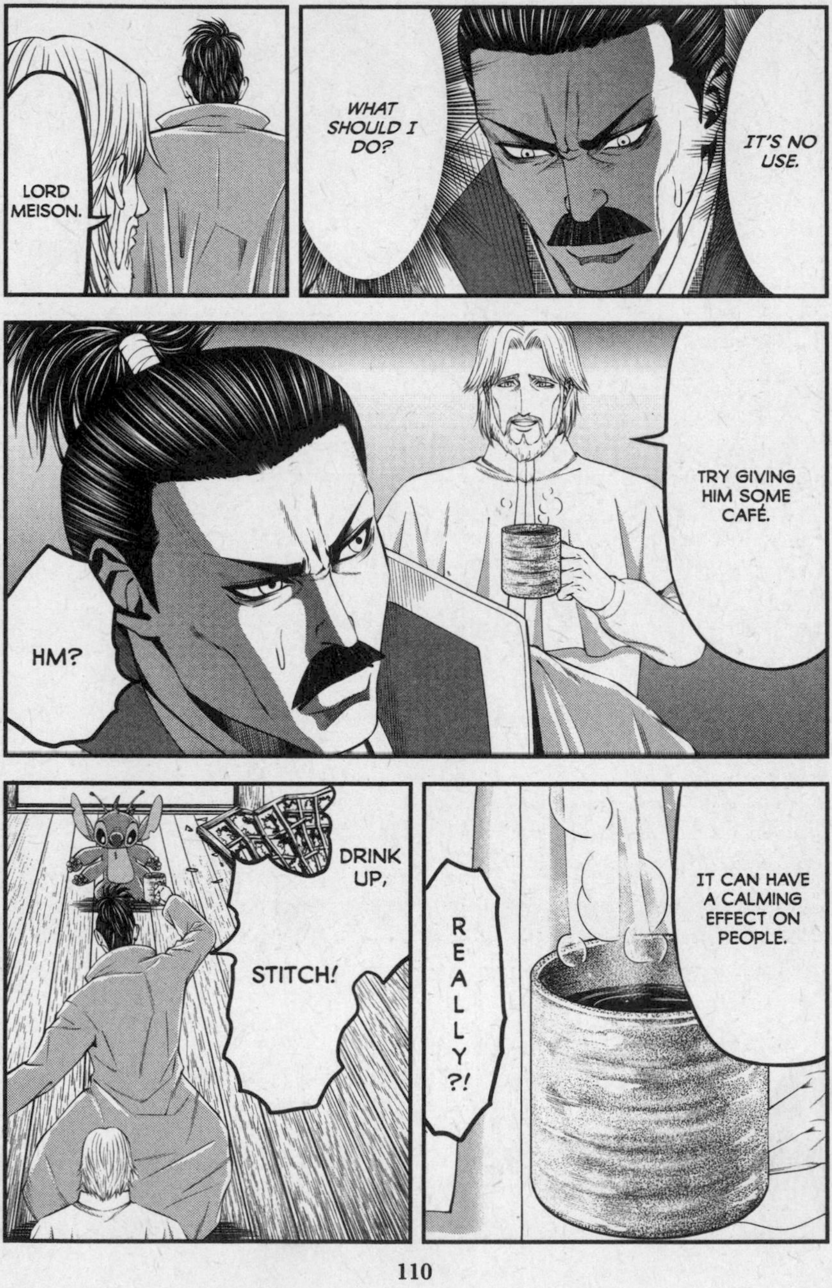
IT'S NO USE.
WHAT SHOULD I DO?
LORD MEISON.
TRY GIVING HIM SOME CAFÉ.
HM?
IT CAN HAVE A CALMING EFFECT ON PEOPLE.
REALLY?!
DRINK UP, STITCH!

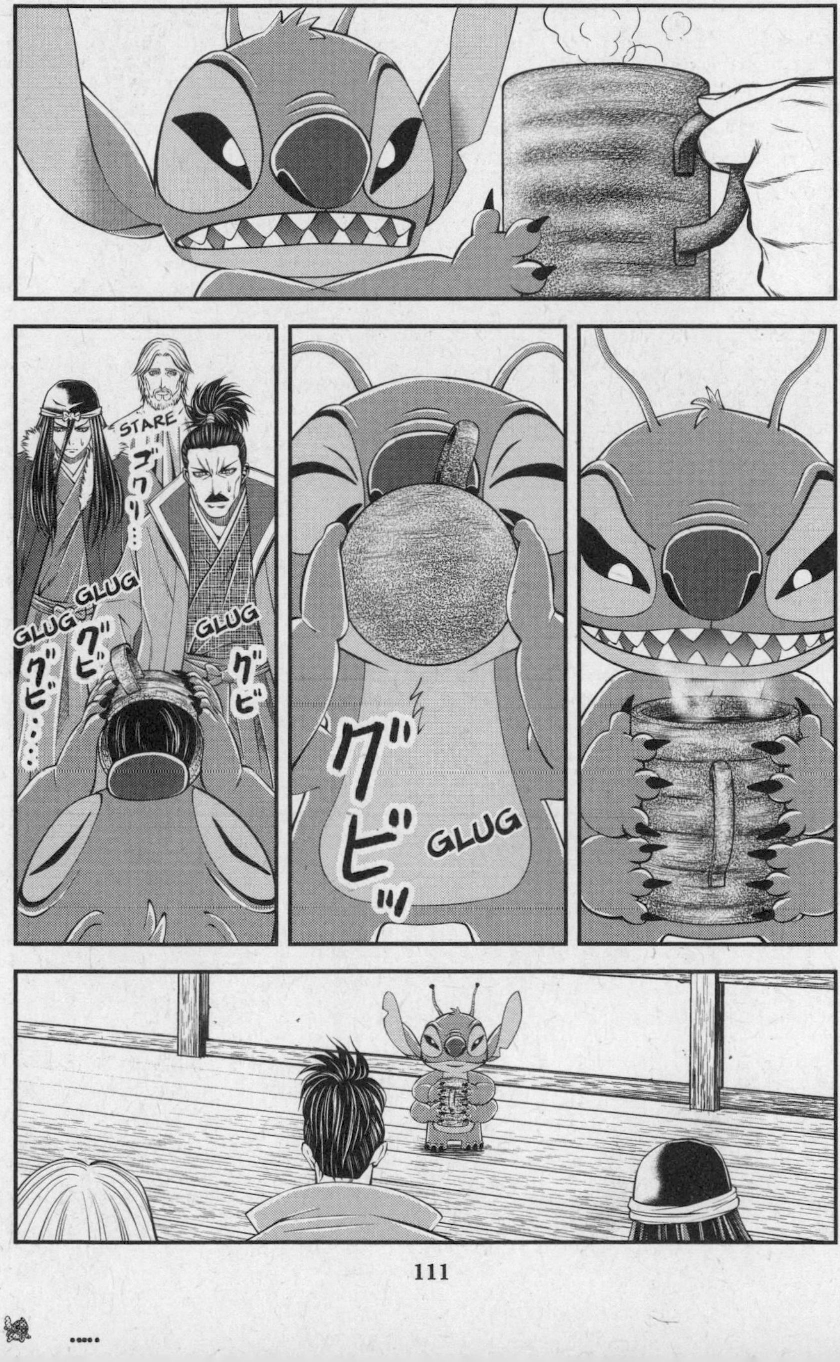
グビッ
GLUG
STARE
ゴクリ…
GLUG
グビ
GLUG
グビ
GLUG
グビ…

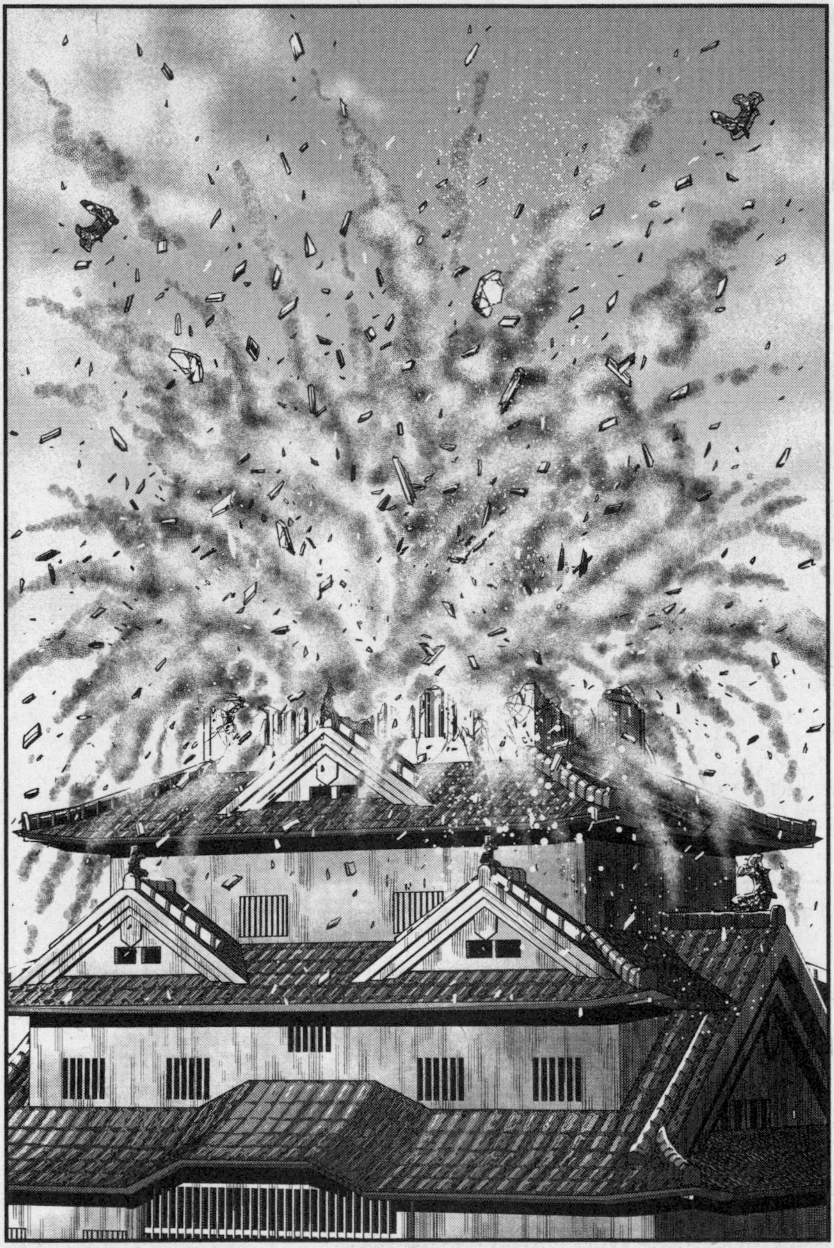

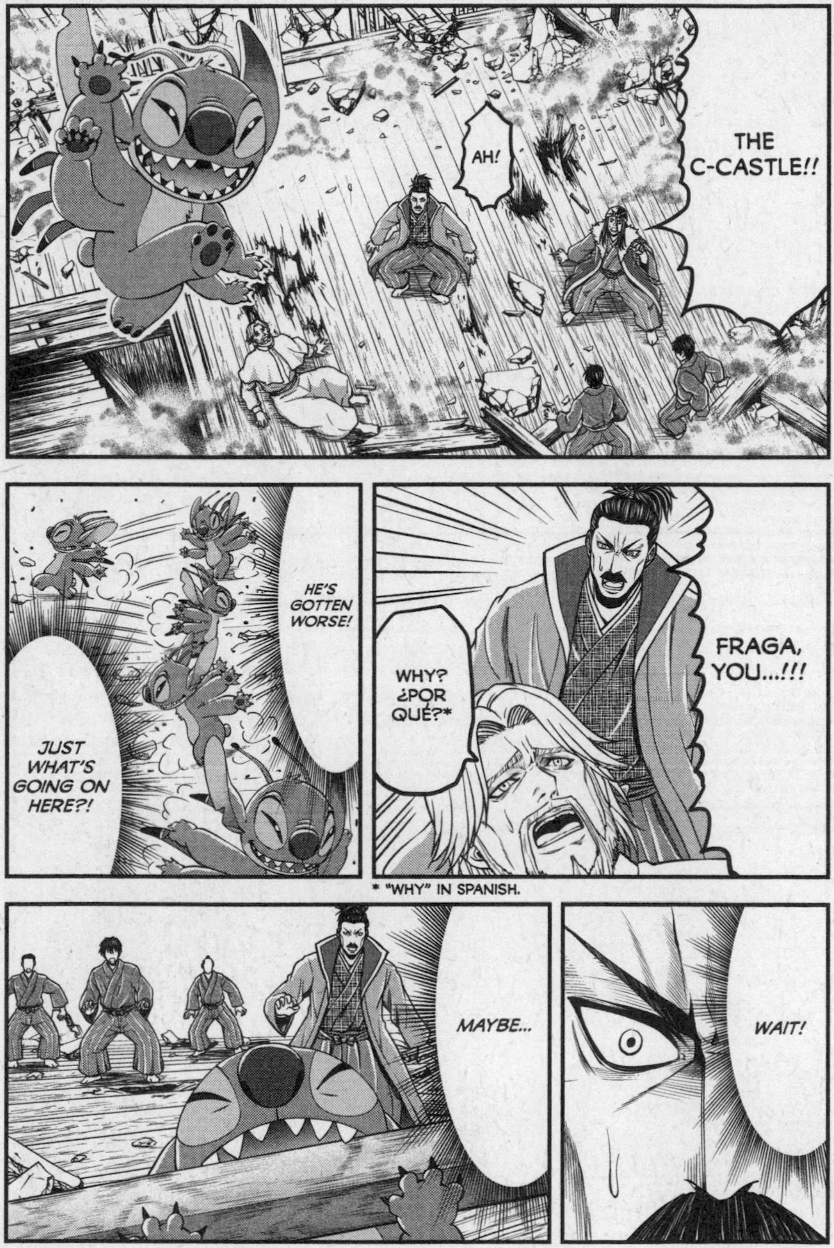
THE C-CASTLE!!
AH!
FRAGA, YOU...!!!
WHY? ¿POR QUÉ?*
HE'S GOTTEN WORSE!
JUST WHAT'S GOING ON HERE?!
* "WHY" IN SPANISH.
WAIT!
MAYBE...

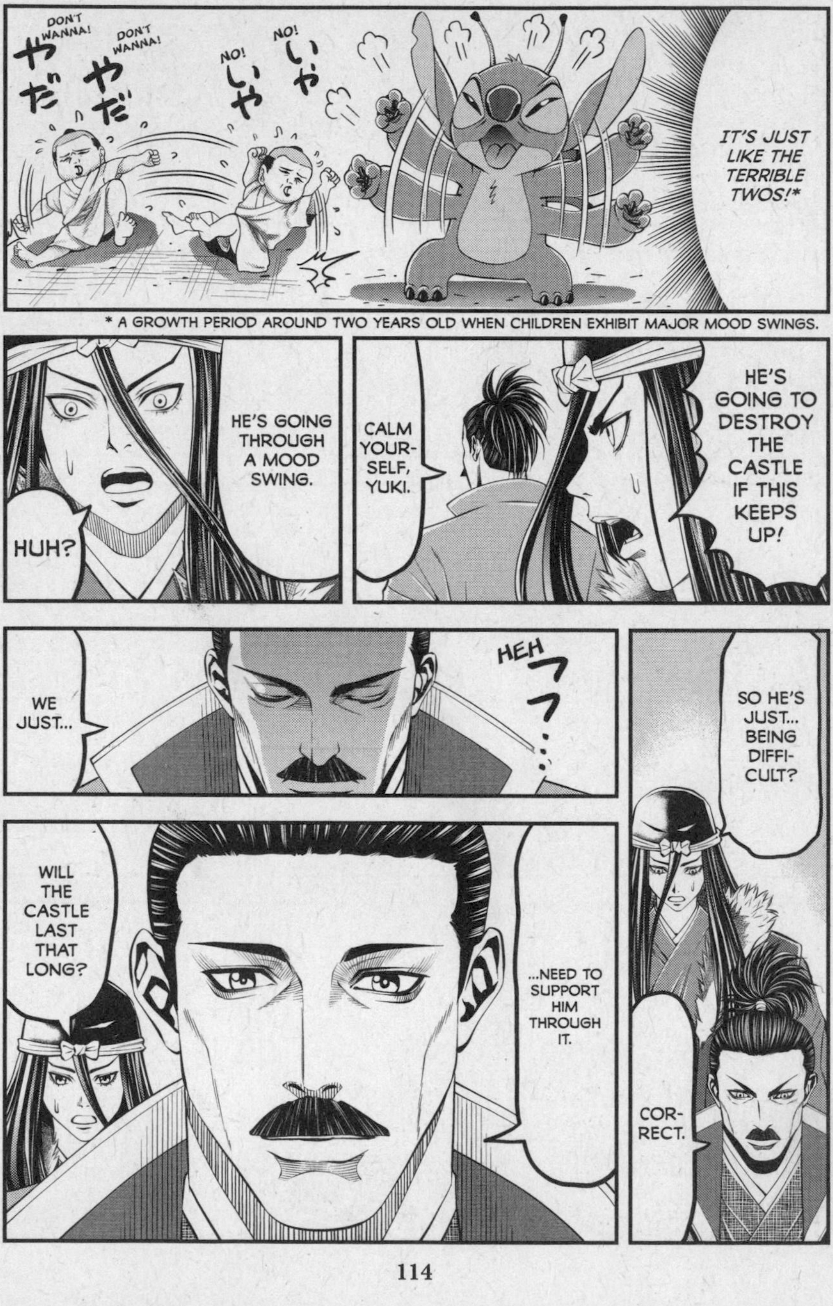
IT'S JUST LIKE THE TERRIBLE TWOS!*
いや NO!
いや NO!
やだ DON'T WANNA!
やだ DON'T WANNA!
HE'S GOING TO DESTROY THE CASTLE IF THIS KEEPS UP!
CALM YOURSELF, YUKI.
HE'S GOING THROUGH A MOOD SWING.
HUH?
SO HE'S JUST... BEING DIFFICULT?
CORRECT.
HEH フフ...
WE JUST...
...NEED TO SUPPORT HIM THROUGH IT.
WILL THE CASTLE LAST THAT LONG?

* A GROWTH PERIOD AROUND TWO YEARS OLD WHEN CHILDREN EXHIBIT MAJOR MOOD SWINGS.

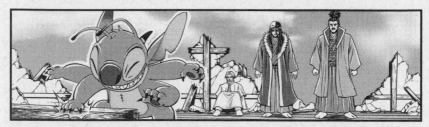

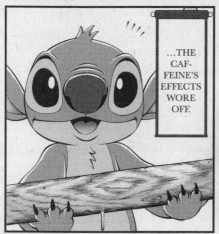

A SHORT TI ME LATER…
ガジ
CHEW
ガジ
CHEW
…THE CAFFEINE'S EFFECTS WORE OFF.
TCHK
トコ
TCHK
トコ
TCHK
トコ…
PLAY! ♪
HUH?!
HE'S ALREADY OVER IT??
CHAPTER 21: FIN

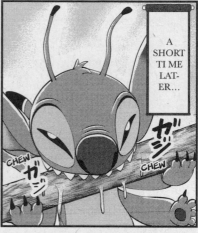

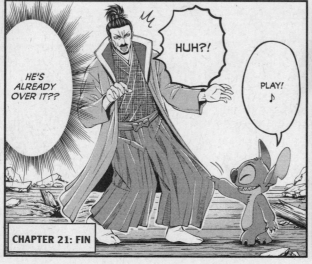

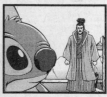

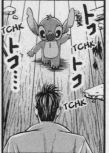

TERRIBLE TWOS

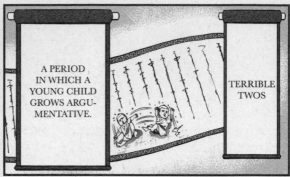

A PERIOD IN WHICH A YOUNG CHILD GROWS ARGU-MENTATIVE.

TERRIBLE TWOS

THIS WAS NOTHING LIKE WHAT STITCH WENT THROUGH.

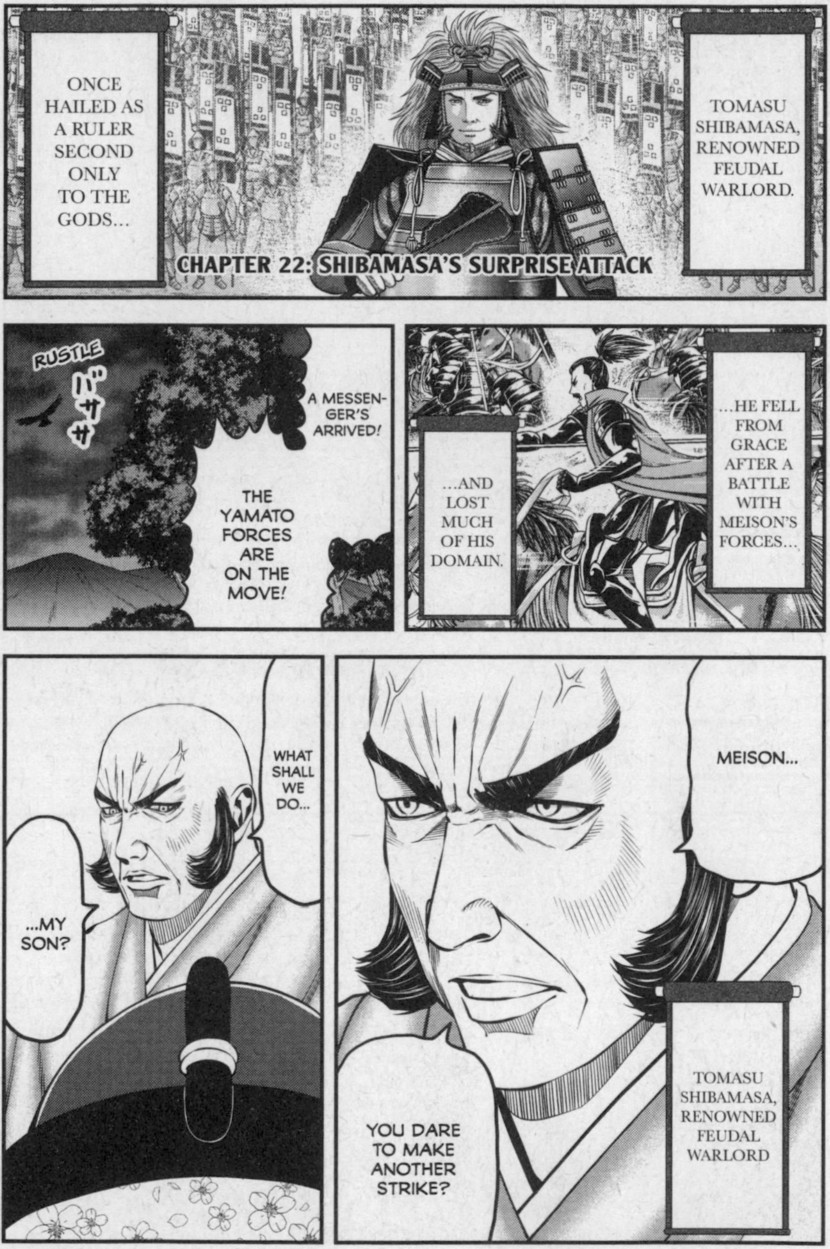
TOMASU SHIBAMASA, RENOWNED FEUDAL WARLORD.
ONCE HAILED AS A RULER SECOND ONLY TO THE GODS...
CHAPTER 22: SHIBAMASA'S SURPRISE ATTACK
...HE FELL FROM GRACE AFTER A BATTLE WITH MEISON'S FORCES...
...AND LOST MUCH OF HIS DOMAIN.
A MESSENGER'S ARRIVED!
THE YAMATO FORCES ARE ON THE MOVE!
RUSTLE
バササ
MEISON...
YOU DARE TO MAKE ANOTHER STRIKE?
TOMASU SHIBAMASA, RENOWNED FEUDAL WARLORD
WHAT SHALL WE DO...
...MY SON?

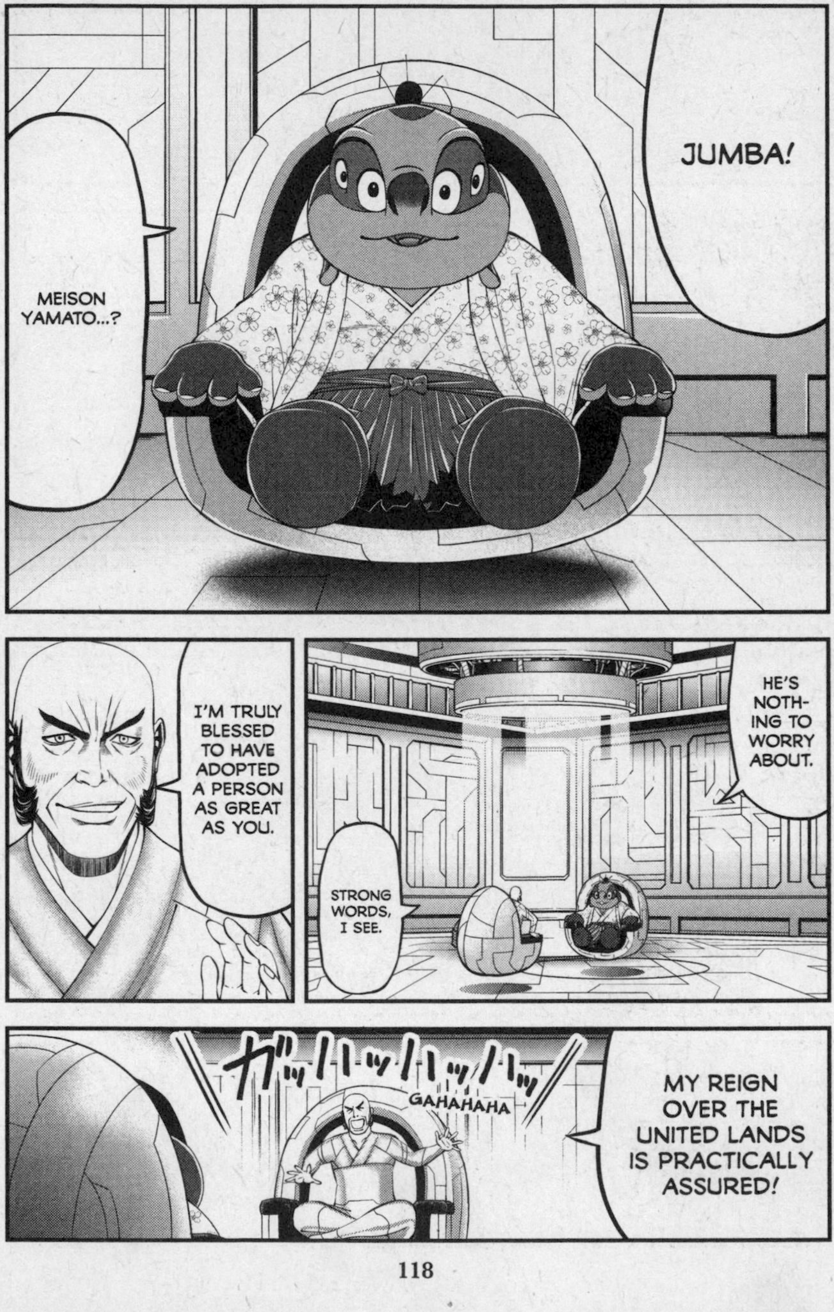
JUMBA!
MEISON YAMATO...?
HE'S NOTH-ING TO WORRY ABOUT.
STRONG WORDS, I SEE.
I'M TRULY BLESSED TO HAVE ADOPTED A PERSON AS GREAT AS YOU.
MY REIGN OVER THE UNITED LANDS IS PRACTICALLY ASSURED!
ガッハッハッハッ
GAHAHAHA

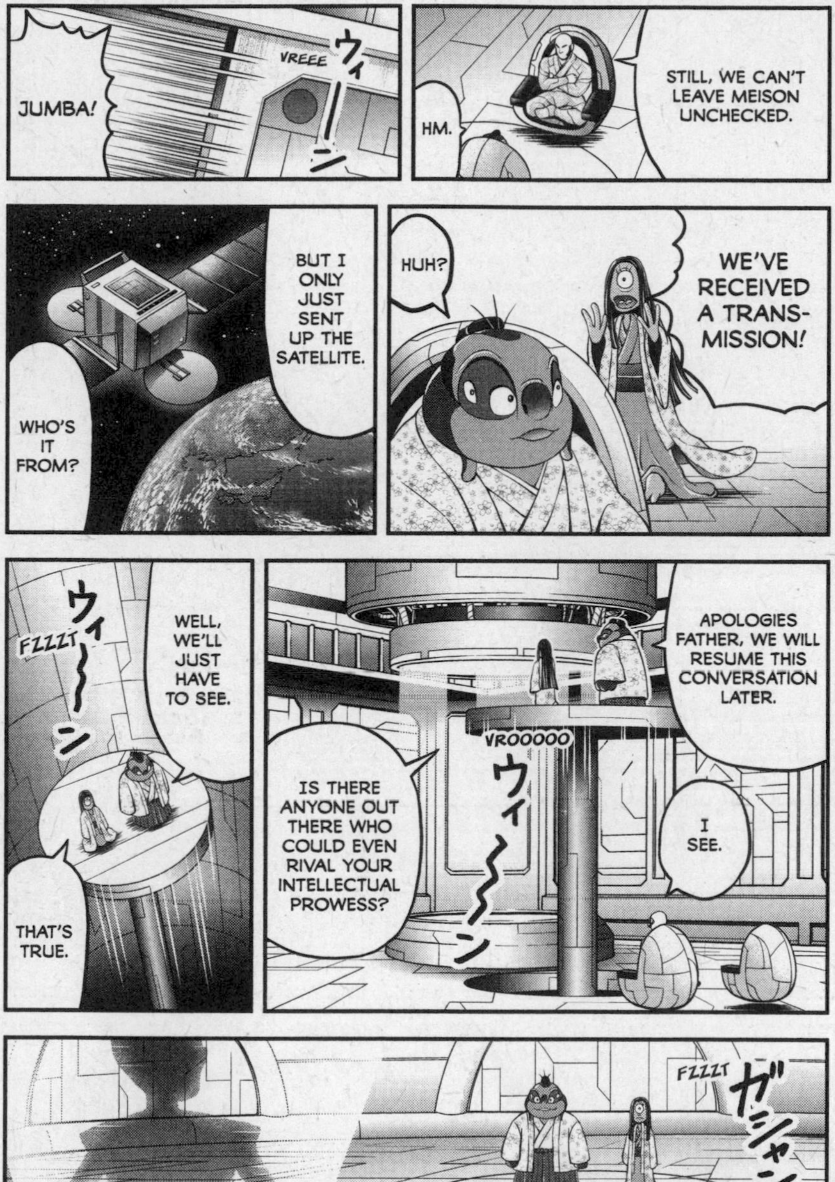
STILL, WE CAN'T LEAVE MEISON UNCHECKED.
HM.
VREEE
ウィーン
JUMBA!
WE'VE RECEIVED A TRANS-MISSION!
HUH?
BUT I ONLY JUST SENT UP THE SATELLITE.
WHO'S IT FROM?
APOLOGIES FATHER, WE WILL RESUME THIS CONVERSATION LATER.
VROOOOO
ウィ～～ン
I SEE.
IS THERE ANYONE OUT THERE WHO COULD EVEN RIVAL YOUR INTELLECTUAL PROWESS?
WELL, WE'LL JUST HAVE TO SEE.
ウィ～ン
FZZZT
THAT'S TRUE.
FZZZT
ガシャン

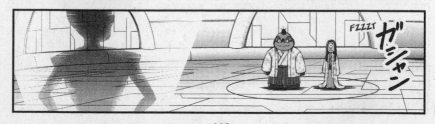

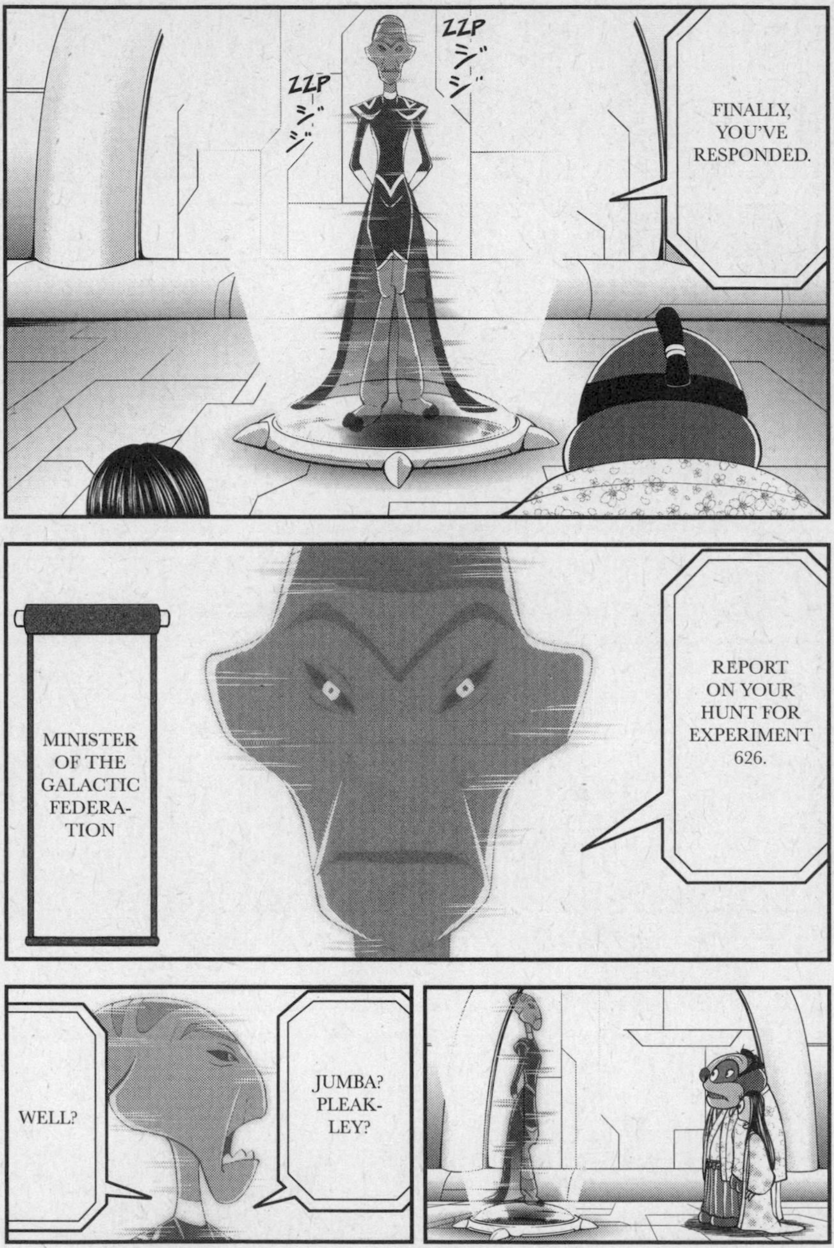
ZZP
ZZP
FINALLY, YOU'VE RESPONDED.
REPORT ON YOUR HUNT FOR EXPERIMENT 626.
MINISTER OF THE GALACTIC FEDERATION
JUMBA? PLEAKLEY?
WELL?

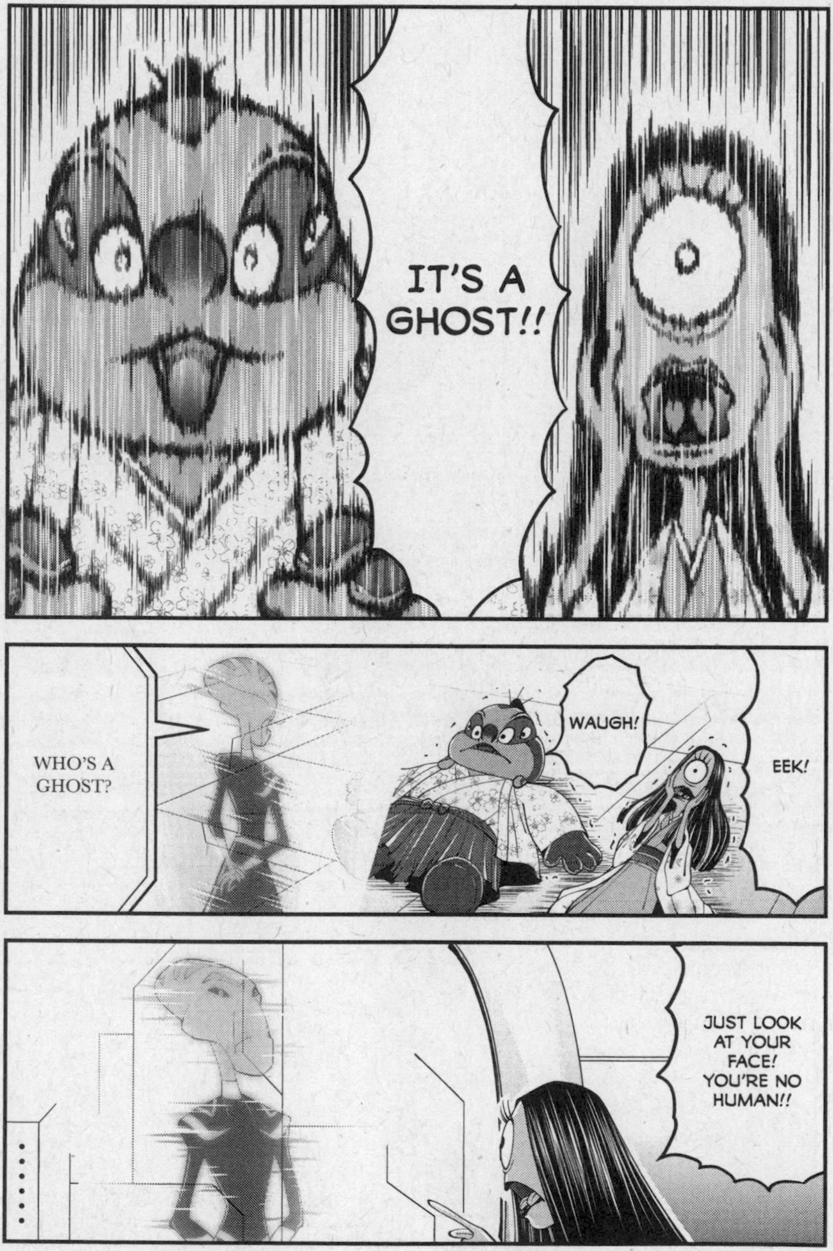
IT'S A GHOST!!
WAUGH!
EEK!
WHO'S A GHOST?
JUST LOOK AT YOUR FACE! YOU'RE NO HUMAN!!
......

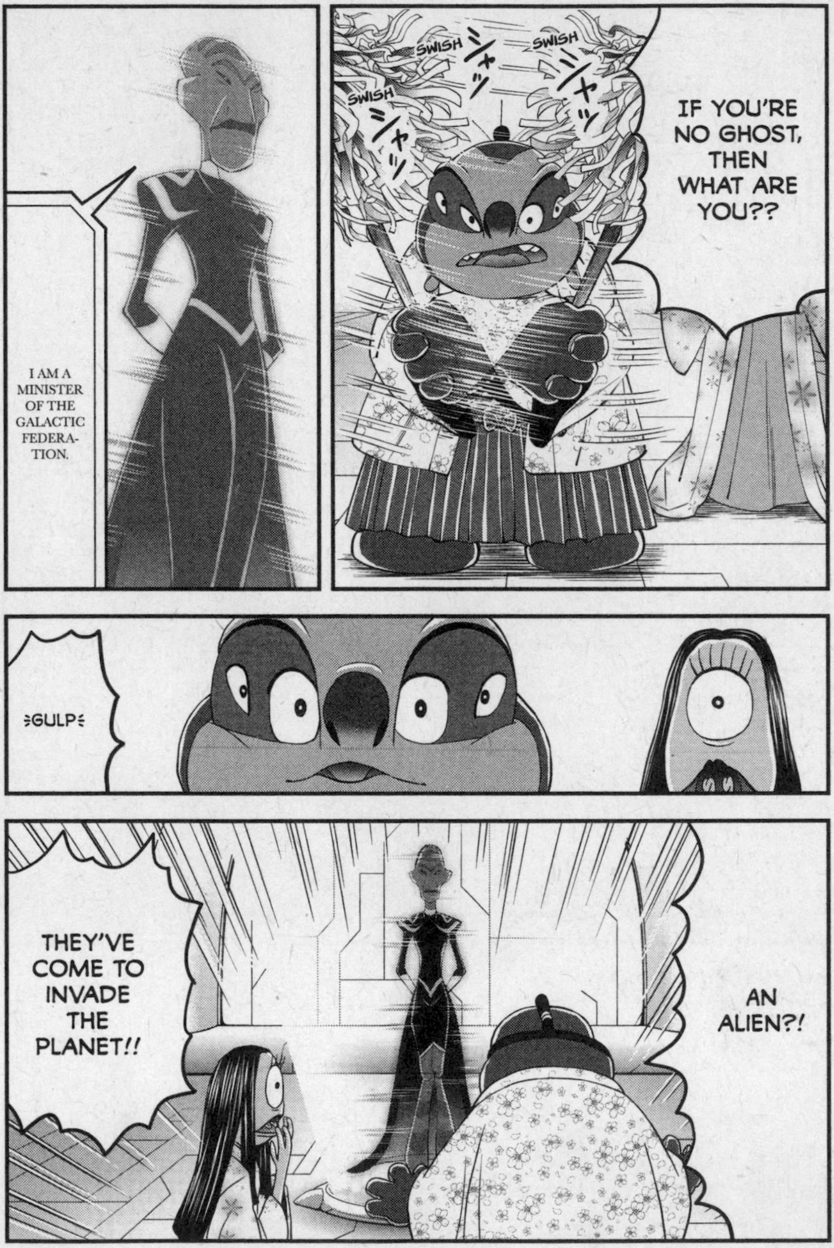
SWISH シャッ
SWISH シャッ
SWISH シャッ
IF YOU'RE NO GHOST, THEN WHAT ARE YOU??
I AM A MINISTER OF THE GALACTIC FEDERATION.
GULP
AN ALIEN?!
THEY'VE COME TO INVADE THE PLANET!!

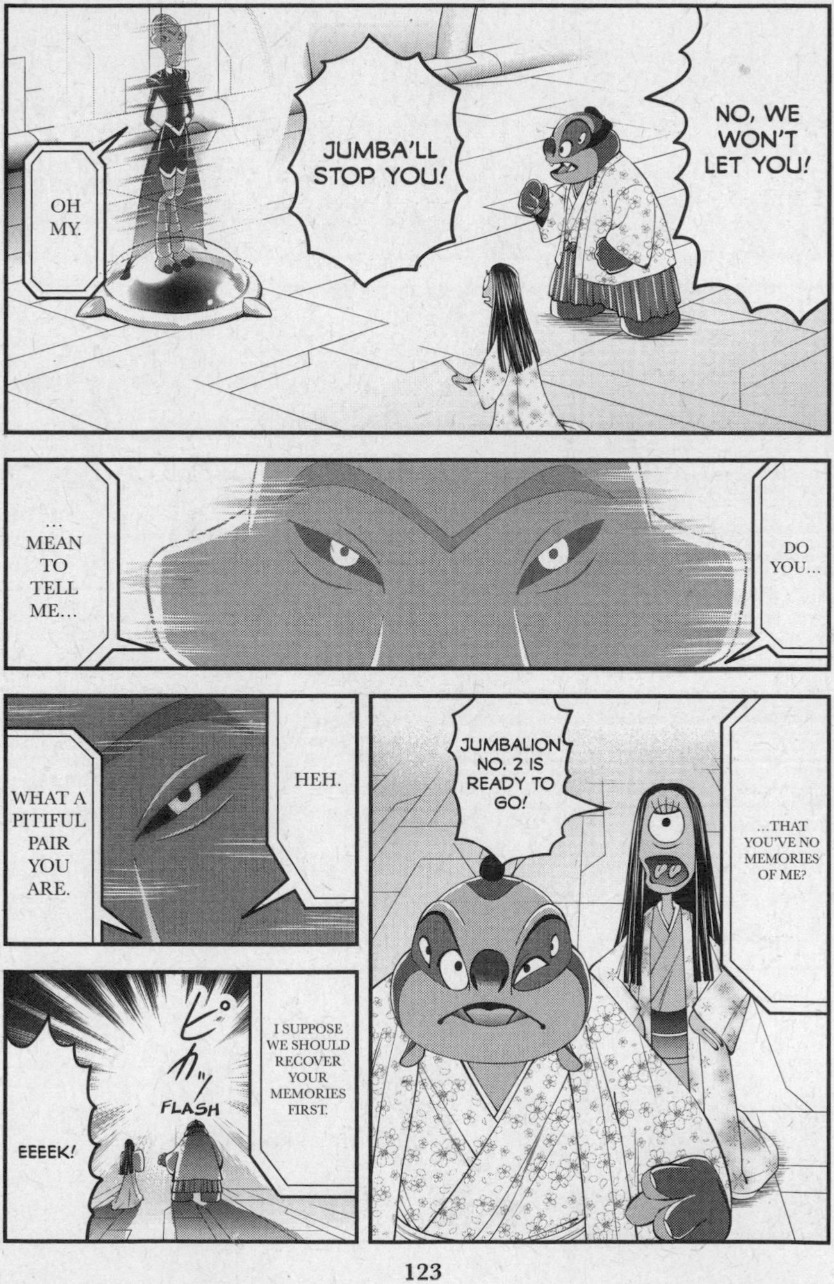
NO, WE WON'T LET YOU!
JUMBA'LL STOP YOU!
OH MY.
DO YOU...
...MEAN TO TELL ME...
...THAT YOU'VE NO MEMORIES OF ME?
JUMBALION NO. 2 IS READY TO GO!
HEH.
WHAT A PITIFUL PAIR YOU ARE.
I SUPPOSE WE SHOULD RECOVER YOUR MEMORIES FIRST.
ピカッ
FLASH
EEEEK!

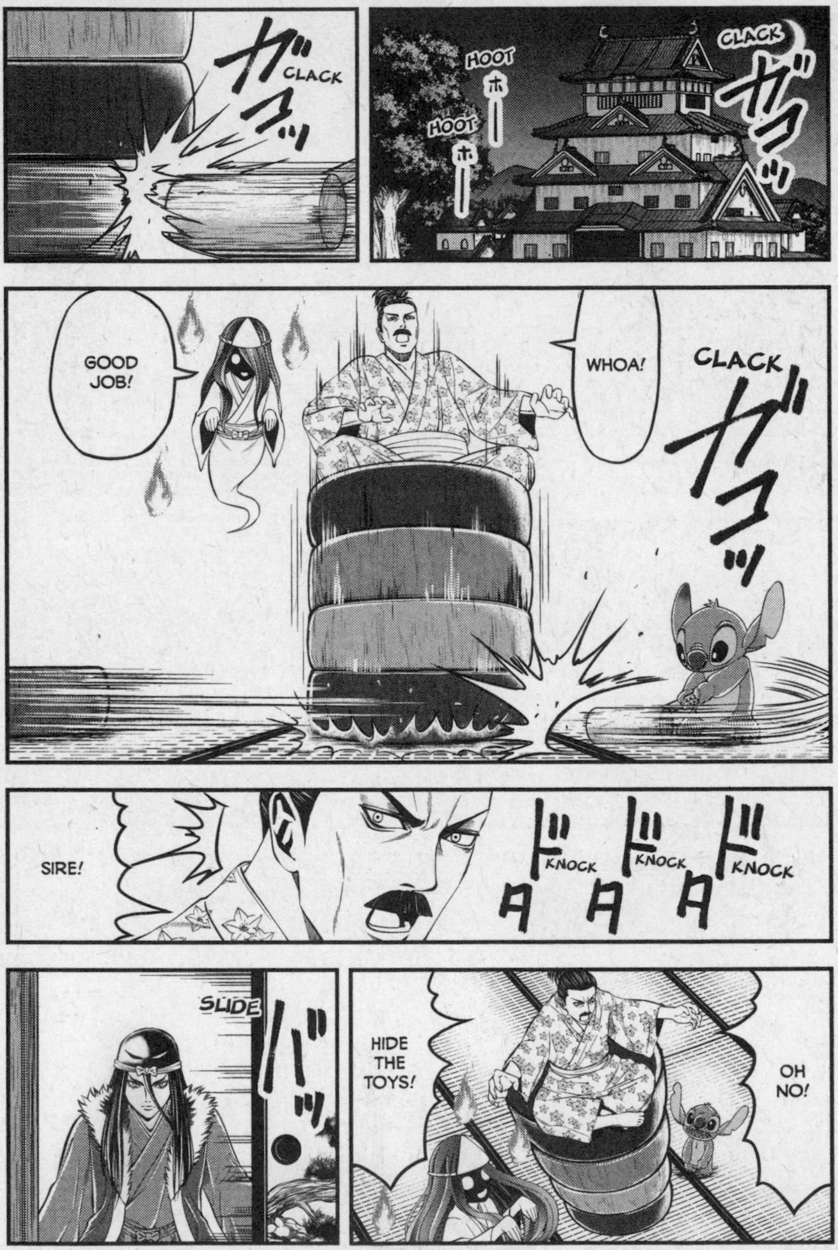
HOOT
ホー
HOOT
ホー
CLACK
ガコッ
CLACK
ガコッ
CLACK
ガコッ
WHOA!
GOOD JOB!
KNOCK
KNOCK
KNOCK
SIRE!
OH NO!
HIDE THE TOYS!
SLIDE
バッ

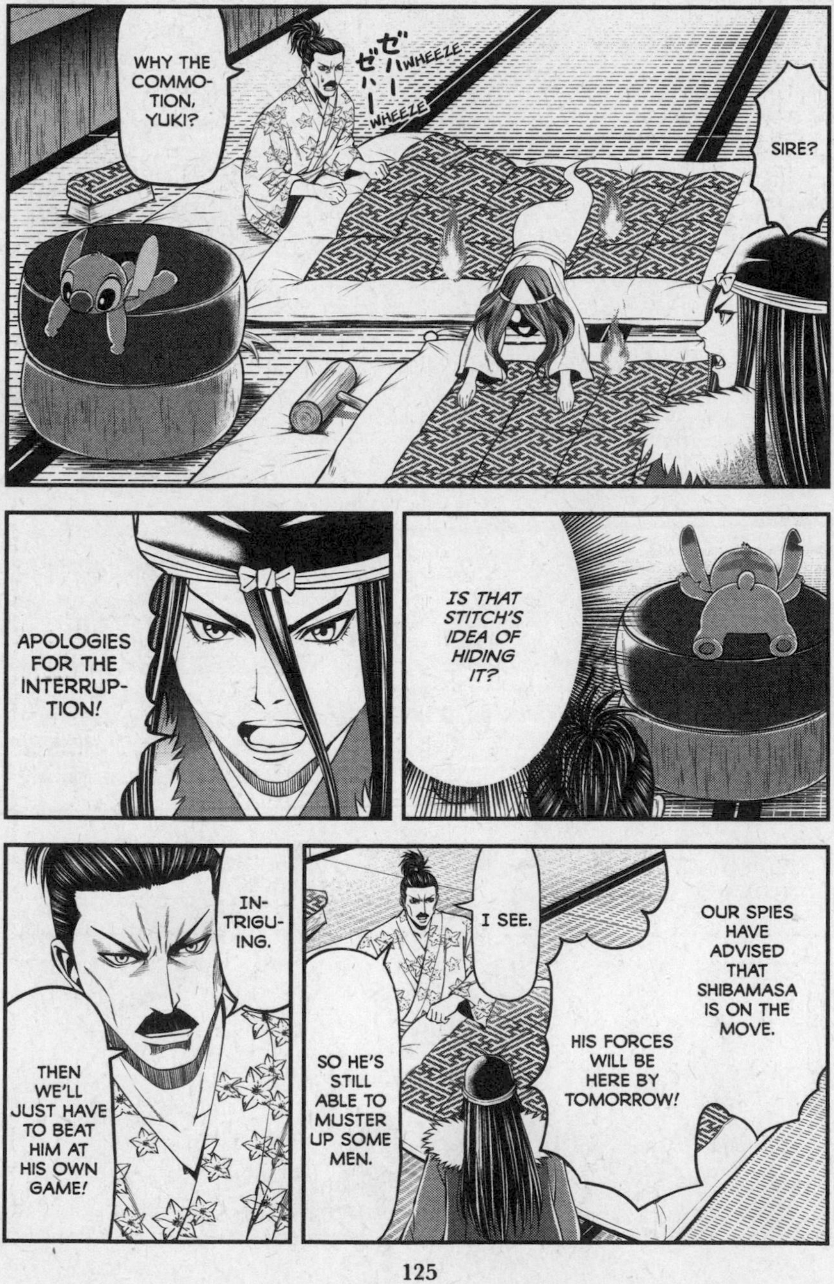
SIRE?
ゼーハー WHEEZE
ゼーハー WHEEZE
WHY THE COMMOTION, YUKI?
IS THAT STITCH'S IDEA OF HIDING IT?
APOLOGIES FOR THE INTERRUPTION!
OUR SPIES HAVE ADVISED THAT SHIBAMASA IS ON THE MOVE.
I SEE.
HIS FORCES WILL BE HERE BY TOMORROW!
SO HE'S STILL ABLE TO MUSTER UP SOME MEN.
INTRIGUING.
THEN WE'LL JUST HAVE TO BEAT HIM AT HIS OWN GAME!

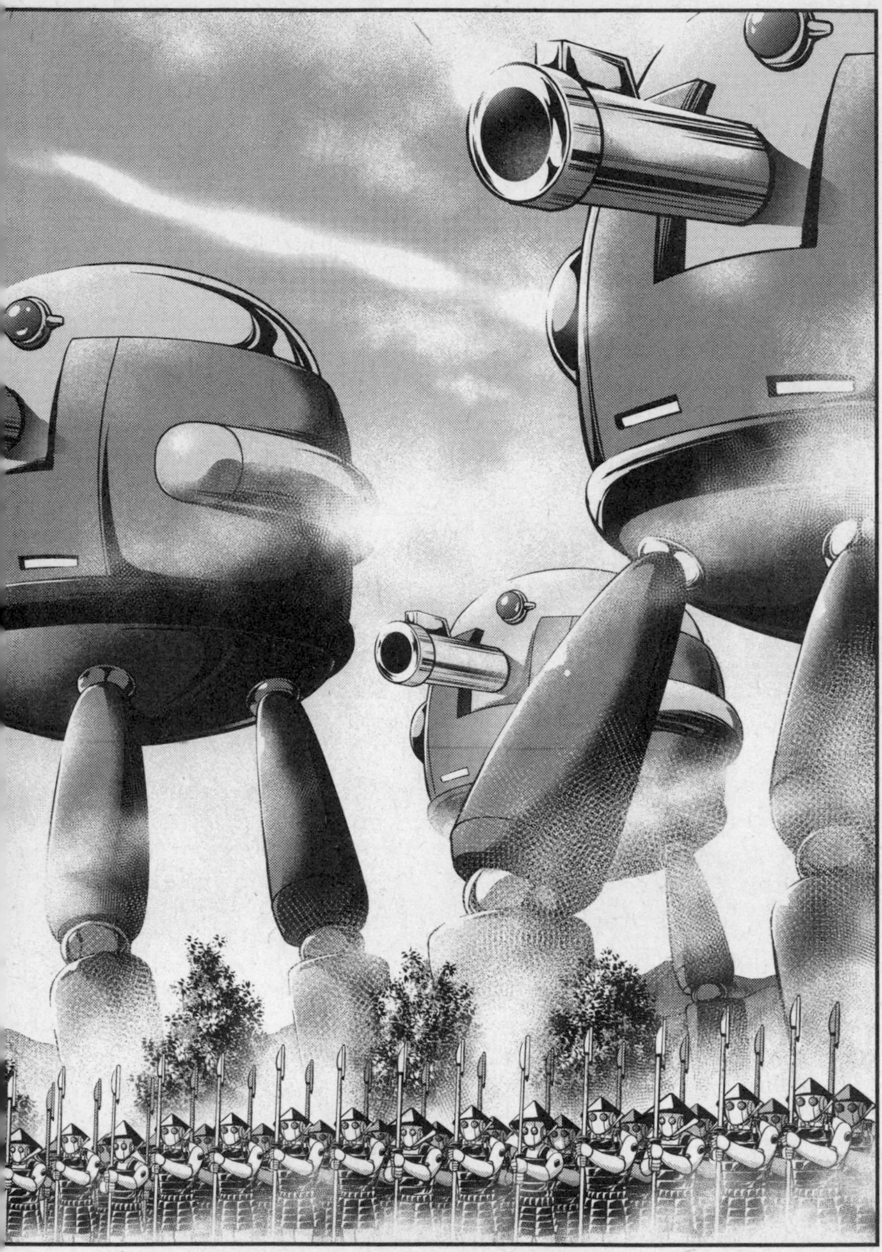

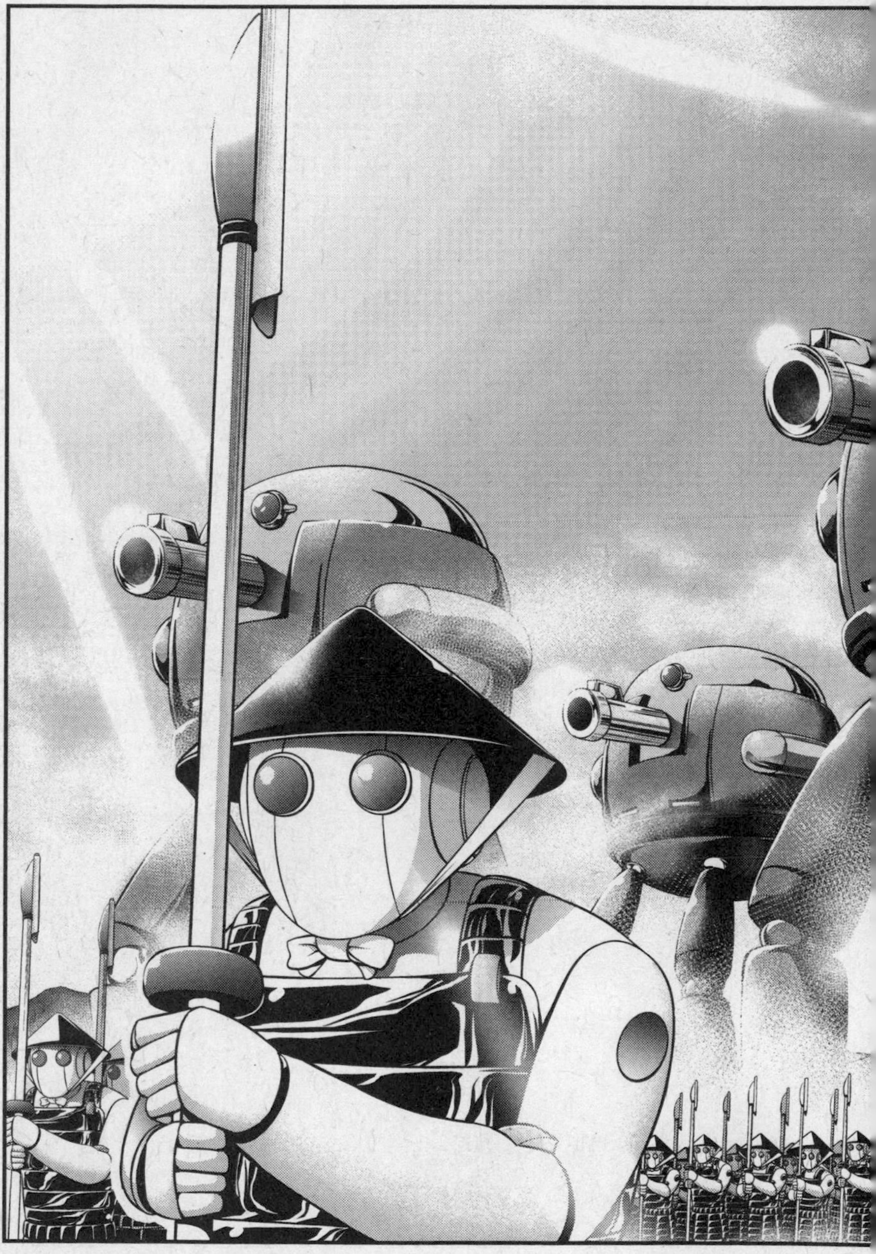

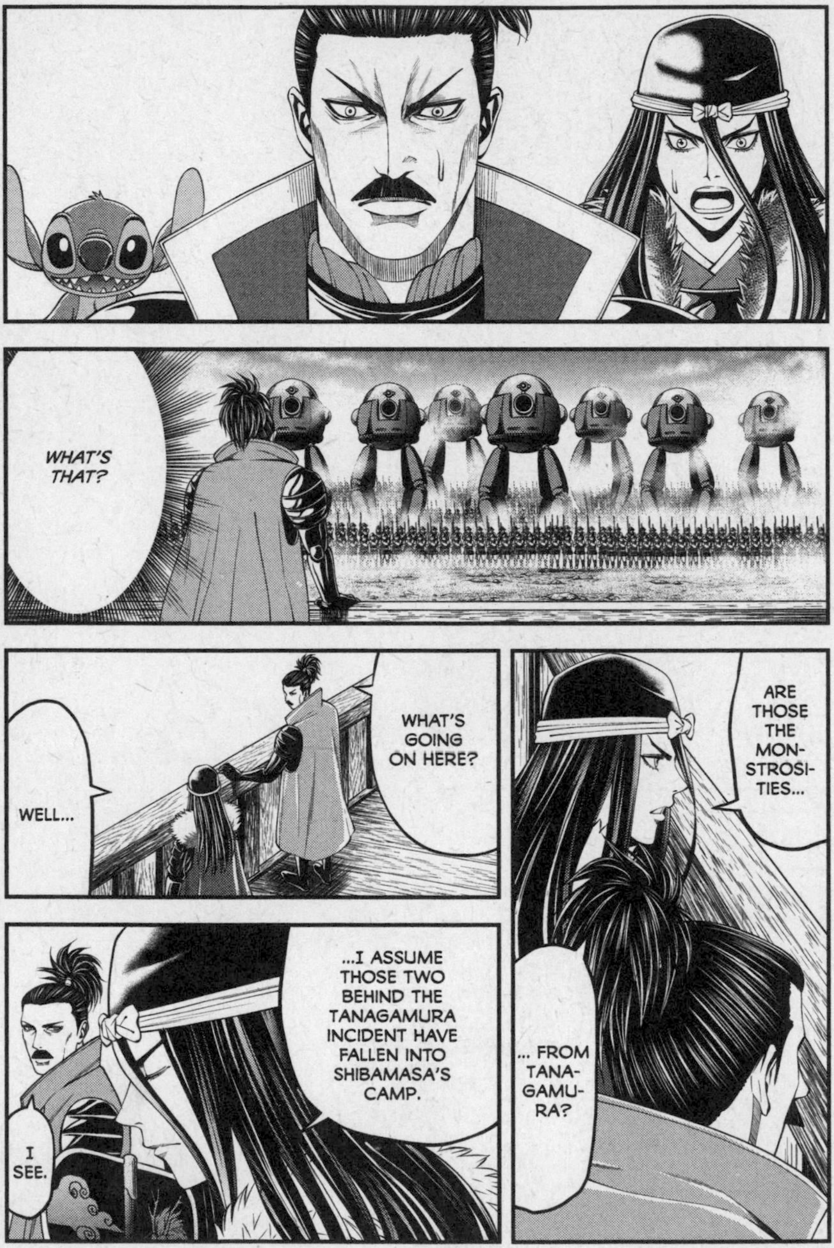
WHAT'S THAT?
ARE THOSE THE MONSTROSITIES...
... FROM TANAGAMURA?
WHAT'S GOING ON HERE?
WELL...
...I ASSUME THOSE TWO BEHIND THE TANAGAMURA INCIDENT HAVE FALLEN INTO SHIBAMASA'S CAMP.
I SEE.

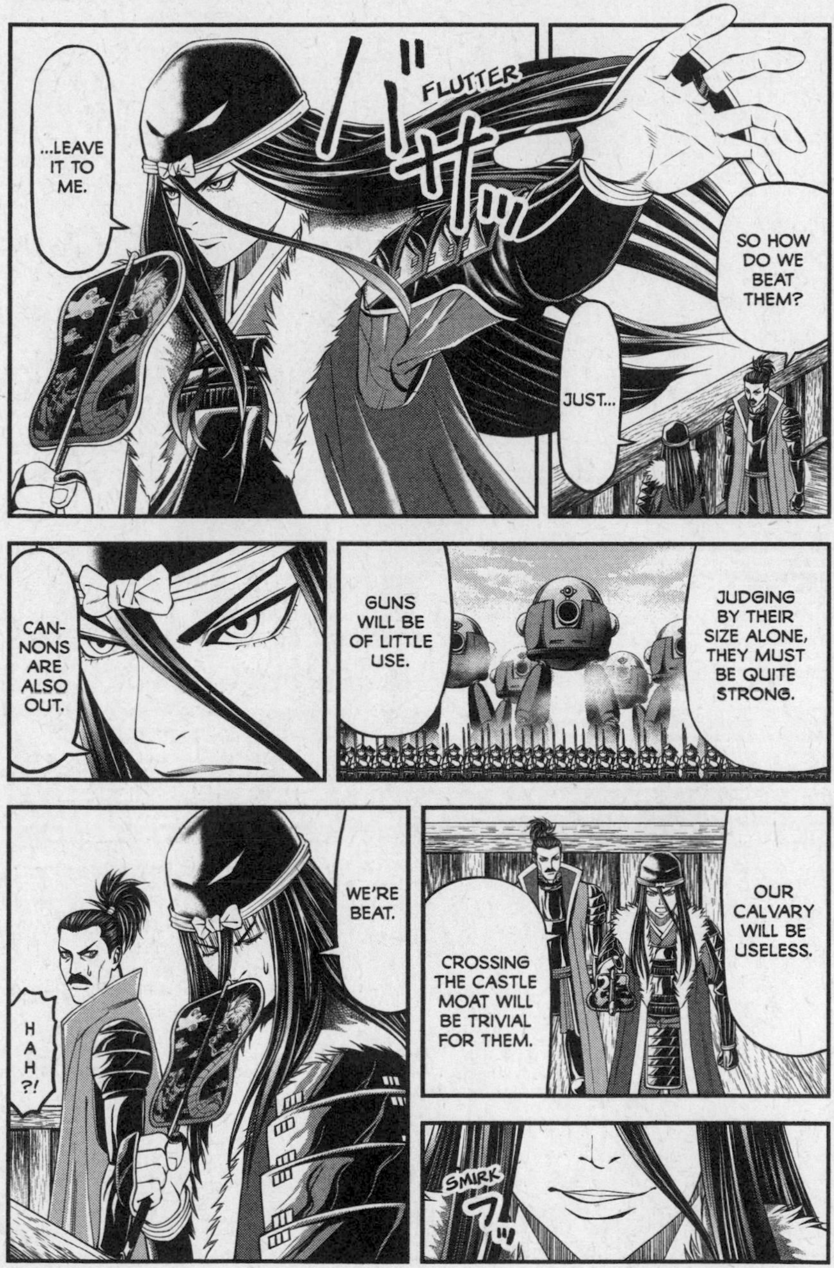
SO HOW DO WE BEAT THEM?
JUST...
FLUTTER
...LEAVE IT TO ME.
JUDGING BY THEIR SIZE ALONE, THEY MUST BE QUITE STRONG.
GUNS WILL BE OF LITTLE USE.
CANNONS ARE ALSO OUT.
OUR CALVARY WILL BE USELESS.
CROSSING THE CASTLE MOAT WILL BE TRIVIAL FOR THEM.
SMIRK
WE'RE BEAT.
HAH?!

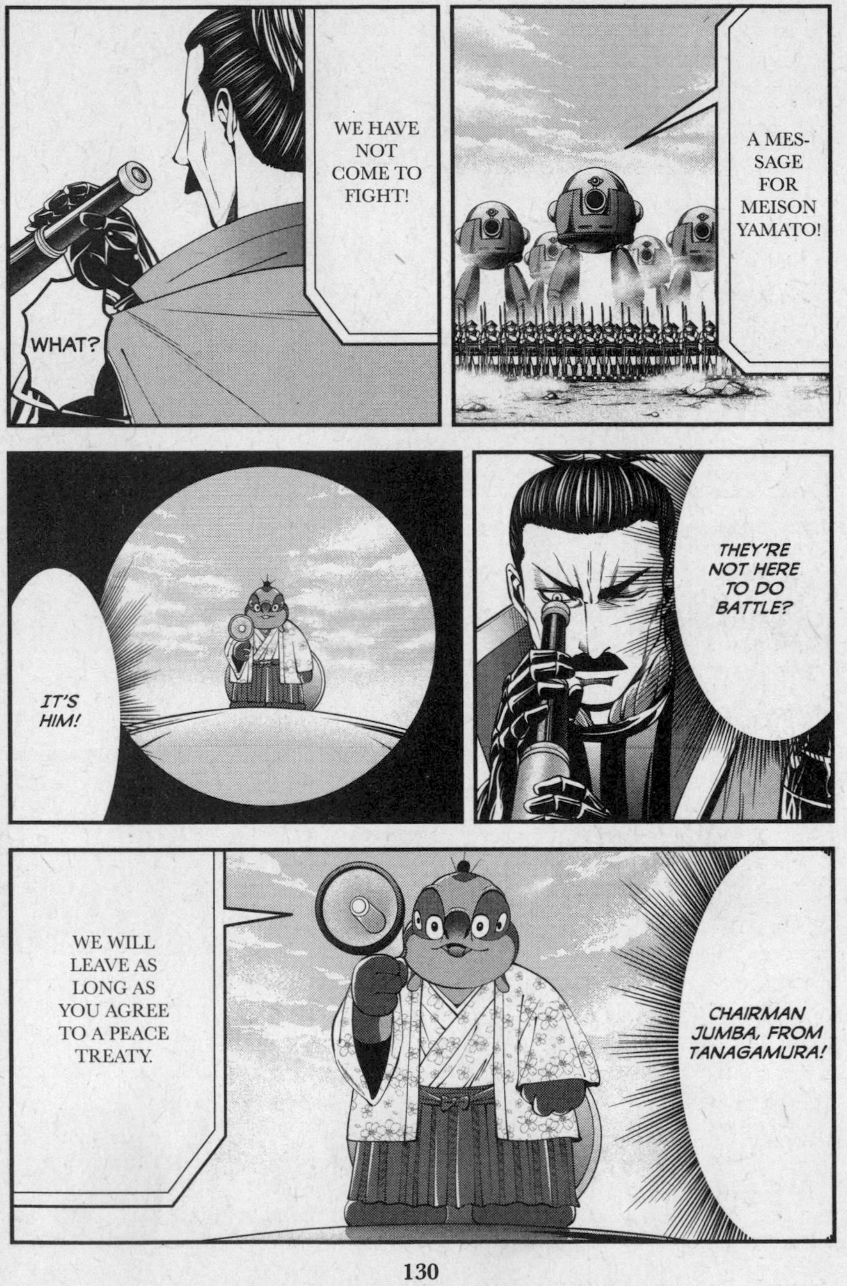
A MESSAGE FOR MEISON YAMATO!
WE HAVE NOT COME TO FIGHT!
WHAT?
THEY'RE NOT HERE TO DO BATTLE?
IT'S HIM!
CHAIRMAN JUMBA, FROM TANAGAMURA!
WE WILL LEAVE AS LONG AS YOU AGREE TO A PEACE TREATY.

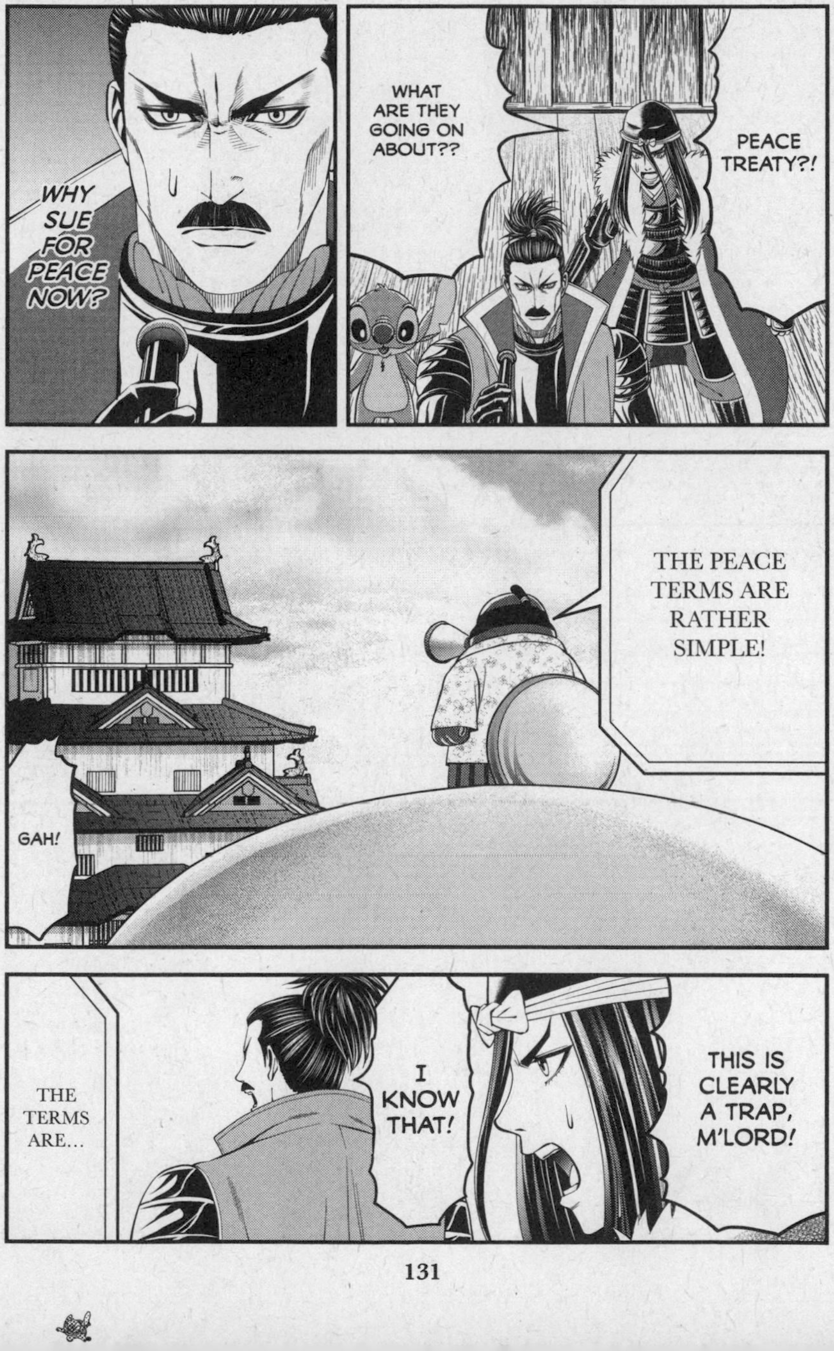
PEACE TREATY?!
WHAT ARE THEY GOING ON ABOUT??
WHY SUE FOR PEACE NOW?
THE PEACE TERMS ARE RATHER SIMPLE!
GAH!
THIS IS CLEARLY A TRAP, M'LORD!
I KNOW THAT!
THE TERMS ARE...

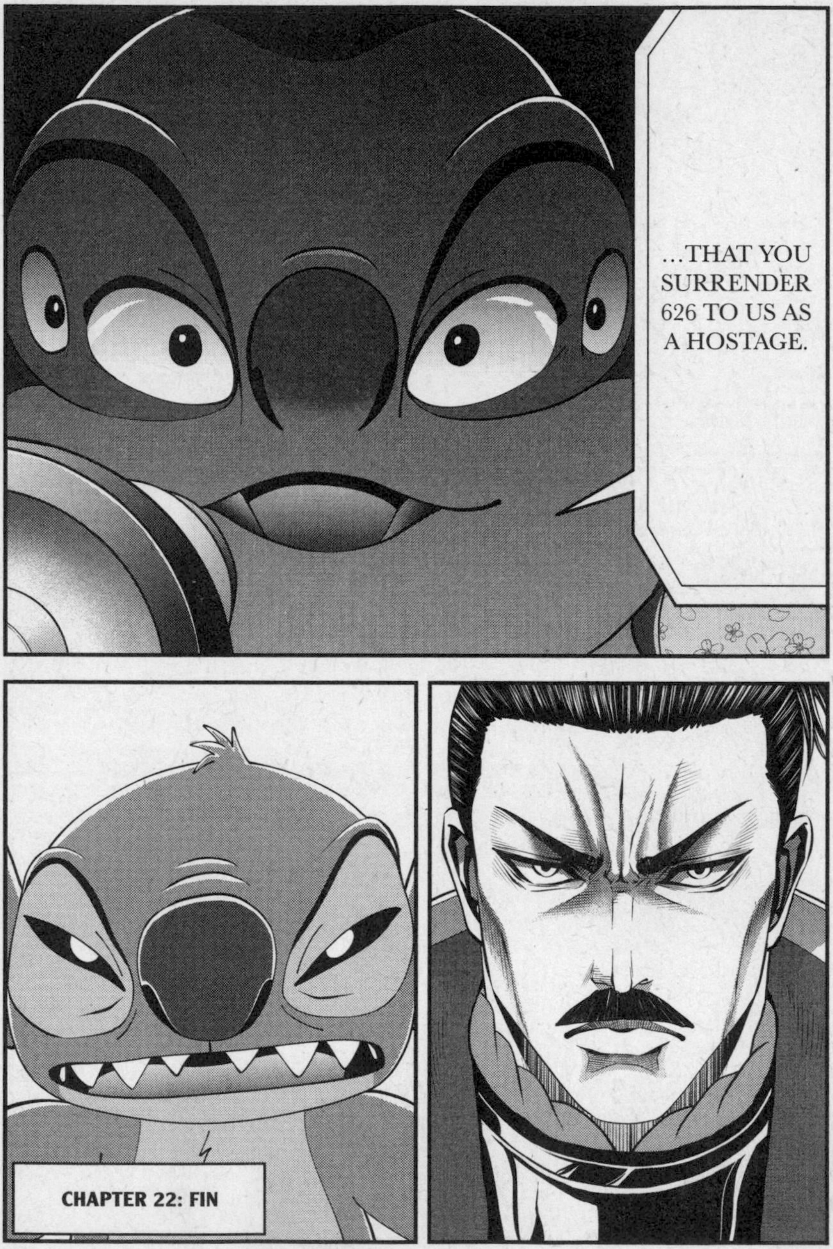
...THAT YOU SURRENDER 626 TO US AS A HOSTAGE.
CHAPTER 22: FIN

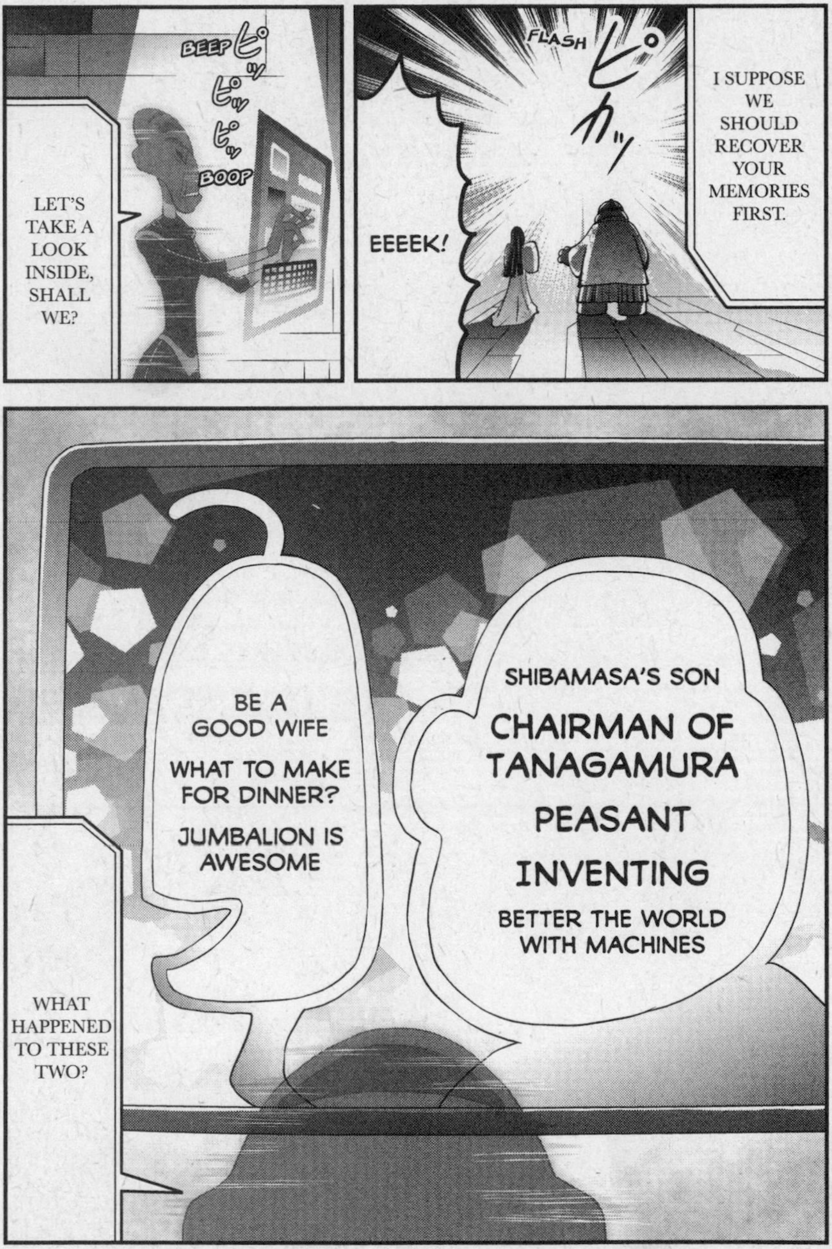
I SUPPOSE WE SHOULD RECOVER YOUR MEMORIES FIRST.
FLASH
EEEEK!
BEEP
BOOP
LET'S TAKE A LOOK INSIDE, SHALL WE?
SHIBAMASA'S SON
CHAIRMAN OF TANAGAMURA
PEASANT
INVENTING
BETTER THE WORLD WITH MACHINES
BE A GOOD WIFE
WHAT TO MAKE FOR DINNER?
JUMBALION IS AWESOME
WHAT HAPPENED TO THESE TWO?

Disney

STiTcH

STITCH & THE SAMURAI

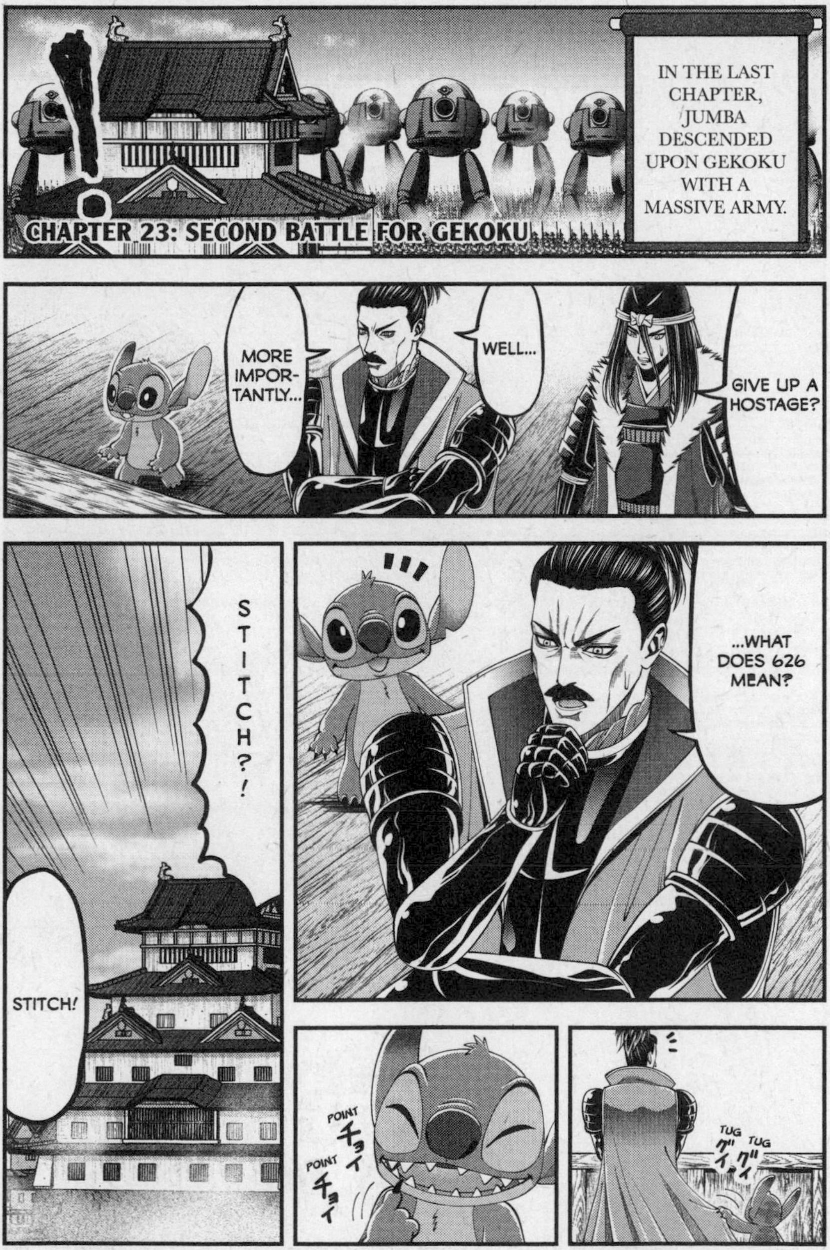
IN THE LAST CHAPTER, JUMBA DESCENDED UPON GEKOKU WITH A MASSIVE ARMY.
CHAPTER 23: SECOND BATTLE FOR GEKOKU
GIVE UP A HOSTAGE?
WELL...
MORE IMPORTANTLY...
...WHAT DOES 626 MEAN?
TUG グイ
TUG グイ
POINT チョイ
POINT チョイ
STITCH?!
STITCH!

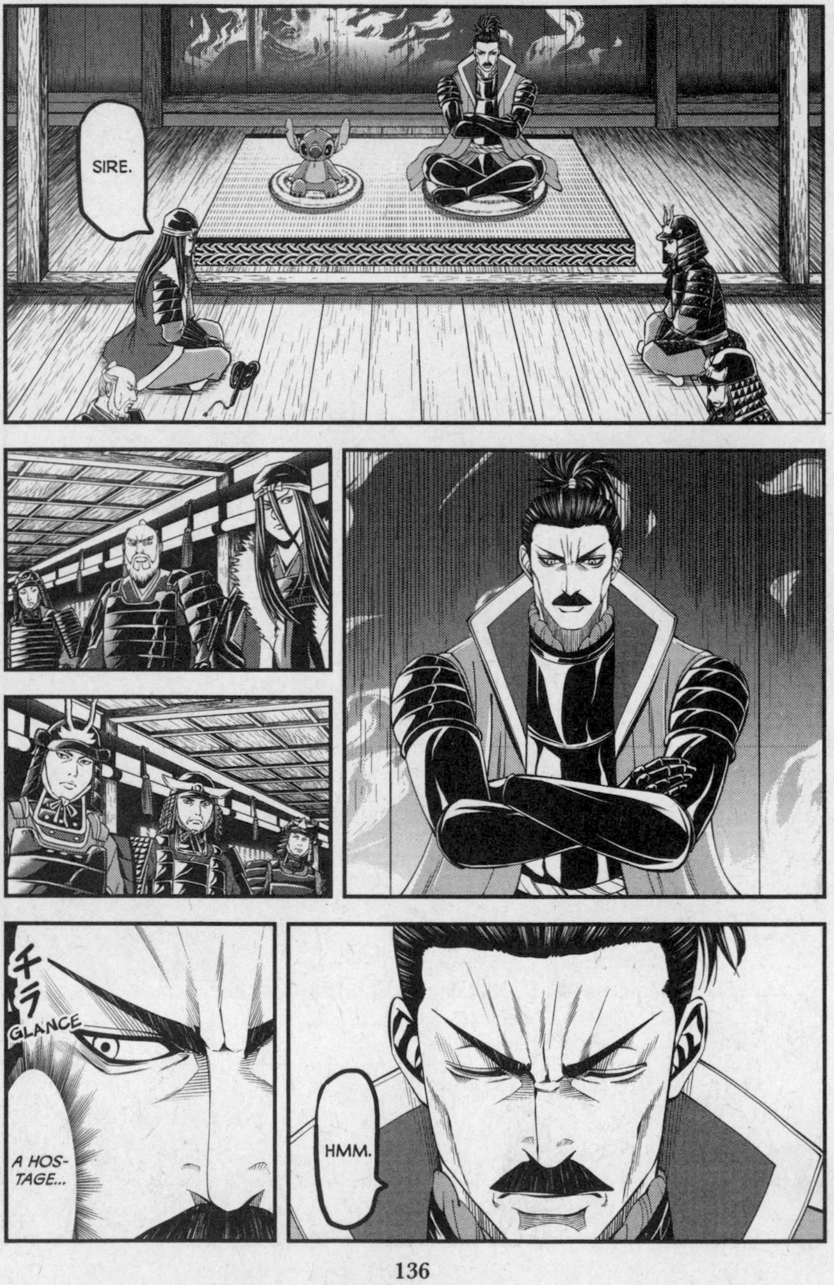
SIRE.
HMM.
チラ
GLANCE
A HOS-
TAGE...

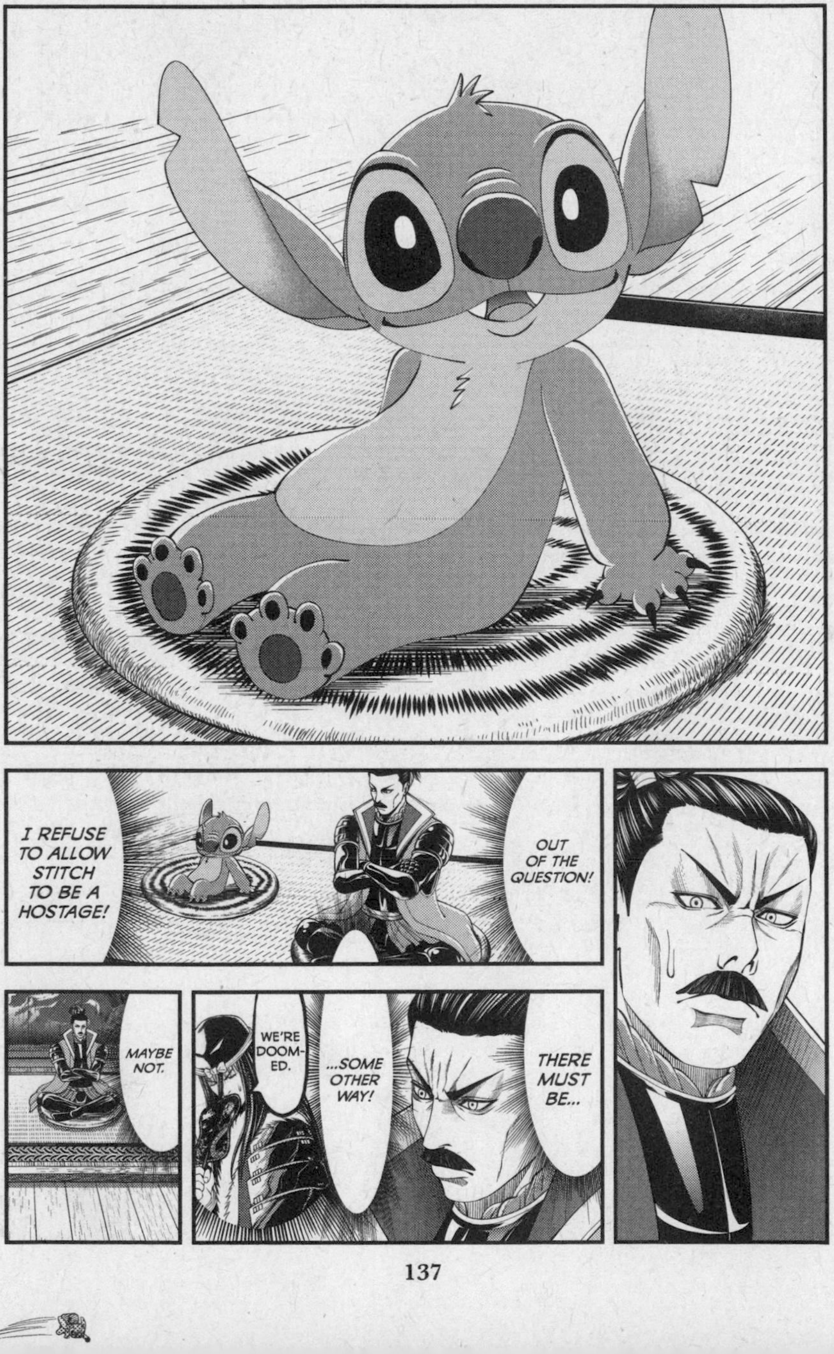
OUT OF THE QUESTION!
I REFUSE TO ALLOW STITCH TO BE A HOSTAGE!
THERE MUST BE...
...SOME OTHER WAY!
WE'RE DOOM-ED.
MAYBE NOT.

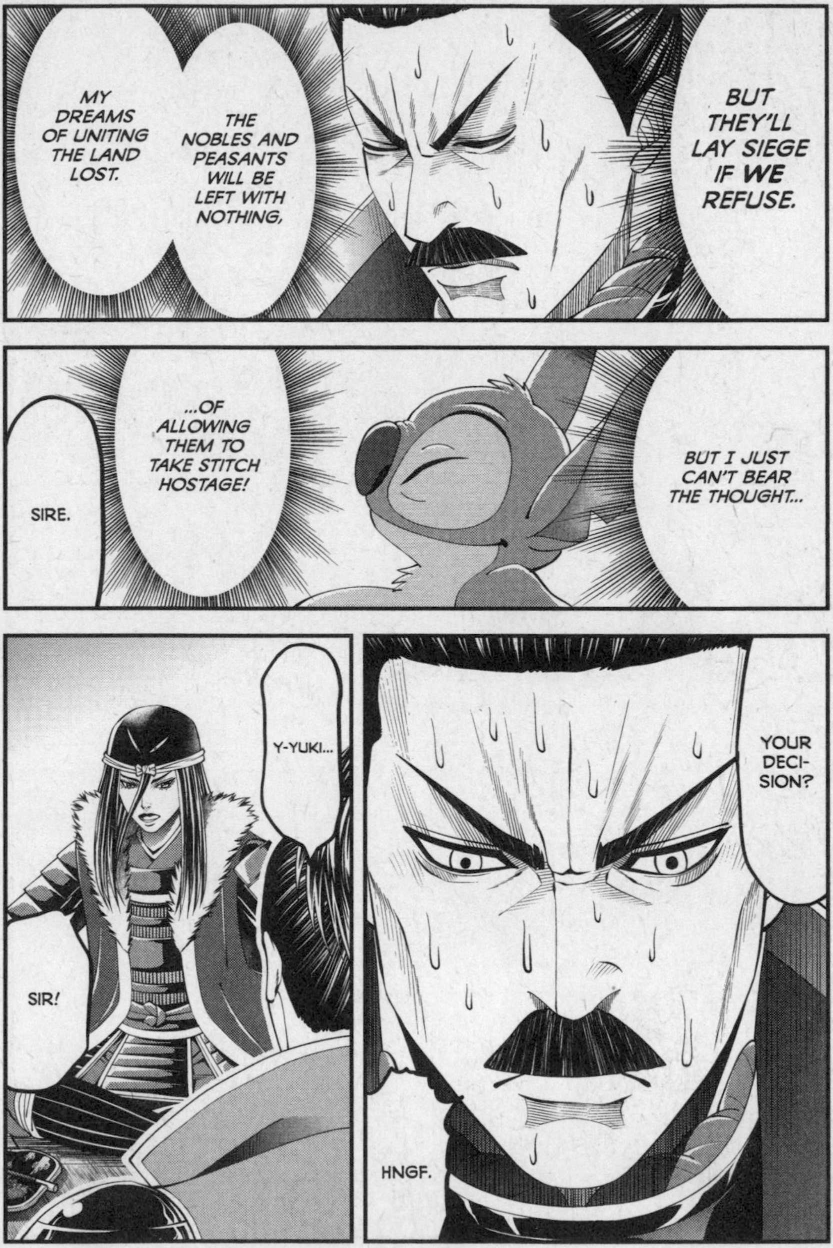
BUT THEY'LL LAY SIEGE IF **WE** REFUSE.
THE NOBLES AND PEASANTS WILL BE LEFT WITH NOTHING,
MY DREAMS OF UNITING THE LAND LOST.
BUT I JUST CAN'T BEAR THE THOUGHT...
...OF ALLOWING THEM TO TAKE STITCH HOSTAGE!
SIRE.
YOUR DECI-SION?
HNGF.
Y-YUKI...
SIR!

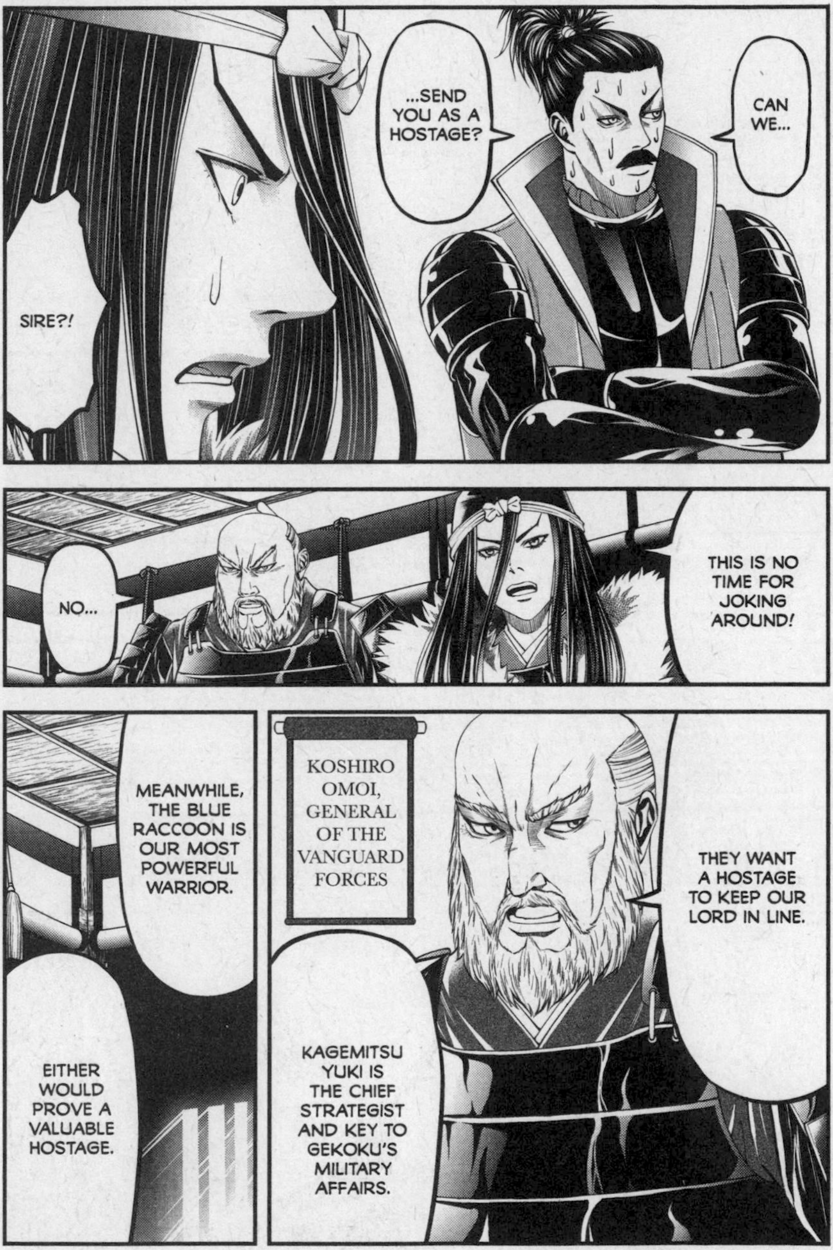
CAN WE...
...SEND YOU AS A HOSTAGE?
SIRE?!
THIS IS NO TIME FOR JOKING AROUND!
NO...
THEY WANT A HOSTAGE TO KEEP OUR LORD IN LINE.
KOSHIRO OMOI, GENERAL OF THE VANGUARD FORCES
KAGEMITSU YUKI IS THE CHIEF STRATEGIST AND KEY TO GEKOKU'S MILITARY AFFAIRS.
MEANWHILE, THE BLUE RACCOON IS OUR MOST POWERFUL WARRIOR.
EITHER WOULD PROVE A VALUABLE HOSTAGE.

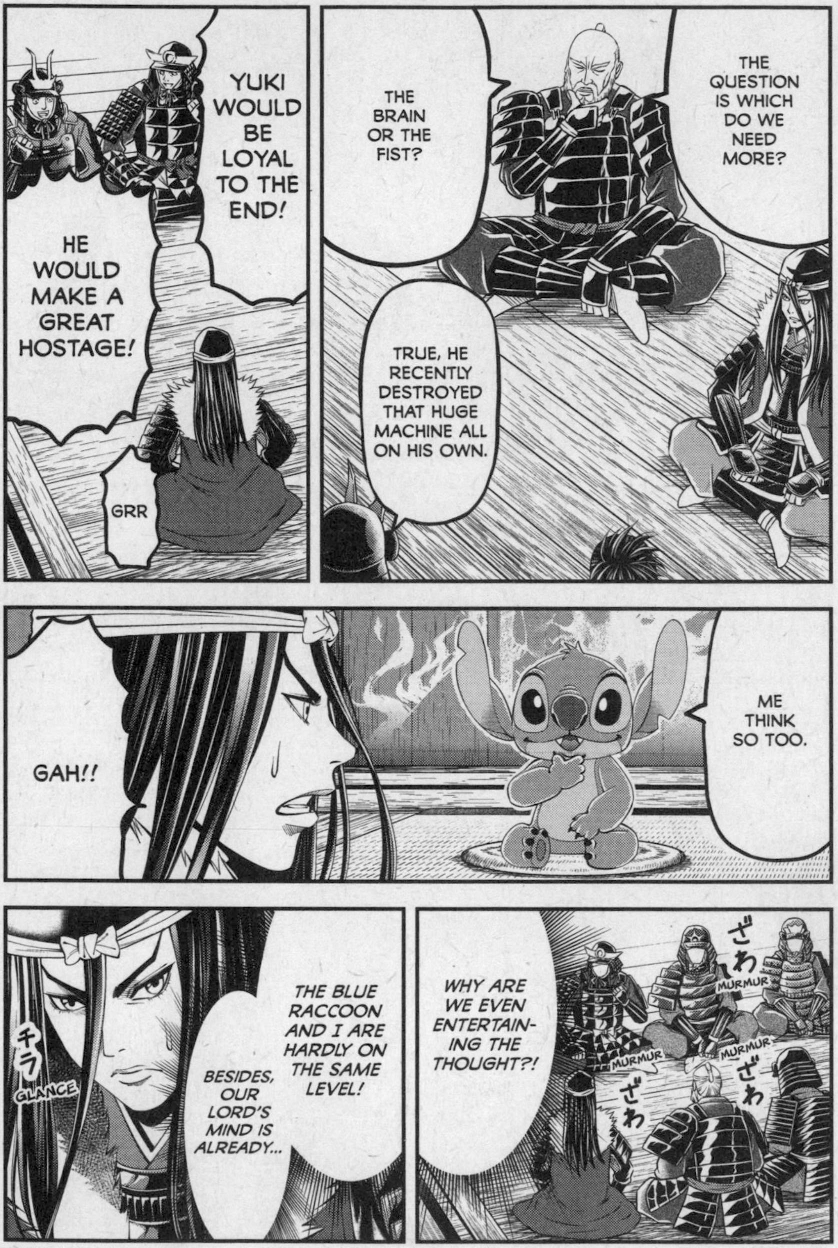
THE QUESTION IS WHICH DO WE NEED MORE?
THE BRAIN OR THE FIST?
TRUE, HE RECENTLY DESTROYED THAT HUGE MACHINE ALL ON HIS OWN.
YUKI WOULD BE LOYAL TO THE END!
HE WOULD MAKE A GREAT HOSTAGE!
GRR
ME THINK SO TOO.
GAH!!
WHY ARE WE EVEN ENTERTAINING THE THOUGHT?!
ざわ
MURMUR
ざわ
MURMUR
ざわ
MURMUR
THE BLUE RACCOON AND I ARE HARDLY ON THE SAME LEVEL!
BESIDES, OUR LORD'S MIND IS ALREADY...
チラ
GLANCE

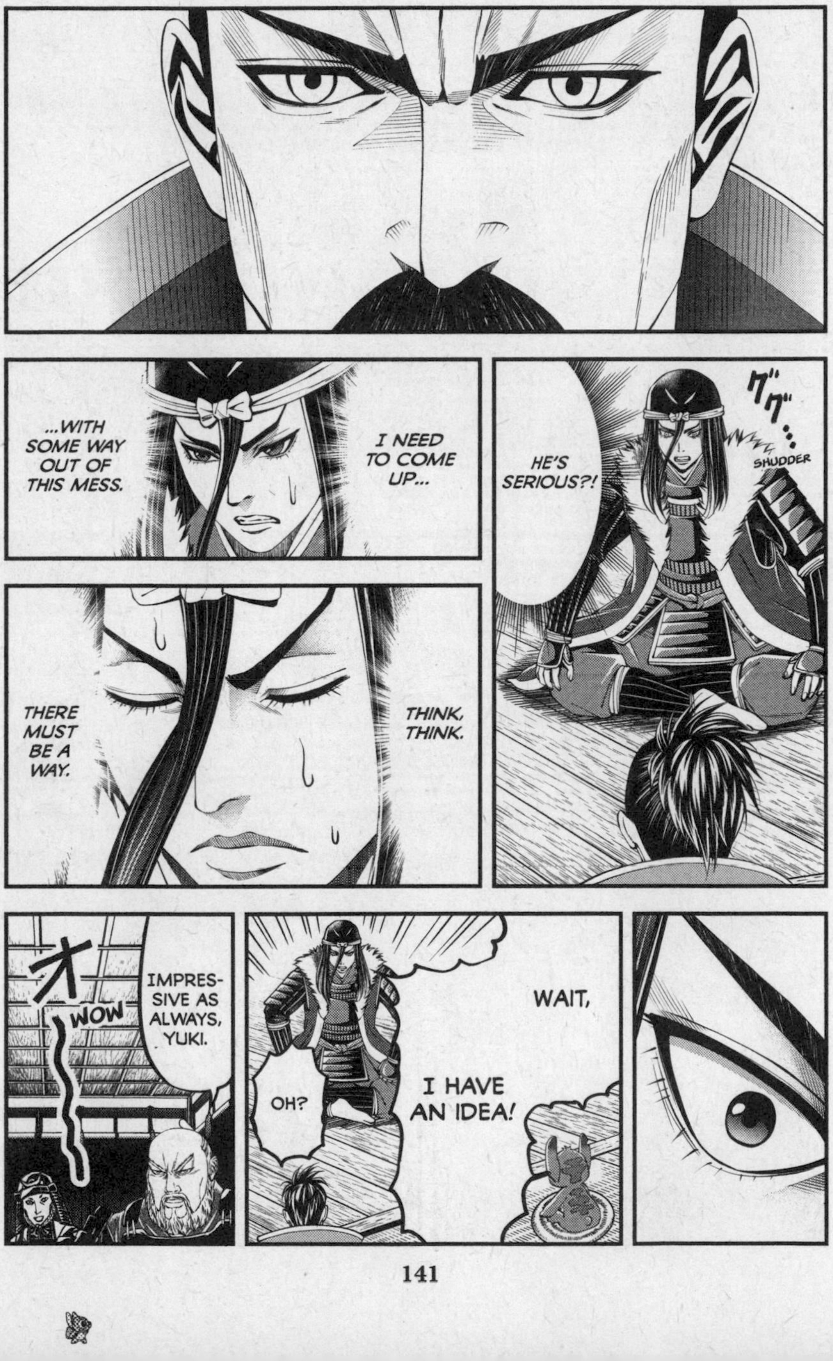
HE'S SERIOUS?!
ググ... SHUDDER
I NEED TO COME UP...
...WITH SOME WAY OUT OF THIS MESS.
THINK, THINK.
THERE MUST BE A WAY.
WAIT,
I HAVE AN IDEA!
OH?
IMPRES-SIVE AS ALWAYS, YUKI.
オ WOW

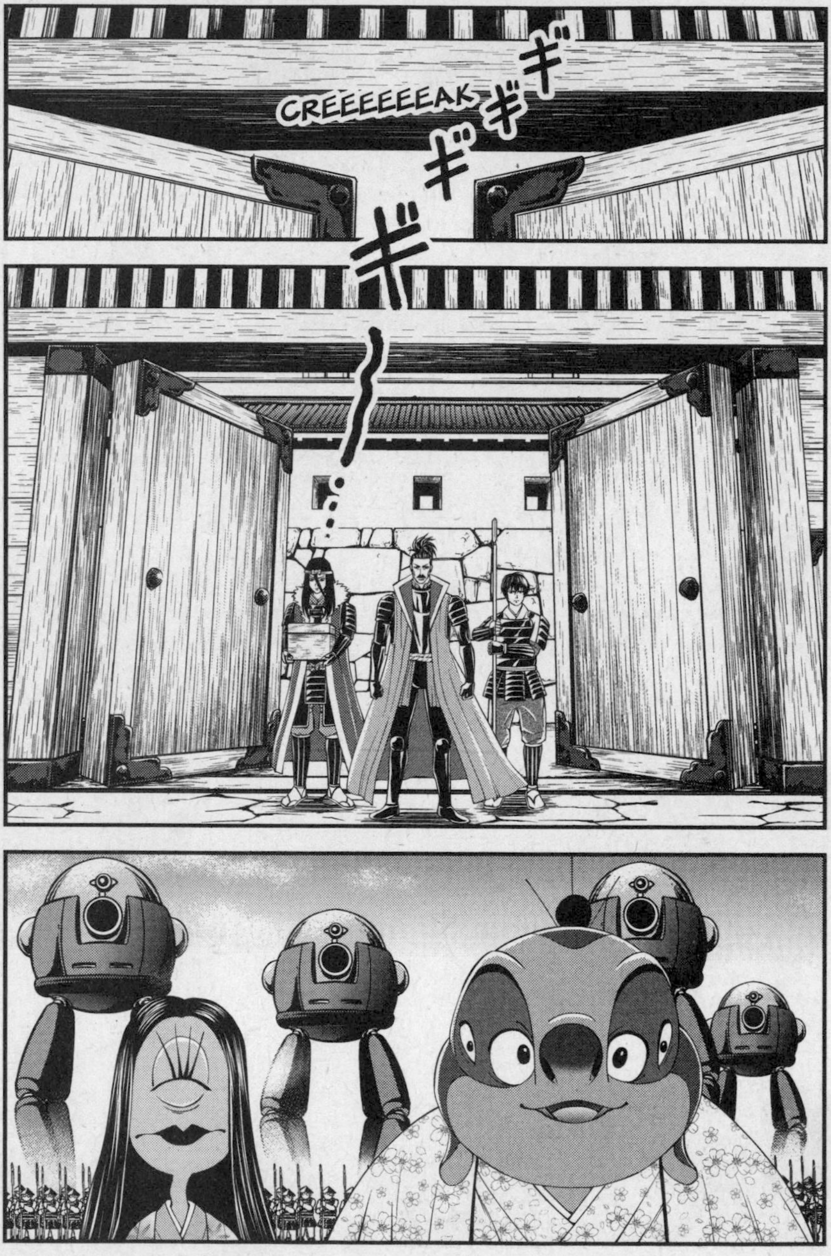
CREEEEEEAK
ギギギギ～…

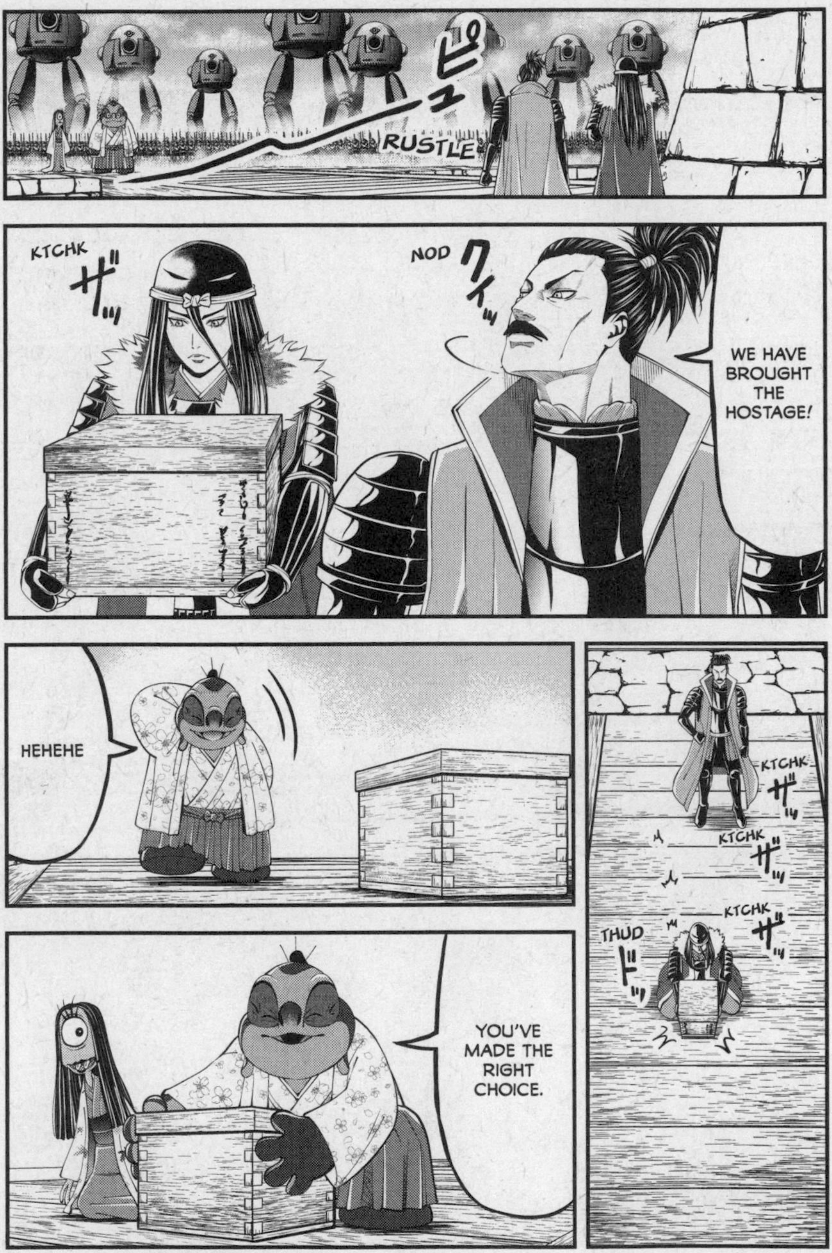
ピュ
RUSTLE
NOD
クイッ
WE HAVE BROUGHT THE HOSTAGE!
KTCHK
ザッ
KTCHK
ザッ
KTCHK
ザッ
KTCHK
ザッ
THUD
ドッ
HEHEHE
YOU'VE MADE THE RIGHT CHOICE.

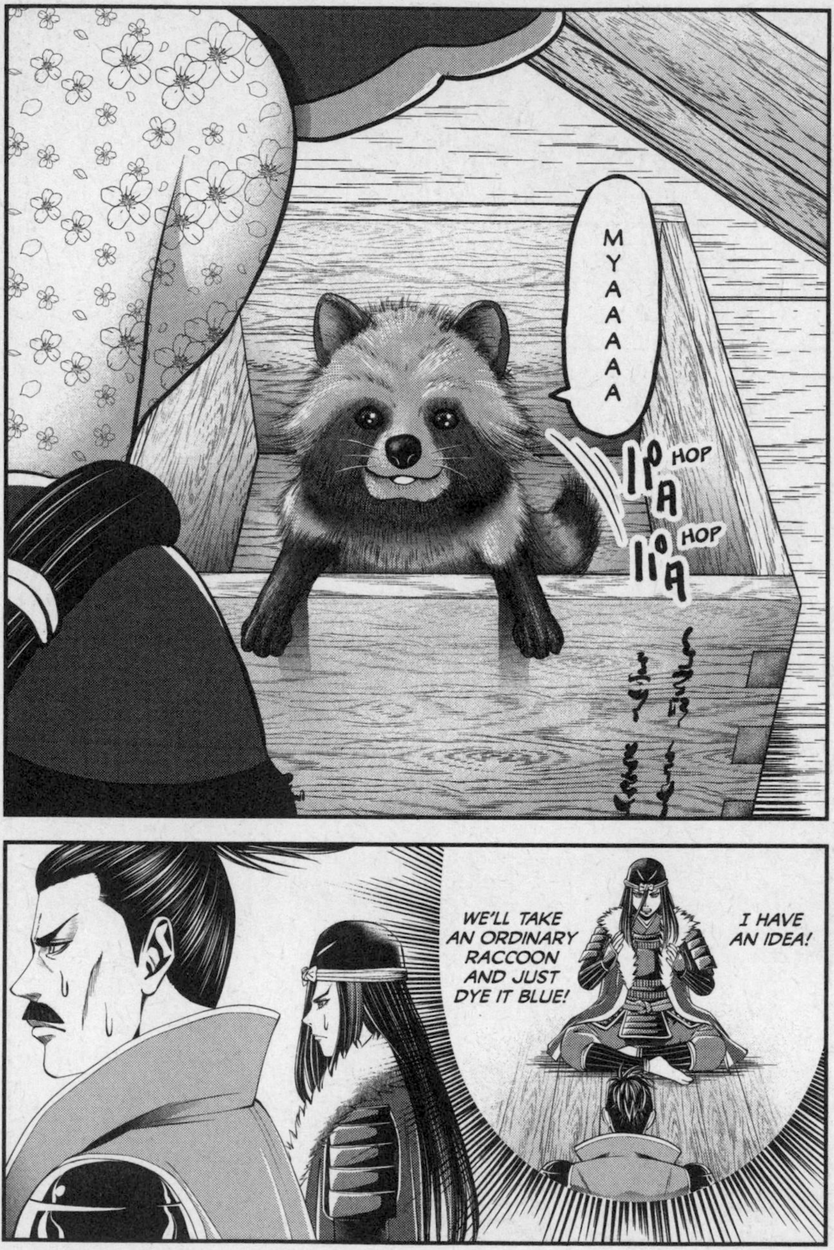
MYAAAAA
HOP
HOP
I HAVE AN IDEA!
WE'LL TAKE AN ORDINARY RACCOON AND JUST DYE IT BLUE!

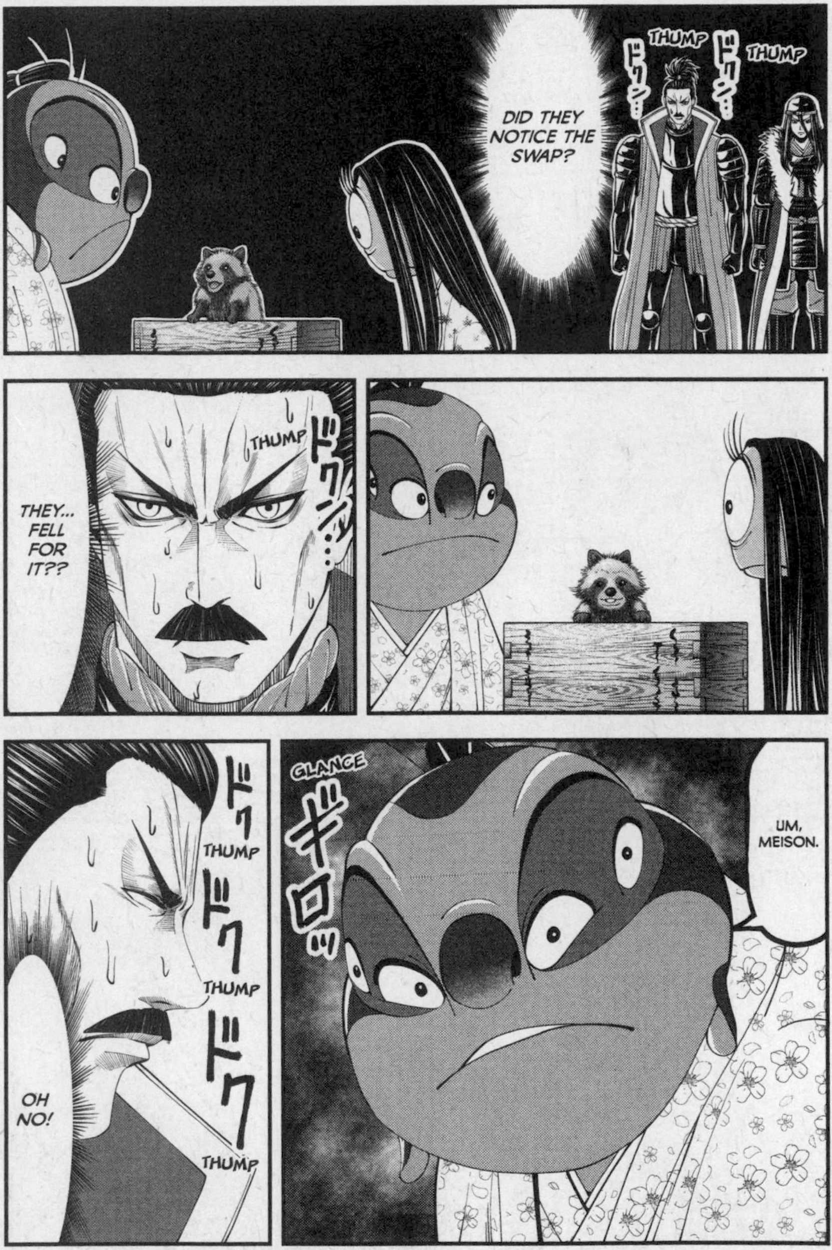
THUMP
ドクン…
THUMP
ドクン…
DID THEY NOTICE THE SWAP?
THUMP
ドクン…
THEY... FELL FOR IT??
UM, MEISON.
GLANCE
ギロッ
ドク
THUMP
ドク
THUMP
ドク
THUMP
OH NO!

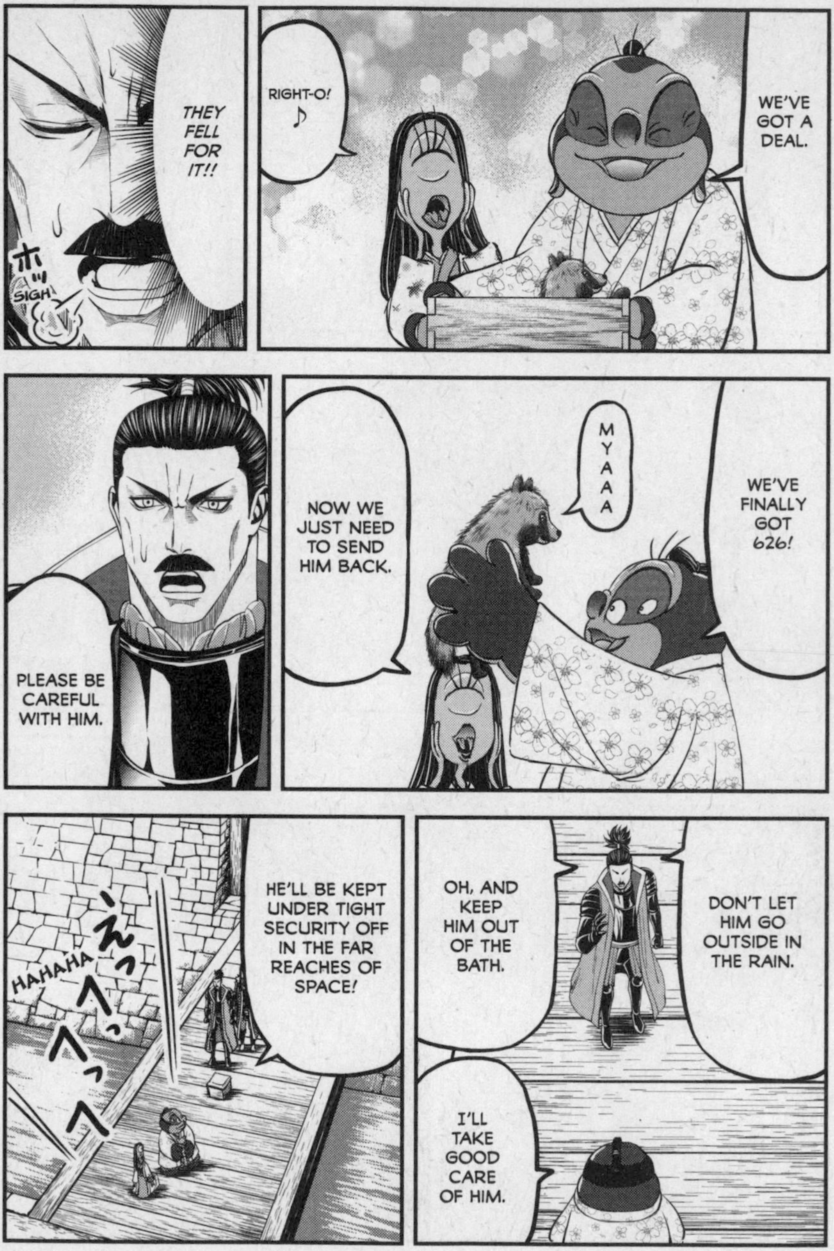
WE'VE GOT A DEAL.
RIGHT-O! ♪
THEY FELL FOR IT!!
ホッ
SIGH
WE'VE FINALLY GOT 626!
MYAAA
NOW WE JUST NEED TO SEND HIM BACK.
PLEASE BE CAREFUL WITH HIM.
DON'T LET HIM GO OUTSIDE IN THE RAIN.
OH, AND KEEP HIM OUT OF THE BATH.
I'LL TAKE GOOD CARE OF HIM.
HE'LL BE KEPT UNDER TIGHT SECURITY OFF IN THE FAR REACHES OF SPACE!
えっへっへっへ
HAHAHA

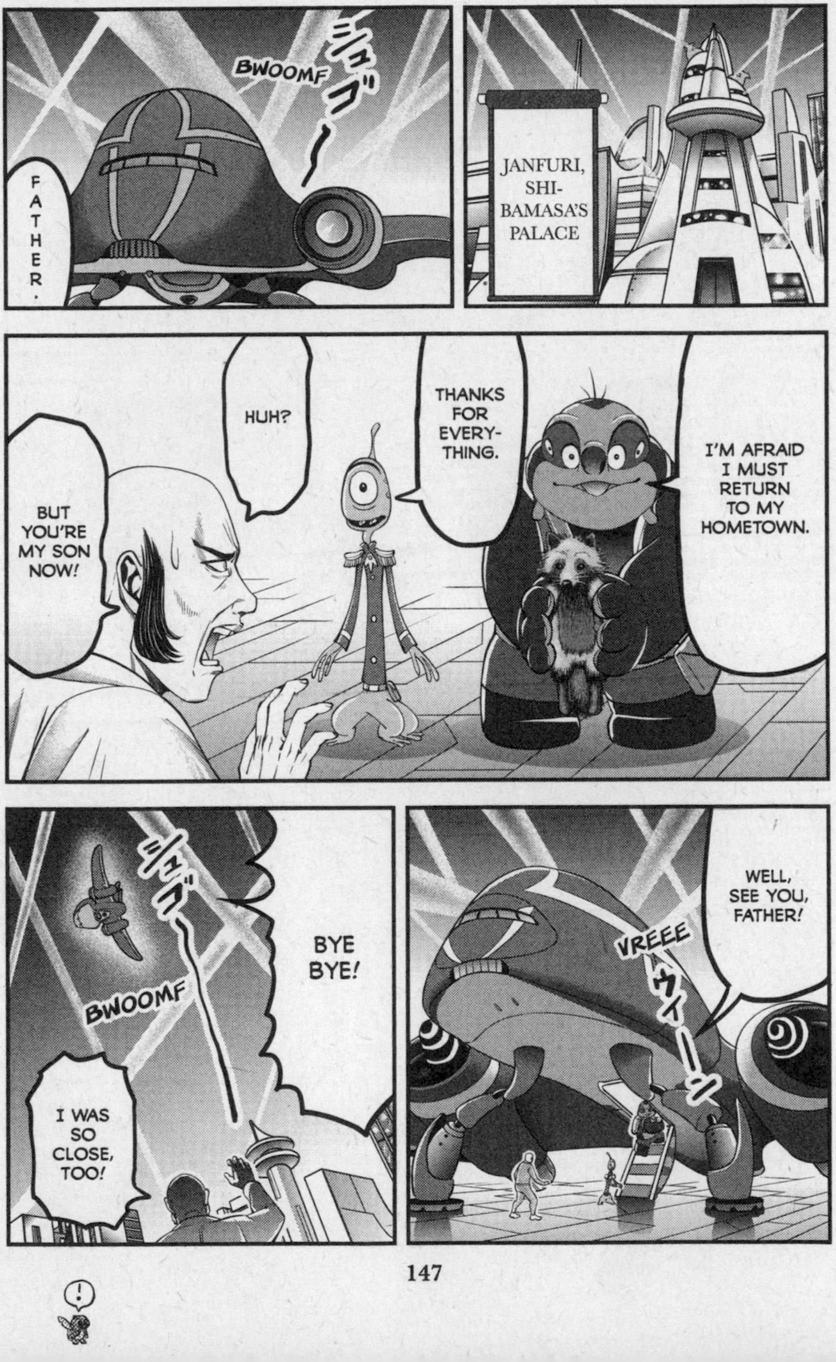
JANFURI, SHI-BAMASA'S PALACE
シュゴー
BWOOMF
FATHER.
I'M AFRAID I MUST RETURN TO MY HOMETOWN.
THANKS FOR EVERY-THING.
HUH?
BUT YOU'RE MY SON NOW!
WELL, SEE YOU, FATHER!
VREEE
シュゴー
BYE BYE!
BWOOMF
I WAS SO CLOSE, TOO!

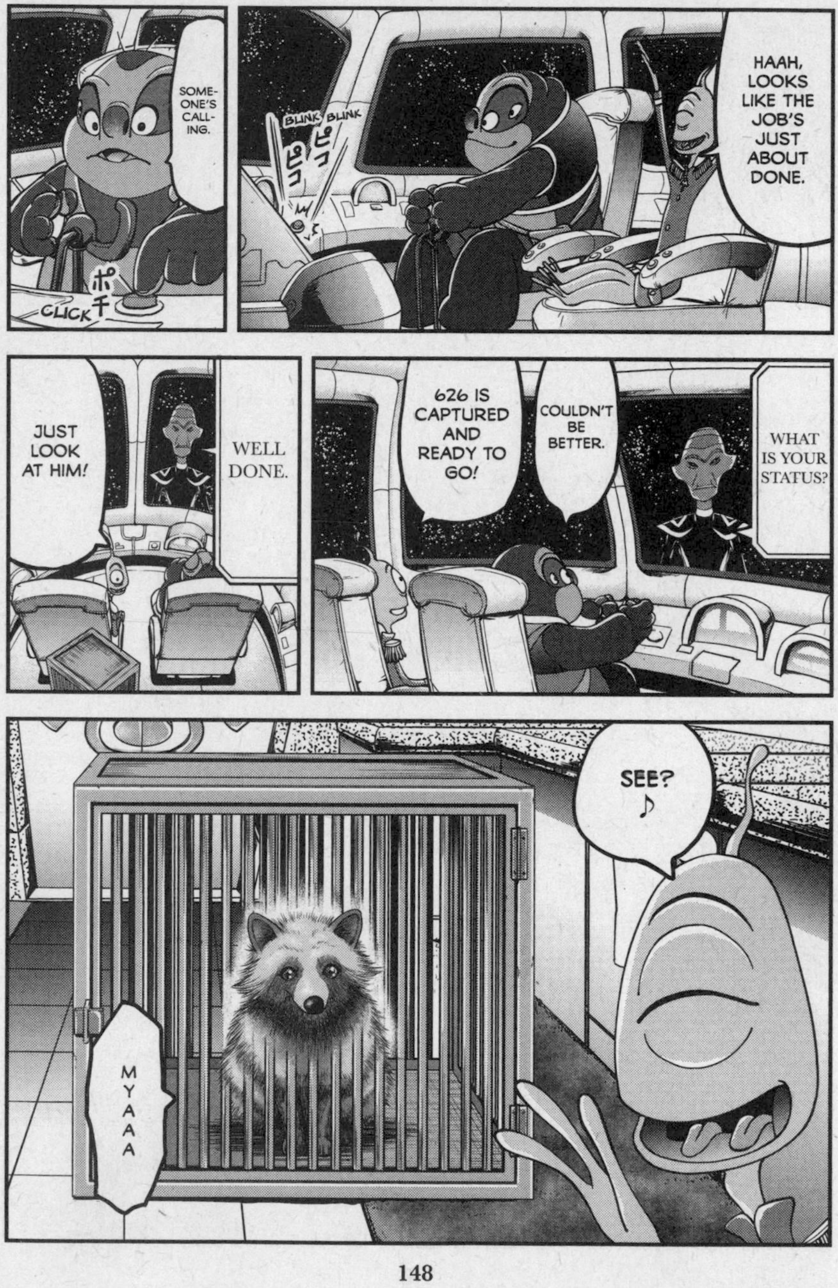
HAAH, LOOKS LIKE THE JOB'S JUST ABOUT DONE.
BLINK BLINK
ピコ ピコ
SOME-ONE'S CALL-ING.
ポチ
CLICK
WHAT IS YOUR STATUS?
COULDN'T BE BETTER.
626 IS CAPTURED AND READY TO GO!
WELL DONE.
JUST LOOK AT HIM!
SEE? ♪
MYAAA

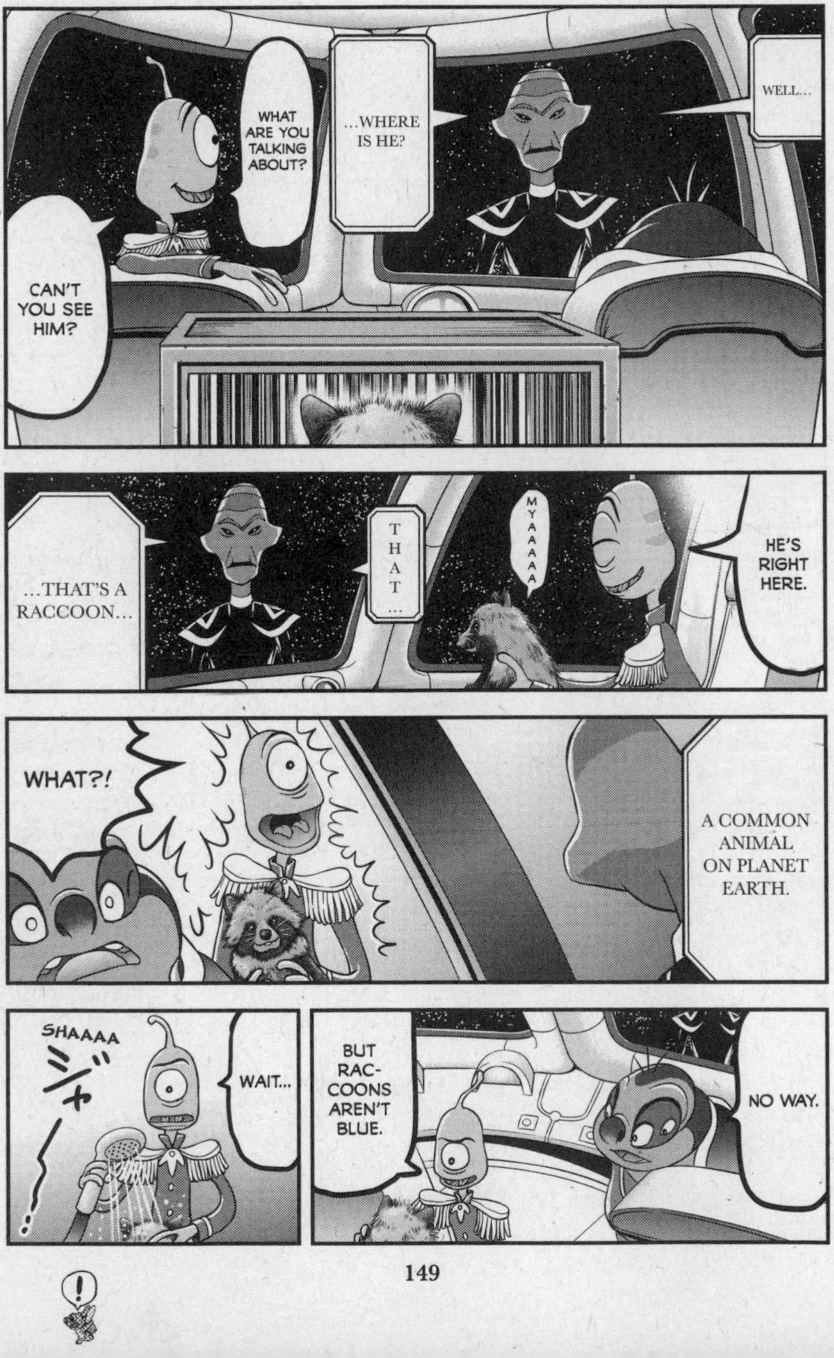
WELL…
…WHERE IS HE?
WHAT ARE YOU TALKING ABOUT?
CAN'T YOU SEE HIM?
HE'S RIGHT HERE.
MYAAAAA
THAT…
…THAT'S A RACCOON…
A COMMON ANIMAL ON PLANET EARTH.
WHAT?!
NO WAY.
BUT RAC-COONS AREN'T BLUE.
WAIT…
SHAAAA

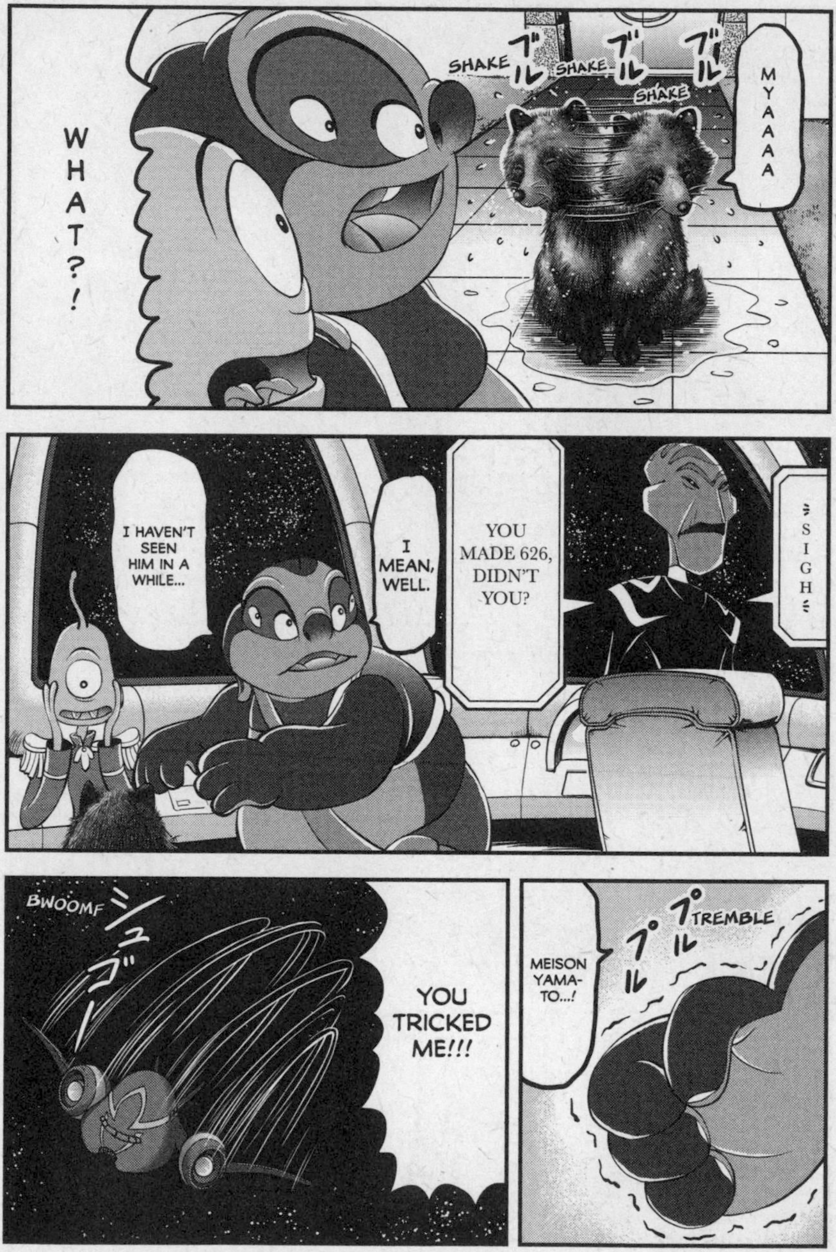
MYAAAA
SHAKE ブル
SHAKE ブル
SHAKE ブル
WHAT?!
SIGH
YOU MADE 626, DIDN'T YOU?
I MEAN, WELL.
I HAVEN'T SEEN HIM IN A WHILE...
TREMBLE プルプル
MEISON YAMA-TO...!
YOU TRICKED ME!!!
BWOOMF

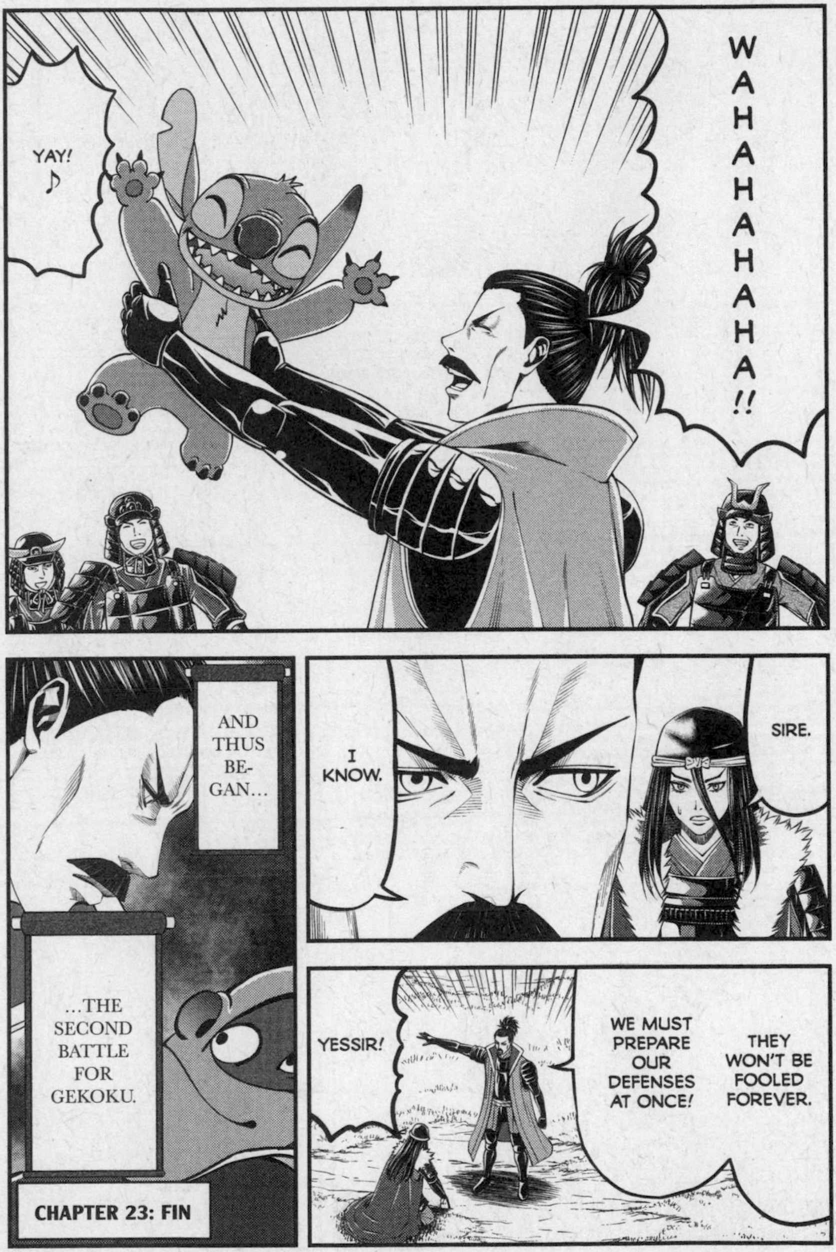
WAHAHAHAHA!!
YAY! ♪
SIRE.
I KNOW.
THEY WON'T BE FOOLED FOREVER.
WE MUST PREPARE OUR DEFENSES AT ONCE!
YESSIR!
AND THUS BE-GAN…
…THE SECOND BATTLE FOR GEKOKU.
CHAPTER 23: FIN

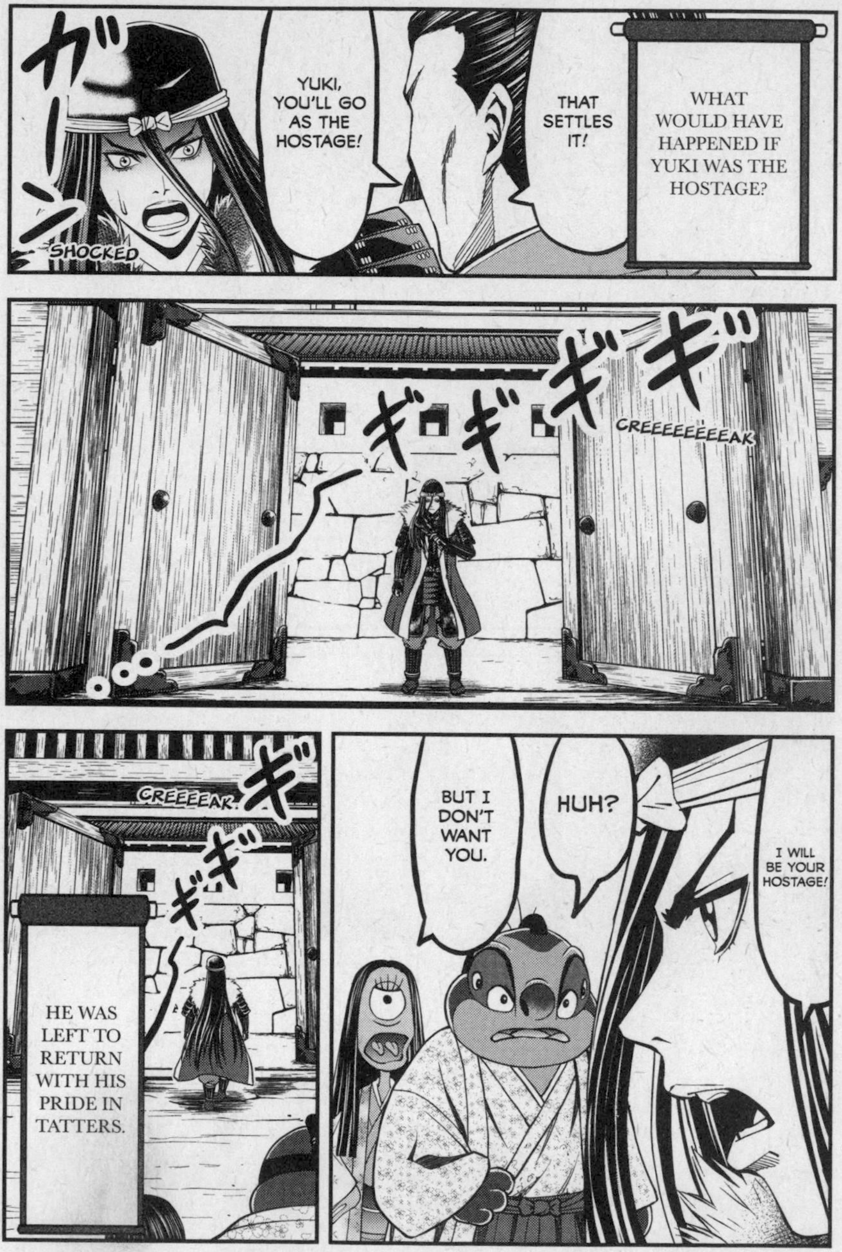
WHAT WOULD HAVE HAPPENED IF YUKI WAS THE HOSTAGE?
THAT SETTLES IT!
YUKI, YOU'LL GO AS THE HOSTAGE!
ガーン
SHOCKED
ギギギギ
CREEEEEEEEEAK
I WILL BE YOUR HOSTAGE!
HUH?
BUT I DON'T WANT YOU.
ギギギ
CREEEEEAK.
HE WAS LEFT TO RETURN WITH HIS PRIDE IN TATTERS.

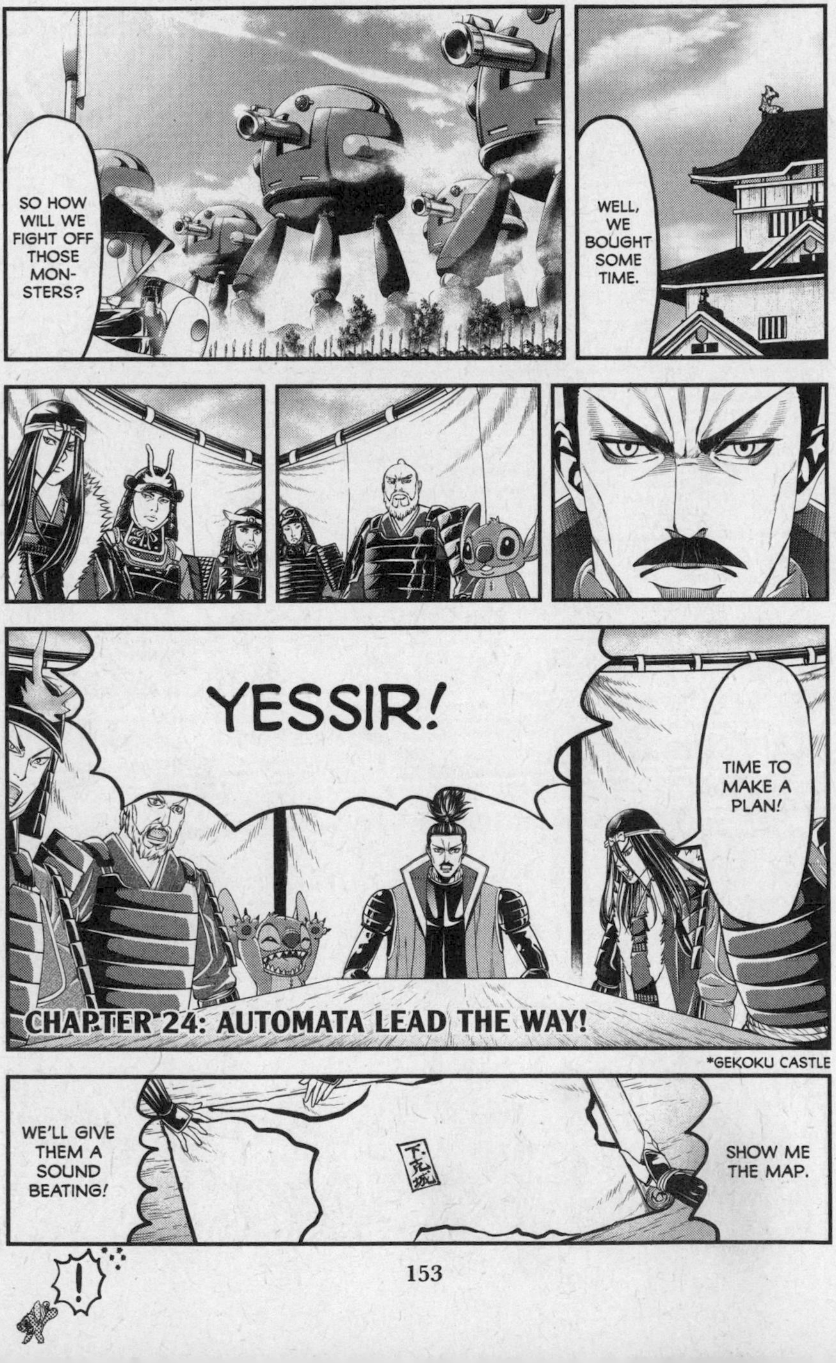
WELL, WE BOUGHT SOME TIME.
SO HOW WILL WE FIGHT OFF THOSE MON-STERS?
TIME TO MAKE A PLAN!
YESSIR!
CHAPTER 24: AUTOMATA LEAD THE WAY!
*GEKOKU CASTLE
SHOW ME THE MAP.
下克城
WE'LL GIVE THEM A SOUND BEATING!

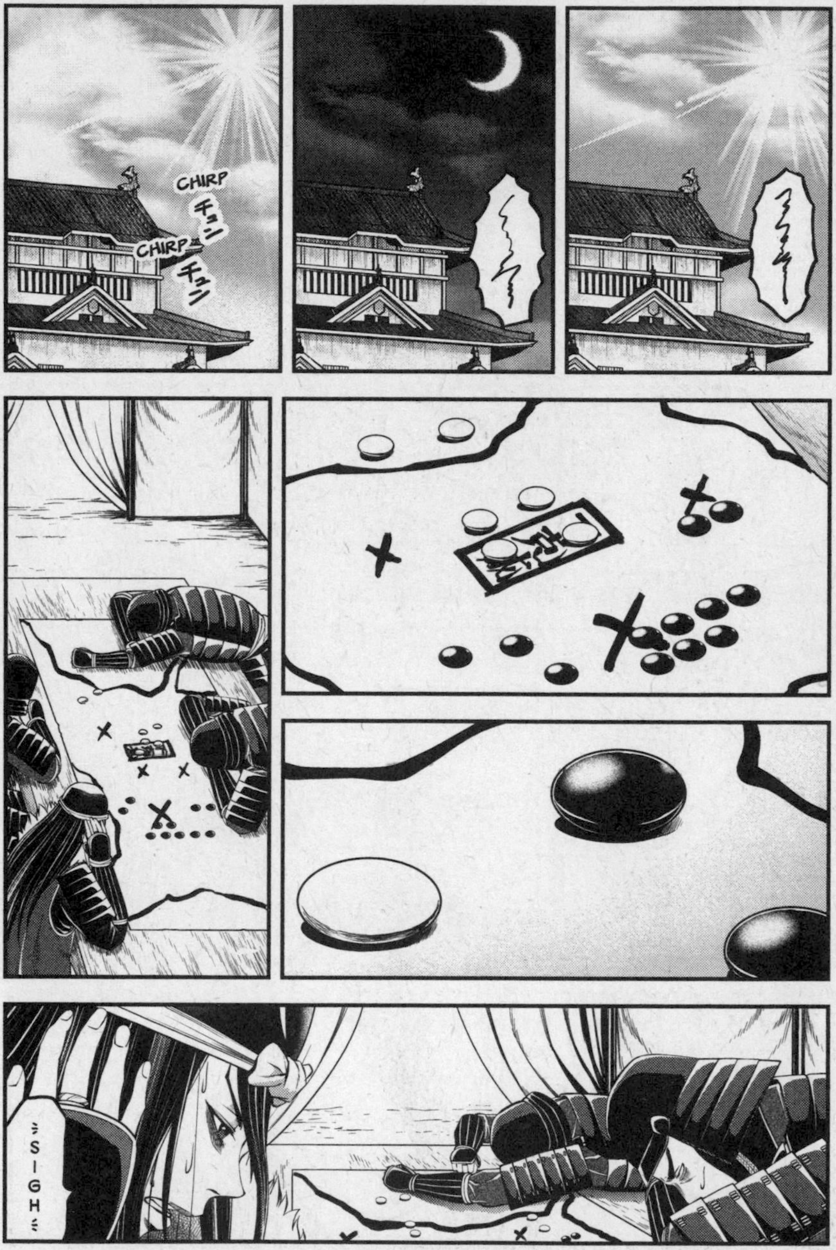
CHIRP
チュン
CHIRP
チュン
SIGH

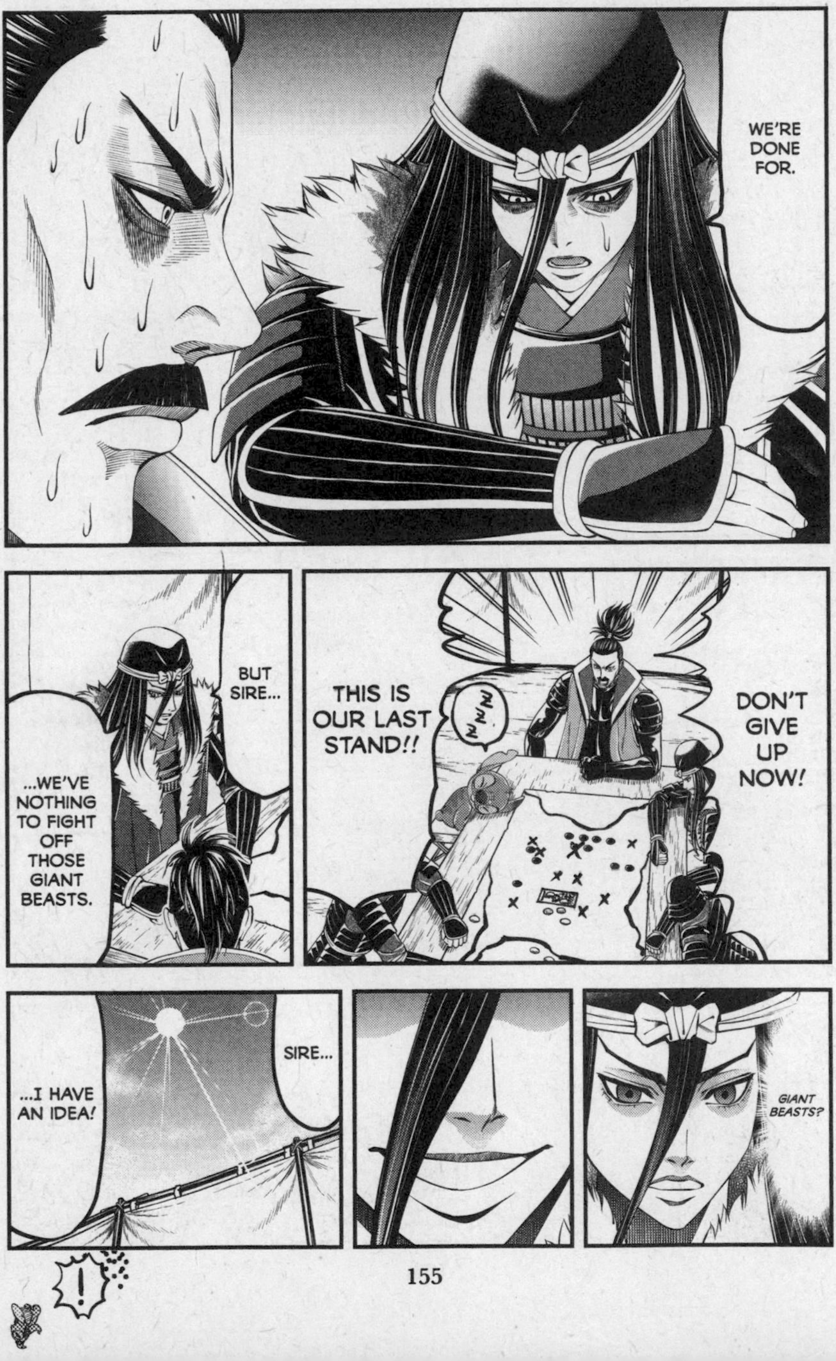
WE'RE DONE FOR.
DON'T GIVE UP NOW!
THIS IS OUR LAST STAND!!
ZZZ
BUT SIRE...
...WE'VE NOTHING TO FIGHT OFF THOSE GIANT BEASTS.
GIANT BEASTS?
SIRE...
...I HAVE AN IDEA!
!

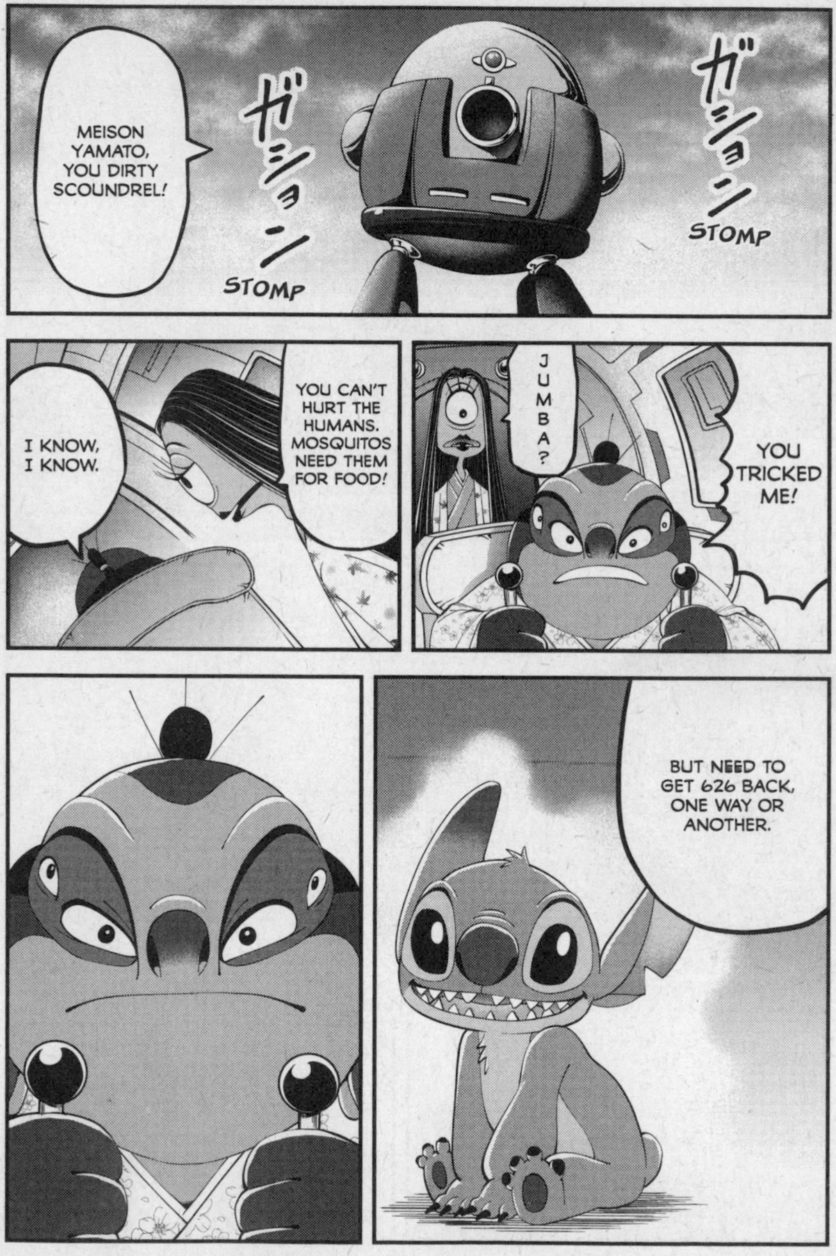
ガション
STOMP
MEISON YAMATO, YOU DIRTY SCOUNDREL!
ガション
STOMP
JUMBA?
YOU TRICKED ME!
YOU CAN'T HURT THE HUMANS. MOSQUITOS NEED THEM FOR FOOD!
I KNOW, I KNOW.
BUT NEED TO GET 626 BACK, ONE WAY OR ANOTHER.

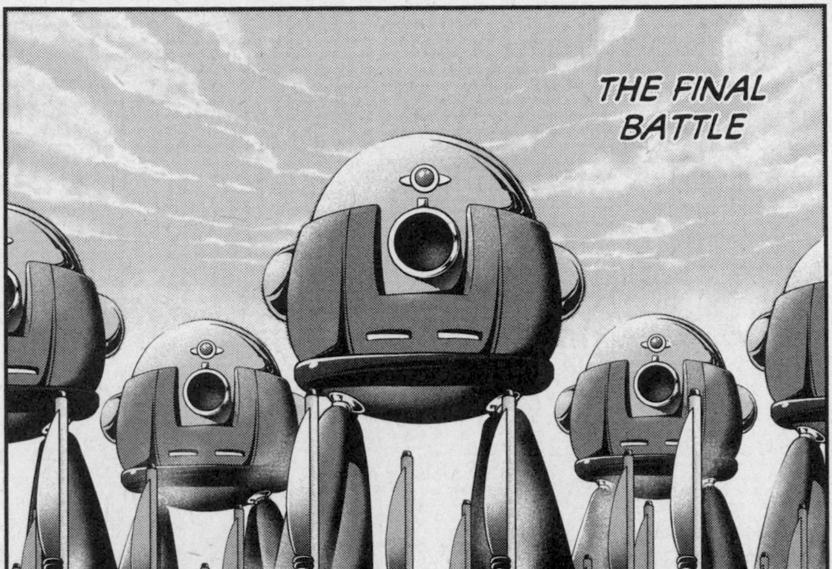
THE FINAL BATTLE
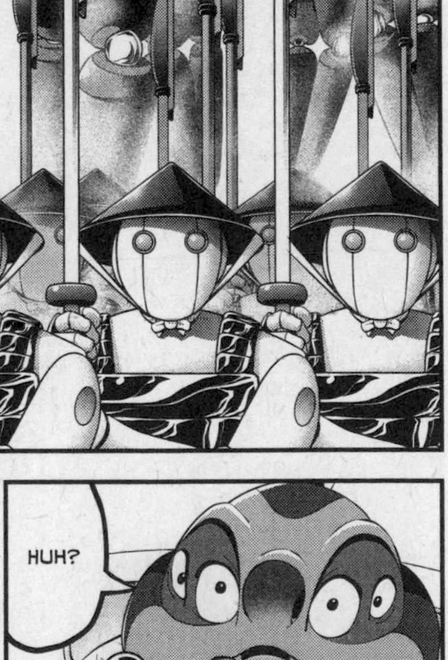
HUH?
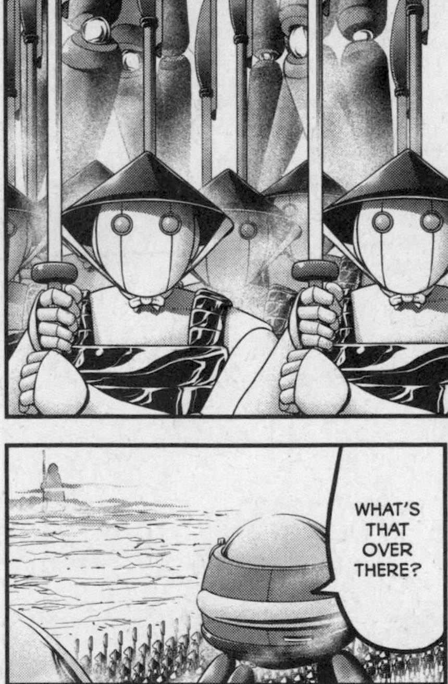
WHAT'S THAT OVER THERE?
!

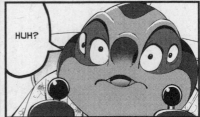

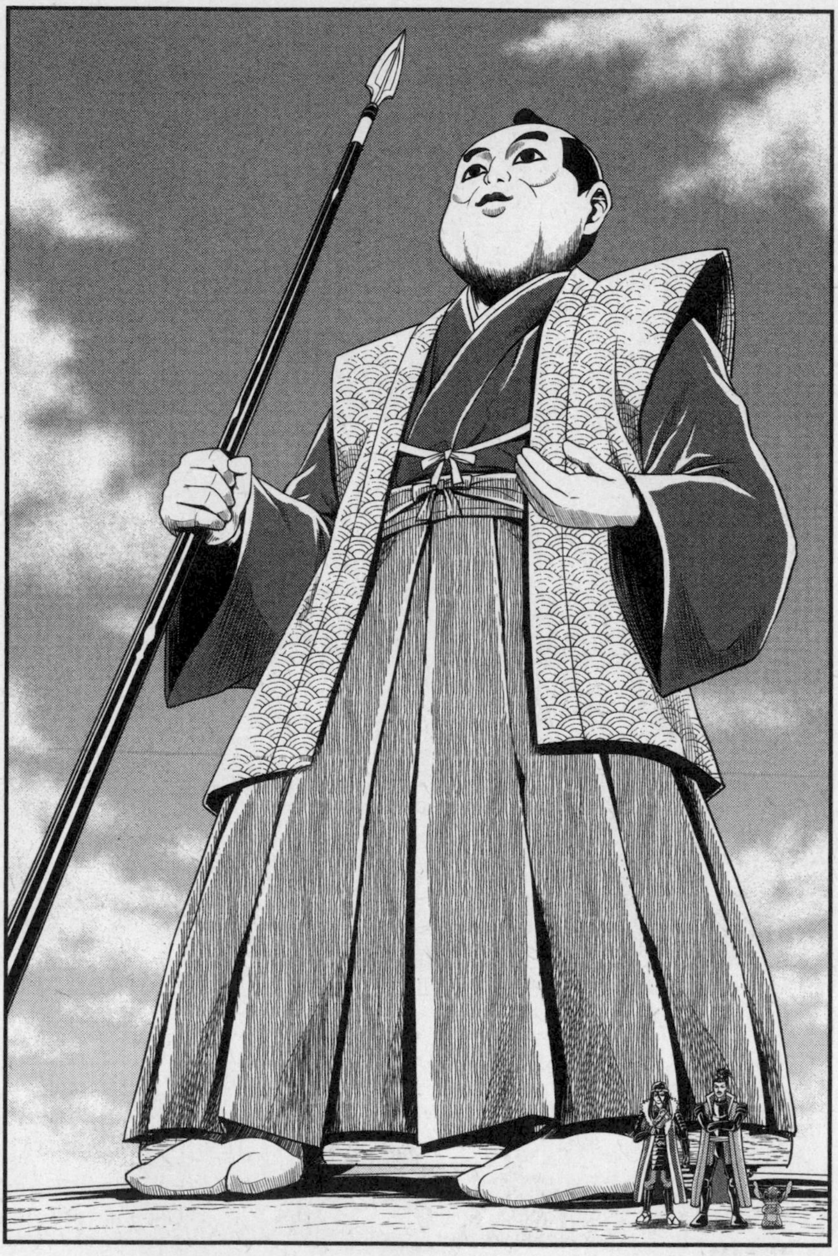

...WHAT'S THAT? WHAT A BIG MAN!

WOW...

WE WILL FIGHT BIG ENEMIES WITH A BIG KARAKURI DOLL!

NOW STRIKE!

INSTEAD OF AN OVERNIGHT CASTLE*, AN OVERNIGHT KARAKURI!

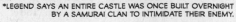

*LEGEND SAYS AN ENTIRE CASTLE WAS ONCE BUILT OVERNIGHT BY A SAMURAI CLAN TO INTIMIDATE THEIR ENEMY.

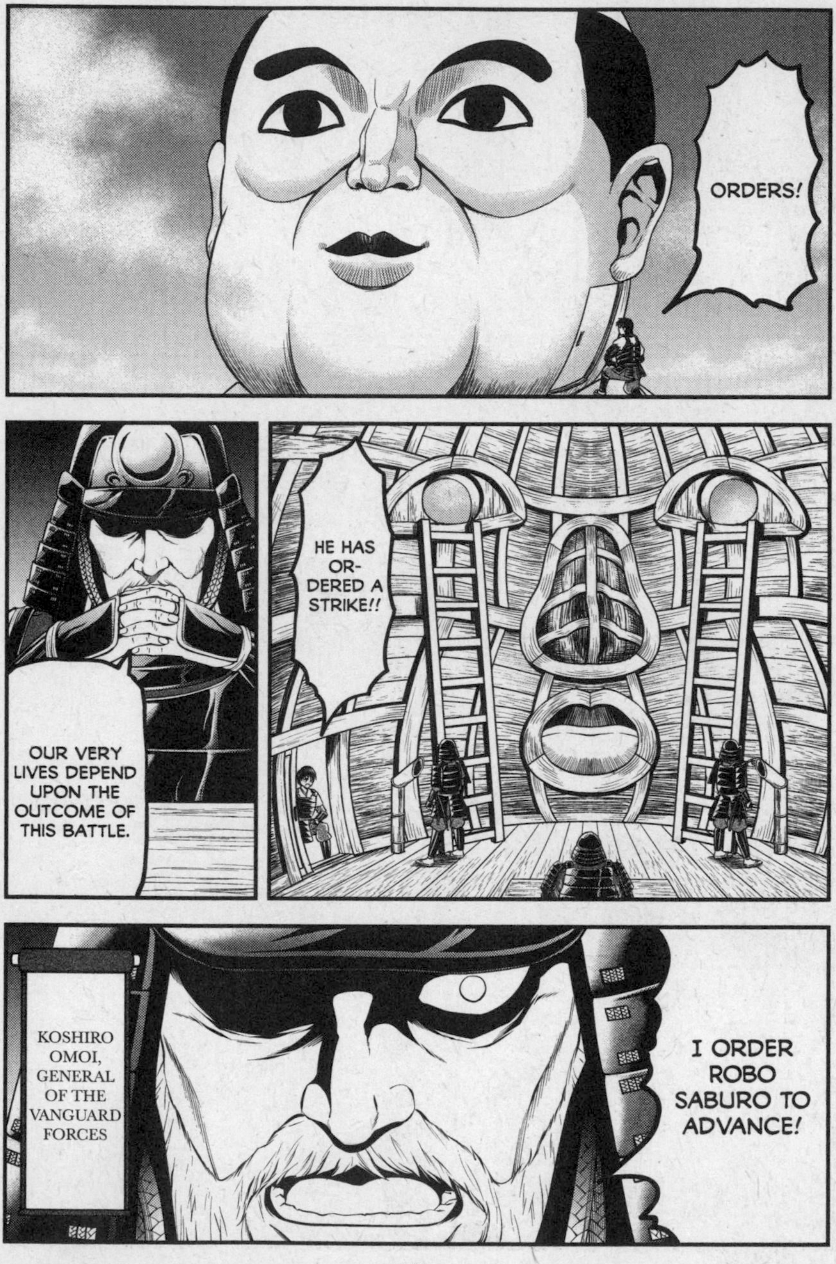
ORDERS!
HE HAS ORDERED A STRIKE!!
OUR VERY LIVES DEPEND UPON THE OUTCOME OF THIS BATTLE.
I ORDER ROBO SABURO TO ADVANCE!
KOSHIRO OMOI, GENERAL OF THE VANGUARD FORCES

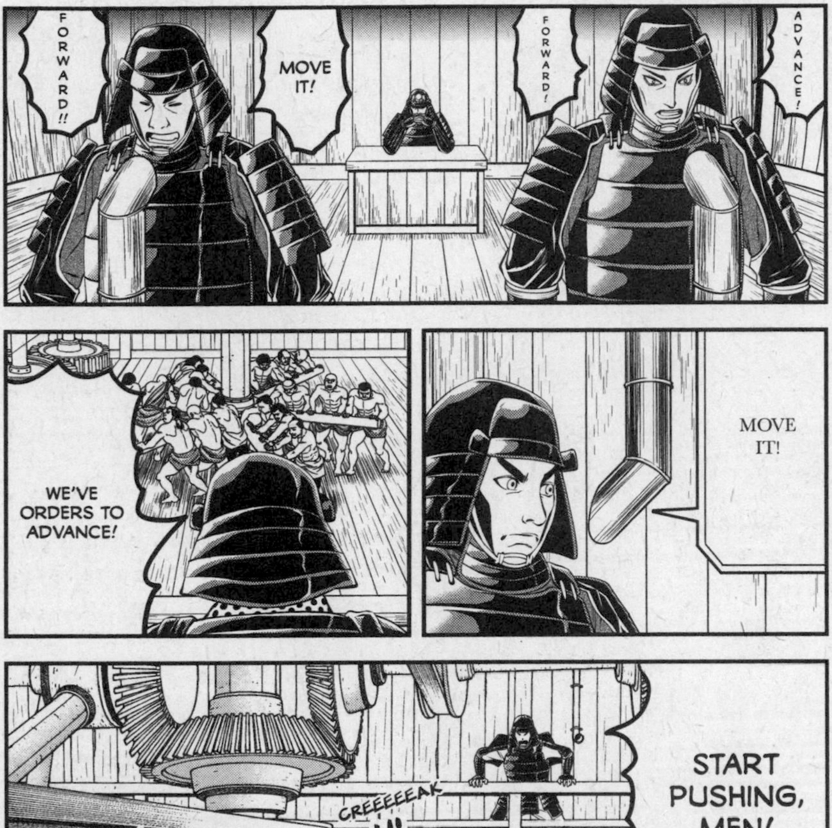
ADVANCE!
FORWARD!
MOVE IT!
FORWARD!!
MOVE IT!
WE'VE ORDERS TO ADVANCE!
START PUSHING, MEN!
CREEEEEAK
ギャリ
CREEEEEAK
ギャリ

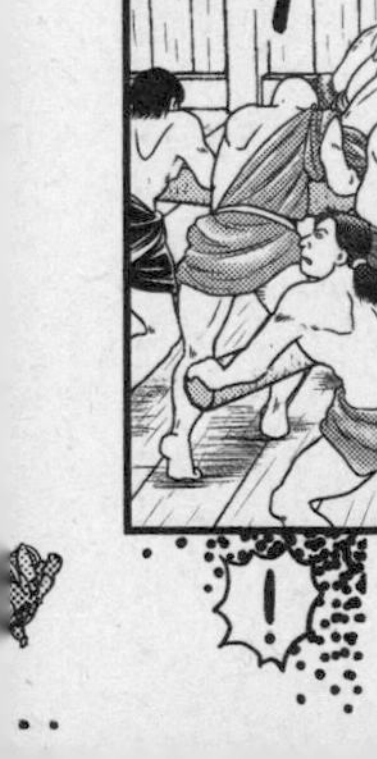
!

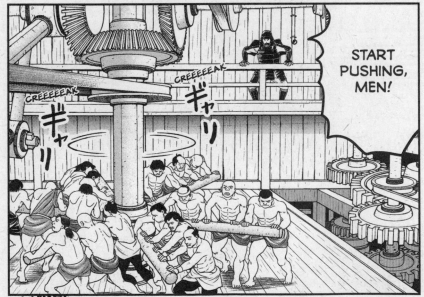

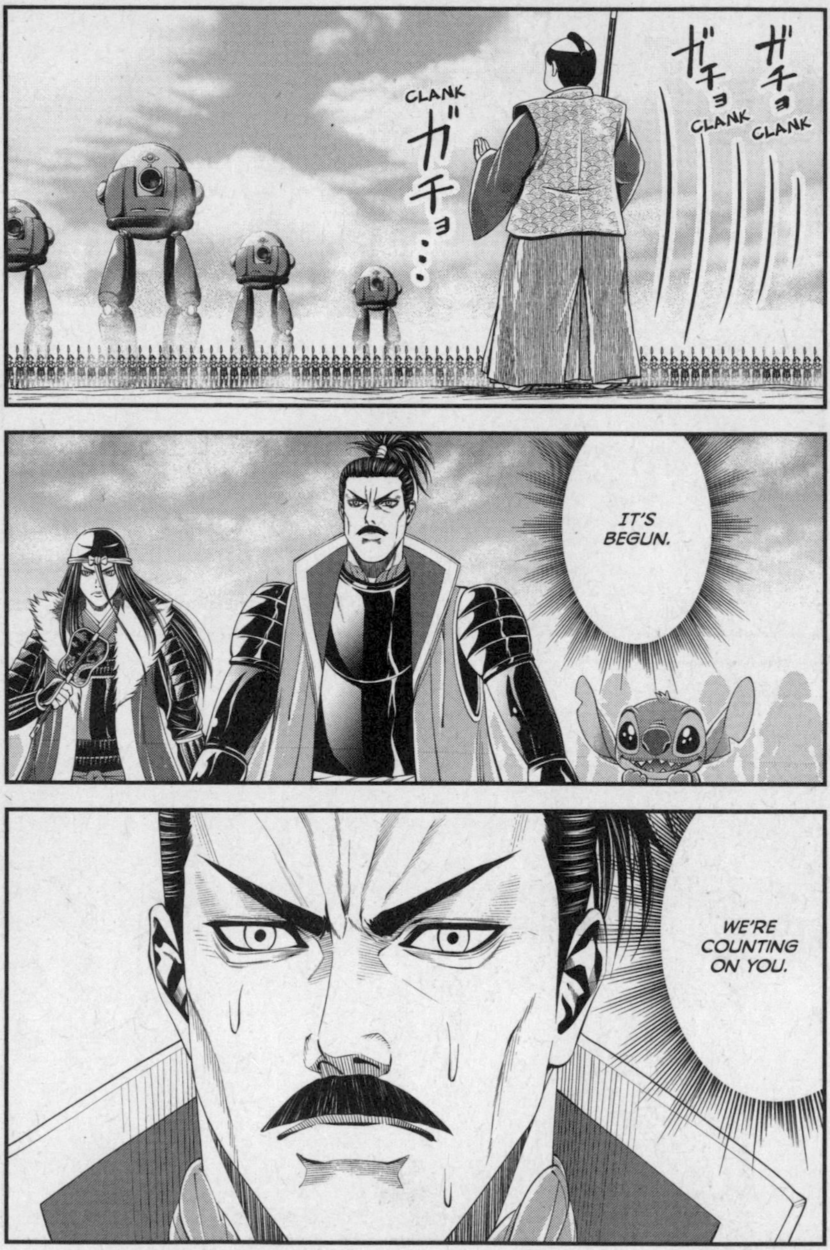
ガチョ
CLANK
ガチョ
CLANK
CLANK
ガチョ・・・
IT'S BEGUN.
WE'RE COUNTING ON YOU.

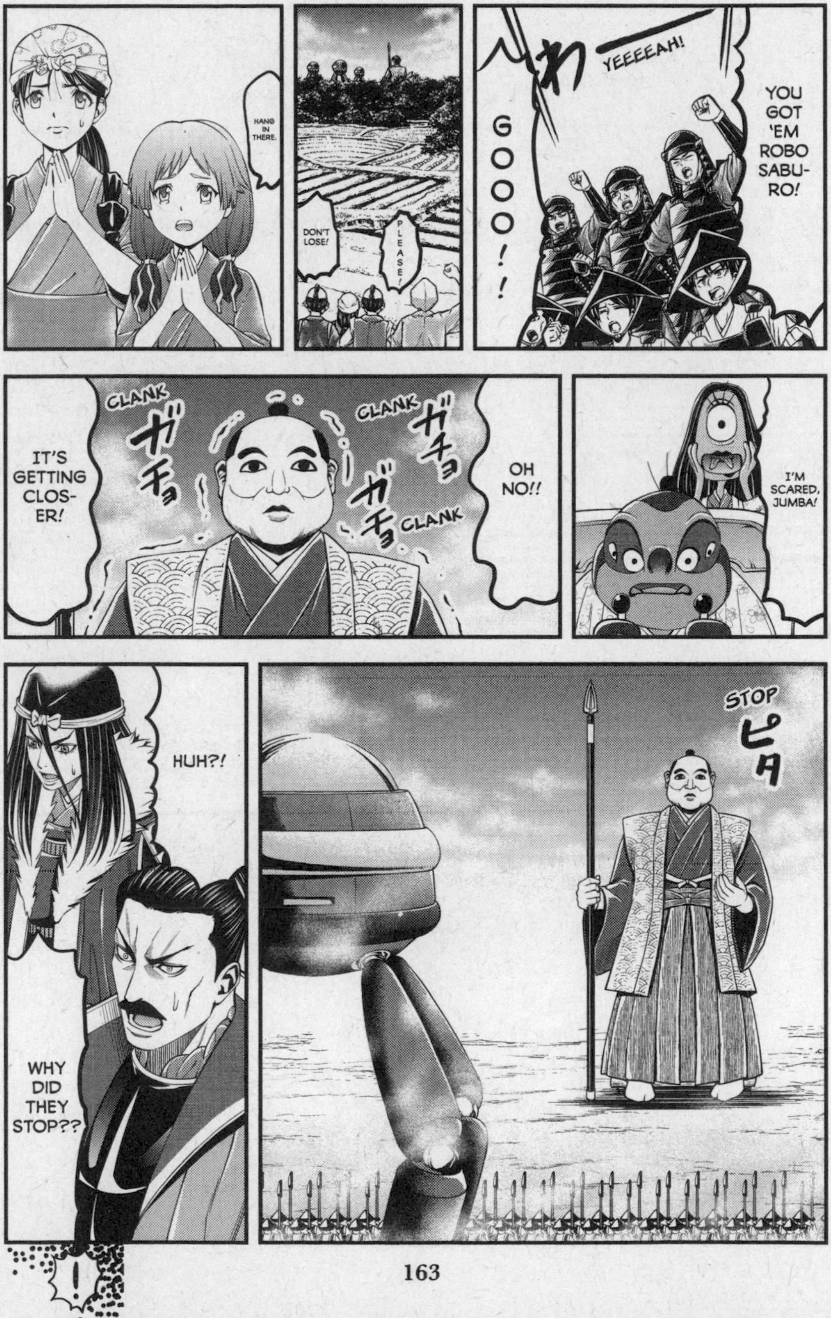

わ
YEEEEAH!
GOOOO!!
YOU GOT 'EM ROBO SABU-RO!
PLEASE!
DON'T LOSE!
HANG IN THERE.
I'M SCARED, JUMBA!
OH NO!!
CLANK
ガチョ
CLANK
ガチョ
CLANK
ガチョ
IT'S GETTING CLOS-ER!
STOP
ピタ
HUH?!
WHY DID THEY STOP??
!

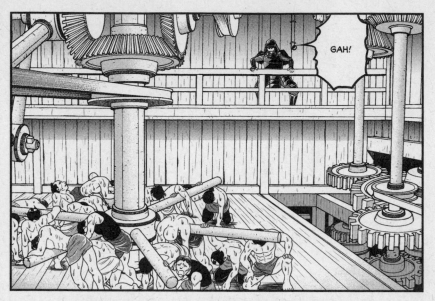

GAH!
QUIT YER WHEEZ-ING!
HUFF
HUFF
HUFF
HUFF
HUFF
HUFF
WE'RE DOING THIS FOR OUR WIVES AND CHILDREN!!
FULL SPEED AHEAD!!
FULL SPEED AHEAD!!
FULL SPEED AHEAD!!

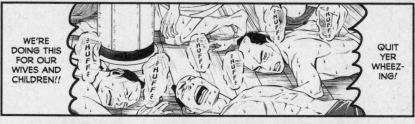

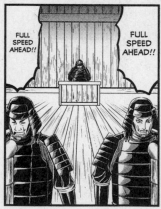

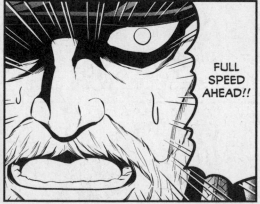

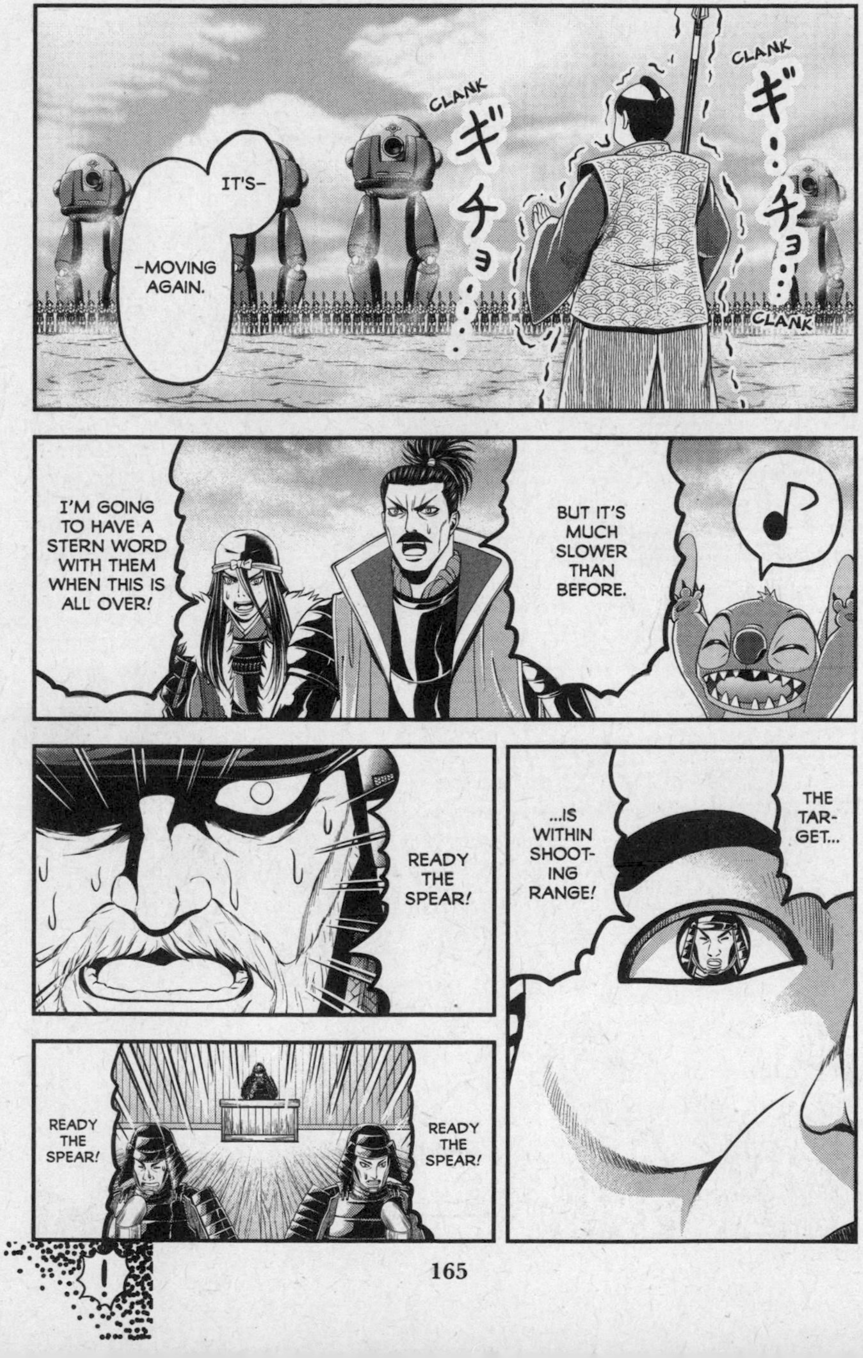
CLANK
ギ・チョ・・・
CLANK
CLANK
ギチョ・・・
IT'S—
—MOVING AGAIN.
♪
BUT IT'S MUCH SLOWER THAN BEFORE.
I'M GOING TO HAVE A STERN WORD WITH THEM WHEN THIS IS ALL OVER!
THE TAR-GET...
...IS WITHIN SHOOT-ING RANGE!
READY THE SPEAR!
READY THE SPEAR!
READY THE SPEAR!
!

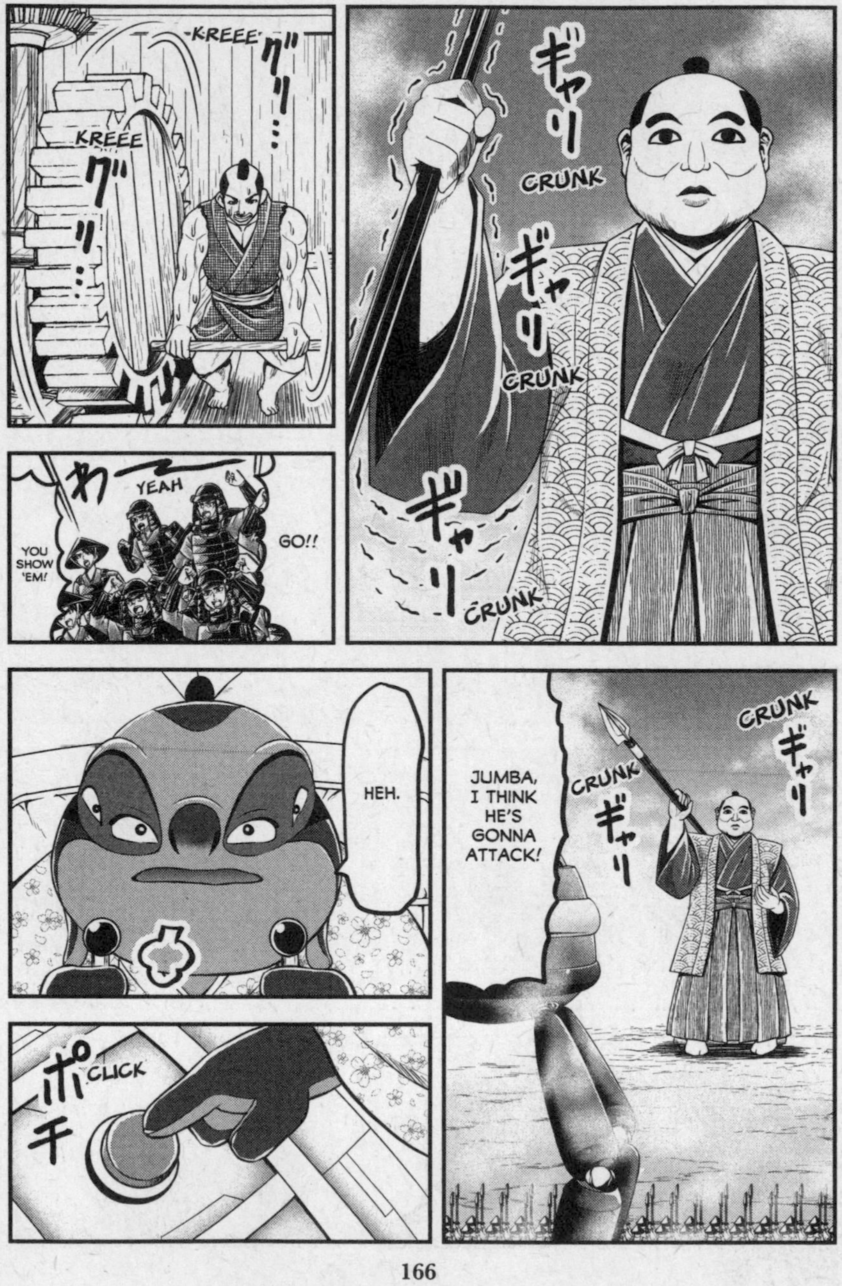
ギャリ
CRUNK
ギャリ
CRUNK
ギャリ
CRUNK
-KREEE-
グリ…
KREEE
グリ…
わー
YEAH
GO!!
YOU SHOW 'EM!
CRUNK
ギャリ
CRUNK
ギャリ
JUMBA, I THINK HE'S GONNA ATTACK!
HEH.
ポチ
CLICK

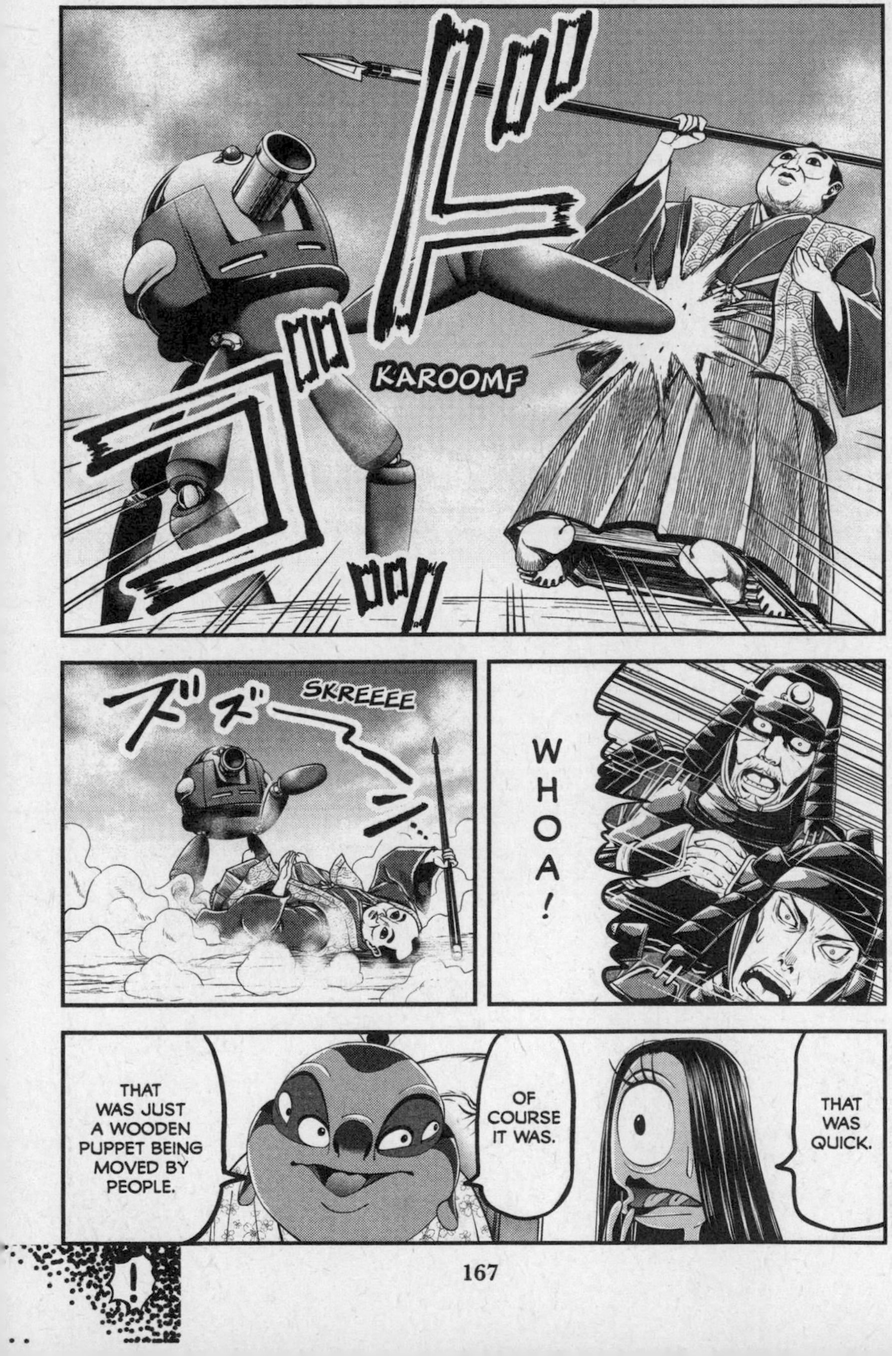
KAROOMF
WHOA!
SKREEEE
THAT WAS QUICK.
OF COURSE IT WAS.
THAT WAS JUST A WOODEN PUPPET BEING MOVED BY PEOPLE.

NO...
...WE'RE DOOMED.
GEKOKU AS WE KNOW IT IS FINISHED!
WE CAN'T BEAT A THING LIKE THAT!
CALM YOUR-SELVES!
WE'LL JUST HAVE TO TRY A NEW PLAN!
ISN'T IT ALREADY TOO LATE?!

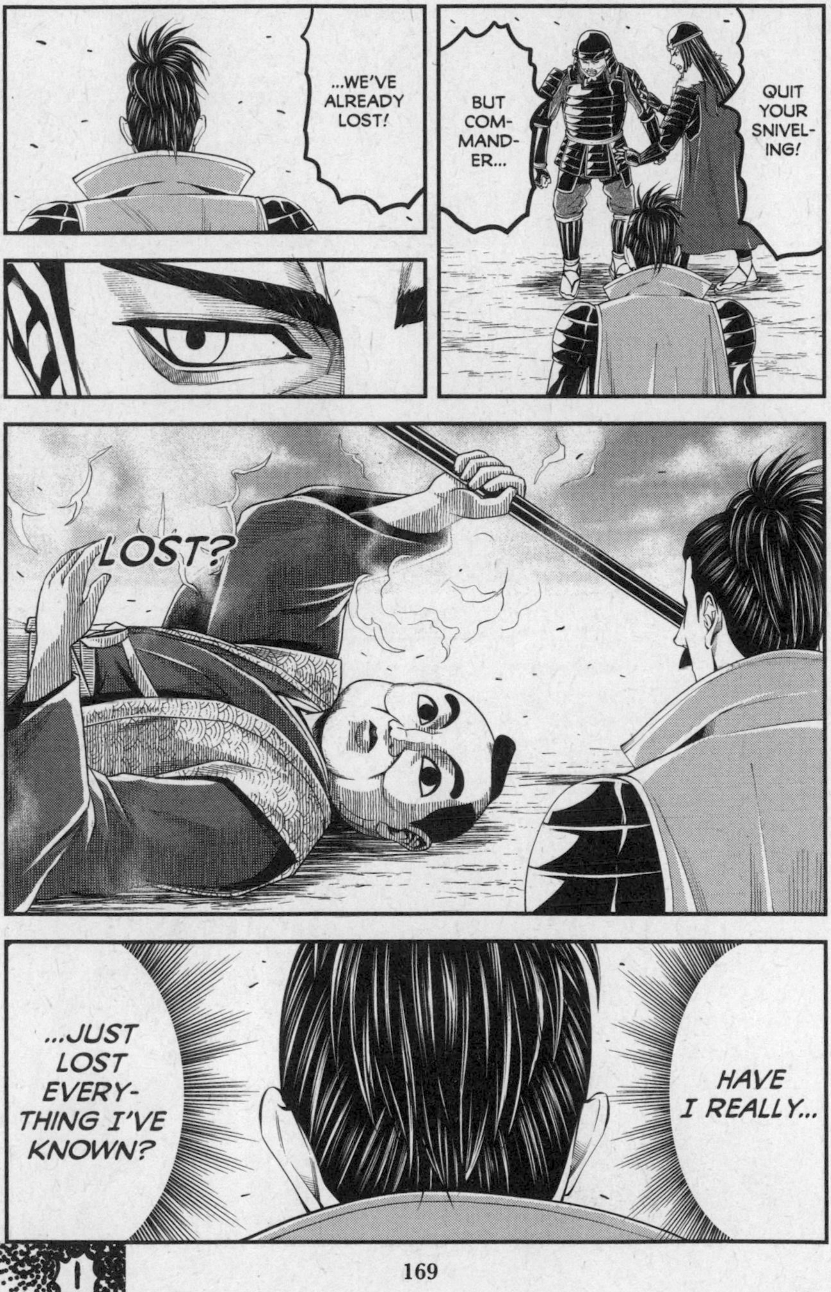
QUIT YOUR SNIVEL-ING!
BUT COM-MAND-ER...
...WE'VE ALREADY LOST!
LOST?
HAVE I REALLY...
...JUST LOST EVERY-THING I'VE KNOWN?
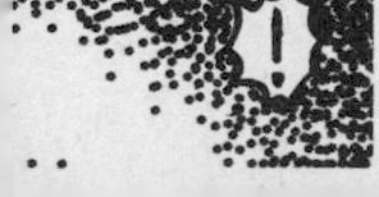
!

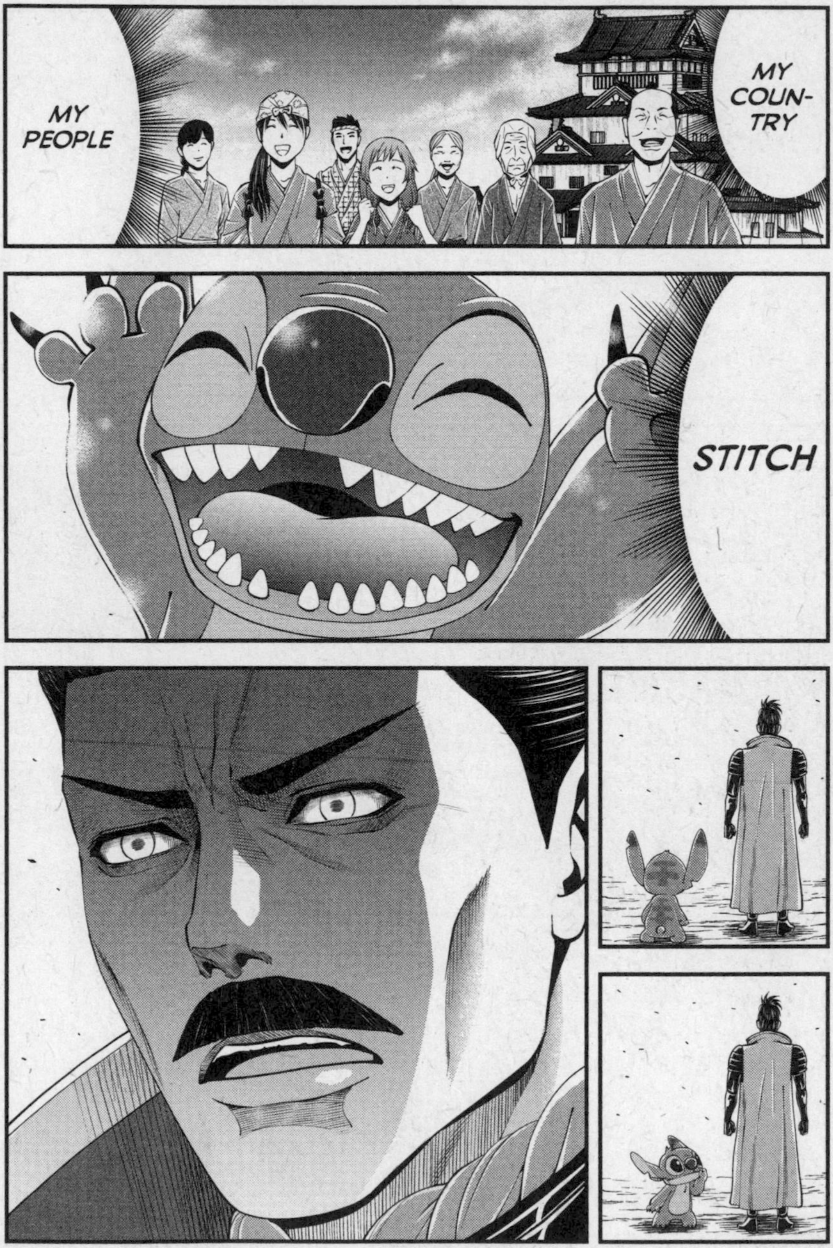
MY COUNTRY
MY PEOPLE
STITCH

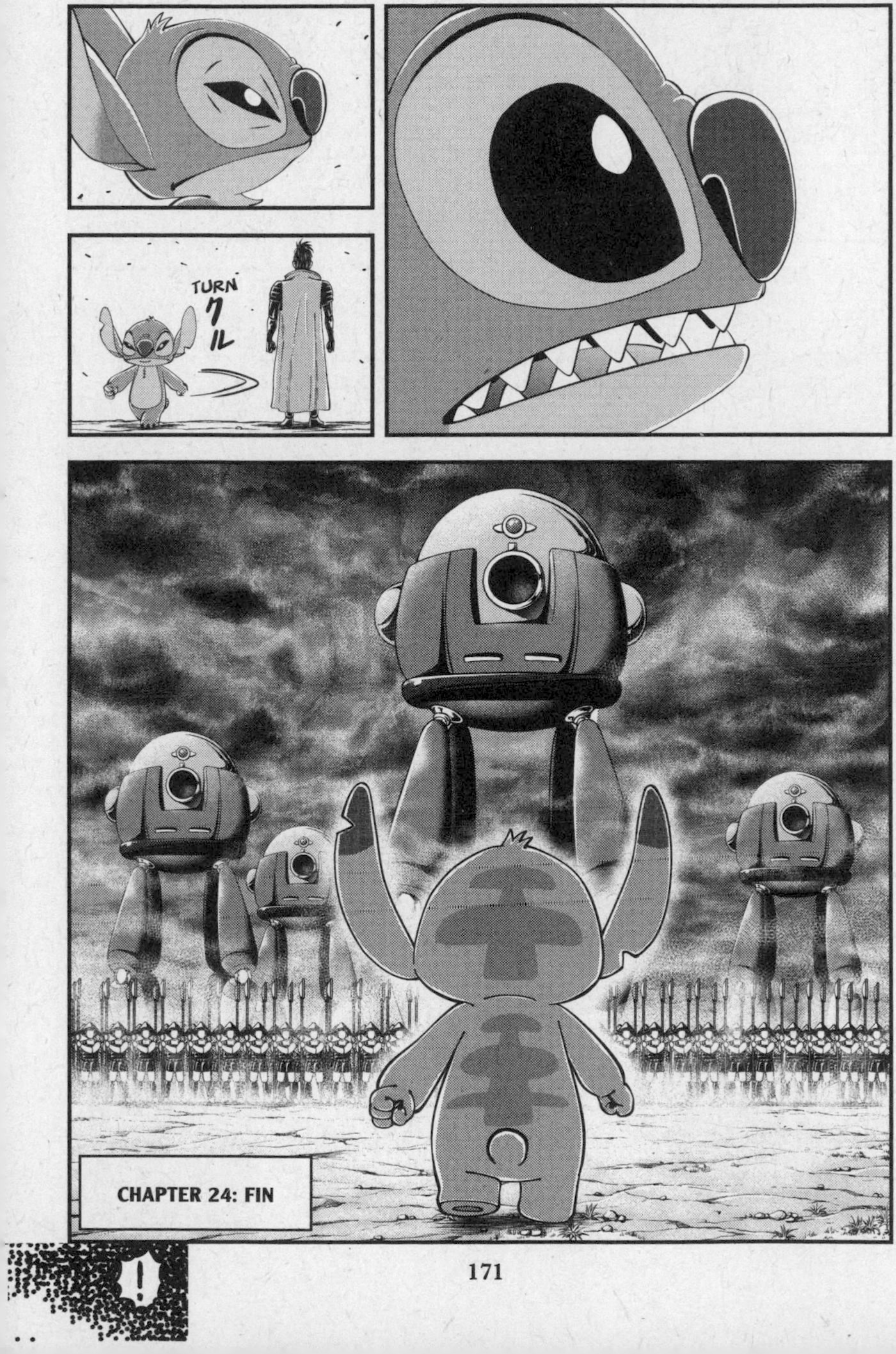
TURN
クル
CHAPTER 24: FIN

FOREBODING PART 2

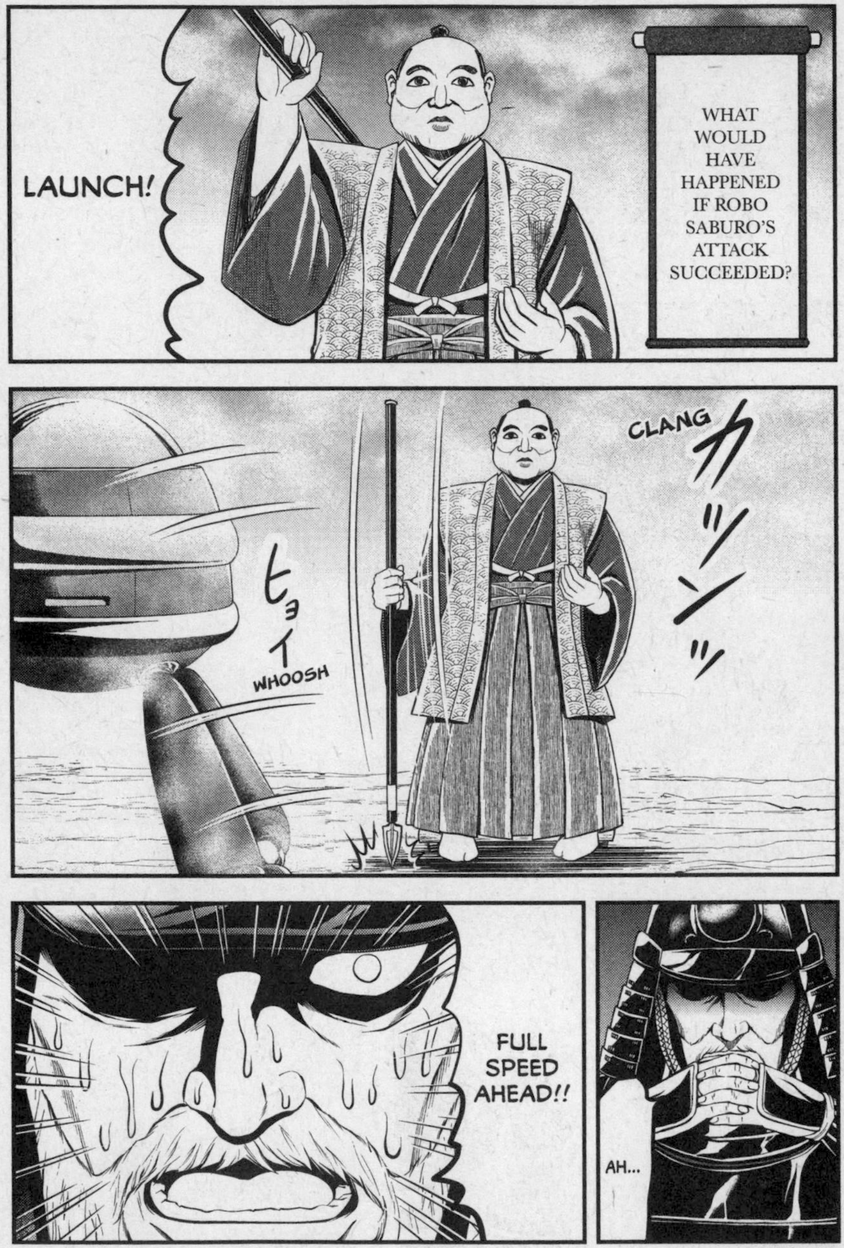
WHAT WOULD HAVE HAPPENED IF ROBO SABURO'S ATTACK SUCCEEDED?
LAUNCH!
CLANG
カッンッ
ヒョイ
WHOOSH
AH...
FULL SPEED AHEAD!!

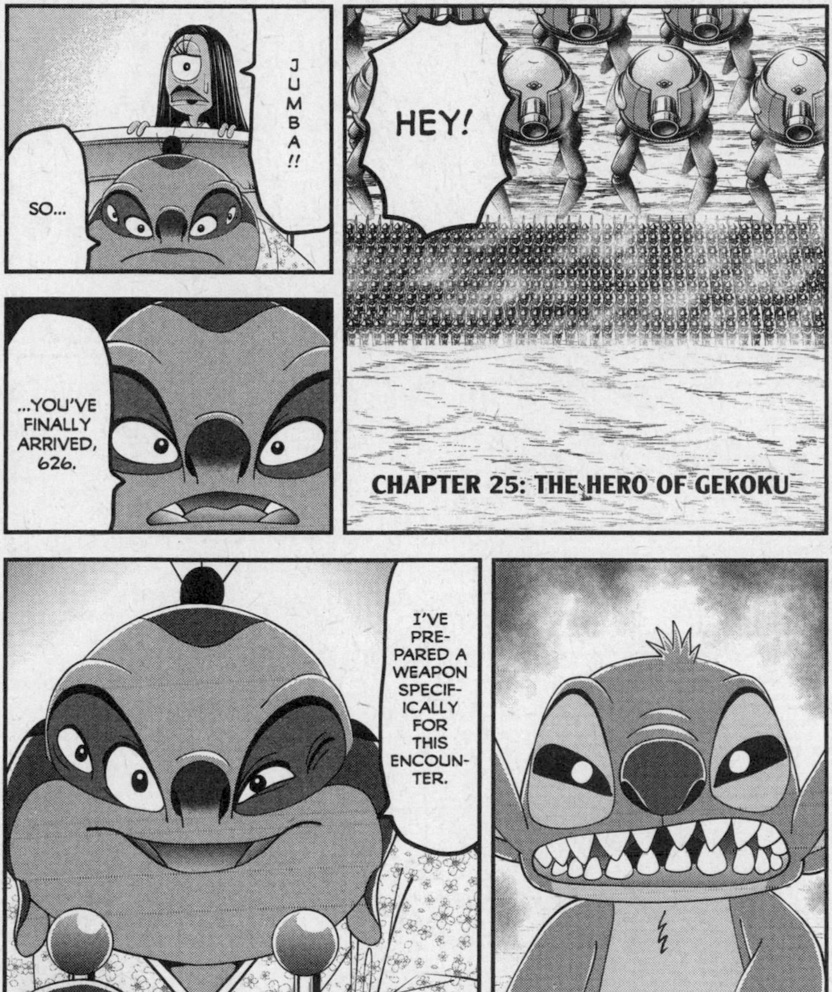
HEY!
CHAPTER 25: THE HERO OF GEKOKU
JUMBA!!
SO...
...YOU'VE FINALLY ARRIVED, 626.
I'VE PREPARED A WEAPON SPECIFICALLY FOR THIS ENCOUNTER.
TAP
ポチ

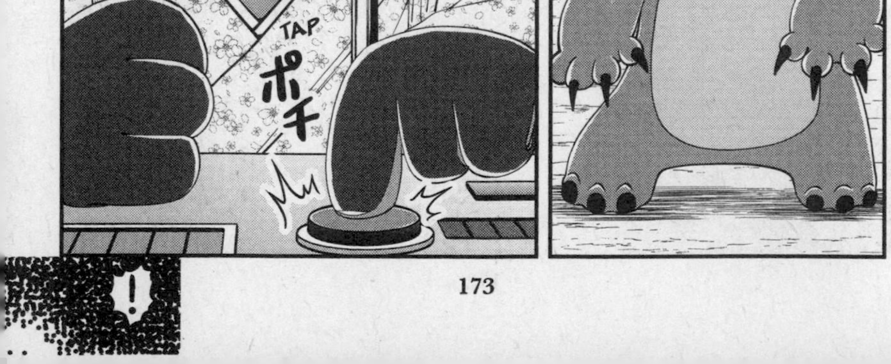
!

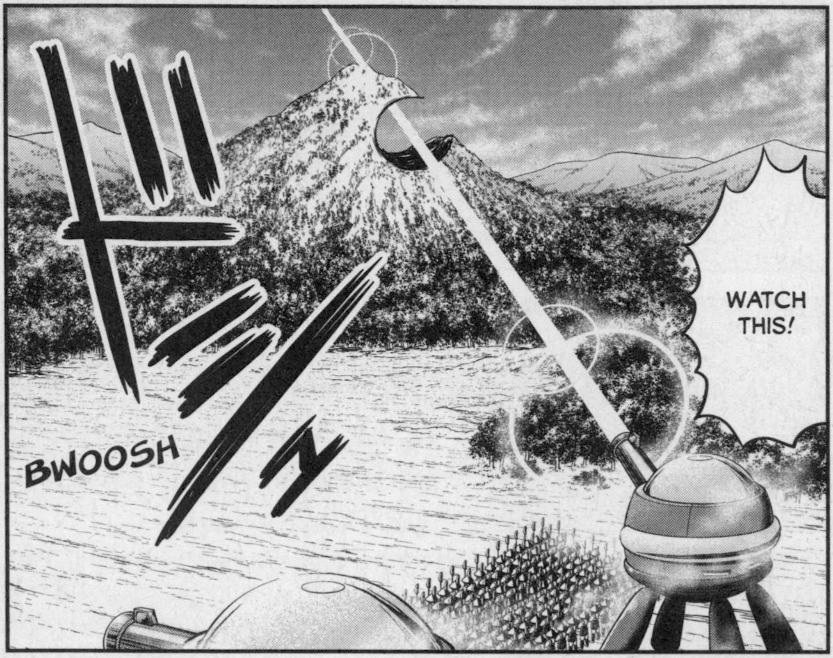
WATCH THIS!
BWOOSH

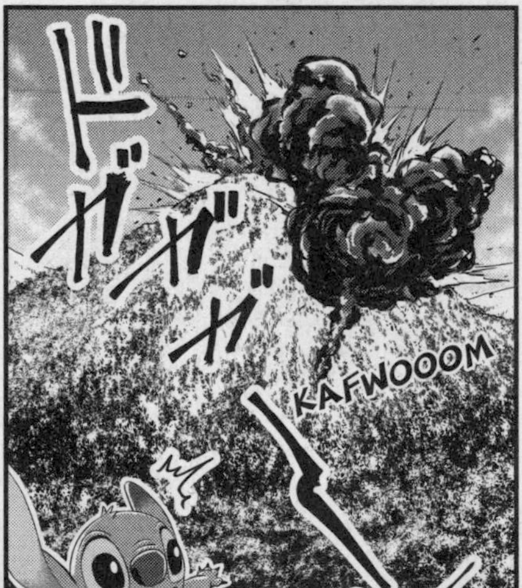
KAFWOOOM

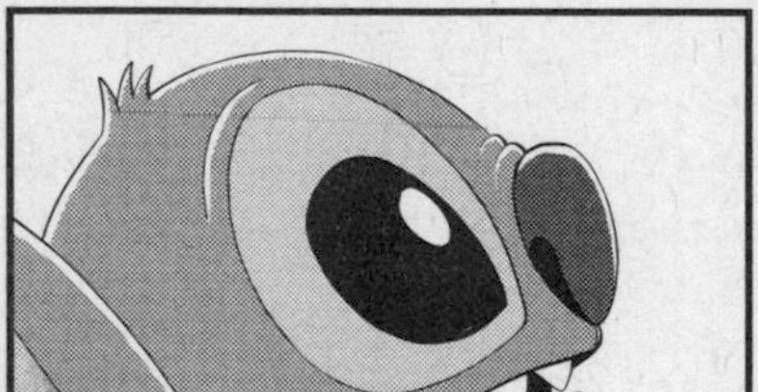

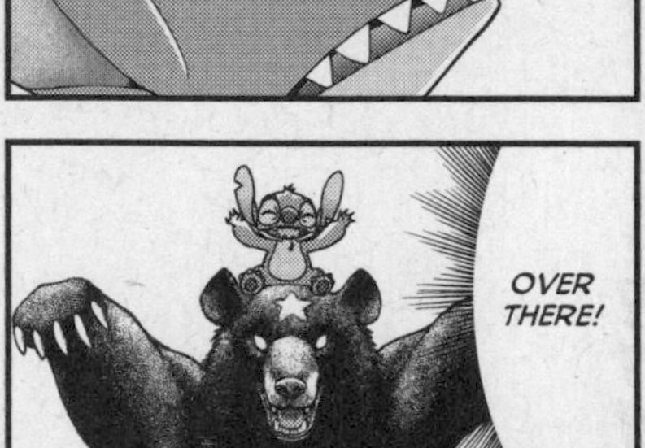
OVER THERE!

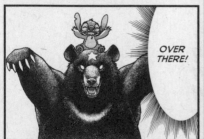

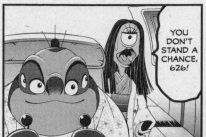

WHAT DO YOU THINK?
STILL WANT TO FIGHT US?
YOU DON'T STAND A CHANCE, 626!
GRRRRRRR!
ググググ…
JUMBA!
I'M WAITING!
SIGH
フ…

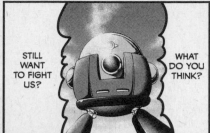

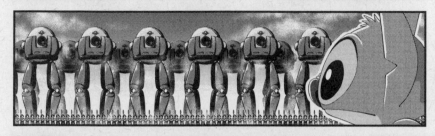

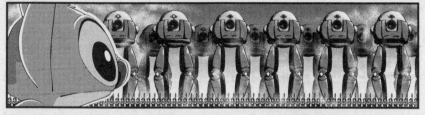

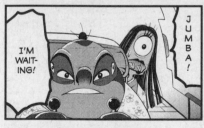

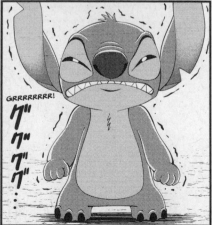

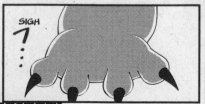

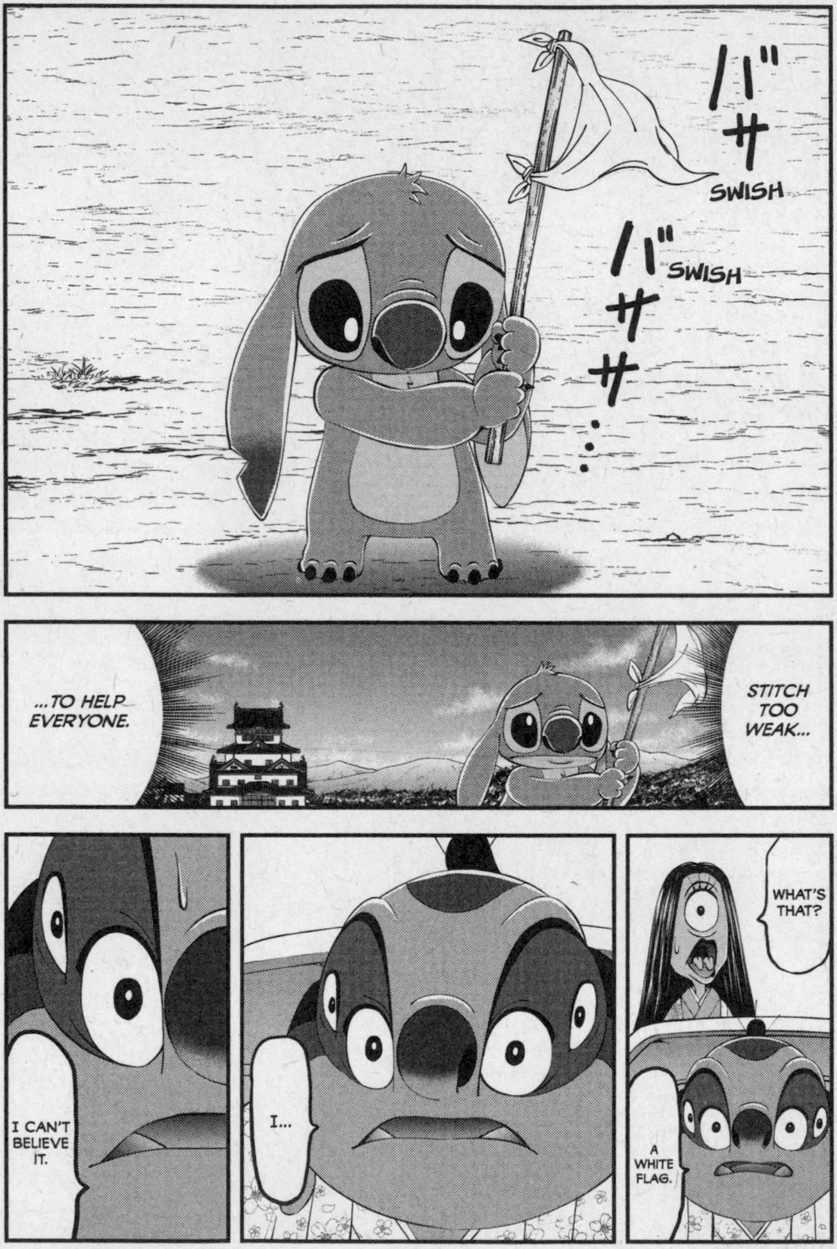
バサ
SWISH
バサササ…
SWISH
STITCH TOO WEAK...
...TO HELP EVERYONE.
WHAT'S THAT?
A WHITE FLAG.
I...
I CAN'T BELIEVE IT.

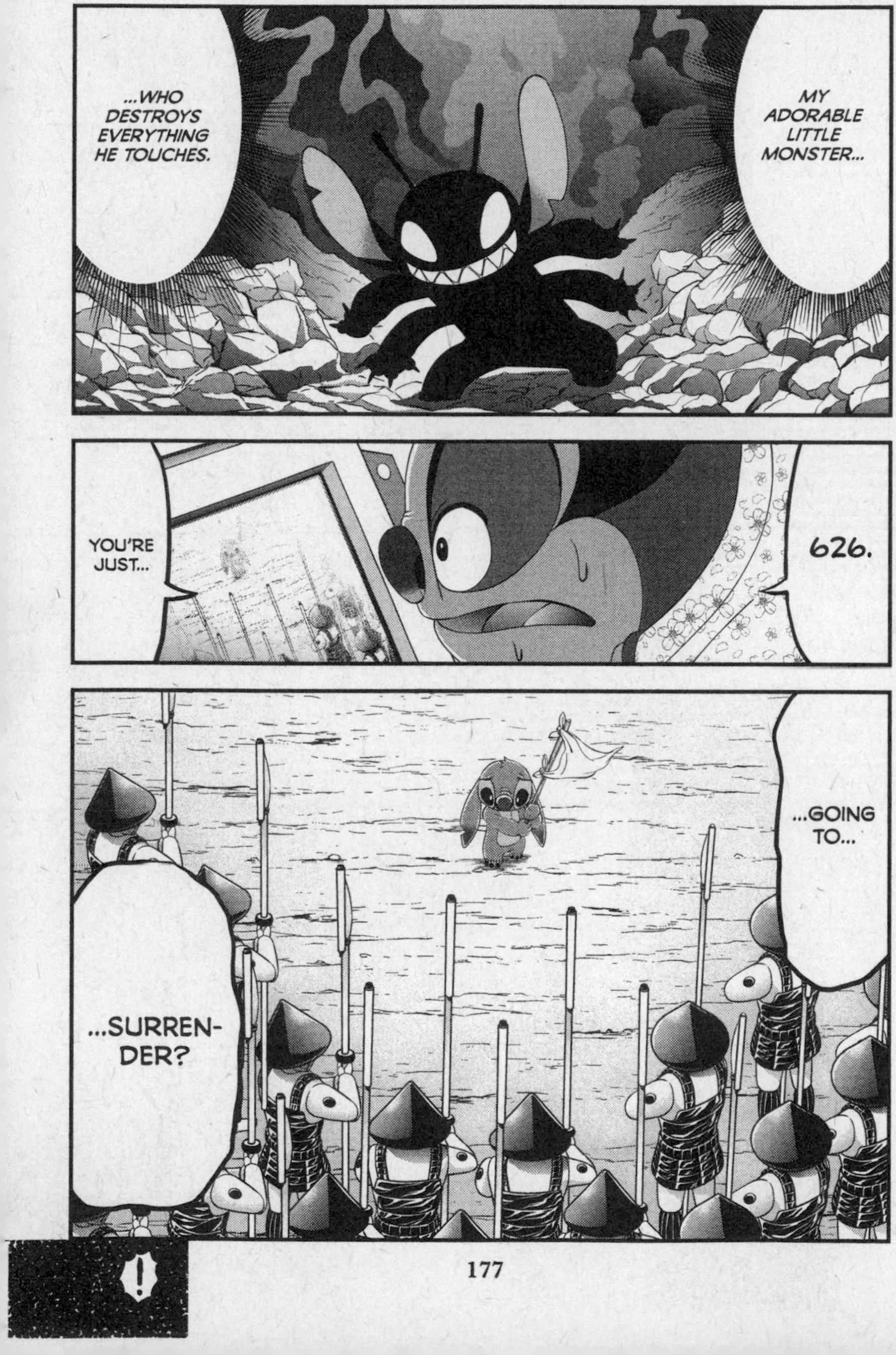
MY ADORABLE LITTLE MONSTER...
...WHO DESTROYS EVERYTHING HE TOUCHES.
626.
YOU'RE JUST...
...GOING TO...
...SURREN-DER?

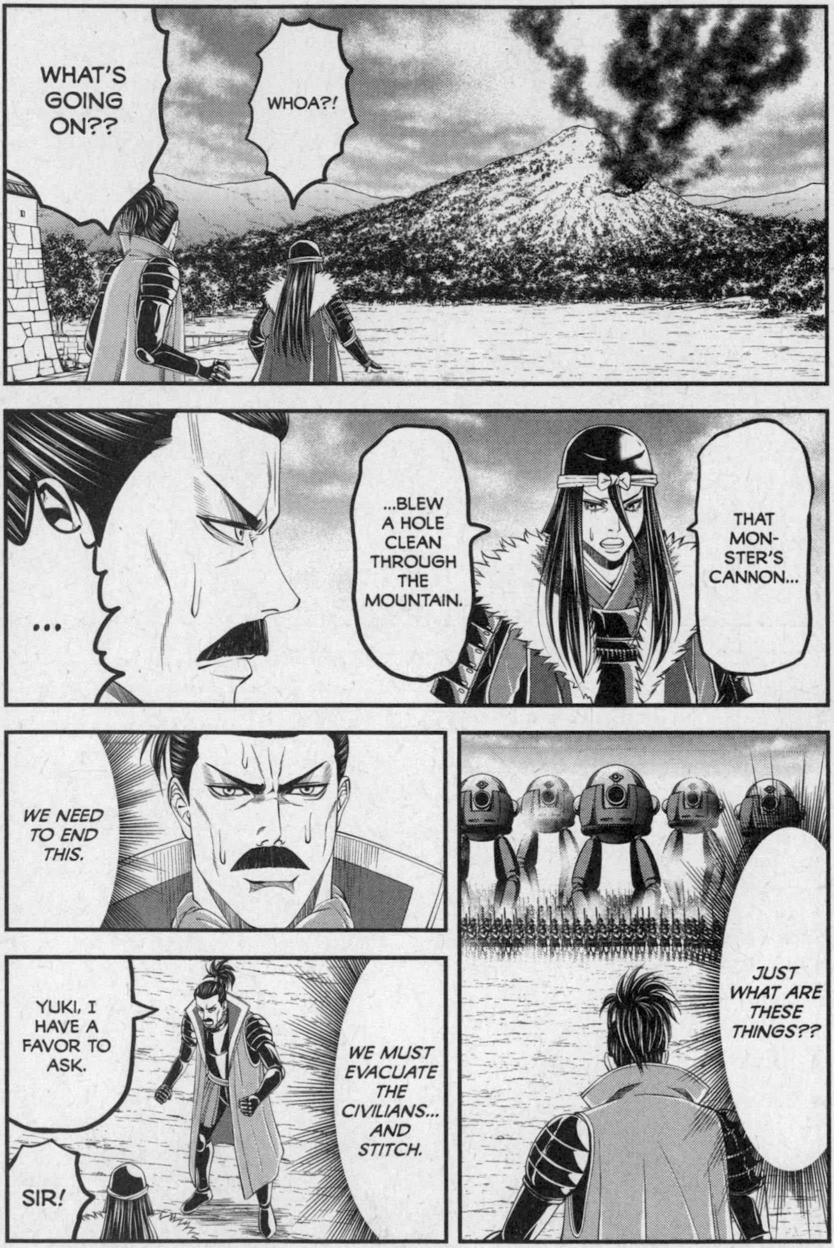
WHOA?!
WHAT'S GOING ON??
THAT MON-STER'S CANNON...
...BLEW A HOLE CLEAN THROUGH THE MOUNTAIN.
...
JUST WHAT ARE THESE THINGS??
WE NEED TO END THIS.
WE MUST EVACUATE THE CIVILIANS... AND STITCH.
YUKI, I HAVE A FAVOR TO ASK.
SIR!

STITCH?

TAKE STITCH AND...

WHERE'S STITCH?!

I... I DON'T KNOW.

626 HAS BEEN SECURED!

STITCH!!

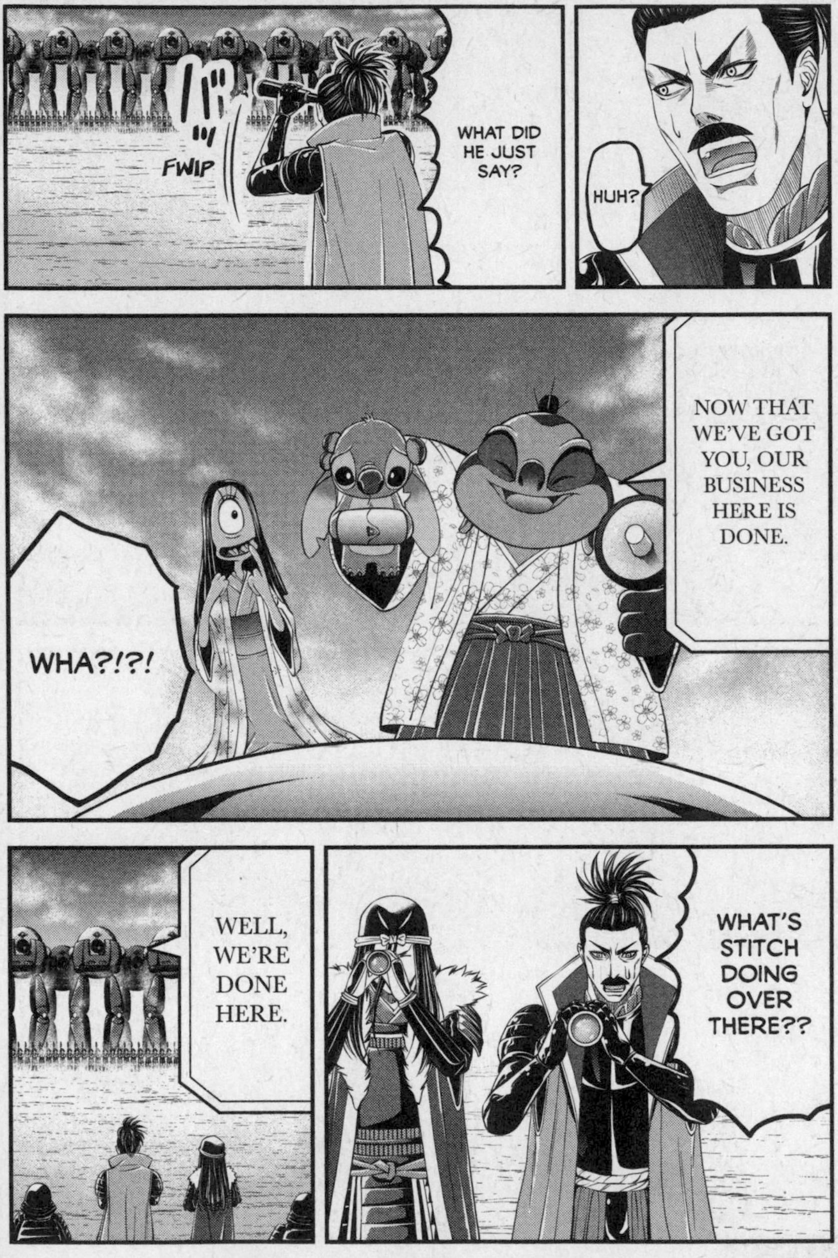
HUH?
WHAT DID HE JUST SAY?
FWIP
NOW THAT WE'VE GOT YOU, OUR BUSINESS HERE IS DONE.
WHA?!?!
WHAT'S STITCH DOING OVER THERE??
WELL, WE'RE DONE HERE.

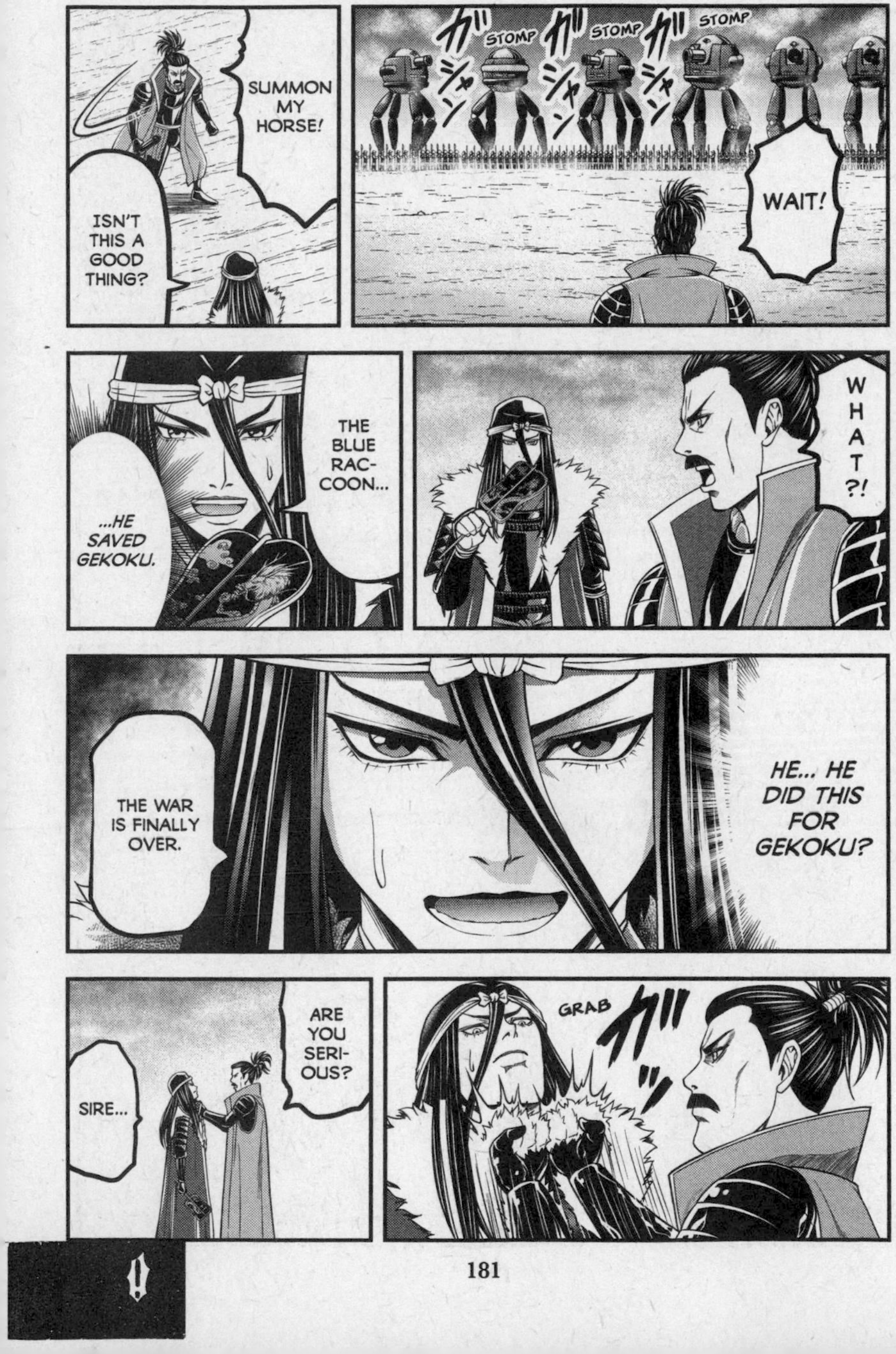
ガシャン
STOMP
ガシャン
STOMP
ガシャン
STOMP
WAIT!
SUMMON MY HORSE!
ISN'T THIS A GOOD THING?
WHAT?!
THE BLUE RACCOON...
...HE SAVED GEKOKU.
HE... HE DID THIS FOR GEKOKU?
THE WAR IS FINALLY OVER.
GRAB
ガッ
ARE YOU SERIOUS?
SIRE...

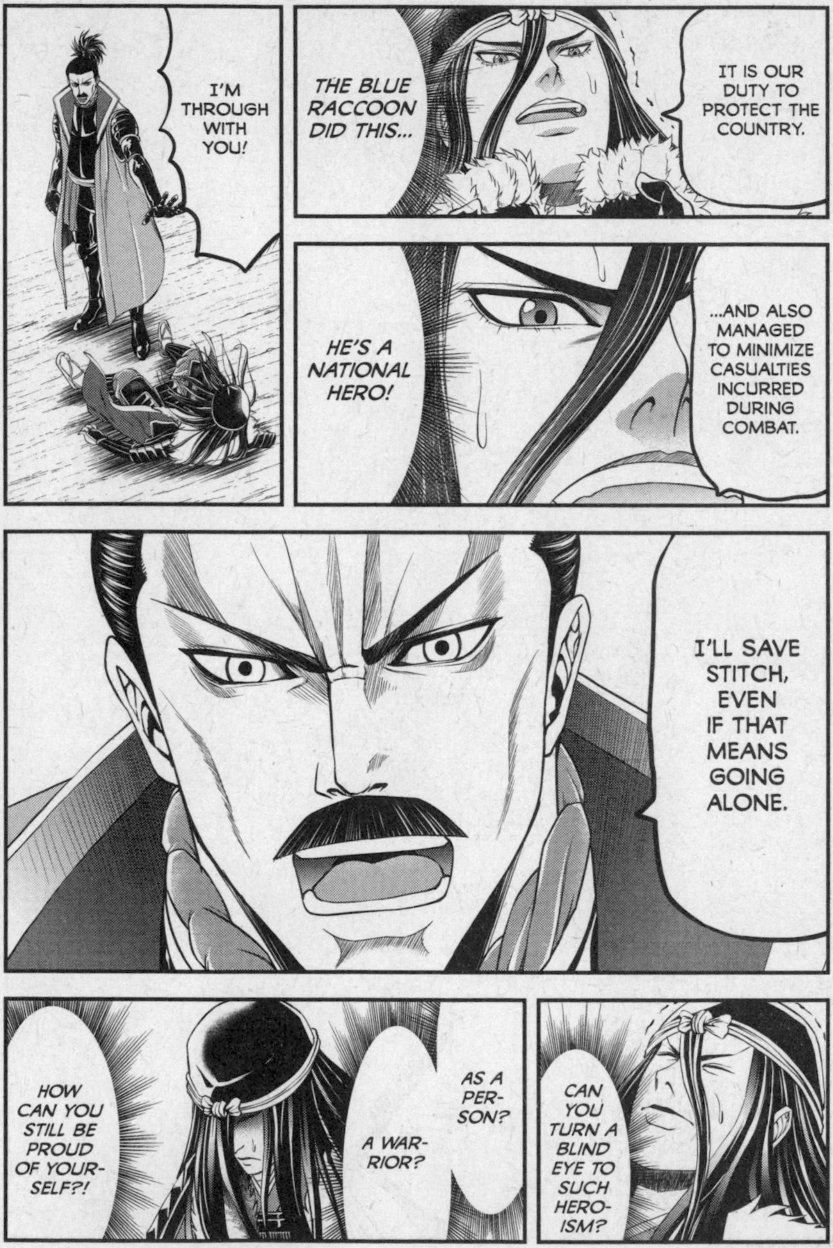
IT IS OUR DUTY TO PROTECT THE COUNTRY.
THE BLUE RACCOON DID THIS...
...AND ALSO MANAGED TO MINIMIZE CASUALTIES INCURRED DURING COMBAT.
HE'S A NATIONAL HERO!
I'M THROUGH WITH YOU!
I'LL SAVE STITCH, EVEN IF THAT MEANS GOING ALONE.
CAN YOU TURN A BLIND EYE TO SUCH HERO-ISM?
AS A PER-SON?
A WAR-RIOR?
HOW CAN YOU STILL BE PROUD OF YOUR-SELF?!

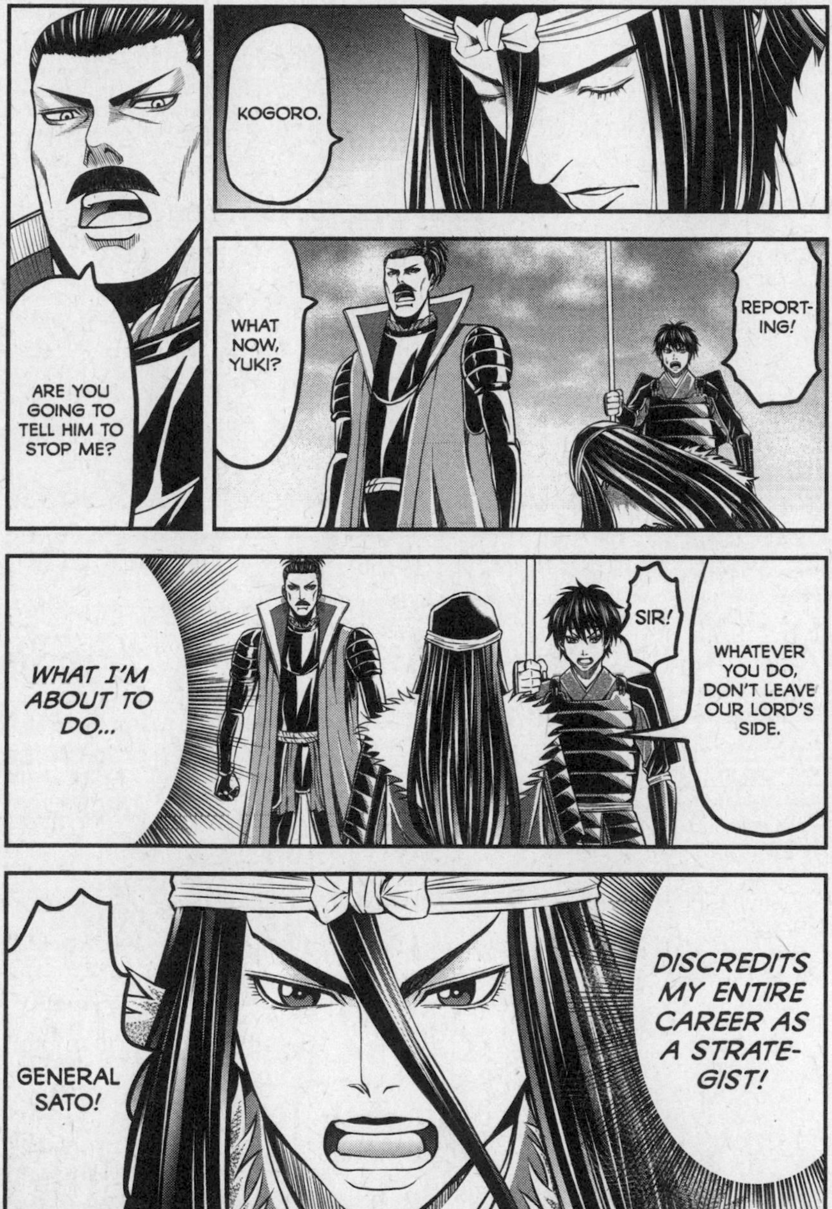
KOGORO.
REPORT-ING!
WHAT NOW, YUKI?
ARE YOU GOING TO TELL HIM TO STOP ME?
SIR!
WHATEVER YOU DO, DON'T LEAVE OUR LORD'S SIDE.
WHAT I'M ABOUT TO DO...
DISCREDITS MY ENTIRE CAREER AS A STRATE-GIST!
GENERAL SATO!

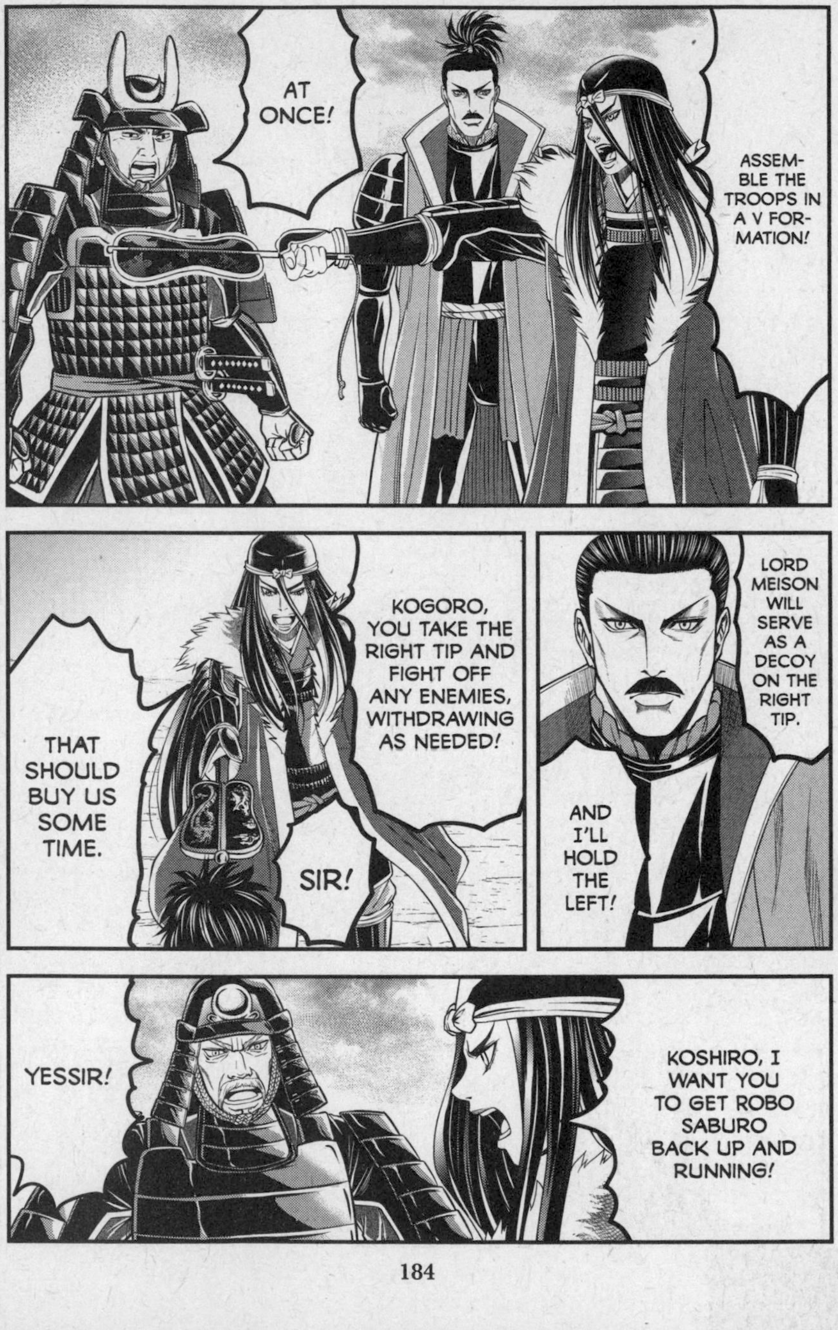
ASSEMBLE THE TROOPS IN A V FORMATION!
AT ONCE!
LORD MEISON WILL SERVE AS A DECOY ON THE RIGHT TIP.
AND I'LL HOLD THE LEFT!
KOGORO, YOU TAKE THE RIGHT TIP AND FIGHT OFF ANY ENEMIES, WITHDRAWING AS NEEDED!
SIR!
THAT SHOULD BUY US SOME TIME.
KOSHIRO, I WANT YOU TO GET ROBO SABURO BACK UP AND RUNNING!
YESSIR!

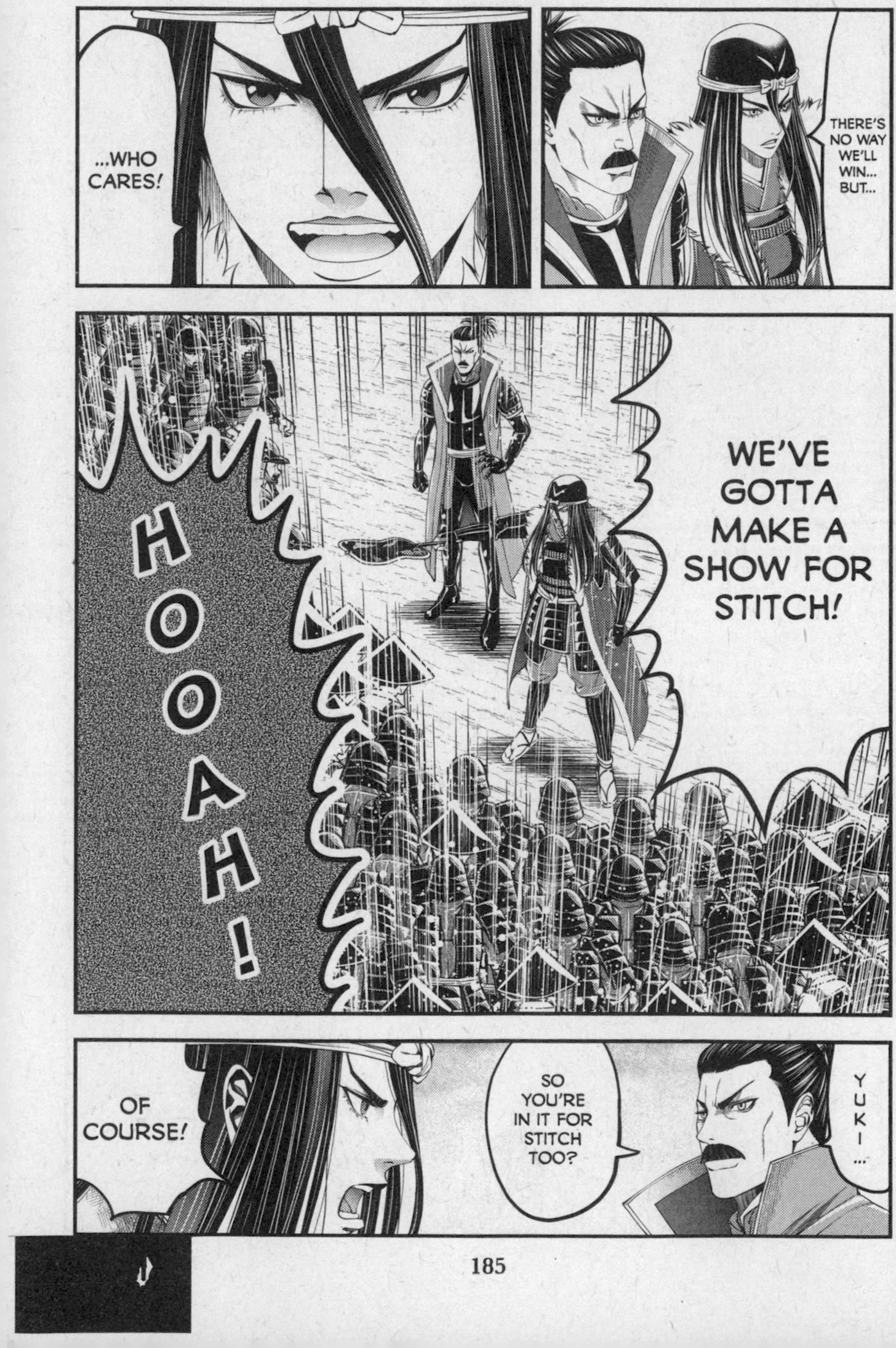
THERE'S NO WAY WE'LL WIN... BUT...
...WHO CARES!
WE'VE GOTTA MAKE A SHOW FOR STITCH!
HOOAH!
YUKI...
SO YOU'RE IN IT FOR STITCH TOO?
OF COURSE!

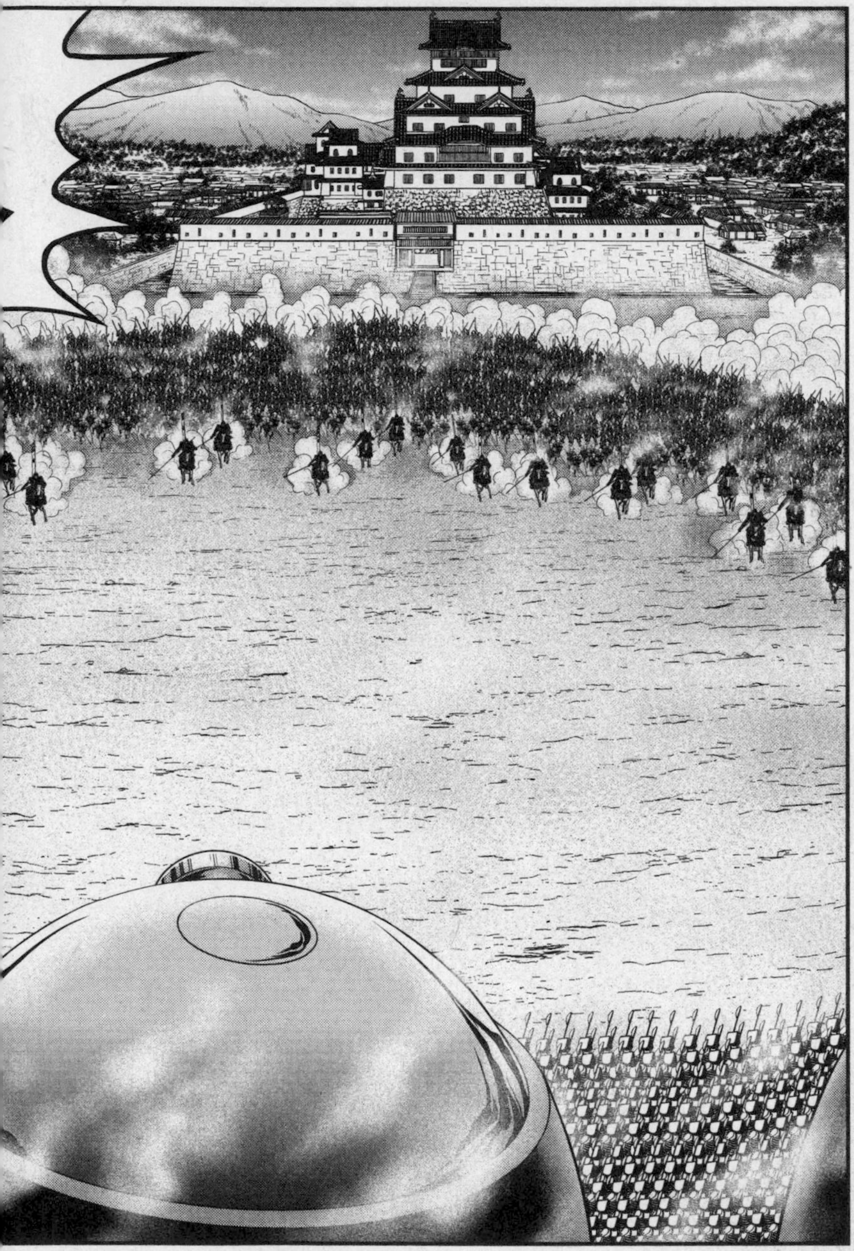

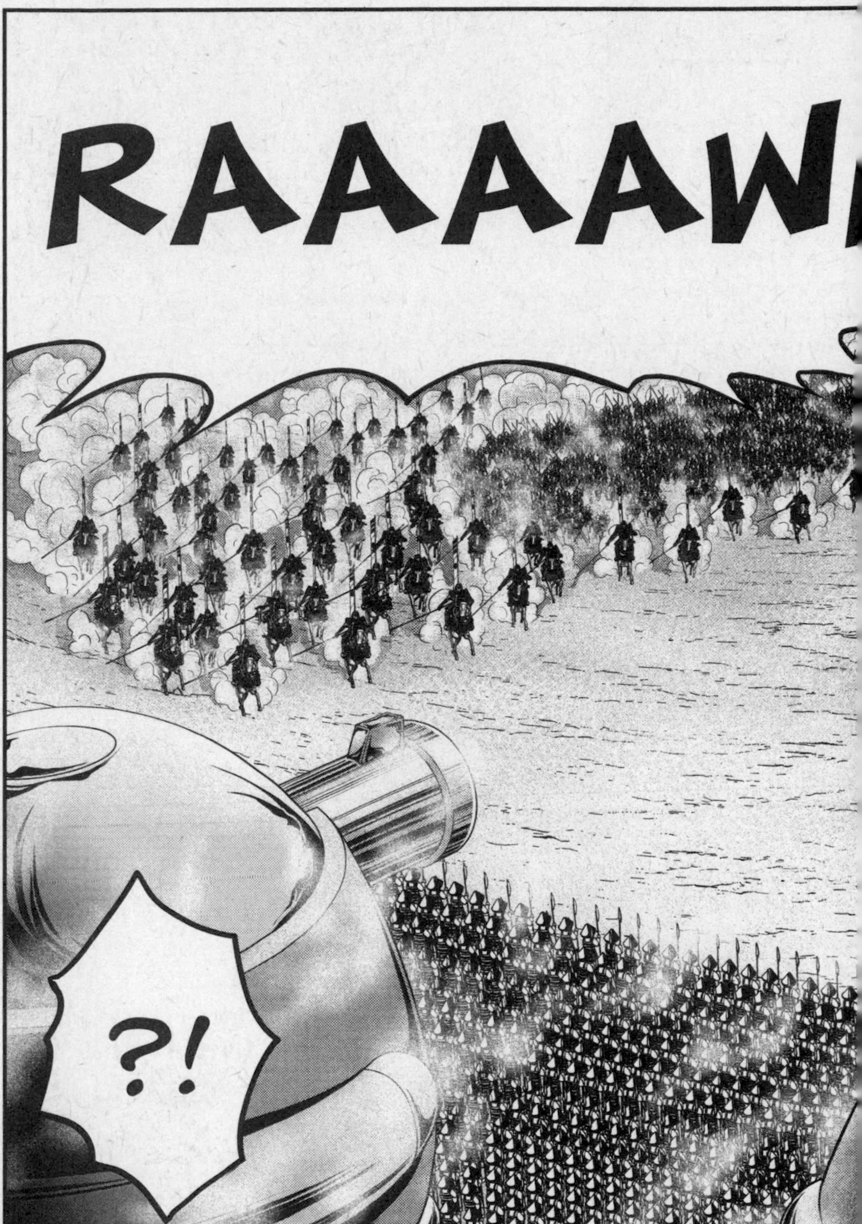
RAAAW
?!

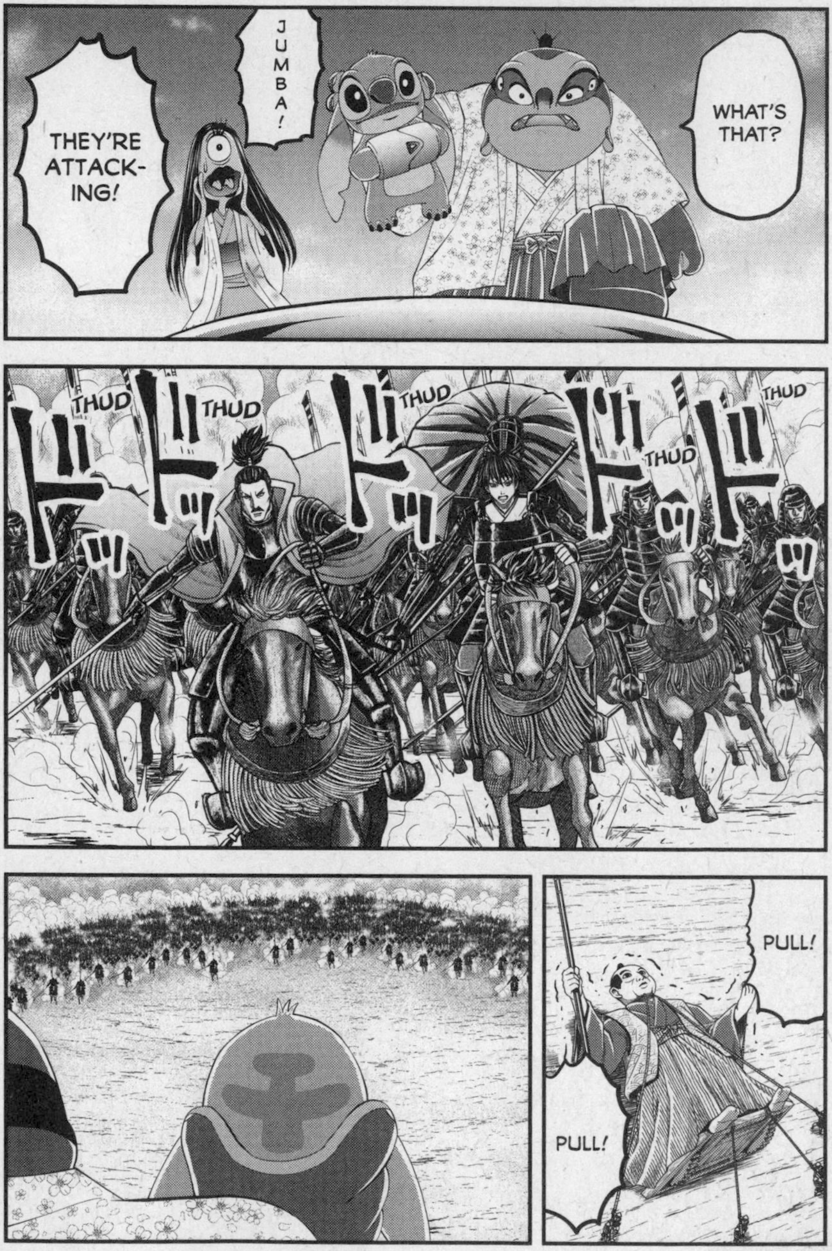
WHAT'S THAT?
JUMBA!
THEY'RE ATTACK-ING!
THUD
THUD
THUD
THUD
THUD
PULL!
PULL!

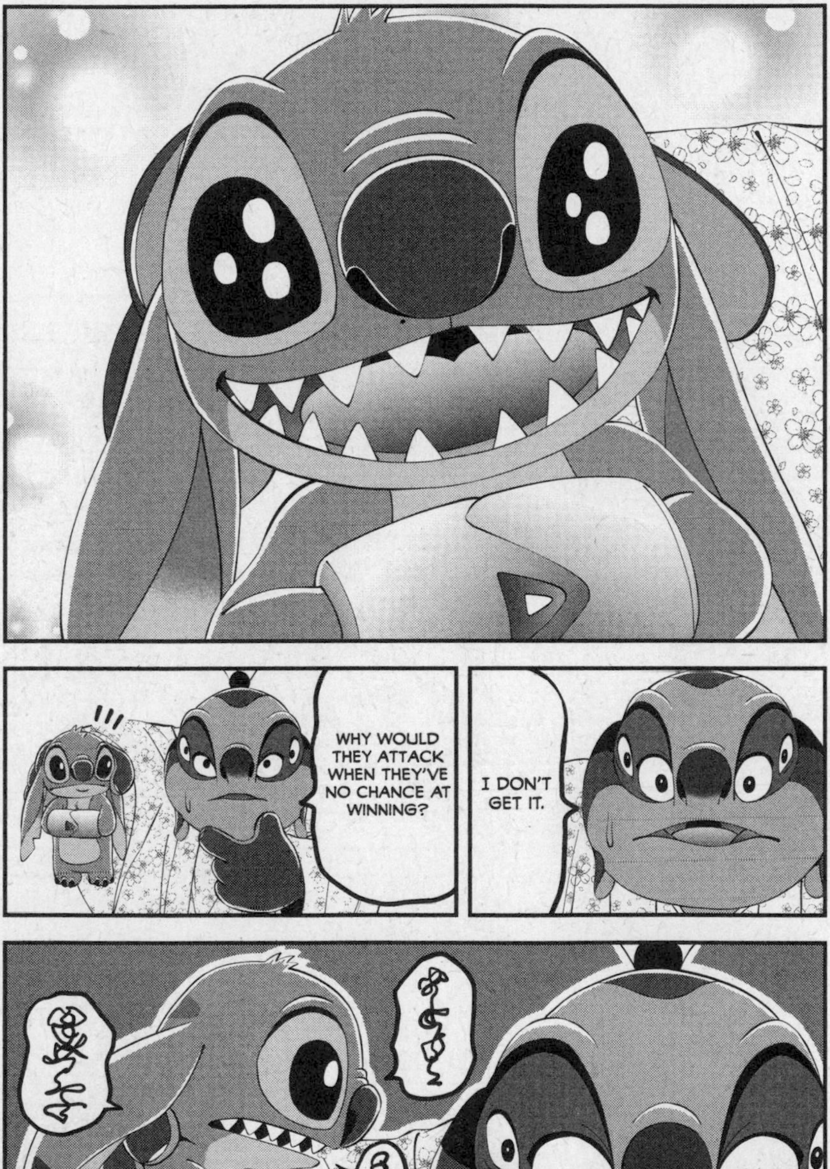
I DON'T GET IT.
WHY WOULD THEY ATTACK WHEN THEY'VE NO CHANCE AT WINNING?

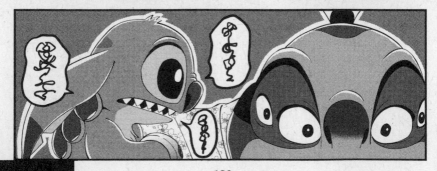

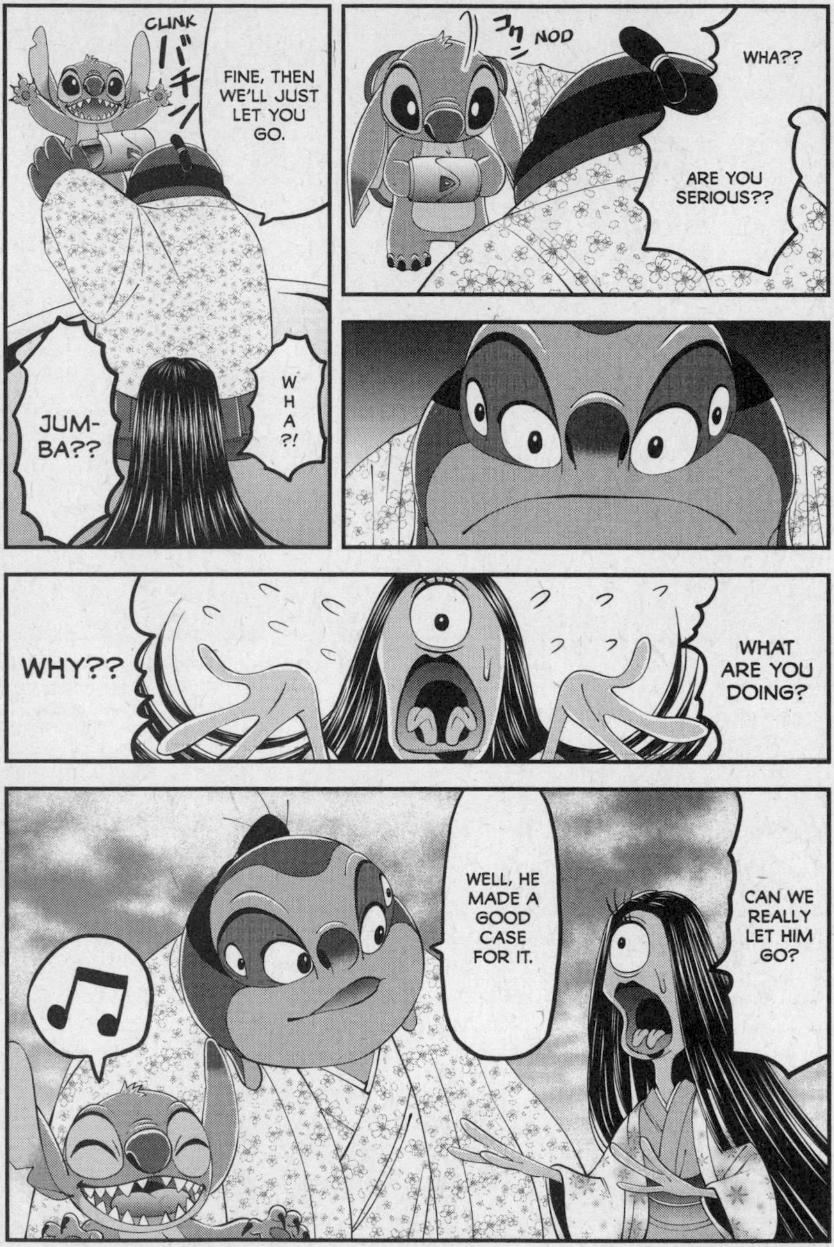
WHA??
ARE YOU SERIOUS??
コク NOD
FINE, THEN WE'LL JUST LET YOU GO.
CLINK バチン
WHA?!
JUMBA??
WHAT ARE YOU DOING?
WHY??
CAN WE REALLY LET HIM GO?
WELL, HE MADE A GOOD CASE FOR IT.
♪

...OF 626 HERE.

...THEY ALL THINK QUITE FONDLY...

IT LOOKS LIKE...

IT'S TIME TO BROKER PEACE WITH MEISON YAMATO.

HAUNG!

FLASH

ピカ

ACK!

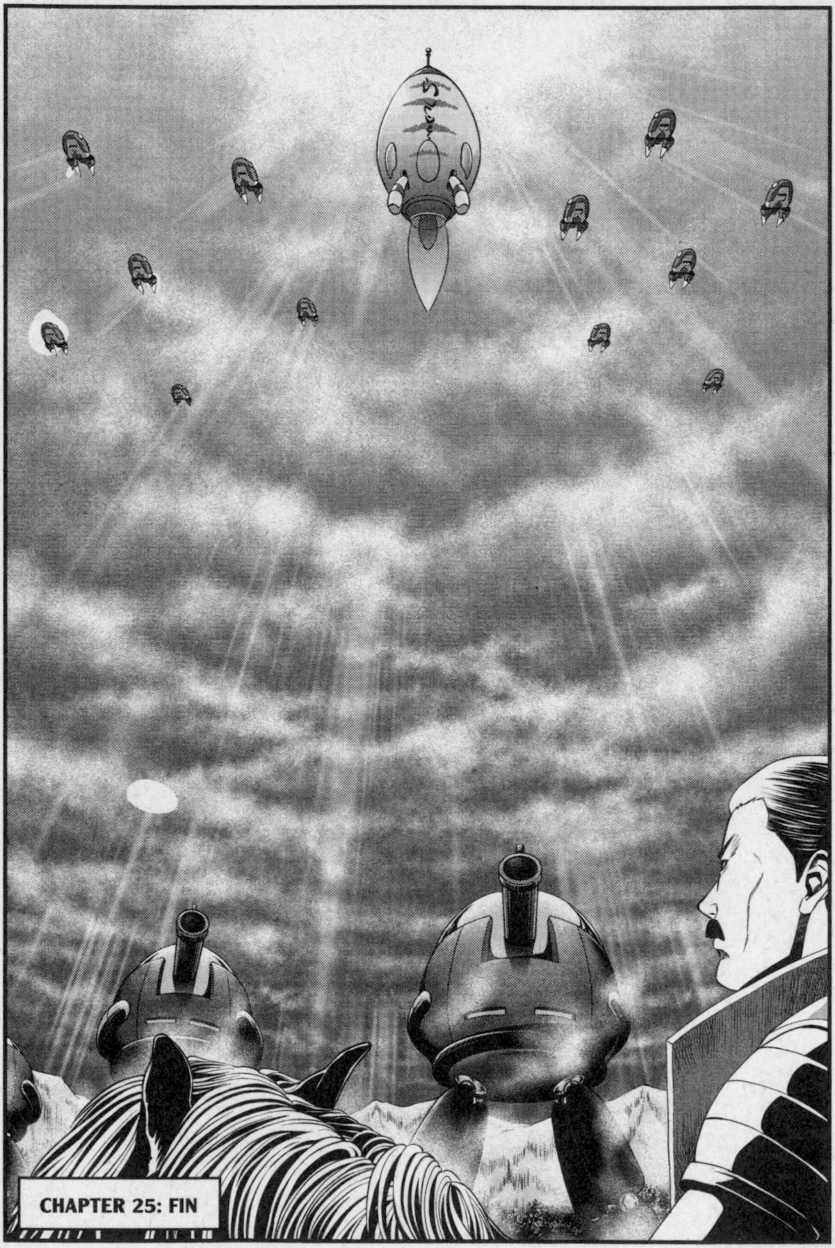
CHAPTER 25: FIN

CLIMAX

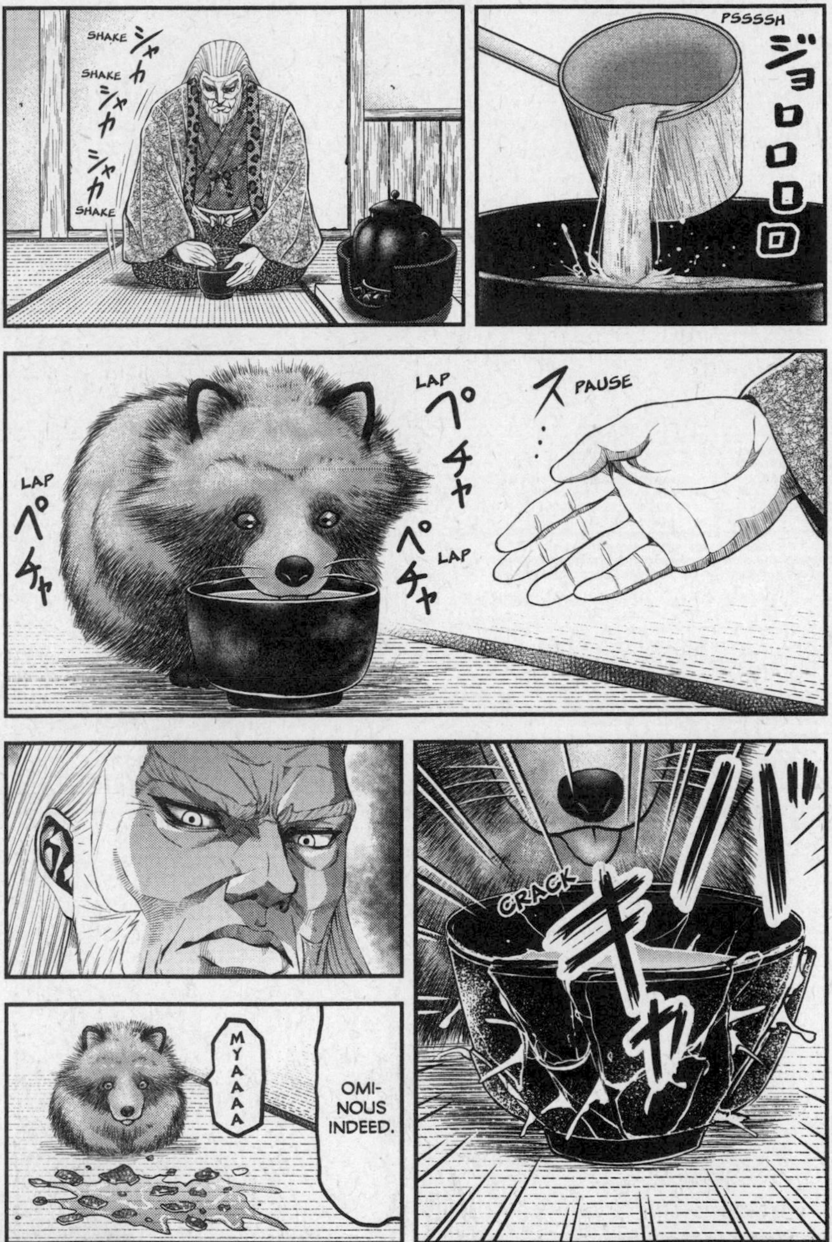
PSSSSH
ジョロロロロ
SHAKE
シャカ
SHAKE
シャカ
シャカ
SHAKE
PAUSE
ス…
LAP
ペチャ
LAP
ペチャ
LAP
ペチャ
CRACK
バキ
MYAAAA
OMINOUS INDEED.

Disney

Stitch

STITCH & THE SAMURAI

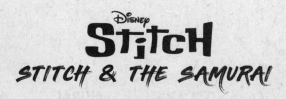

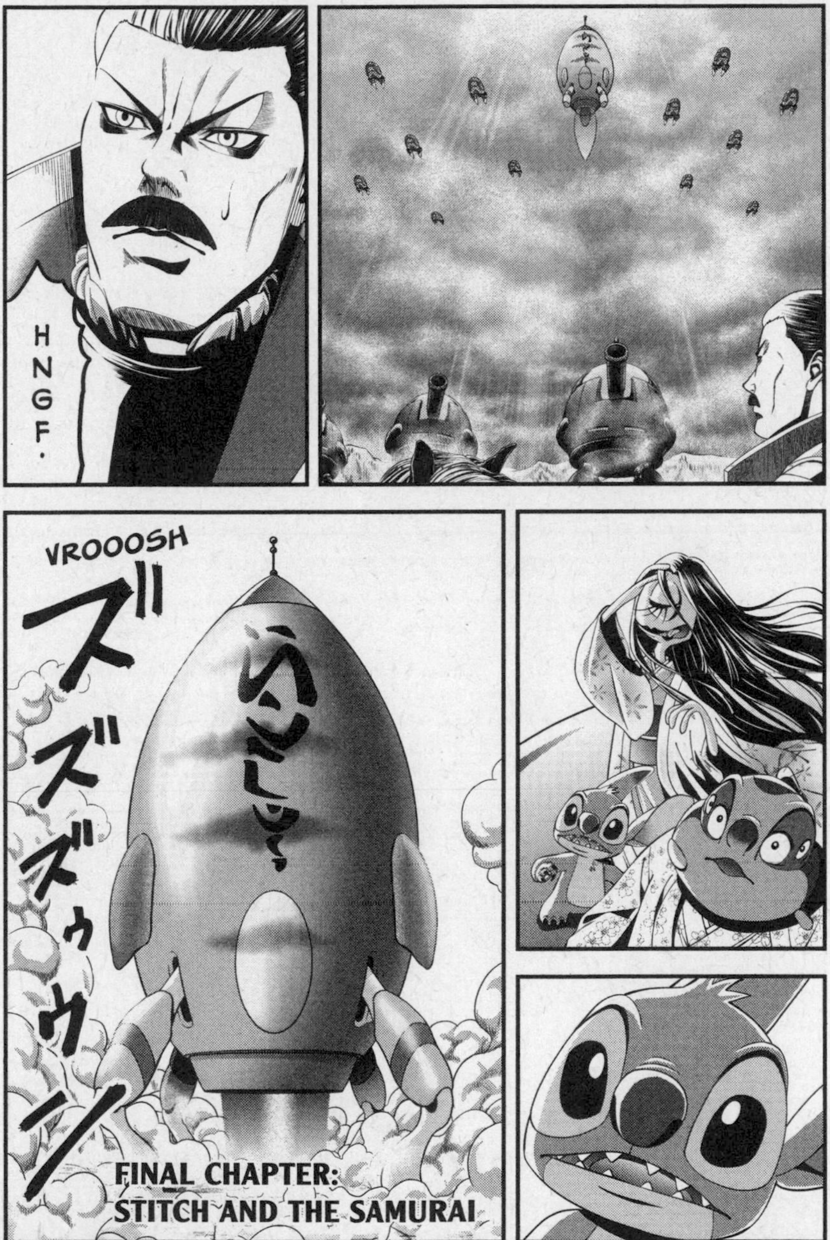
HNGF.
VROOOSH
ズズズゥウン
FINAL CHAPTER:
STITCH AND THE SAMURAI

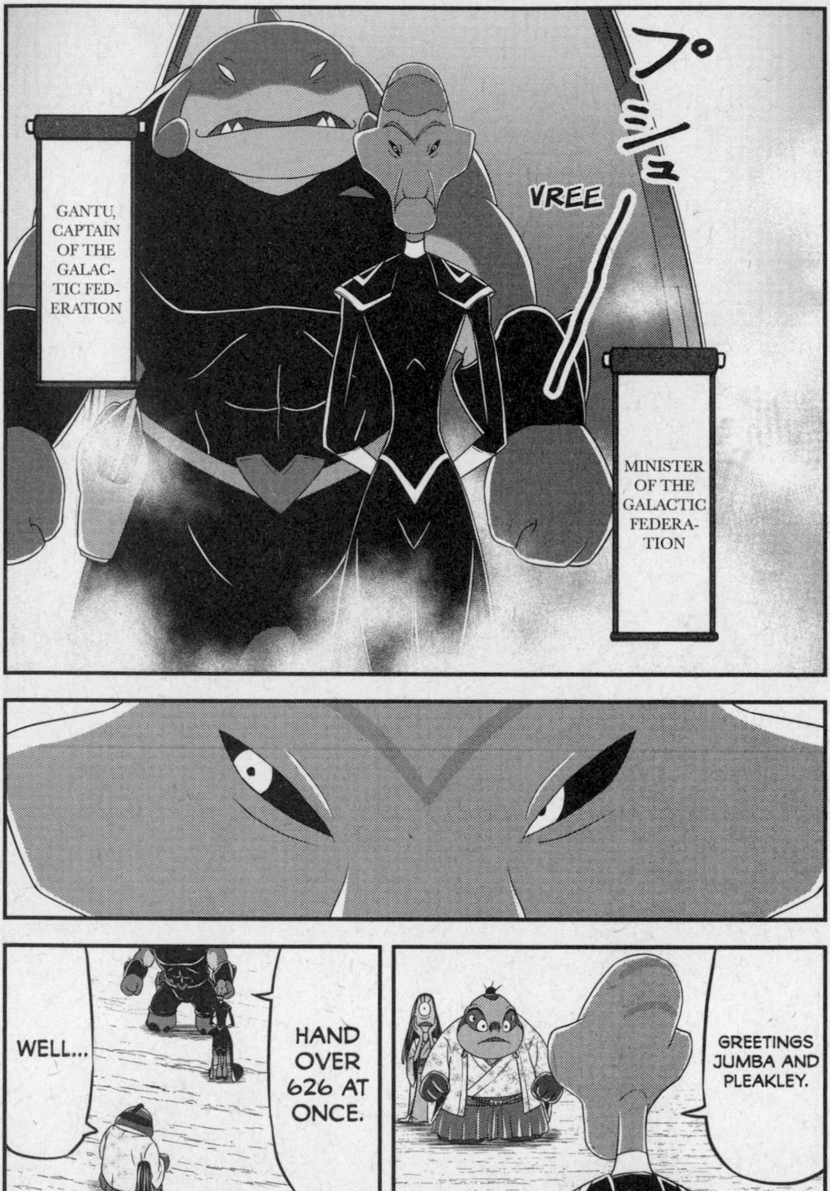
プシュ
VREE
GANTU, CAPTAIN OF THE GALACTIC FEDERATION
MINISTER OF THE GALACTIC FEDERATION
GREETINGS JUMBA AND PLEAKLEY.
HAND OVER 626 AT ONCE.
WELL...

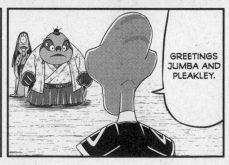

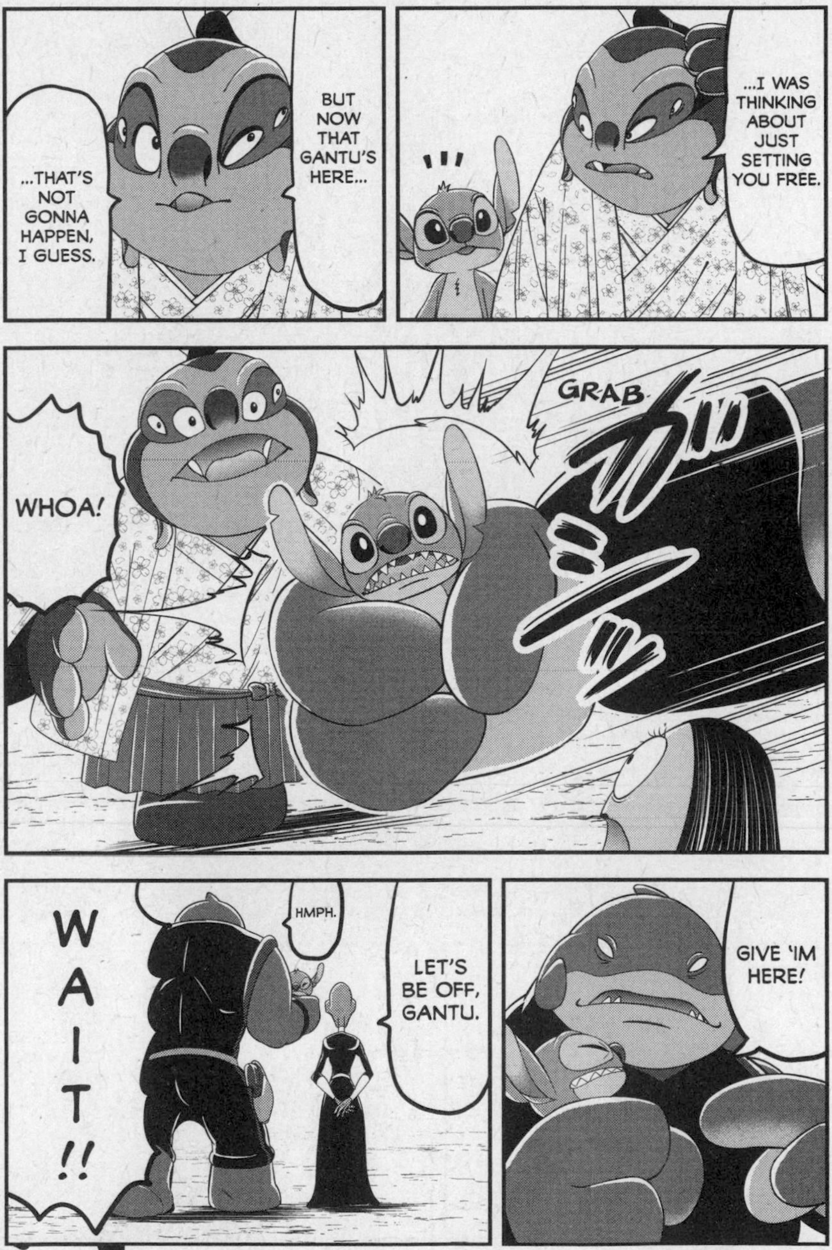
...I WAS THINKING ABOUT JUST SETTING YOU FREE.
BUT NOW THAT GANTU'S HERE...
...THAT'S NOT GONNA HAPPEN, I GUESS.
GRAB
WHOA!
GIVE 'IM HERE!
HMPH.
LET'S BE OFF, GANTU.
WAIT!!

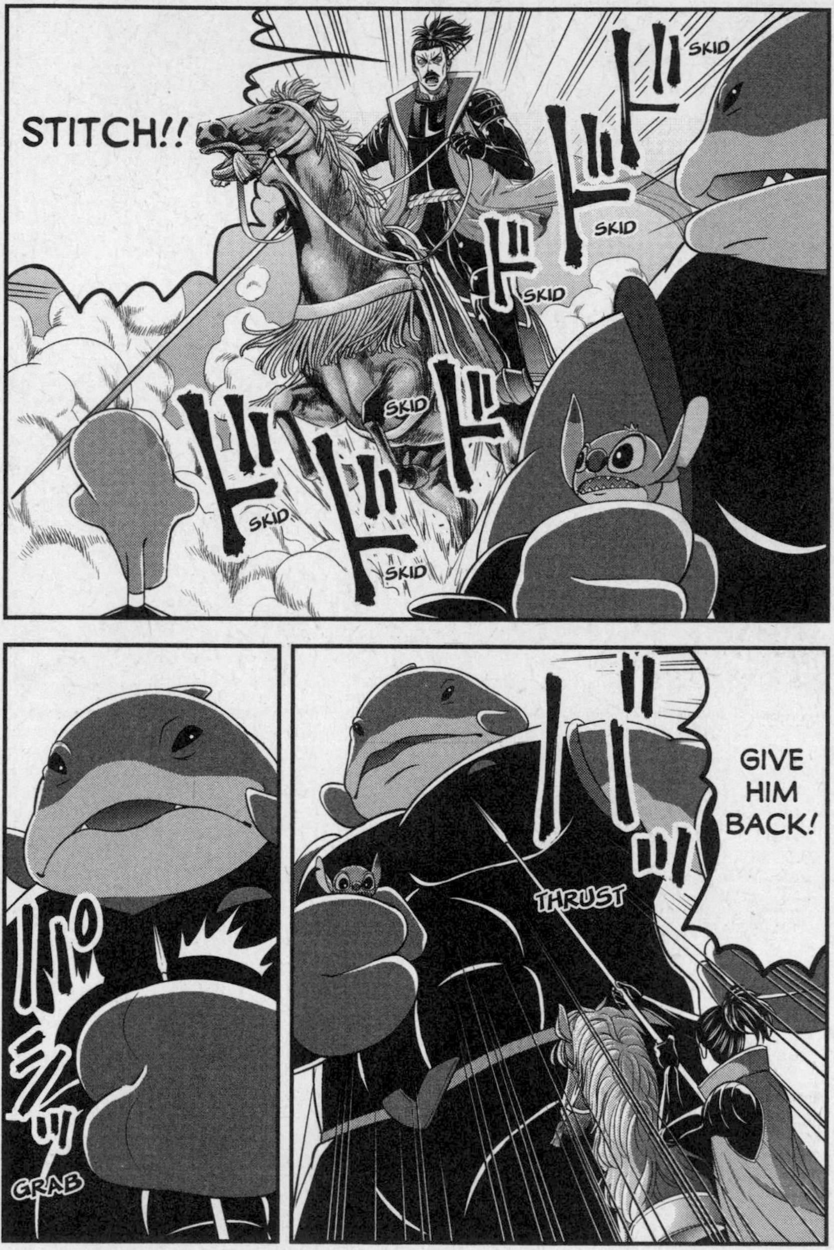
SKID
STITCH!!
SKID
SKID
SKID
SKID
SKID
GIVE HIM BACK!
THRUST
GRAB

WHO ARE YOU?!

AUNGH!

グイッ

YANK

THUD THUD THUD THUD THUD THUD THUD

WE'RE HERE TO SAVE YOU, M'LORD!

THAT'S WHAT THEY CALL 626.

BUT WHY ARE THEY COMING TO SAVE HIM?

I SEE.

WHAT'S THAT?

STITCH?

199

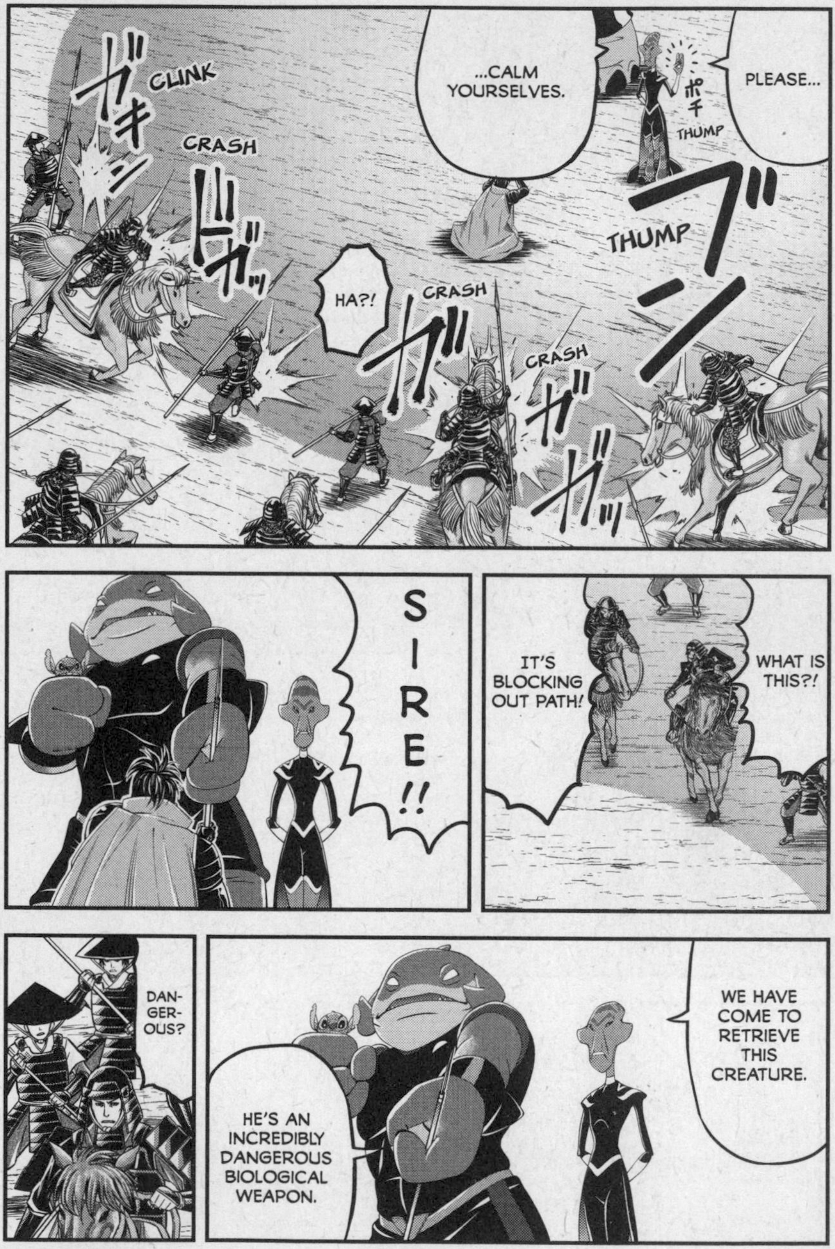
PLEASE...
ポチ
THUMP
...CALM YOURSELVES.
ブン
THUMP
ガキン
CLINK
CRASH
ドガッ
HA?!
CRASH
ガッ
CRASH
ガガッ
WHAT IS THIS?!
IT'S BLOCKING OUT PATH!
SIRE!!
WE HAVE COME TO RETRIEVE THIS CREATURE.
HE'S AN INCREDIBLY DANGEROUS BIOLOGICAL WEAPON.
DAN-GER-OUS?

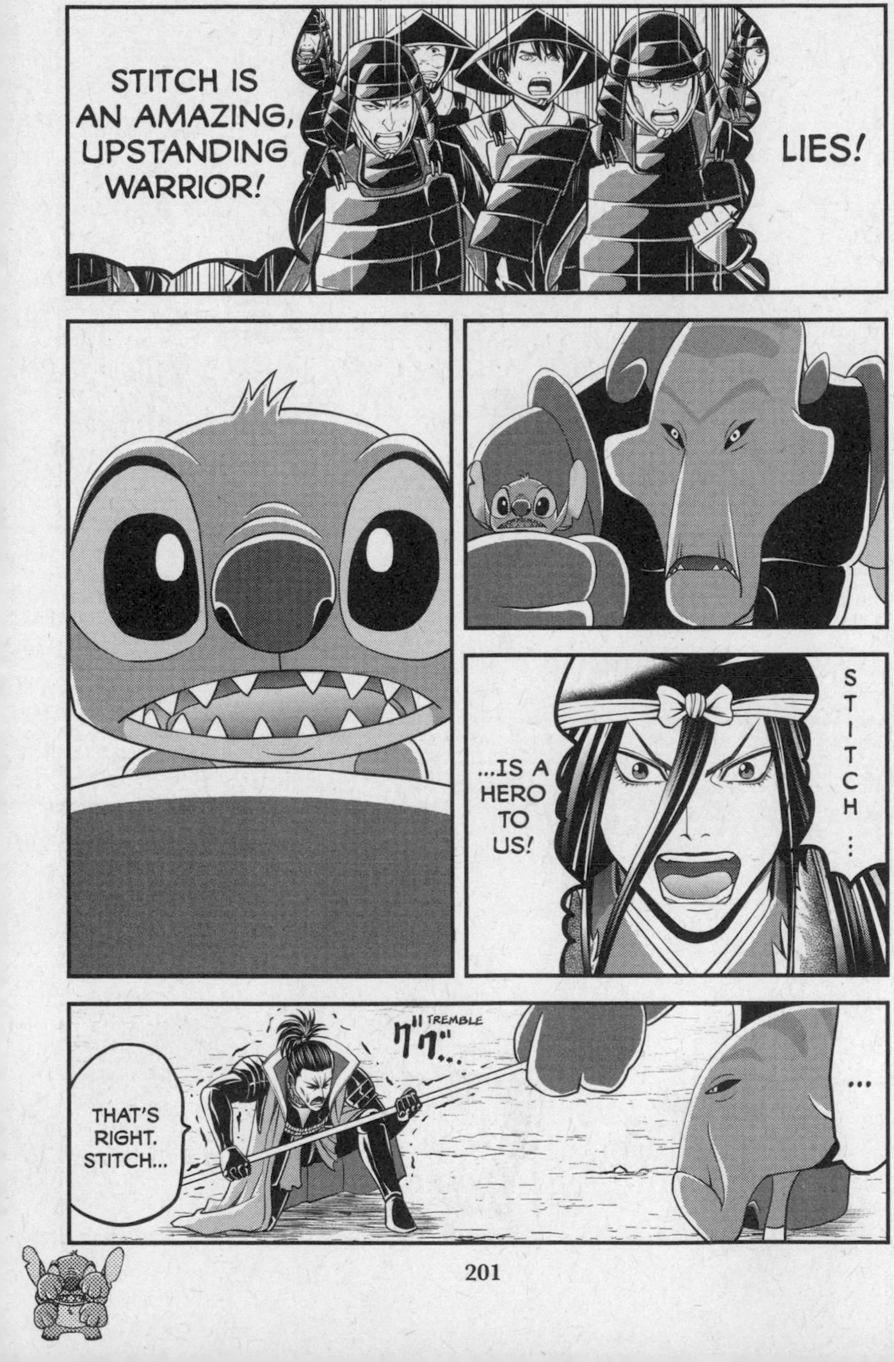
STITCH IS AN AMAZING, UPSTANDING WARRIOR!
LIES!
STITCH...
...IS A HERO TO US!
...
ググ...
TREMBLE
THAT'S RIGHT. STITCH...

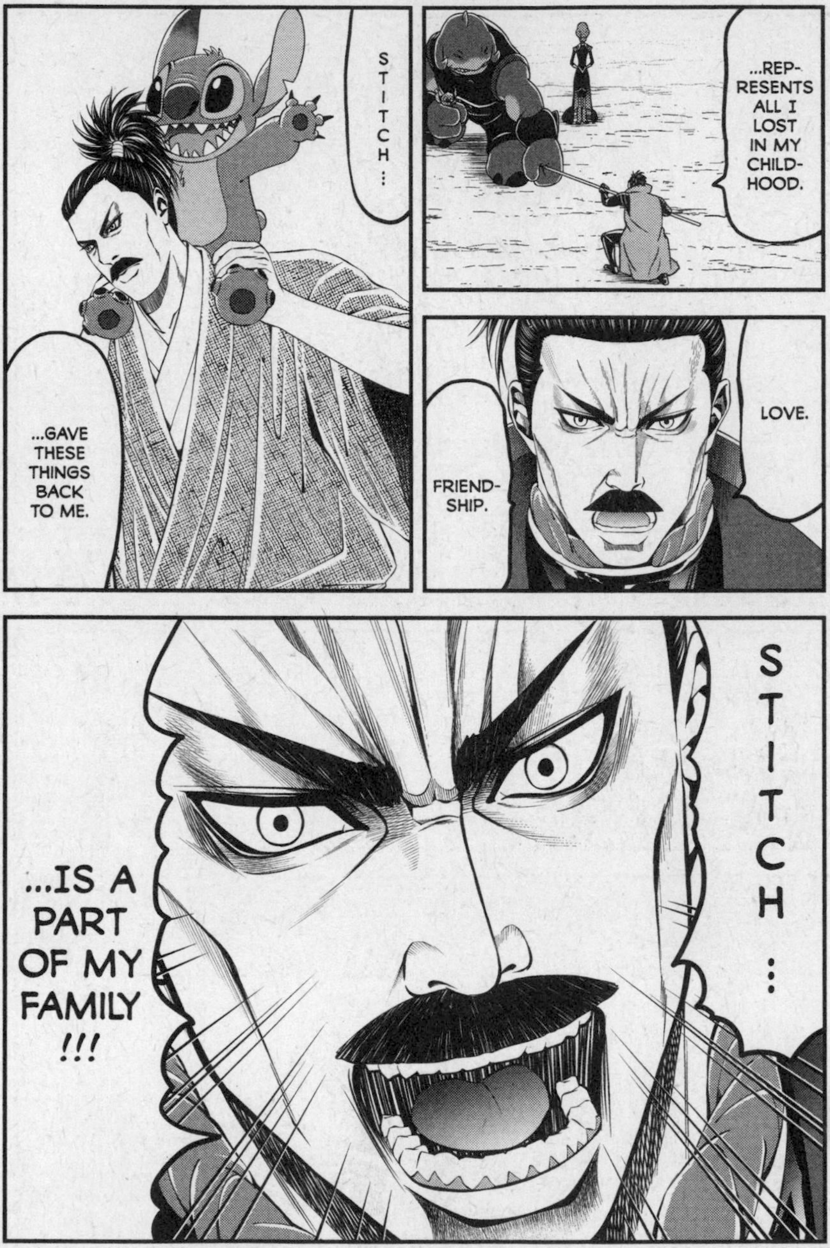
...REP-RESENTS ALL I LOST IN MY CHILD-HOOD.
LOVE.
FRIEND-SHIP.
STITCH...
...GAVE THESE THINGS BACK TO ME.
STITCH...
...IS A PART OF MY FAMILY!!!

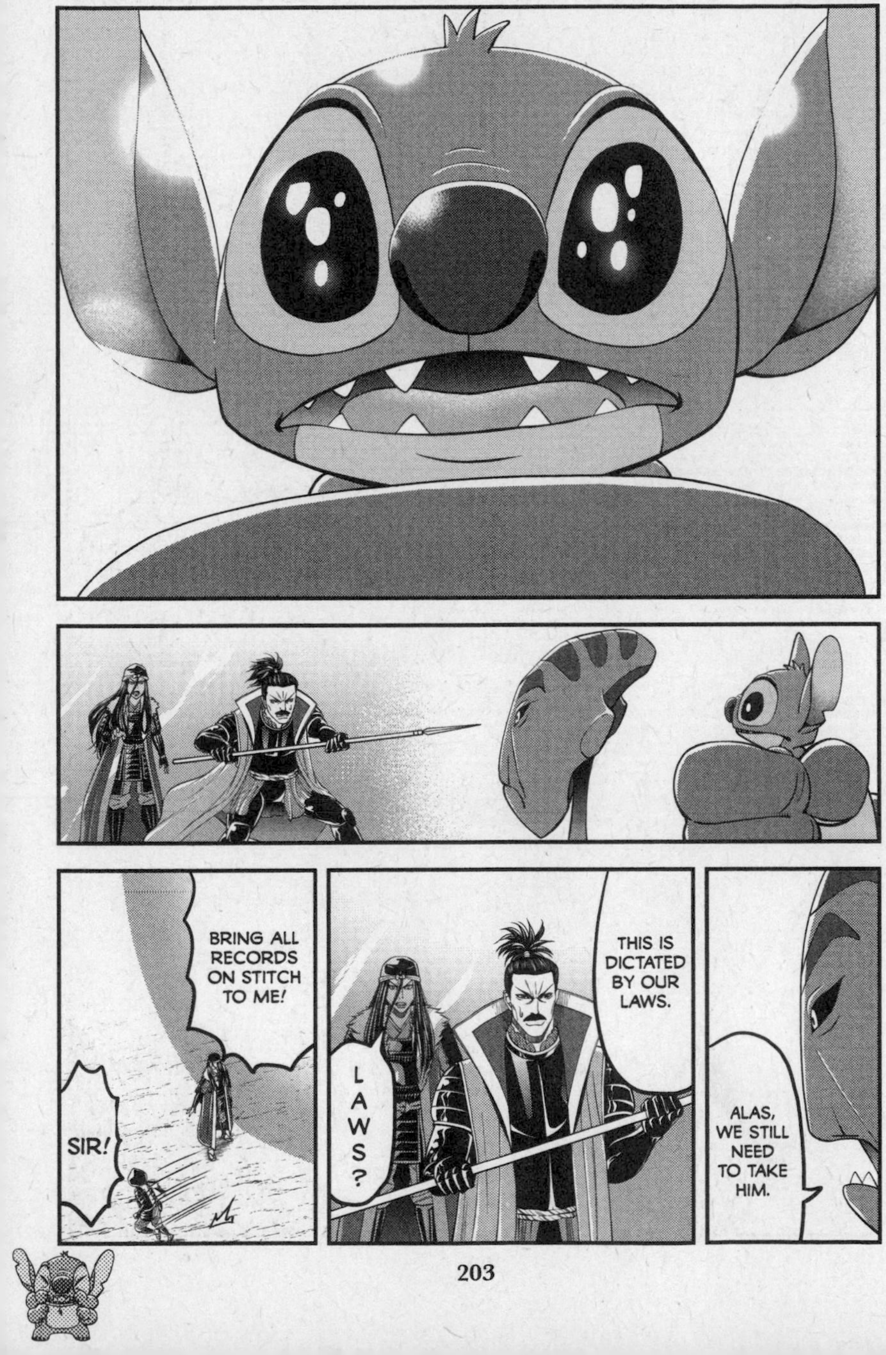
ALAS, WE STILL NEED TO TAKE HIM.
THIS IS DICTATED BY OUR LAWS.
LAWS?
BRING ALL RECORDS ON STITCH TO ME!
SIR!

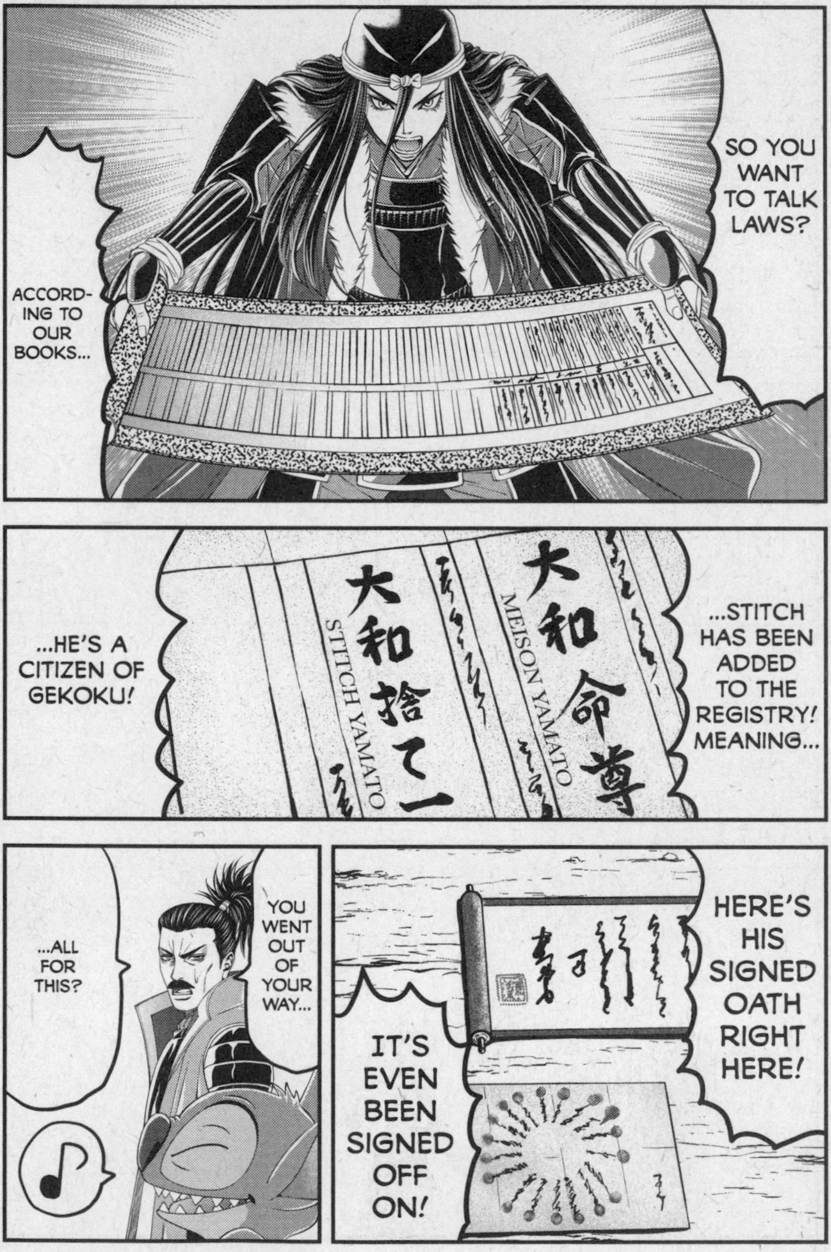
SO YOU WANT TO TALK LAWS?
ACCORDING TO OUR BOOKS...
...STITCH HAS BEEN ADDED TO THE REGISTRY! MEANING...
大和命尊
MEISON YAMATO
大和捨て一
STITCH YAMATO
...HE'S A CITIZEN OF GEKOKU!
HERE'S HIS SIGNED OATH RIGHT HERE!
IT'S EVEN BEEN SIGNED OFF ON!
YOU WENT OUT OF YOUR WAY...
...ALL FOR THIS?
♪

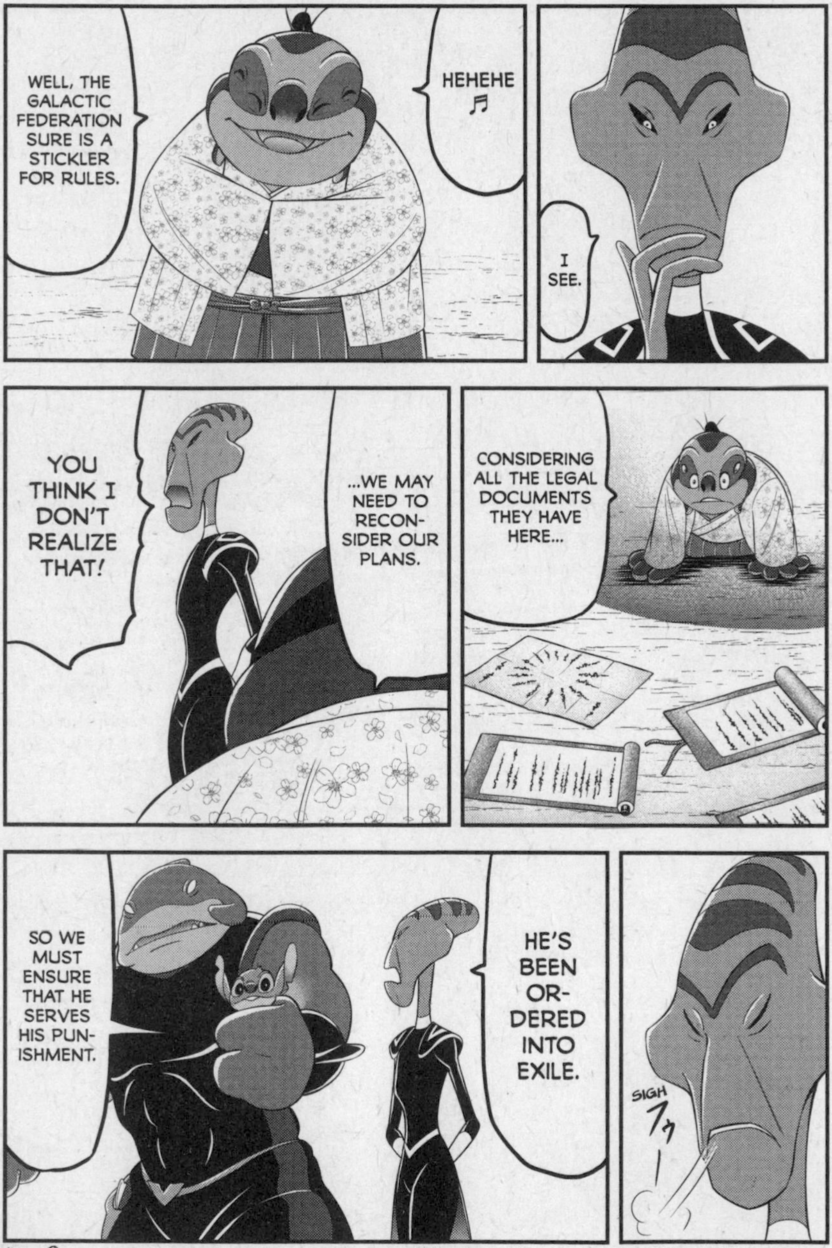
I SEE.
HEHEHE ♬
WELL, THE GALACTIC FEDERATION SURE IS A STICKLER FOR RULES.
CONSIDERING ALL THE LEGAL DOCUMENTS THEY HAVE HERE...
...WE MAY NEED TO RECONSIDER OUR PLANS.
YOU THINK I DON'T REALIZE THAT!
SIGH
HE'S BEEN ORDERED INTO EXILE.
SO WE MUST ENSURE THAT HE SERVES HIS PUNISHMENT.

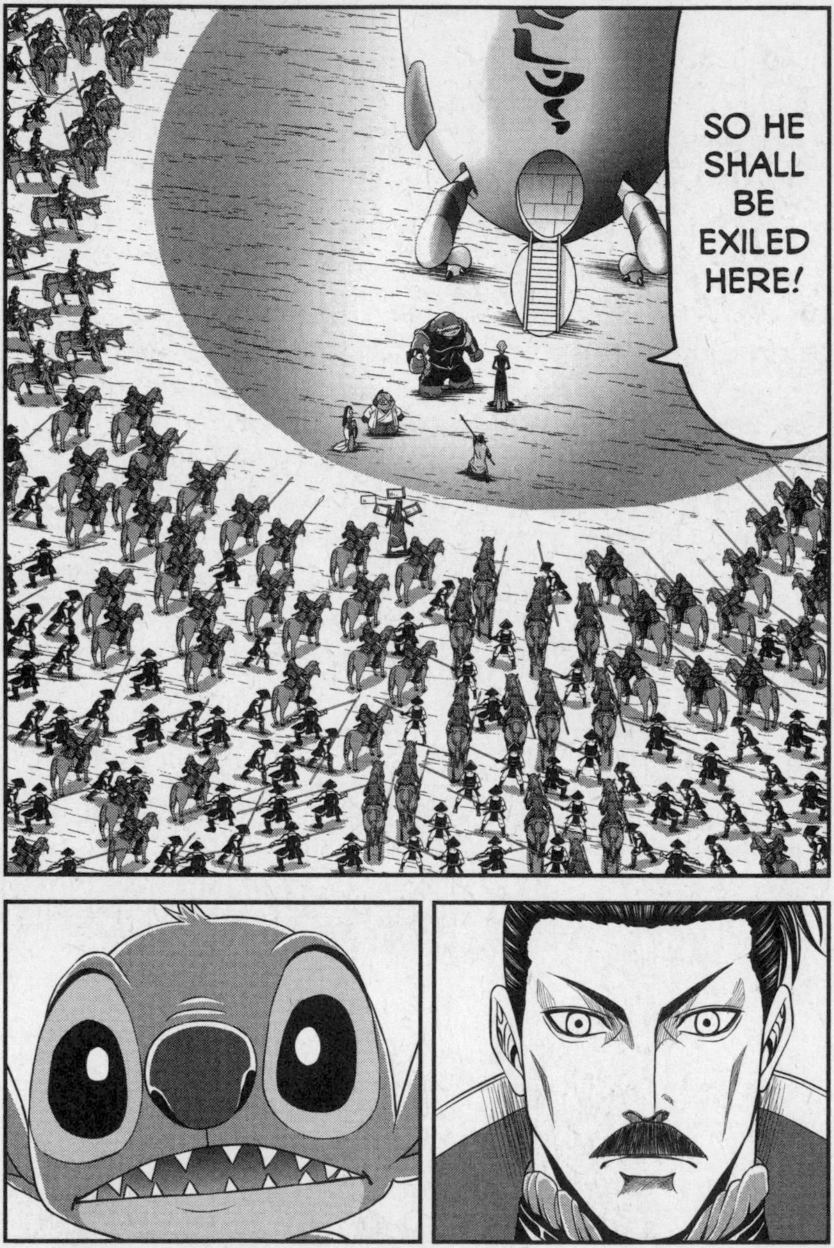
SO HE SHALL BE EXILED HERE!

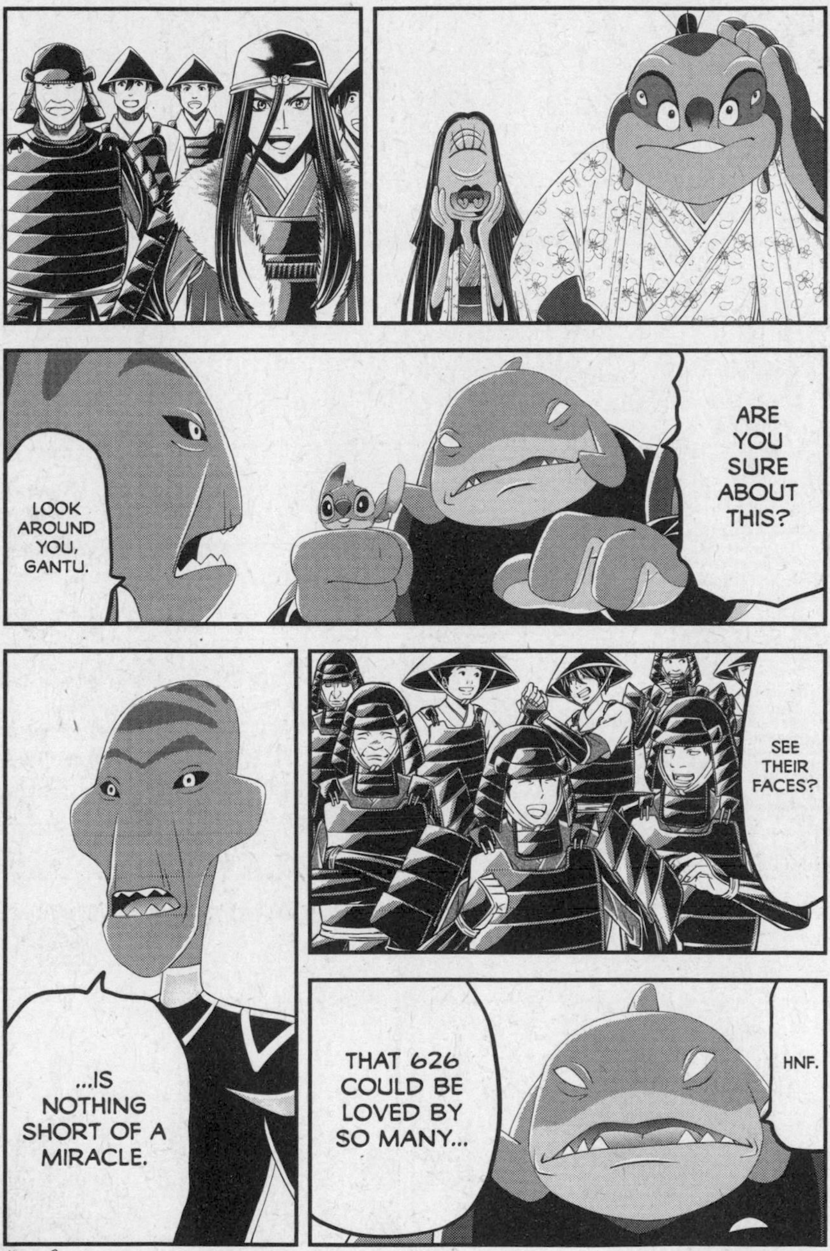
ARE YOU SURE ABOUT THIS?
LOOK AROUND YOU, GANTU.
SEE THEIR FACES?
HNF.
THAT 626 COULD BE LOVED BY SO MANY...
...IS NOTHING SHORT OF A MIRACLE.

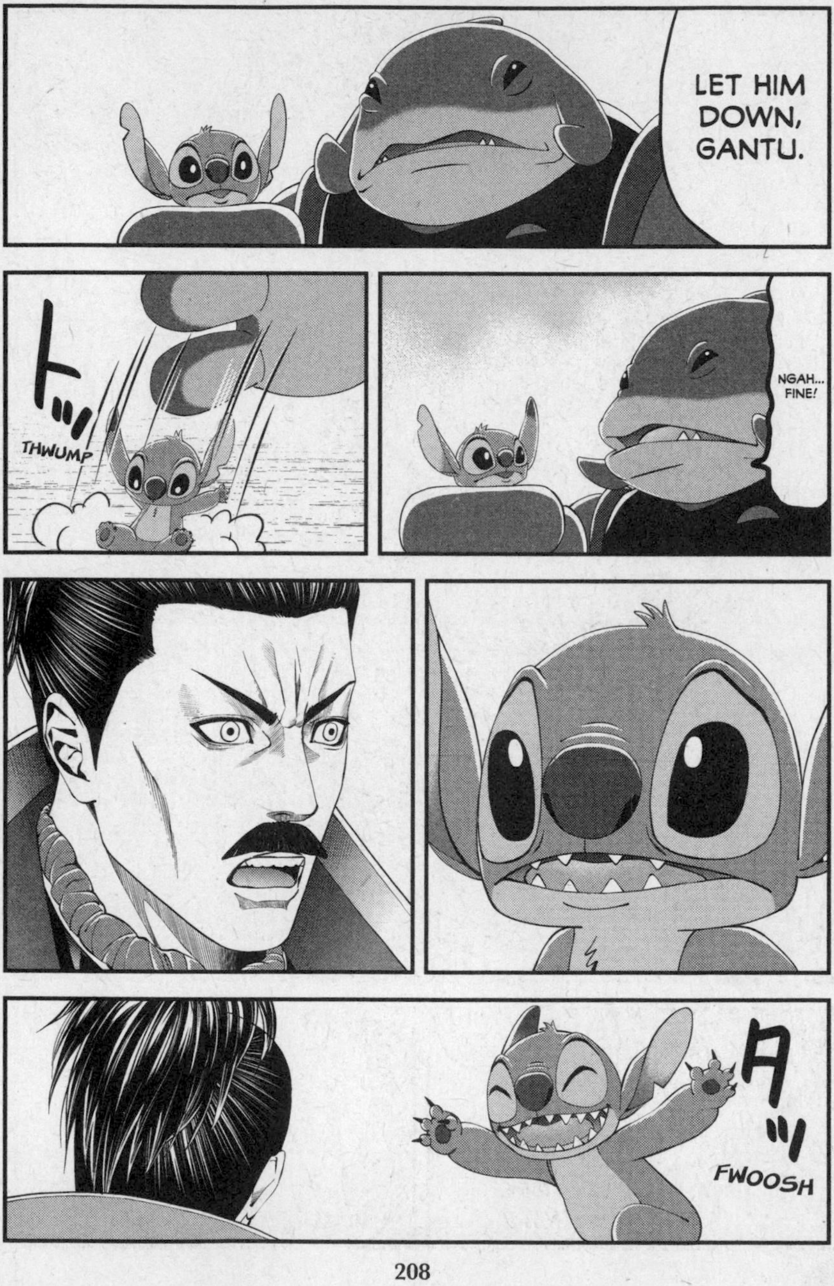
LET HIM DOWN, GANTU.
NGAH... FINE!
THWUMP
FWOOSH

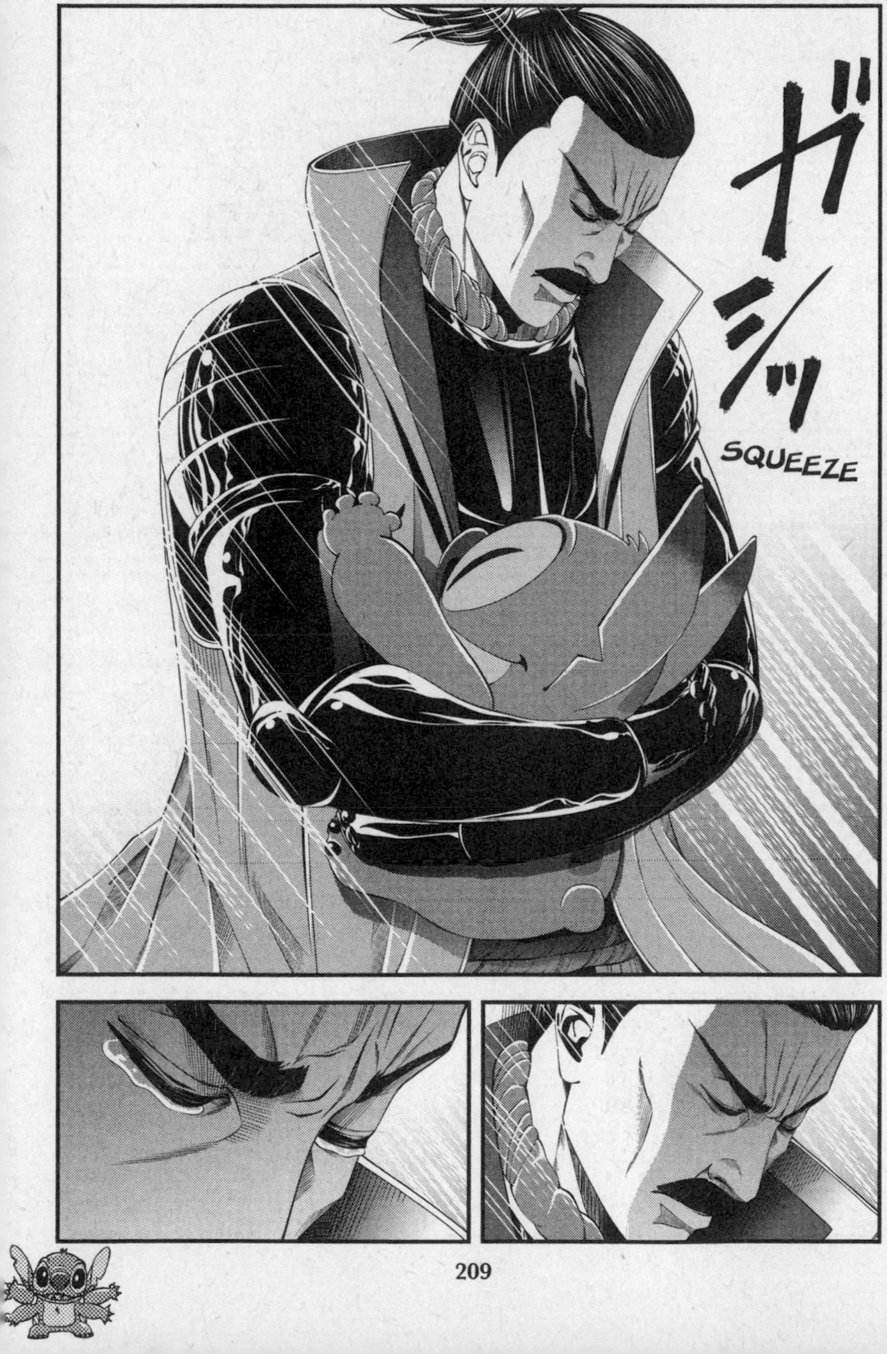
ガシッ
SQUEEZE

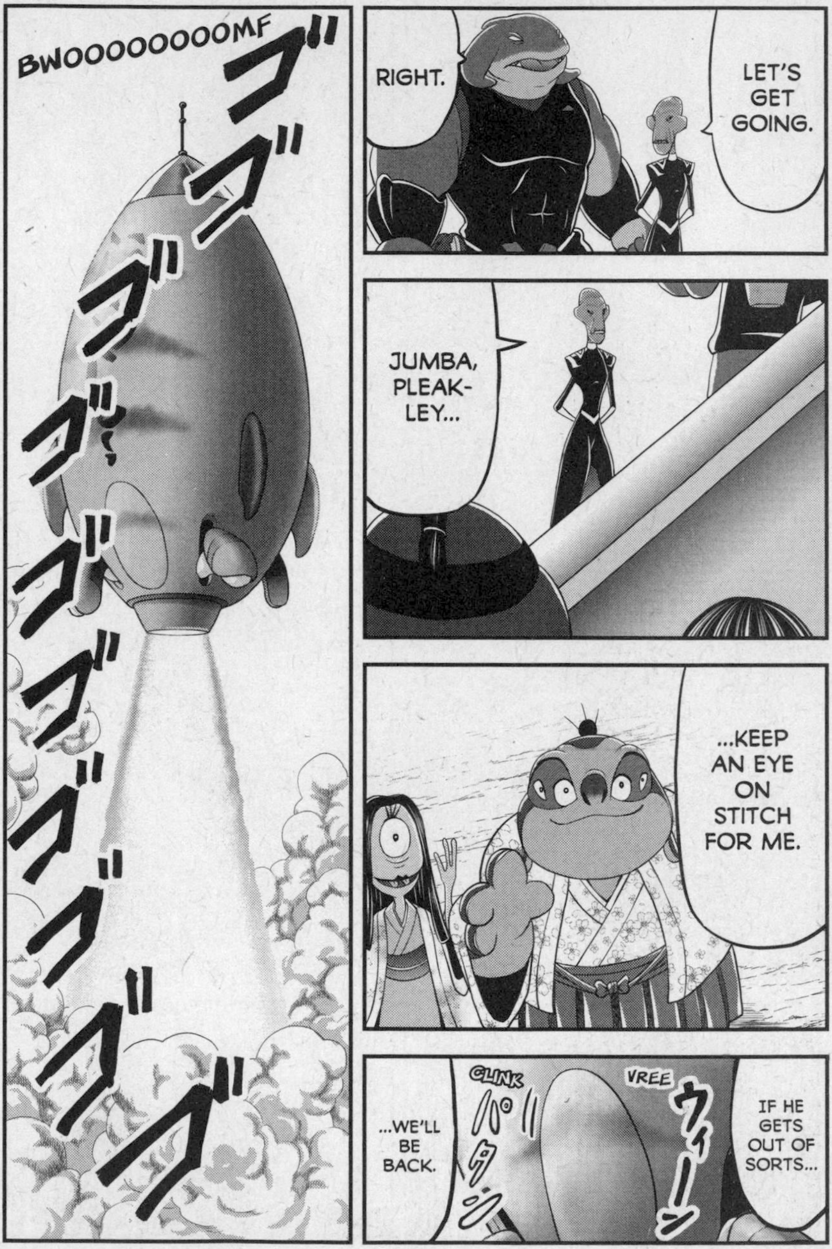
LET'S GET GOING.
RIGHT.
JUMBA, PLEAK-LEY...
...KEEP AN EYE ON STITCH FOR ME.
IF HE GETS OUT OF SORTS...
VREE
ウィーン
CLINK
パタン
...WE'LL BE BACK.
BWOOOOOOOOMF

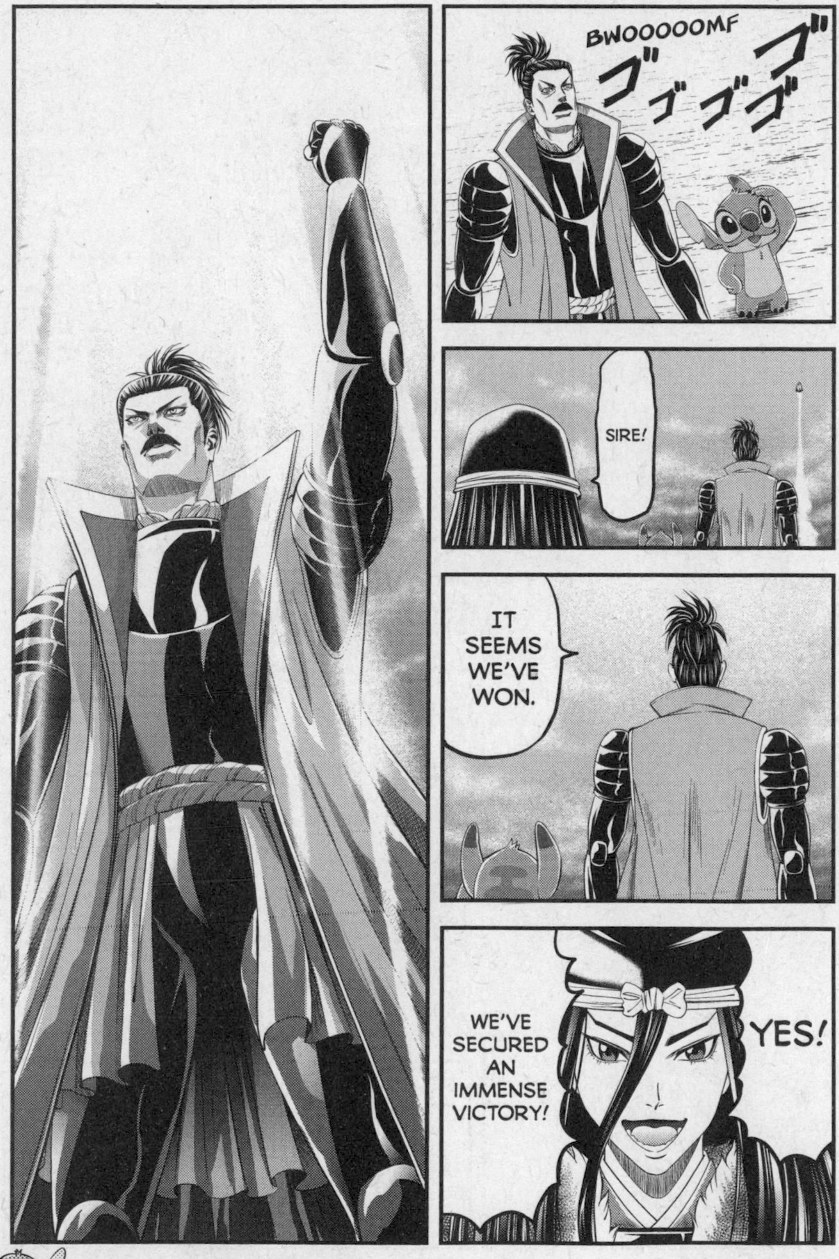
BWOOOOOMF
ゴゴゴゴ
SIRE!
IT SEEMS WE'VE WON.
YES!
WE'VE SECURED AN IMMENSE VICTORY!

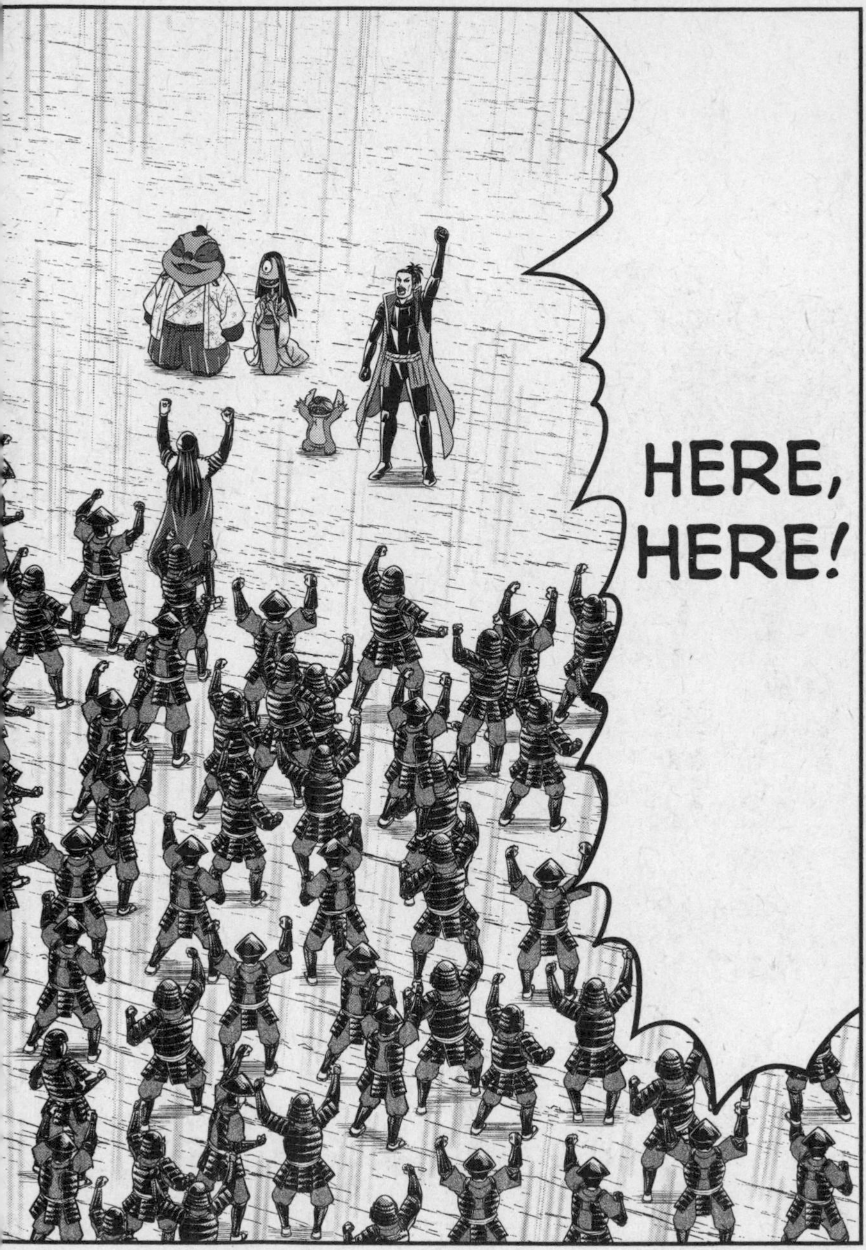
HERE, HERE!

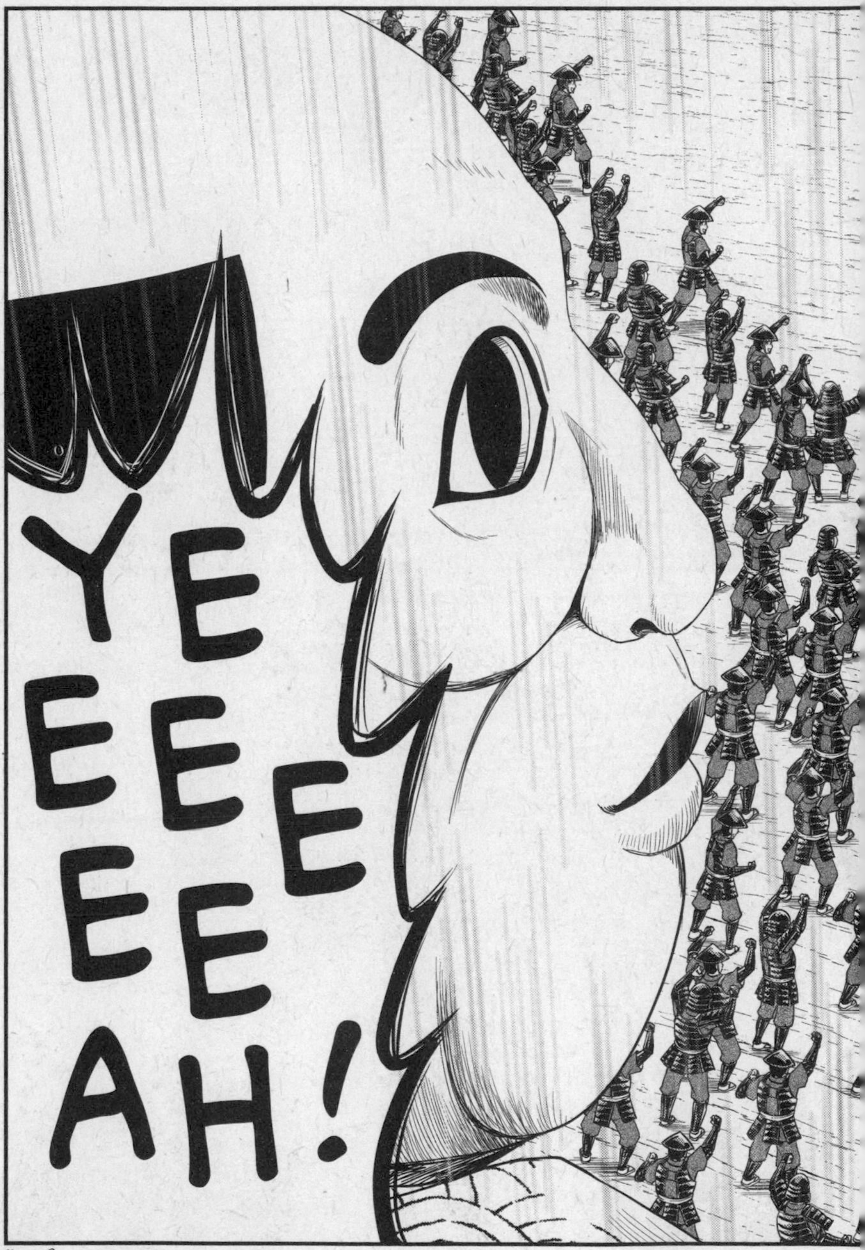
YEEEEEEEAH!

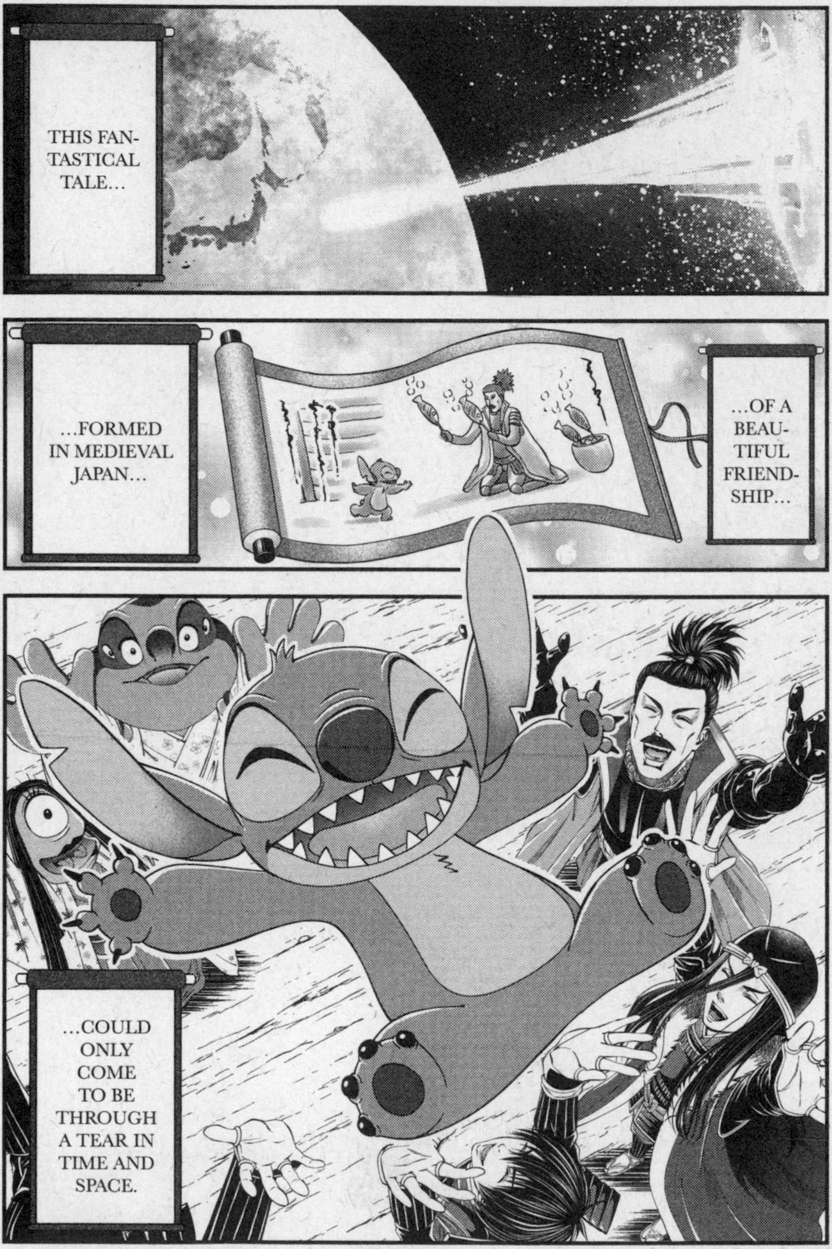
THIS FAN-
TASTICAL
TALE…
…OF A
BEAU-
TIFUL
FRIEND-
SHIP…
…FORMED
IN MEDIEVAL
JAPAN…
…COULD
ONLY
COME
TO BE
THROUGH
A TEAR IN
TIME AND
SPACE.

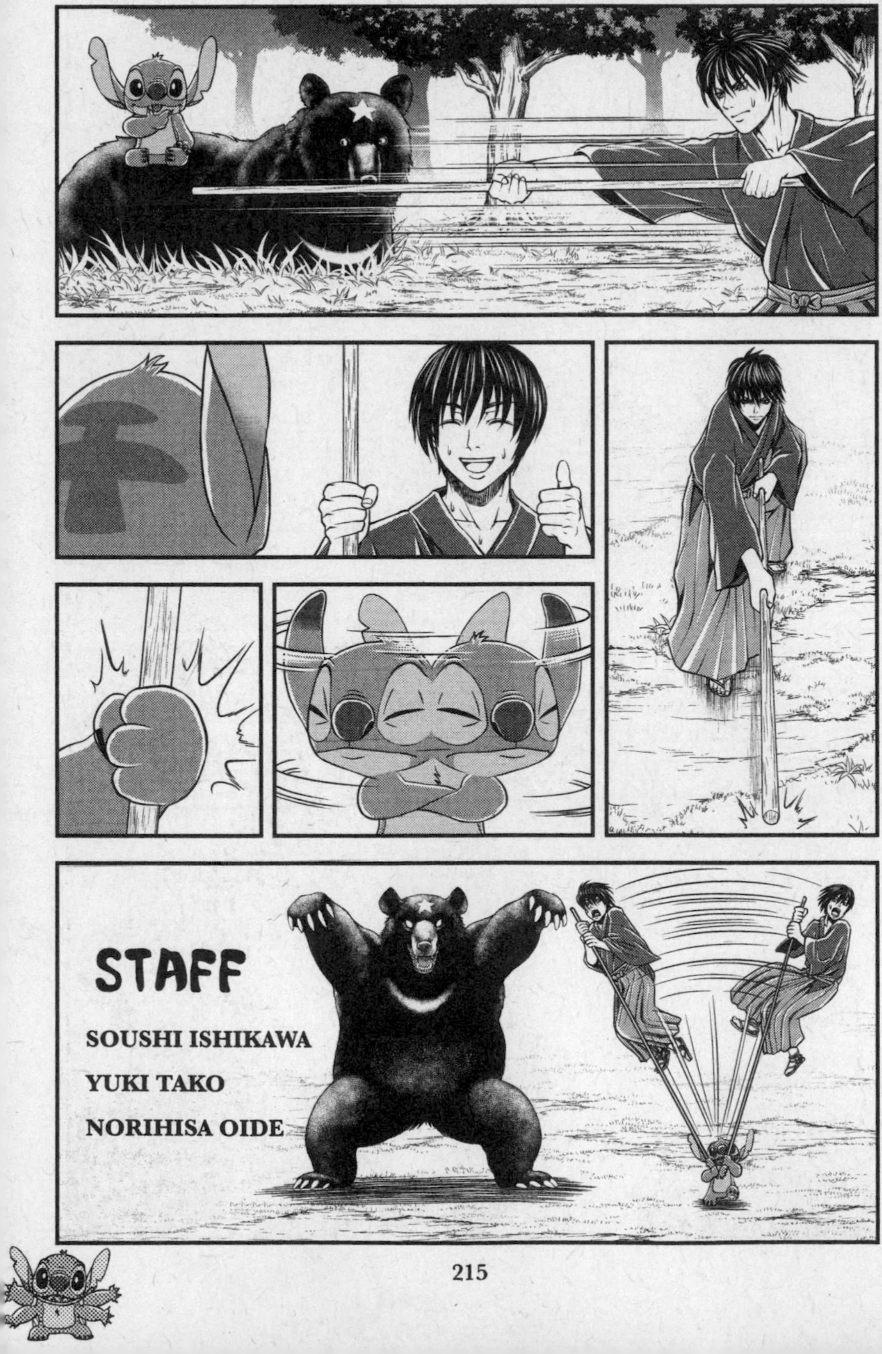
STAFF
SOUSHI ISHIKAWA
YUKI TAKO
NORIHISA OIDE

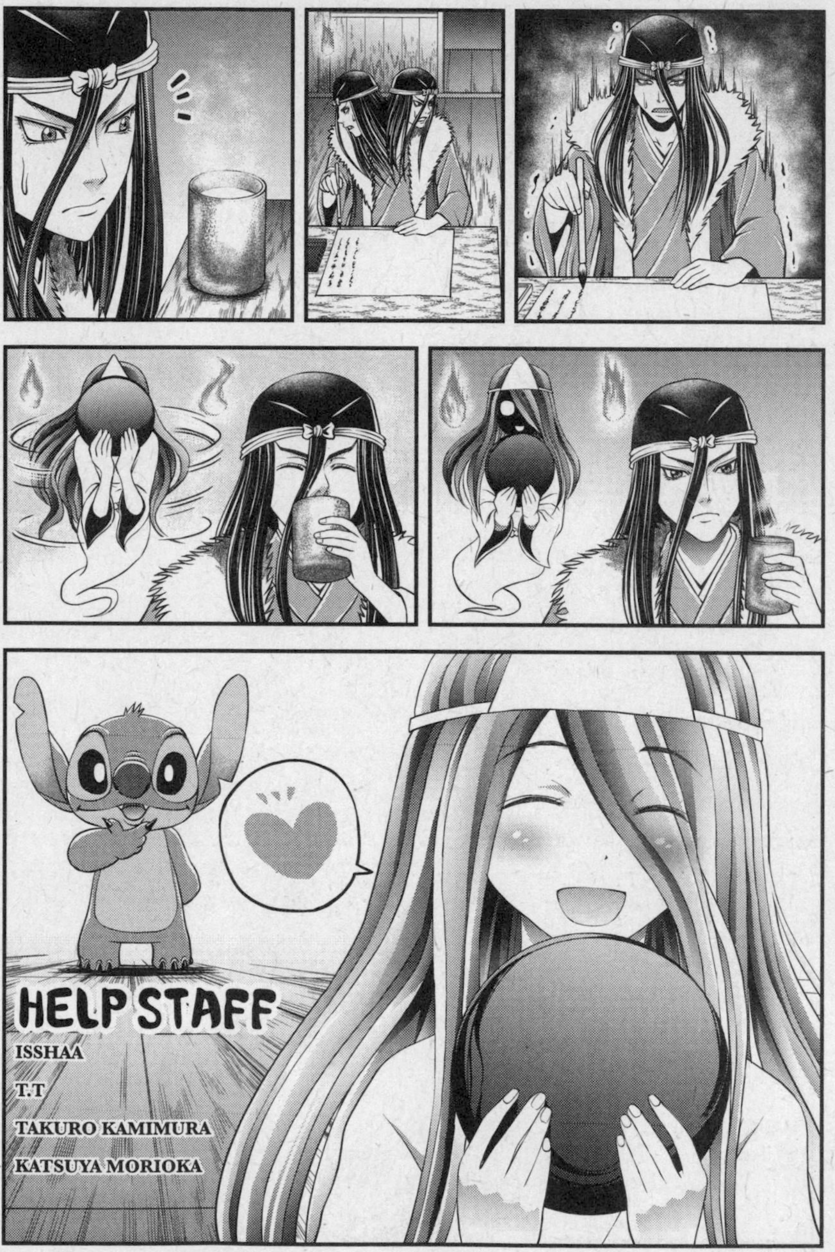
HELP STAFF
ISSHAA
T.T
TAKURO KAMIMURA
KATSUYA MORIOKA

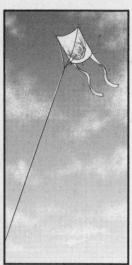

SPECIAL HELP STAFF

MANABU AKISHIGE

TAKANORI YASAKA

CHIWA OMATSU

TAKESHI HIRAI

EDITOR

MITSUHIRO MURAMATSU

KOKI TOKUDOME

RYUSUKE SHIBATA

MANGA
HIROTO WADA

ピーヒョロ……

WE'RE
HERE.

FLUTTER

SPECIAL THANKS

WALT DISNEY JAPAN

WALT DISNEY COMPANY

HIDEKI MIYASHITA DAIJU YANAUCHI

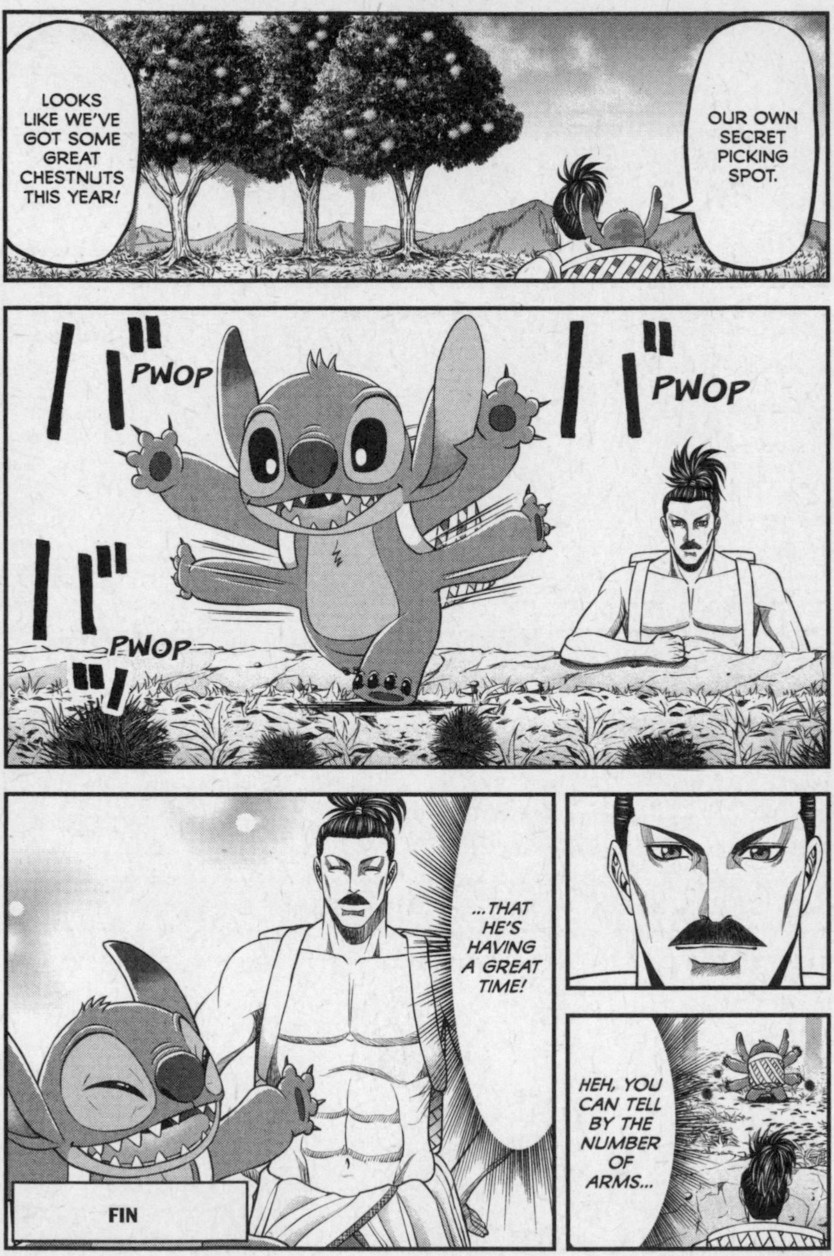
OUR OWN SECRET PICKING SPOT.
LOOKS LIKE WE'VE GOT SOME GREAT CHESTNUTS THIS YEAR!
PWOP
PWOP
PWOP
HEH, YOU CAN TELL BY THE NUMBER OF ARMS...
...THAT HE'S HAVING A GREAT TIME!
FIN

FOREVER

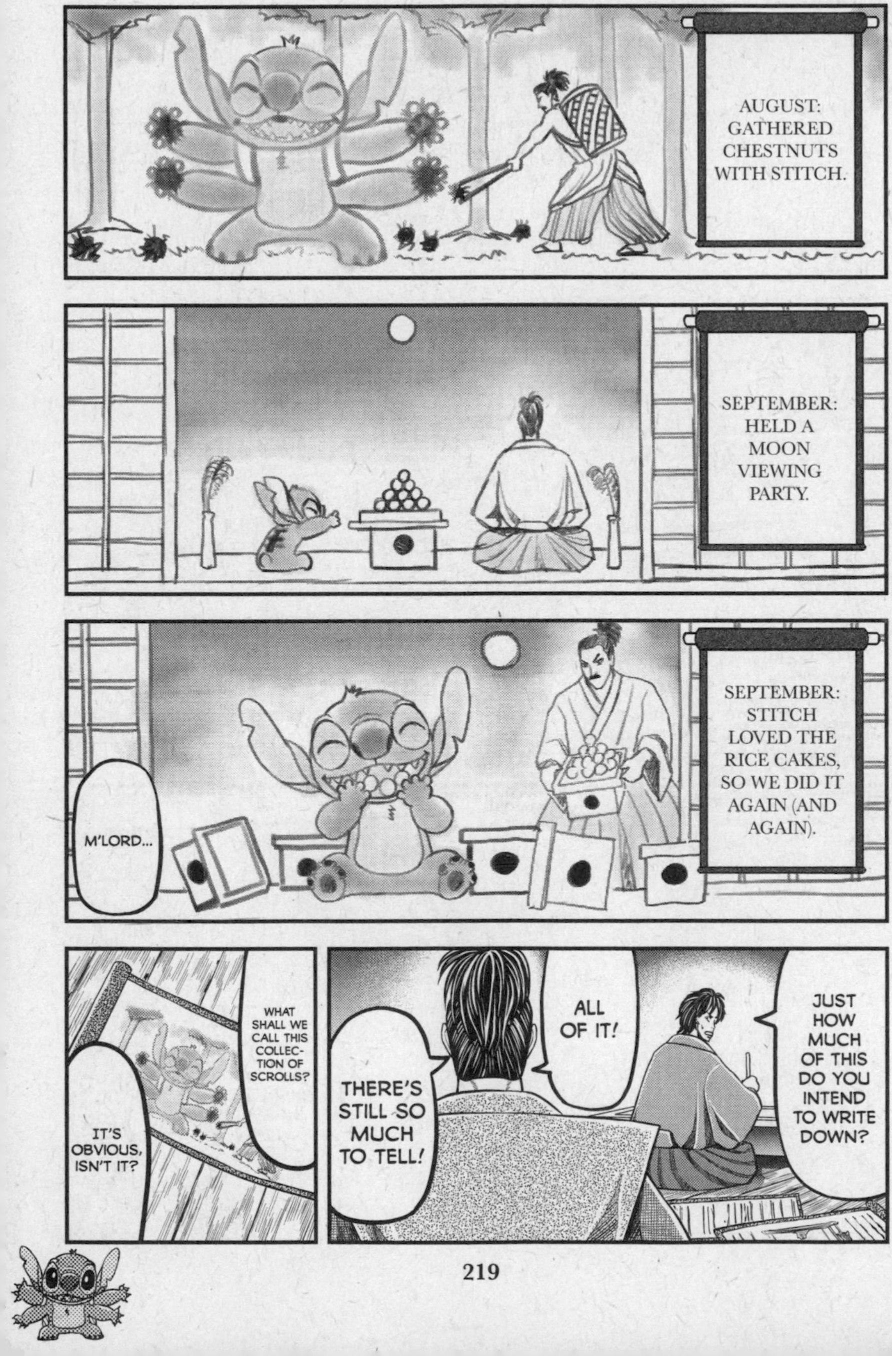
AUGUST: GATHERED CHESTNUTS WITH STITCH.
SEPTEMBER: HELD A MOON VIEWING PARTY.
SEPTEMBER: STITCH LOVED THE RICE CAKES, SO WE DID IT AGAIN (AND AGAIN).
M'LORD...
JUST HOW MUCH OF THIS DO YOU INTEND TO WRITE DOWN?
ALL OF IT!
THERE'S STILL SO MUCH TO TELL!
WHAT SHALL WE CALL THIS COLLECTION OF SCROLLS?
IT'S OBVIOUS, ISN'T IT?

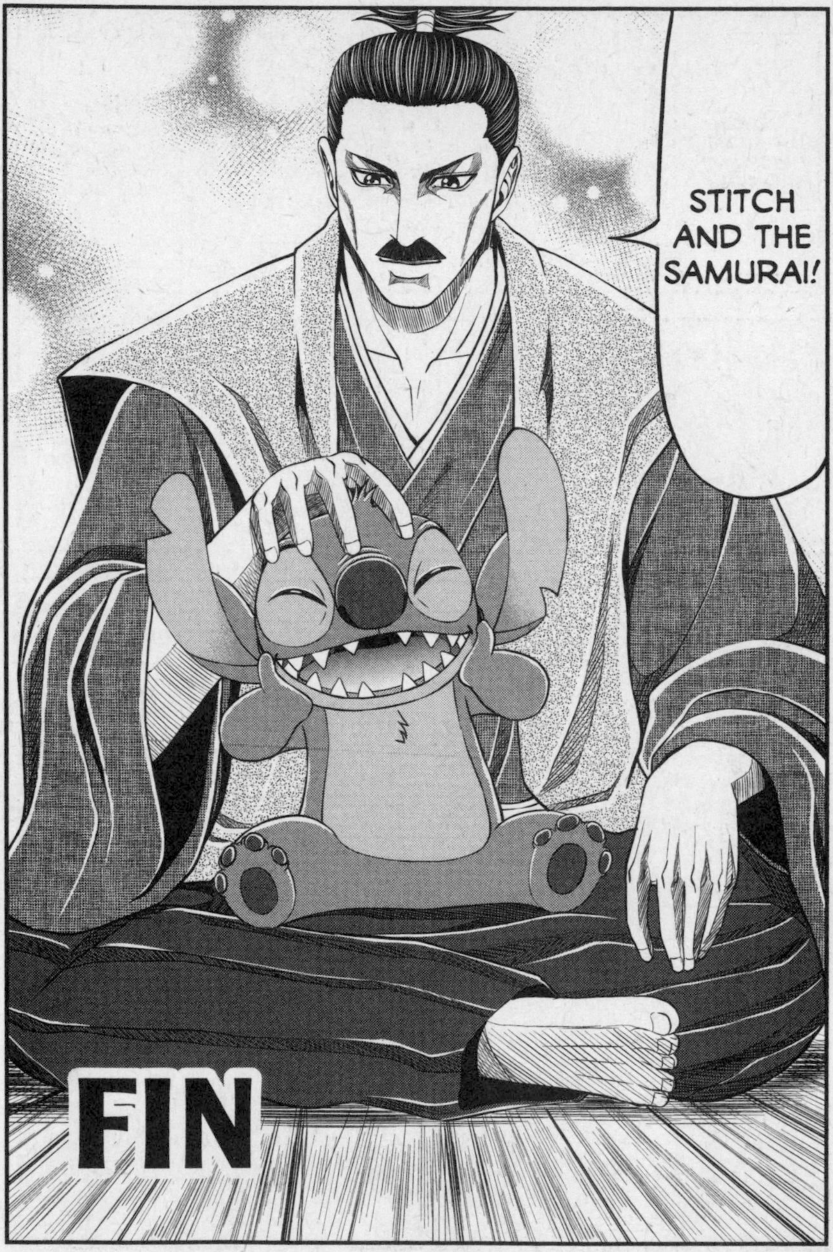
STITCH AND THE SAMURAI!
FIN

AFTERWORD

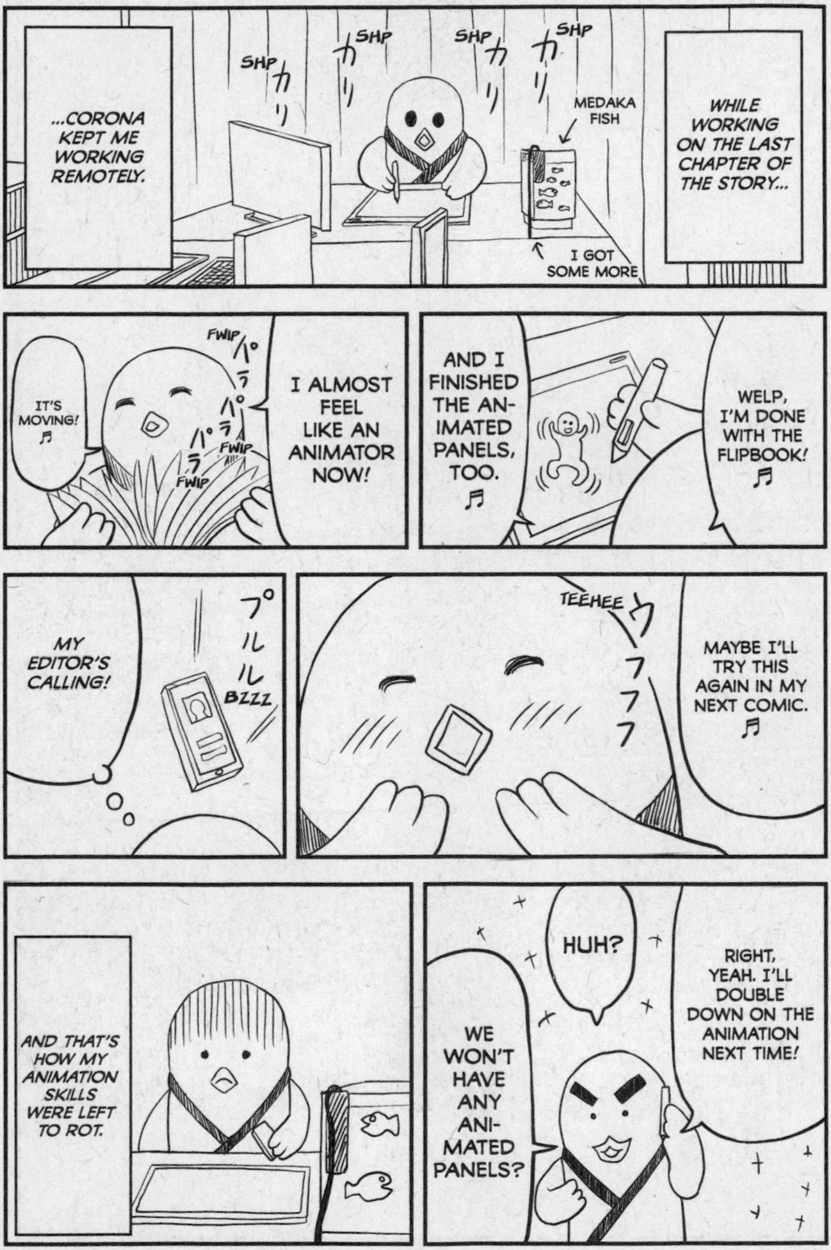
WHILE WORKING ON THE LAST CHAPTER OF THE STORY...
SHP カリ
SHP カリ
SHP カリ
SHP カリ
MEDAKA FISH
I GOT SOME MORE
...CORONA KEPT ME WORKING REMOTELY.
WELP, I'M DONE WITH THE FLIPBOOK!
AND I FINISHED THE ANIMATED PANELS, TOO.
I ALMOST FEEL LIKE AN ANIMATOR NOW!
FWIP パラ
FWIP パラ
FWIP パラ
IT'S MOVING!
MAYBE I'LL TRY THIS AGAIN IN MY NEXT COMIC.
TEEHEE ウフフフ
プルル BZZZ
MY EDITOR'S CALLING!
RIGHT, YEAH. I'LL DOUBLE DOWN ON THE ANIMATION NEXT TIME!
HUH?
WE WON'T HAVE ANY ANIMATED PANELS?
AND THAT'S HOW MY ANIMATION SKILLS WERE LEFT TO ROT.

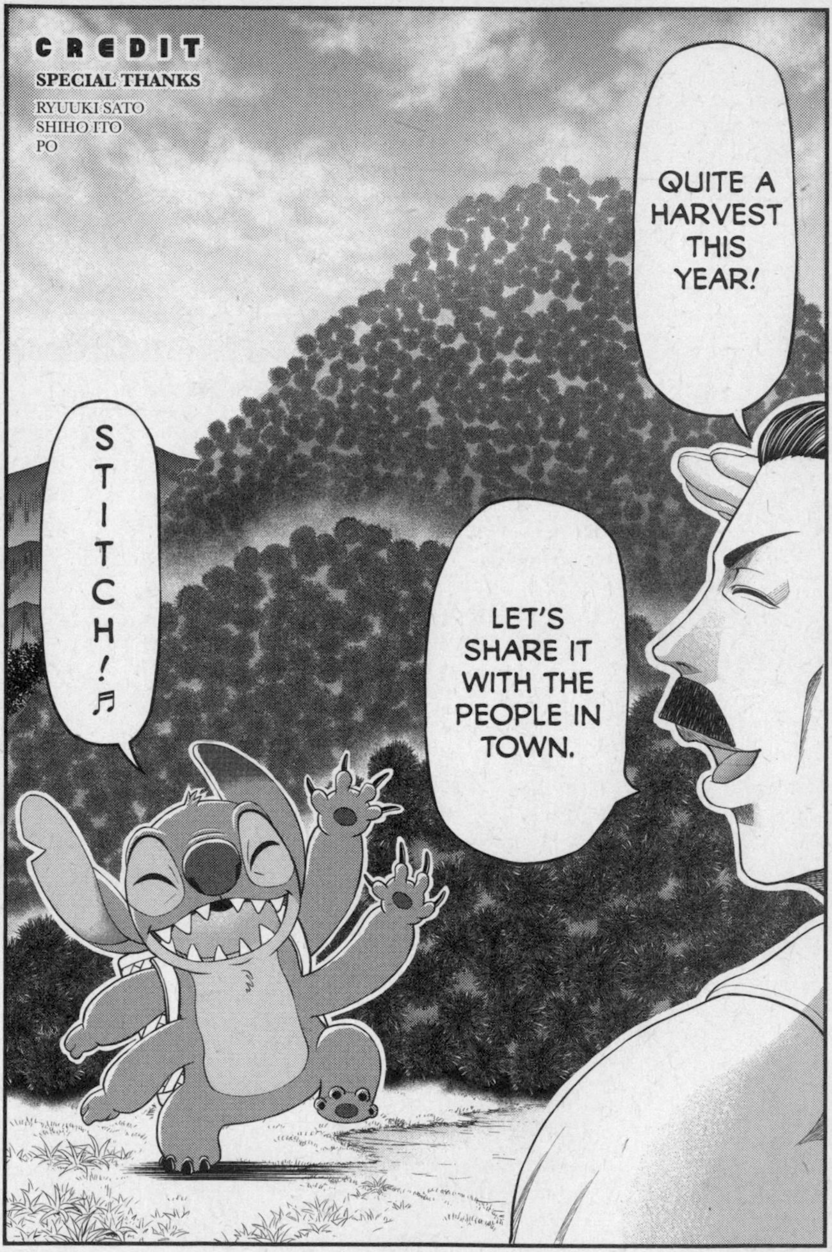
QUITE A HARVEST THIS YEAR!
LET'S SHARE IT WITH THE PEOPLE IN TOWN.
STITCH!♬
CREDIT
SPECIAL THANKS
RYUUKI SATO
SHIHO ITO
PO

Disney Stitch and the Samurai, Volume 3
Art by Hiroto Wada

Editorial Associate	-	Janae Young
Marketing Associate	-	Kae Winters
Translator	-	Jason Muell
Copy editor	-	Sean Doyle
Graphic Designer	-	Sol DeLeo
Retouching and Lettering	-	Vibrraant Publishing Studio
Editor-in-Chief & Publisher	-	Stu Levy

A  Manga

TOKYOPOP and ☜ are trademarks or registered trademarks of TOKYOPOP Inc.

TOKYOPOP Inc.
5200 W. Century Blvd. Suite 705
Los Angeles, 90045

E-mail: info@TOKYOPOP.com
Come visit us online at www.TOKYOPOP.com

f www.facebook.com/TOKYOPOP
🐦 www.twitter.com/TOKYOPOP
📷 www.instagram.com/TOKYOPOP

ISBN: 978-1-4278-6884-8
First TOKYOPOP Printing: October 2021
Printed in CANADA

STOP

THIS IS THE BACK OF THE BOOK!

How do you read manga-style? It's simple! To learn, just start in the top right panel and follow the numbers: